Other companies can waste your time,

we know how valuable it is.

But don't just take our word for it:

"Sema Group has exceptionally aggressive recruitment targets for 1998, and is confident that Hunterskil Howard will work with us and contribute towards achieving them.

We have found that Hunterskil Howard's strengths lie in their ability to supply us with good quality senior candidates who are relevant to our needs. Sema Group has expanded its recruitment function, restructured it to match our lines of business and implemented a Preferred Supplier List which is regularly reviewed. Hunterskil Howard have been appointed as a Preferred Supplier, an indication of the success they have enjoyed to date."

Sema Group

"Dominic, in any career-change situation, the most difficult aspects for a potential candidate to deal with are impatience and frustration. Time-frames appear to be very different for the candidate, for the move and for the potential new employer. A great deal of patience and faith is needed.

From the moment that you first approached me, you have impressed me with your absolute determination to keep me informed of developments and to always do what you say, at the time that you said that you would. This is both admirable and rare!

I would like to offer my thanks and appreciation for your professionalism and enthusiasm."

David Beynon
(former CEO J. Rothschild International Assurance and MD Midland Bank Personal Financial Services)

Clients: Big 6 and leading IT and Strategy Consulting Firms.
Disciplines: Financial Services, Package, Change/BPR, IS/IT Strategy, Technical Architecture, Outsourcing, Project/Programme Managers, IT Technical Specialists.
Attributes: Excellent academics, blue-chip experience, high achiever, likely to be aged 27-45.

For further information please contact Dominic Trillo or Natalie Frost at the following address: Hunterskil Howard, Project House, 110-113 Tottenham Court Road, PO Box 1BX, London W1A 1BX. Tel: 0171 383 3888   Fax: 0171 387 2048
Email: natalie.frost@hunterskil-howard.com

Hunterskil Howard

HUMAN RESOURCE SERVICES

P   R   E   C   I   S   E   L   Y

Good recruitment practice is not a necessity, it's a strategic essential

- **Does my recruitment consultancy add measurable value to the HR process?**
- **Do they understand the commercial impact that poor recruitment practice has on my bottom line?**
- **Do they challenge and recommend change based on real-world criteria?**

At Hunterskil Howard we develop a deeper more strategic understanding of our clients' business. Then, and only then, will we select and forward candidates who meet the brief - people with the right track record and the enthusiasm to deliver results.

We will tell you if your 'Brand' image matches candidate perceptions. We will assess your recruitment process and identify the shortfalls - response time analysis, candidate briefing papers, assessment procedures, post interview analysis - they will all be scrutinised.

A partnership based relationship depends on this approach and we deliver it. We will not waste your time and we will not let you waste the candidate's - a more fexible and responsive recruitment strategy will enable you to identify, assess and secure the best candidates. Base your recruitment targets on a more numbers oriented strategy and it will ultimately severely limit the pool of talent available for you to select from.

As the recruitment market place continues its competitive upward spiral, both clients and candidates can ill afford to make mistakes. Reputation is hard to build and is easily damaged. At Hunterskil Howard we have built ours by working with clients and candidates - precisely.

Discover the Hunterskil Howard approach to human resourcing by contacting Dominic Trillo or Natalie Frost at the following address: Hunterskil Howard, Project House, 110-113 Tottenham Court Road, PO Box 1BX, London W1A 1BX.

Tel: 0171 383 3888. Fax: 0171 387 2048.
Email: natalie.frost@hunterskil-howard.com

MANAGEMENT CONSULTANCY

a handbook of best practice

EDITED BY PHILIP SADLER

KOGAN
PAGE

YOURS TO HAVE AND TO HOLD
BUT NOT TO COPY

First published in 1998

Reprinted 1999 (twice)

Kogan Page Limited
120 Pentonville Road
London N1 9JN

© Philip Sadler and named contributors, 1998

British Library Cataloguing in Publication Data

A CIP record for this book is available from the British Library.

ISBN 0 7494 2448 6

Typeset by Saxon Graphics Ltd, Derby
Printed and bound in Great Britain by Biddles Ltd, Guildford and King's Lynn

Contents

Contents

Contents

Contents

Contents

Contents

Part 6 Different fields of consulting activity

Contents

Contents

Foreword

I am delighted to welcome this pioneering text, which is the product of an inspired vision for an MSc in contemporary consulting practice by distance learning.

This book, like the postgraduate programme design that prompted it, aims to approach consultancy practice by exploring the principles that stand behind the application of specialized management techniques. It also seeks to emphasise and pursue an understanding of what is really driving the dynamics of the consulting relationship in a particular client business context.

Certified Management Consultants and those preparing for the qualification in the 25 different countries internationally where it is awarded, will find the text essential reading for their continuing professional development and certification.

It will be particularly useful to consultants who are sole practitioners or who are with small firms that do not have access to the highly systematic proprietary training programmes run by the brand name management consulting houses. It will be of equal interest and value to those working within the larger consultancies who are taking charge of their own careers and managing their own learning within a framework of career opportunity and professional development resources provided by their employers.

The Institute of Management Consultants in the UK (IMC), and its fellow members of the International Council of Management Consulting Institutes (ICMCI) maintain the same standards for the CMC qualification globally. They require that qualified consultants should demonstrate ongoing competence in the principles and practice of consultancy, as well as in general business management and their functional management specialisms.

Foreword

In particular, Certified Management Consultants attest to a Professional Code of Conduct and Ethical Guidelines reflecting such principles of good practice.

We see the MSc in Management Consultancy from the Management Consultancy Business School in collaboration with the University of Surrey of which this book is a part as ideal stepping stones across the Uniform Body of Knowledge in Management Consultancy, which underpins the CMC qualification.

However, as consultancy skills increasingly become core competencies or life skills for effectiveness and survival in a wide range of professional service and managerial positions, this book will become a *vade mecum* for a broad range of careers in the post-employment and portfolio labour markets of the future.

Barry Curnow
Principal, Maresfield Curnow School of Management Consulting
Past President, Institute of Management Consultants (UK)
Secretary-designate, International Council of Management
Consulting Institutes

Foreword

I welcome this opportunity to write the Foreword to this invaluable book that succinctly describes the management consultancy industry. Indeed I would congratulate the authors on even attempting to do so, for today the spectrum covered by the term 'management consultancy' embraces so much, with one end of the structure having little similarity with the other. What does the sole practitioner or academic selling his or her valuable professional services at an hourly rate have in common with a multinational organization claiming to provide value added on a £100 million contract? I suspect it is little more than the brand name management consultancy and the belief that if you are a participant in one of the 'camps' then those who are not with you are not deemed management consultants. As a student of management consultancy you are faced, therefore, with a dilemma before your studies have even begun. But do not worry, management consultancy is all about challenge and providing the answers. Management consultancy is about investment in the future: it is the means by which new ideas, new skills new technology are disseminated through the community. Consultants are unrecognized as wealth creators in an economy: they are catalysts and multipliers and this is their value, whether we relate them to global, regional or national markets.

Management consultancy has moved great distances since its originators in the late nineteenth century set up their professional stall. In the UK for the next half a century its efforts were concentrated on organization and methods, and the leading companies of that time such as PA (Personnel and Administration) and PE (Product and Engineering) demonstrated that focus. The sixties saw the first evolution in the business when accountancy-based consultancies entered the market, demonstrating that consultancy should have a 'bottom line' focus too. The multi-national dimension of accountants drove consultancy into the international arena, and for the next quarter century the driving force in management consulting was provided by these practices.

Now we are facing a second evolution. As clients increasingly understand not only the value of outside 'bought in' advice, they also, through their regular use of management consultancy, understand the service that is on offer. Management consultancy nowadays is no longer solely about diagnosis and identification, recommendations and implementation, but it is about the provision of complete business solutions. Such solutions involve the omnipresence of technology. The drivers therefore in the industry today are those organizations with technology expertise written into their structure.

No one can really estimate the size of today's global management consultancy market. We believe that in the UK it amounts to around £2.7 billion depending on how purist one is in defining it: in Europe the market is seen as being around £14 billion while globally it is probably around £60 billion in value. Having said this, over 80 per cent of management consultancy is still performed nationally, and even in a global market it is fairer to say that it is sold internationally but still performed nationally. It is fair to add that at the top of the market local performance is tempered by the fact that international experts are flown in to service the national market.

Management consultancy is an industry that thrives on discontinuity (change) but not insecurity and uncertainty. It is a partnership between client and consultancy, the former being clear as to this objective, the latter upon the means of getting there. There is a cliché often used, which says that you cannot do a 'good consultancy for a bad client, or a bad consultancy for a good client'. Irrespective of whether the statement is true or not, it does underline one truism – unless client and consultancy work together on a constant basis, the likelihood of real added value resulting is debatable.

This book deals with the 'nuts and bolts' of management consultancy. This is important, but never forget that when you enter the 'wide and wicked' commercial world management consultancy is not only about process expertise but brain power as well. Management consultancy cannot be priced as if it is a commodity, and consultants valued by the string of initials and qualifications they possess after their name. It is about not only having a focus but also a breadth of knowledge and a vision. Not everyone possesses these two great forces and, too often in my experience, individuals at all levels of the consultancy industry are unable to demonstrate a breadth of vision outside of their expertise. To be successful, management consultancy has to be outward rather than inward looking. I hope this book sets you on the correct path.

Brian O'Rorke
Former Executive Director
Management Consultancies Association

Hewitt

www.hewitt.com

Where people make a difference

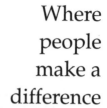

Organisations can have the most advanced technologies and the best products on the market – but without people working together, they still won't be successful.

For over fifty years, we have been helping clients engage their people to gain a competitive advantage. Our mission is clear: "To excel, around the world, at helping our clients and their people succeed together." How do we deliver on this? By following our own advice and maintaining an open, team-oriented environment where people can play to their strengths and give their best.

We know that the only way to realise our full potential as a firm is by helping our people to realise their own. Which means we are always looking for talented individuals who thrive on professional challenge, respond to opportunities and want to grow. Most of all, we're looking for people who can make a difference.

Please send your CV, with covering letter, to: Helen Coe, Hewitt Associates, Prospect House, Abbey View, St Albans, Hertfordshire AL1 2QU. Tel: 01727 888226. E-mail: hbcoe@hewitt.com

Preface

This book, which has been produced as a textbook for an MSc in Management Consultancy, is the product of a unique threefold collaboration.

- The book was commissioned by the publishers in co-operation with the Management Consultancy Business School, as a textbook for this degree programme.
- The Business School brought together representatives from both the Management Consultancies Association (MCA) and the Institute of Management Consultants (IMC), with a representative from Kogan Page (the Publishers) and academics from the University of Surrey in order to prepare the content of the programme – therefore Management Consultants have been involved in preparing the degree programme itself and, indirectly, the contents of this book.
- The Business School and the University of Surrey, through its School of Educational Studies, have entered a collaborative arrangement so that the whole of the degree programme is an internal degree of the University.

In the opening chapters of the book, there is reference to the perennial debate as to whether Management Consultancy is an industry or a profession. Of course this debate will continue, but the real concern of Management Consultants should perhaps be about their own professionalism, irrespective of the status of the occupation. Naturally, the occupation's status matters a great deal, but it will certainly be enhanced if its practitioners exhibit all the characteristics of professionals.

The MSc programme is concerned that practitioners should acquire a greater level of knowledge, so that they begin to be even more professional in practice. Consequently, the course is very practical, and that is why it is being run mostly by distance, and is part-time. It is for practitioners who can try out ideas that they gain, from the course, from this text-book and from their peers working with them in workshops during the programme.

In the well known tradition of professions, they need to have a body of knowledge, but conditions are changing rapidly. Indeed, knowledge is changing rapidly, so that a stable body of knowledge is much harder to ascribe to. The Institute of Management Consultants have tried hard to build such a body of knowledge and informed practitioners need to enter the debate about what constitutes the foundations of their occupation.

In contrast, Brian O'Rorke, formerly from the Management Consultancies Association, has always been more concerned about the whole occupation, including the Management Consultancy companies, and so he has regarded the occupation as an industry. Of course he is also right – this is one of the interesting things about different ways of looking at the same occupation – different interpretations can be made about it.

The Management Consultancy Business School which commissioned this book in the first instance shares the concern about increasing the level of professionalism in this highly sophisticated industry: that is why it has both commissioned the book and initiated the collaboration with the University of Surrey. This points towards the future: industry and higher education collaborating together to draw theory from practice and to enhance practice through creating more reflective practitioners who can also test out theoretical ideas. It has to be recognized that theory comes out of best practice and that best practice can be generated and enhanced when practitioners are prepared to try out theoretical ideas to see if they actually work.

Of course this book also stands alone. It can and should be read and used by management consultants, irrespective of whether or not they pursue the master's degree programme. It has been produced for practitioners as much as it has as a course text. The fact that it is a stand-alone book is important and we from the Management Consultancy Business School, the University of Surrey and the publishers would like your comments on the book, even if you are not following the Master's degree programme. Those comments will certainly help us, as we consider future editions to this book and new developments within the master's degree programme.

Preface

We are grateful to everybody who has been involved in the production of the book and hope that it serves professionals in the industry well.

Peter Jarvis
Professor of Continuing Education, University of Surrey
Non-Executive Director of the Management Consultancy Business School

Elizabeth Gluck
Managing Director, Management Consultancy Business School.

Part 1

Management consultancy today

1

The management consultancy industry

Clive Rassam

Introduction

This chapter sets out the context within which management consultants work. It defines the practice of consultancy, puts this into an historical framework, explains the structure of the consultancy industry and its markets, profiles the major consultancies and then takes a look at the consultancy trade associations. It concludes by returning to the present and suggesting where this industry is heading.

Definitions of consultancy

There are almost as many definitions of consultancy as there are consultants; each consultant and consultancy has their own slant on the work they do. In recent years, consultancy has become such an all-embracing pursuit, for a variety of reasons, that it is impossible to define consultancy as precisely as we would wish. However, here are three definitions that together sum up what consultancy is all about.

> The rendering of independent advice and assistance about management issues. This typically includes identifying and investigating problems and/or opportunities, recommending appropriate action and helping to implement those recommendations.
>
> *The Management Consultancies Association (MCA), which represents the major*
> *UK consultancy firms*

> The service provided to business, public or other undertakings by an independent and qualified person or persons in identifying and

investigating problems concerned with policy, organization, procedures and methods, recommending appropriate action and helping to implement those recommendations.

The Institute of Management Consultants

Management consulting is an advisory service contracted for and provided to organizations by specially trained and qualified persons who assist, in an objective and independent manner, the client organization to identify problems, analyse such problems, recommend solutions to these problems and help, when requested, in the implementation of solutions.

L Greiner and R Metzger, *Consulting to Management* (1983)

Within these all-encompassing definitions there are three important themes:

- identifying a problem
- recommending a solution
- helping with implementation.

These three characteristics of consultancy necessitate different roles and require very different competences on the part of the consultant. Thus, the consultant will sometimes adopt the role of mentor, at other times the role of creator, while on other occasions the consultant is, in reality, a leader.

Consultants have also been called 'company doctors', which is apt because the very term 'management consultant' appears to have originated from the medical profession. If you are ill you might seek out a consultant physician, maybe in his or her 'consulting' rooms. The word 'consultant' first came to mean someone whose advice you sought. It was then a short step to creating the term management consultant, that is, someone whom you looked to in order to counsel you on managing your business.

Implicit in all the definitions we have looked at is the notion that the consultant advises and encourages but never actually manages. There is one exception to this – outsourcing. When a management consultant takes on an outsourcing contract, they are very clearly entering the realms of management. Whether outsourcing is part of management consultancy is still being questioned, but what cannot be denied is that outsourcing is what management consultancies are increasingly offering.

A profession or an industry?

The very breadth of consultancy activity raises the question as to whether consultancy is a profession or an industry. This question has been asked for decades. Stanley Hyman, in his book, *An Introduction to Management Consultancy* (1961), questioned whether or not consultants could rightly call themselves a profession, and set out 'to see if the management consultant conforms to the criteria of professional conduct.' Then, Patricia Tisdall, in her book *Agents of Change* (1982), commented that neither consultants nor their clients are quite sure whether consultancy is 'a profession or a business'.

Tisdall's perceptive comment still holds true in the 1990s. Consultants remain divided as to how to define the sociological status of the consultant. Brian O'Rorke (1997), former Executive Director of the Management Consultancies Association, for example, claimed that consultancy is an industry 'because the services it needs to provide to a client are much broader than a personal service can offer'.

However, others, such as Vernon Ellis, head of Andersen Consulting's Europe/Middle East division, argues that it is very much a profession. As he said to me:

> I can understand Brian's starting point: consultancy has become almost industrialized in terms of its scale and its marketing. Also, the trend towards doing implementation work for clients has broadened consultancy away from the traditional role of the professional as someone who just offers advice, and then, too, the shift from the view that the consultant should be paid by the hour regardless of their output to the view that consultants' pay should be oriented a bit more towards the value of what they can do is a departure from the conventional role of a professional. Yet, I still think there are enduring professional attributes in consultancy. These are a sense of independence, of objectivity and doing what is best for the client. Admittedly, you could argue that the concept of independence is in practice questionable because, in many cases, a consultancy has a continuing relationship with their clients or there may be the prospect that this might happen, so in that sense they are not independent. But I still feel that we can call ourselves a profession.

He adds, 'I would say we are a profession as well as an industry'.
When Hyman asked himself the same question, nearly 40 years ago, he concluded that consultancy was not yet a profession but that it could become one. He maintained that there are four essential characteristics of a profession:

- it is concerned with a body of established knowledge
- it involves the training of recruits in this knowledge
- it implies a concern with extending this knowledge
- it demands a sense of responsibility towards the clients.

He argued that on all these four counts consultancy was not yet a profession, but much has changed since he put pen to paper. Using Hyman's categorizations, how well does consultancy fit into them today?

The body of knowledge has certainly become much more extensive, but it has not been universally accepted by all those who call themselves consultants. Another and much deeper problem is that consultancy training is still conducted on an *ad hoc* basis, and there is far too little attention paid to professional development. Most consultants do have a sense of responsibility towards their clients, but this is sometimes tempered by conflicts of interest, especially in the IT sector.

Hyman concluded by suggesting that a number of procedures and institutions were necessary 'to transform consultancy into a respectable profession.' These were:

- a satisfactory registration procedure for both experienced and apprentice consultants
- the protection by law of the term 'consultant'
- a system of training and examinations
- a disciplinary body
- a professional journal
- a professional training college.

A year after Hyman's book was published, the Institute of Management Consultants (IMC) was founded. Today the IMC does have its own registration procedure, but membership is entirely voluntary. There is also now a recognized industry journal, called simply *Management Consultancy*, and the IMC has its own publication. As far as training and training institutions are concerned, however, this is only just beginning to happen in a systematic way. So, maybe consultancy is set to become more of a profession than an industry.

A brief history of management consultancy

The origins of management consultancy are essentially Anglo-American. The industry was founded by pioneers in the USA in the late nineteenth and early twentieth centuries and by leading management thinkers and businessmen in the UK from the 1920s onwards.

The first management consultants came into being between 1870 and 1914 in the USA, and their main role then was to help manufacturing companies become more productive and more efficient. They were especially active in the steel and engineering companies in the north-west of America. They were not called management consultants then – no one would have known what that term meant – but 'industrial engineers'. They were seen as time and motion men, and this picture of management consultants prevailed right up until the 1960s.

Among the early pioneers were Charles Sampson, Frederick Taylor, Frank and Lillian Gilbreth, Arthur D Little and Edward Booz. They were all American and were management researchers just as much as they were management consultants.

Frederick Taylor left a particular legacy. Taylor's prescriptions have caused him to be called the father of 'scientific management'. Taylor was essentially concerned with what was later called organization and methods. His views on the simplification of complicated manufacturing tasks, clear modes of supervision and the raising of productivity were highly influential in the USA and Europe, and remained so right up until the 1970s.

Frank and Lillian Gilbreth are also important in the history of consultancy. The Gilbreths, like Taylor, were fascinated by the interplay between man and machine – or, more often than not, by the apparent *lack* of interplay. However, unlike Taylor, their starting point was the human factor rather than the mechanical one. They were enthusiasts and evangelists for their ideas and their 'sheer exuberance had a profound effect on the development of management consultancy' (Tisdall, 1982). Their consultancy, Gilbreth Inc, which lasted until Frank Gilbreth's death in 1924, had clients in the UK and Germany as well as in the USA.

After World War I, management consultants played a big part in the development and restructuring of American industry. General Motors, for example, hired Arthur D Little to set up its research and development centre, while the US government bought the services of Booz. Allen & Hamilton.

In the 1920s, management consultancy, which was still American-inspired, began to be influenced by the early motivational, industrial psychologists like Elton Mayo and Mary Parker Follett. These thinkers put issues of efficiency into a wider organizational perspective. The human factors at work began to be taken a little more seriously.

It was also in the 1920s that the first UK consultancies were formed. Here again, there was an American influence at work, for the two principal British pioneers had seen at first hand the work of consultancies in the USA. Each of them began their own consultancies in the USA and then transferred the focus of their business to the UK.

The first of these pioneers was a French-born engineer called Charles Bedeaux. He had emigrated to America in 1906, almost penniless, at the age of 20. He went on to found his own consultancy, basing his approach on work study principles adapted from Taylor and Gilbreth. He then came over to the UK to set up the British Bedeaux Company. Bedeaux's UK clients reported major productivity improvements of up to 40 per cent. As his fame spread, ably helped by his flamboyant personality, so his company grew.

The second pioneer was Dr Harold Whitehead, who first set up a consulting practice in Massachusetts, specializing in sales and marketing. He founded Harold Whitehead and Partners in the UK in 1929.

The British Bedeaux Company left a long legacy, for it spawned three major post-war consultancies. The company itself was to change its name to Associated Industrial Consultants (AIC), which later underwent a further change of name, becoming Industrial and Business Consultants, better known as Inbucon. Two of Bedeaux's staff went on to found their own consultancies. Robert Bryson started Production Engineering Consultants, known as P-E Consultants, in 1934, and then, in 1943, Ernest Butten established Personnel Administration Consultants (now PA Consulting Group).

These three companies – AIC, P-E and PA – represented three of the big four UK consultancy companies in the early post-war years. The fourth was Urwick Orr and Partners, founded by Lyndall Urwick and Leslie Orr in 1934.

With the setting up of these four consultancies, management consultancy in the UK widened its focus. Not only was it concerned with efficiency, it also dealt with leadership and the needs of individuals and groups of workers. This move towards a larger territory in which to practise consultancy was epitomized in the name Personnel Administration Consultants, with its implicit recognition that people matter just as much as mechanical systems.

Urwick Orr played an important part in this development. Lyndall Urwick was deeply influenced by his association with the Rowntree company. He worked there as a young man and imbibed the humanitarian views of Seebohm Rowntree. Urwick has said that his days at Rowntree's York factory were, for him, 'a practical university of management.'

Until 1959, the UK consultancies mentioned so far had the UK market to themselves, but in that year McKinsey set up its first European office in London. Over the next few years, other US consultancies, such as Arthur D Little, set up in the UK, too. These consultancies entered the market armed with different experience and new ideas. They broadened the remit of consultancy to include advice on strategy and organizational structure. McKinsey, for example, became known for recommending a multidivisional structure when companies reorganized.

Consultancy boomed in the 1960s in response to a rapidly changing industrial and economic structure. There was a big rise in the number of US-owned companies in the UK, and the remaining independent UK companies rationalized themselves in almost every sector. This was the era when GEC merged with AEI, when British Motor Holdings joined forces with Leyland Motors, when Cadbury got together with Schweppes, and when Rowntree teamed up with Mackintosh. These two trends – US companies setting up in the UK and the rationalization of UK firms – increased the demand for consultancy.

Also in the 1960s – as the first real, widely spread consumer society took shape – the importance of advertising and marketing began to be appreciated. Here, too, the US consultancies were influential. Many of their consultants had been trained in such firms as Procter & Gamble, long regarded as a kind of business school of marketing. Thus, the management consultants helped companies to respond to the new marketing techniques.

The 1960s represent a turning point in the received wisdom concerning leadership, motivation and organizational structures. The traditional UK view of management used somewhat military terms, with the notion that leaders are born and not made, that simple command structures make for the best kind of organization and that, to be effective, an organization must practise good communications from the top down. However, the US view of management, which was shaped by the new ideas coming from such thinkers as Herzberg, McGregor and Leavitt, was essentially more democratic and more open-minded. Leadership could be learned and organizations required two-way communications to be truly effective. Thus, the so-called behavioural sciences began to impact management thinking and management consultancy.

The 1960s was also the era when the concept of 'management by objectives', as outlined by John Humble at Urwick Orr, was taken up in a big way. Put very simply, Humble's thesis was that the secret of good management lay in setting clear corporate objectives, with measurable targets and agreement on how the results could be obtained. He later said, 'It seemed to me that the future of consultancy had to lie, at any rate in the foreseeable future, in being able to see the relationship between the parts (of the management process) and not just the parts themselves' (Tisdall, 1982). This approach to management fitted well into the management culture of the time, which highlighted long-range planning, manpower planning and so on. However, this view of management was soon to be blown away forever in favour of a new approach that recognized the business world had entered a much more turbulent and unpredictable period.

What shattered all previous assumptions about the management of business was the oil price crisis of the 1970s. Between 1973 and 1978, world oil prices were twice raised to unheard of heights. These price rises, which ushered in two recessions, dramatically shifted business priorities. Financial performance became the top concern, while another pressing problem was an improvement in industrial relations, which in the UK reached their lowest ebb since 1945. Concepts such as worker participation, productivity improvement and enhanced financial performance dominated much management thinking of the time. When financial return on capital became much more critical, what could be more natural than for the accountants to start offering consultancy advice in a significant way? The accountancy firms began to take the consultancy market seriously. By the end of the 1970s the accountancy firms had a sizeable share of the market.

The 1970s were a time when Japanese, and, to an extent European, competition began to unnerve British businesses. The motor industry was indicative of what was happening. In 1970, UK manufacturers had 97 per cent of the UK car market, but by the end of the decade this had fallen to about 60 per cent. Cheaper imports of cars and other products – partly accelerated by a depreciating currency – brought home to UK businesses that they had to cut their costs. So, again, financial performance acquired a new criticality. This factor also helped the accountancy firms to gain consultancy business.

During the 1980s, there was a series of developments in management thinking that affected the consultancy world. First, as Japanese companies took a bigger share of world markets in automotive products, consumer electronics, semiconductors and computers, one response was to try and imitate Japanese management methods. Thus, Japanese approaches to production involving flexible manufacturing systems and, above all, quality management became extremely influential. For a while, manufacturing systems/technology and total quality management were the fastest-growing segments of the UK consultancy market. Second, the liberalization of financial markets, the lowering of international tariff barriers and the internationalization of businesses created the need for global corporate and marketing strategies. Into this new business environment stepped Michael Porter with his seminal work, *Competitive Advantage* (1985).

The management consultancy industry

Porter was an early exponent of the need for firms to 'add value'. In particular, he introduced the concept of the 'value chain', where each activity performed by a firm can be analysed in order to show how it interacts with other activities. He explained, 'A firm gains competitive advantage by performing these strategically important activities more cheaply or better than its competitors.'

Porter's books have encouraged companies to examine not only all their internal activities but also their external relationships, and crucial to such an examination is a review of relationships with suppliers.

Following on from Porter's thesis, the concept of business process re-engineering was the logical next step. Mike Hammer and James Champy's book *Re-engineering the Corporation* (1993), which admonishes managers to focus on processes and not functions, has galvanized a large number of companies into totally restructuring themselves. In practically every case they have done so with the aid of consultants.

This emphasis on organizational self-assessment has also led to other developments, namely a trend towards concentrating on those 'core' businesses that the organization is best fitted or most 'competent' to manage and a corollary move towards subcontracting or 'outsourcing' those activities that are not central to the business. Management consultancies have led the way in advising companies on what and how to outsource, and then increasingly to manage the outsourced activities themselves – if they are IT-related. And mention of IT brings us to the remaining major development in consultancy.

If there is one factor that is changing management consultancy more than any other it is IT. Back in the early 1980s, IT assignments accounted for less than 10 per cent of the market. Today, they represent 25 per cent or more. For some of the larger consultancies, IT brings in as much as 50 per cent of their revenue. All the business developments of the 1980s have pushed IT to the forefront of the management process, from Just-in-Time methods to 24-hour customer care services. The pervasiveness of IT means that there are now very few management issues where IT does not have an impact. This also means that the structure of the industry is changing rapidly as more and more IT-based consultancies become predominant in the industry.

The structure of the industry

The structure of this industry has changed enormously, both in response to the needs of clients and as a result of major new entrants into the market. Client demand for more IT expertise has encouraged the large IT companies to come into the market in a very significant way. Having done so on the back of IT, many of these companies have begun to offer services in other sectors of consultancy, so their growing presence in the market is changing the shape of the industry.

The current structure of the industry is therefore highly complicated, with many suppliers earning their revenues from non-consultancy work as well as consultancy and with suppliers overlapping each other in what they offer. It is often difficult to categorize particular consultancies because even if they are specialists they still stray into what for them are non-specialist sectors.

In order of size, the industry has eight kinds of operators:

- accountancy-based firms
- IT companies
- US-based consultancies
- small- to medium-sized independent consultancies
- actuarial firms
- business school-based consultants
- small consultancies
- sole practitioners.

Accountancy-based firms

The accountancy-based firms include what used to be known as the 'Big Six': Arthur Andersen, Andersen Consulting, Coopers & Lybrand, KPMG, Ernst & Young, Price Waterhouse and Deloitte & Touche. Now Price Waterhouse and Coopers & Lybrand have merged to form Price Waterhouse Coopers, and Andersen Consulting and Arthur Andersen seem destined to split. All these firms have substantial consultancy earnings. They differ from one another in terms of their internal structure. Since 1989 Andersen Consulting has led a wholly separate existence within Andersen Worldwide. Meanwhile, accountancy Arthur Andersen has built up its own business consultancy unit. Similarly, the consulting businesses of Deloitte & Touche now operate quite independently of their owner's other activities. At Coopers & Lybrand, Ernst & Young, KPMG and Price Waterhouse, however, the consultancy and the accountancy business are part of the same organizational structure. Other accountancy-based firms include Grant Thornton, BDO Stoy Hayward and Moores Rowland.

The accountancy-based firms – especially the old Big Six – provide services across the whole spectrum of consultancy.

IT companies

The number of IT companies in this sector is increasing all the time. They currently include IBM, EDS (which acquired the venerable US consultancy, A T Kearney), Unisys, Sema, Cap Gemini, ICL, CMG and Logica.

Sema and Cap Gemini are French companies. Cap Gemini UK PLC is the new name for Hoskyns, which was acquired in 1990 but only changed its name to that of its parent in 1996.

These companies predominantly provide IT consultancy, while an additional service that many of them offer is financial administration and systems advice. ICL has plans to enter another market, namely human resource management consultancy.

US-based consultancies

The US-based consultancies are seen as another type of consultancy. With these consultancies the accent is on strategic advice, including marketing and brand management, but they have also been active in the organizational development sector, especially business process re-engineering. These companies also have strong links with US academic centres and are known to have a preference for hiring graduates with MBAs.

Examples of US consultancies include McKinsey, The Boston Consulting Group, Bain and Arthur D Little. Arthur D Little is unusual in that it has its own technology subsidiary called Cambridge Consultants.

Small- to medium-sized independent consultancies

There are also a few middle-ranking consultancies, such as PA Consulting Group and Hay Management Consultants, but they are diminishing in number, not just in the UK but all over Europe. P-E International, for example, which used to be independent, was bought by Cray Electronics in 1989 and then sold to Lorien in 1996.

PA Consulting Group is the largest independent firm and operates in all the main consultancy sectors. Its strengths lie in IT, change management and technology, that is, product development.

Hay Management Consultants – founded by Edward Hay in the USA in 1947 – is now based in Holland with its European headquarters in London. It specializes in human resource management and change management consulting.

Actuarial firms

Actuarial firms are also in the consultancy market. Beginning with consultancy on employee benefits and remuneration, they have moved into the wider area of human resource management. Leading actuarial firms include Towers Perrin Tillinghast (based in the UK), which bought a small change management consultancy – Kinsley Lord – in the early 1990s, Mercer Management Consultants (based in the USA), Watson Wyatt (based in the USA) and Sedgwick Noble Lowndes (based in the UK). Three of these companies – Mercer Management Consultants, Watson Wyatt and Sedgwick Noble Lowndes – are part of the insurance industry. Mercer Management is owned by US insurance broker Marsh McLennan, and Sedgwick Noble Lowndes is part of the US broking company Sedgwick Group.

A big advantage that these firms have is that they are able to use their international insurance networks to sell on their consultancy services.

Business school-based consultancies

Business schools are also represented in the consultancy market, though not usually under their own name. Generally speaking, individual lecturers and researchers will take on consultancy assignments and, although they will do so from their academic base, the consultancy fees will be paid to them and not to the business school. One business school that has set up its own consultancy business is Ashridge Management College, which has established the Ashridge Consulting Group.

The fact that very few business schools have a central unit for consultancy has always made it difficult for commentators to assess their importance in the consultancy market. Indeed, the role of business schools in the market is quite often ignored. Business school-based consultancy tends to focus more on research and analysis than on implementation.

Small consultancies

There is also a large number of quite small consultancies, employing up to ten people or so. They may work on their own or they may collaborate with research consultants in business schools or sometimes with consultants in the larger firms. Small consultancies also network with each other.

Sole practitioners

Finally, there is a substantial number of sole practitioners. They may have come from a large consultancy or straight from a managerial position in business or industry.

Just how many there are is debatable. The IMC has suggested that there are around 20,000 sole practitioners, but this is very likely an underestimate. Key Note Publications has estimated that there are prob-ably as many as 40,000. However, most of them practise consultancy along with other activities, such as training and writing.

Suppliers from outside the industry

As the management consultants have moved into newer areas, such as strategic marketing, IT and outsourcing, other professional groups are moving into consultancy.

- *Designers and technologists* are offering product development and design consultancy. Britain's top design companies do not just put a pretty face onto products already designed by their clients, though that does happen, they are also in the forefront of engineering and electronics product design.
- *Corporate identity companies* are offering marketing and communica-tions consultancy. The best example is the Wolff Olins company. In many ways Wolff Olins acts just like a consultancy in that it scruti-nizes a client's brief, examines the client's corporate culture by means of a quite detailed analysis and then suggests how the new corporate identity should reflect the changing company culture and objectives.
- *Advertising and marketing agencies* are also providing consultancy ser-vices in marketing, advertising strategy and brand management.
- *Executive search companies and employment agencies* are offering consul-tancy advice on human resource management.
- *Environmental consultancies* are providing consultancy advice that inevitably overlaps with the kind of work that consultants provide in manufacturing.

This, therefore, is an industry with very loose boundaries. It also means that the market for consultancy is much bigger than is generally assumed.

The industry today

The industry today has a strong IT bias. This is reflected in every analy-sis of its revenues. *Management Consultancy* magazine's report, 'Current Trends in Management Consultancy' (1995) estimated that, in 1994, the origin of the UK industry's fees in the UK market were as follows:

- IT   31%
- corporate strategy   12%
- business process re-engineering   6%
- change management   5%
- project management   4%
- financial consultancy   3%
- product and service management   3%
- other kinds of consultancy
  (such as human resource management, marketing,
  communications)   36%

The latest available figures from the Management Consultancies Association (MCA; referring to 1996) show that IT remains the single most important sector in revenue terms, accounting for 42 per cent of MCA members' UK revenues in 1996, but that corporate strategy and organizational development combined represented 21 per cent of MCA members' UK revenues. The MCA figures also show a higher preponderance of financial consultancy, showing that in 1996 this accounted for 12 per cent of MCA members' revenue in the UK.

In terms of the economic sectors that the consultancy industry operates in, three are dominant:

- financial services
- utilities
- local and central government.

According to the report by *Management Consultancy* magazine mentioned above, these three sectors accounted for 61 per cent of the UK industry's UK revenue in 1994. The MCA's figures for the economic sector for 1996, which are structured in a slightly different way to those of *Management Consultancy* magazine, suggest that this figure is now slightly lower, but the broad picture of sectoral demand is still the same, with financial services and public-sector work continuing to be major sources of business.

The issues facing the industry are fourfold according to a report in 1996 by Datamonitor – *Management Consultancy in Europe*. These issues are:

- differentiation
- innovation
- globalization
- evaluation

The Datamonitor report explains that 'the consulting profession itself is undergoing rapid and radical change across international borders', and it argues that consultancies will have to address each of these issues in order to survive.

First, they will have to decide how they will differentiate themselves and whether this means that they specialize or become generalists. The report suggests that 'large firms will tend to become generalist in nature given the absence of many of the constraints on growth experienced by smaller operations', and that 'smaller firms are more likely to become niche players and grow within that particular area.'

Second, consultancy firms will need to devote more time and resources to innovation and the sharing of knowledge concerning innovation. This, therefore, is a double-fronted issue for them:

- innovation
- the management of innovation and information.

Third, they will be driven to become global enterprises. Client demand, a desire to expand into fresh markets and the saturation of their domestic market will pressure them into expanding and deepening their presence internationally. This will pose strategic as well as management problems for consultancy firms.

Fourth, consultants will have to evaluate their output much more than they have up to now. Clients will scrutinize much more the economic value of consultancy. At the same time, consultancies themselves need to evaluate the profitability of their assignments, especially in the long term.

The report argues that undertaking projects where the client is virtually in a state of dependency on the consultancy does not necessarily bring in long-term financial rewards for the consultancy. It explains, 'Client dependency fuels a short-term demand for consulting services but where satisfaction is low, and additional spending is required to fulfil a project, the attractiveness of such consultancy services diminishes rapidly.'

So, the message is that consultancies need to think through much more carefully what kind of clients they take on and what assignments they will do, so as to provide good value to the client and a good financial return to the consultants.

Consultancy markets and suppliers

The world market

The world market for management consultancy in 1995 was estimated to have been $40 billion – or around £25 billion – by the Gartner Group.

This figure substantially underestimates the world market for consultancy. Most market figures are based on the estimates provided by trade associations, which in turn are founded on the reported earnings of their members. However, none of the trade associations, including that of the USA (Acme), represents all the industry. For example, there are some big firms such as McKinsey that are not members of consultancy trade associations in any country.

Another reason for market estimates usually underestimating the value of the market is that they are focused on mainstream consultancy earnings: they exclude the consultancy income of those firms that are outside the consultancy industry. In other words, they are based on notions of consultancy industry income and not on consultancy demand.

The size of the world market in 1995 was more likely to have been £50 billion, and quite possibly the figure was even bigger. The value of the world market in 1997 was probably between £60 and £80 billion.

The world's largest consulting firms

Table 1.1 The world's largest consulting firms in 1996, ranked by revenue (*Management Consultant International*, June 1996)

Consultancies	$million
1 Andersen Consulting	5,300.0
2 Ernst & Young	2,010.4
3 McKinsey & Co	2,000.0
4 KPMG	1,860.0*
5 Deloitte Touche Tomatsu	1,550.0
6 Coopers & Lybrand	1,422.0
7 Arthur Andersen	1,379.6
8 Price Waterhouse	1,200.0
9 Mercer Consulting Group	1,159.2
10. Towers Perrin	1,001.3
11 Booz., Allen & Hamilton	980.0
12 AT Kearney	870.0
13 American Management Systems	812.2
14 IBM Consulting Group	730.0e
15 Watson Wyatt Worldwide	656.0
16 The Boston Consulting Group	600.0
17 Gemini Consulting Group	600.0e
18 Hewitt Associates	568.0
19 Aon Consulting	490.0
20 Bain & Co	459.4e

* = gross fee income
e = estimated

The management consultancy industry

Table 1.1 is indicative of what has happened to the structure of the consultancy industry. Of the top ten companies, nine are part of worldwide firms that derive a major source of their revenue either from accountancy or from actuarial or insurance activities. The exception is McKinsey. Andersen Worldwide is represented twice, first by Andersen Consulting, which is its consultancy business, and then by Arthur Andersen, which is its accountancy business.

Of those firms in the second group of ten, two are IT-based – IBM and Cap Gemini, while another two come from the world of insurance – Aon Consulting and Watson Wyatt Worldwide.

Four of the firms – McKinsey & Co, Booz, Allen & Hamilton, The Boston Consulting Group and Bain & Co – are based in what is perceived as a niche area – strategy, and yet they have made it to the top 20. Their success lies in their strong corporate cultures, their international networks and their ability to help companies make corporate transformations. Booz. Allen & Hamilton has made a name for itself as an adviser on mergers and acquisitions.

The European consultancy market

The European consultancy market was probably worth around £20 billion in 1995, and £23 billion in 1997. The largest markets are the UK and Germany. Consultancy has always been strongest in the northern parts of Europe – the UK, Germany, Netherlands and Scandinavia. These markets are also the most international, with strong performances by the US consultancies.

The largest consulting firms in the European market

Table 1.2 Europe's largest consulting firms in 1995, ranked by revenue (*Management Consultant International*, July 1996)

Consultancies	$million
1 Andersen Consulting	1,366.0
2 McKinsey & Co	620.6*
3 Coopers & Lybrand	546.0
4 KPMG Management Consulting Europe	451.0
5 Ernst & Young	322.0
6 Gemini Consulting Group	321.0
7 Deloitte Touche Tomatsu	290.0
8 The Boston Consulting Group	281.0

Consultancies	$million
9 CMG	245.1
10 Price Waterhouse	
Management Consultants	245.0
11 Mercer Consulting Group	240.6
12 AT Kearney	232.5*
13 PA Consulting Group	224.7
14 Roland Berger and Partner	217.5
15 Sedgwick Nobel Lowndes	200.2
16 Arthur D Little	178.0
17 Bossard Consultants	140.6
18 American Management Systems	139.0
19 Watson Wyatt Worldwide	136.8
20 Bain & Co	124.6*

Key
* = Estimated by MCI

In the European as in the world market, the accountancy-based firms are predominant among the top ten. Two US firms – McKinsey & Co and The Boston Consulting Group – are also in the top ten. Sedgwick Noble Lowndes is the actuarial, pay and benefits division of the UK-based Sedgwick Group, which ranks as the third largest insurance broker in the world after Marsh McLennan and Aon Corporation. Sedgwick Group acquired Noble Lowndes at the end of the 1980s in order to have one stream of income that would not be buffeted by the deep peaks and troughs of the insurance market. It has proved an extremely wise buy as it contributed about one third of total revenue in 1996.

Gemini Consulting Group, founded in the USA in the 1980s, is now part of the French-owned Cap Gemini group, formerly known as Cap Gemini Sogeti.

Only three of the firms listed in Table 1.2 are from the old established nationally-based management consultancy fraternity. These are PA Consulting Group, which is largely owned by a private trust, Roland Berger, which is owned by Deutsche Bank, and Bossard Consultants, which is now no longer independent, having been bought by Cap Gemini in 1996. These three firms were once the premier consultancies in their home market. They are now dwarfed by much larger and much more international competitors.

Since the figures given in Table 1.2 were collated, several IT companies have raised their European consultancy income considerably. These include IBM, EDS, Unisys and Cap Gemini. At least one of these – IBM – would now rank among the top 20 consultancies in Europe.

The UK market

As with the estimates given for the world market in Table 1.1, almost all estimates for the size of the UK market have traditionally underestimated its true value. Key Note Publications has estimated that the market value for UK consultancy in 1996 was £5.55 billion, of which 31 per cent came from IT and outsourcing work. This seems a much more realistic figure than those given by some other sources. The MCA's Executive Chairman, Brian O'Rorke, now agrees that the UK market in 1996 was worth at least £5 billion.

The largest consulting firms in the UK market

Table 1.3 The top 15 consulting firms in the UK in 1996, ranked by fee income (Key Note Publications)

Consultancies	£ million
Andersen Consulting	350.0e
Coopers & Lybrand	187.0
PA Consulting Group	120.0e+
IBM Consulting Group	115.0e
KPMG Management Consulting	106.7
Price Waterhouse	100.0e+
Gemini Consulting Group	100.0e
Deloitte & Touche	90.0e+
Cap Gemini UK PLC	85.0e
McKinsey & Co	84.0e
Ernst & Young	77.4
ICL	65.0e
Capita Group	60.0e+
Sema Group UK	60.0e+
Arthur D Little	46.0e

Key
e = Key Note Publications' estimate
+ = consultancy income only

Again, the accountancy-based firms are very strong in the UK market. However, there are also other important competitors, such as PA Consulting Group, once the market leader, IBM Consulting Group, which has sited its European consultancy HQ in the UK and France-based Cap Gemini Sogeti, which is represented by Gemini Consulting Group and Cap Gemini UK PLC (formerly known as Hoskyns).

What is also interesting is that the top six companies are all important IT consultancies, which underlies the growing significance of IT in the consultancy market. Indeed, of the 15 firms listed, 5 are IT-based – IBM Consulting Group, Cap Gemini UK PLC, ICL, Capita Group and Sema Group UK – while another 5 are leaders in IT consultancy – Andersen Consulting, Coopers & Lybrand, PA Consulting Group, KPMG Management Consulting and Price Waterhouse (now merged with Coopers & Lybrand).

Consultancy profiles

Andersen consulting

Andersen Consulting is the world's largest management and IT consultancy. It grew out of the accountancy firm Arthur Andersen & Co, and eventually became a wholly separate business within what is now called Arthur Andersen Worldwide.

Andersen's growth has been phenomenal. Between 1989 and 1995, its worldwide revenue quadrupled from around $1 billion to $4.2 billion, and in 1996 its revenue rose by a further 26 per cent to $5.3 billion. It is a major outsourcing company, too, and outsourcing revenues rose by 46 per cent in 1996 to $582 million.

The company has a reputation for its methodical approach to problems and for its commitment to training and research. It is said to spend around 20 per cent of its profits on research and training. According to *The Economist* (1996), what has made the company so successful 'is its machine-like reliability. Andersen's core business is advising clients on how to use IT, and although it has diversified into the more airy-fairy bits of the discipline, such as strategic consulting, it still maintains some of that practical touch.'

In 1997, tensions between Andersen Consulting and Arthur Andersen led to the firms entering an arbitration process, which will probably lead to the break up of the Andersen Worldwide organization.

Ernst & Young

Ernst & Young, another accountancy-based firm, is the result of the merger in 1989 of UK-based Ernst & Whinney and US-based Arthur Young. The merger resulted in a massive reduction in partners, from 8000 to 6500 in 1996. The firm has deliberately set out to expand into the consultancy arena since the merger. In the UK, consultancy revenues accounted for 17 per cent of total revenues in 1996, and much of this came from big clients spending £1 million or more.

In July 1997, Ernst & Young in the UK announced that it was ending its alliance with Kalchas, the strategy consultancy, and that it was seriously looking for an acquisition to boost its consultancy revenues in 1997/98. Consultancy income is Ernst & Young's fastest-growing business in the UK, but, for a generalist consultancy, it is regarded as being too small to survive in the long run. In 1997, merger talks began with KPMG, but these were swiftly called off. Although this was described as an 'accountancy merger' it is clear that the real motivation was to achieve critical mass in consultancy.

McKinsey & Co

McKinsey & Co was founded by James O'McKinsey in 1926, and is now arguably the most famous management consultancy in the world. Insiders call it 'The Firm' and those who leave it are still bound to it inasmuch as they feature in the firm's alumni book, which is updated each year.

McKinsey's main focus is on corporate strategy, for which it charges the highest fees in the consultancy industry. It also has the highest revenues per consultant in the industry. Thus, although it only had around 4000 consultants in 1997 compared with Ernst & Young's 11,000 (which is its nearest competitor in size), its worldwide income was almost equal to that of Ernst & Young.

McKinsey is known for its 'cool, analytical approach to management that challenges assumptions and rejects wishful thinking,' and for its 'ruthless logic' (Byrne and McWilliams, 1993).

KPMG

KPMG, an accountancy-based firm, is the result of a series of mergers in the 1980s. The original constituent parts include Peat Marwick Mitchell and Thomson McLintock, which merged in 1988.

KPMG is a leading consultancy in finance, IT, strategy and production management. In the UK, management consultancy revenue accounted for 17 per cent of its total income in 1996. Between October 1996 and March 1997, its UK consultancy revenue rose by 30 per cent to £73 million.

The aborted merger with Ernst & Young appears to have inspired a period of soul-searching at KPMG and a determination to relaunch itself as a truly global practice while avoiding an Andersen-style split.

Deloitte Touche Tomatsu

Like KPMG, this accountancy-based firm is the result of a series of mergers. In this case, it was Deloitte, Haskins & Sells (except for the UK partnership, which joined Coopers & Lybrand) and Touche Ross, plus the Japanese firm Tomatsu International.

The consultancy business of Deloitte Touche Tomatsu International in 1996 represented 24 per cent of its total revenue.

During 1996, the consulting business was restructured into a truly global practice, following the integration of the US and UK consultancy divisions. However, Braxton Associates, the US strategy firm bought in 1984, retains its organizational independence.

Price Waterhouse Coopers

Coopers & Lybrand was the UK's largest accountancy firm, with its revenue totalling £701 million for the year to April 1996. Around 27 per cent of its income came from its management consultancy activities, which reported fee revenue of £187 million, a 10 per cent increase on 1994/95. The firm is a leading consultancy in finance, IT, strategy and business process re-engineering.

Like many of its competitors, it has been engaged in substantial restructuring in order to create a really international practice. As part of its drive for further expansion, the firm is putting extra resources into three consultancy activities: strategy, business process re-engineering and systems integration.

Price Waterhouse claims to have been the first accountancy-based consultancy in the market, doing consultancy work in the UK in the 1920s and then formally establishing a consultancy practice in 1948. The firm was started in 1849.

The consultancy business really took off in the 1980s, first as a result of a big investment and expansion into IT consulting and second because of the acquisition of Urwick Orr, which had been a leader in manufacturing and human resource management consultancy. In the 1990s, IT has remained a key sector for the firm, and it has also launched itself into outsourcing.

The management consultancy industry

In the year ending June 1996, worldwide management consultancy earnings rose 20 per cent. In the USA and Europe, the firm's consultancy business grew faster than its accountancy and tax revenue during the same period.

The merged firm will be the largest accountancy/consulting concern in the world, with consultancy revenues comparable to Andersen Consulting.

Arthur Andersen & Co

Arthur Andersen & Co is the accounting business within Arthur Andersen Worldwide.

Founded in 1913, Arthur Andersen started consultancy work in the 1950s, formally established Andersen Consulting in the USA in 1954 and then set up in the UK in 1957. The consultancy business grew to such an extent that it was hived off as a separate organization in 1989, but the accountancy business has continued to operate in the consultancy market.

Within Andersen Worldwide, Arthur Andersen & Co contributed 47 per cent of the total revenue of $5.59 billion between August 1996 and February 1997, but it contributed two-thirds of the group's partners. This disparity in partner representation, plus the fact that Arthur Andersen & Co has been tendering for business in competition with Andersen Consulting, had caused tension between the two wings of Andersen Worldwide.

In March 1997, Arthur Andersen & Co announced that it was setting up a separate consultancy business called Arthur Andersen Knowledge Enterprises to address the needs of the knowledge industries. This will clearly compete head on with Andersen Consulting, which has already developed some services in this area.

The firm clearly wishes to grow aggressively in the consultancy market, but this may be stalled by the arbitration battle with Andersen Consulting.

Mercer Consulting Group

Mercer Consulting Group is owned by Marsh McLennan, the world's largest insurance broker, which is based in the USA. Mercer Consulting Group is comprised of three companies:

- Mercer Management Consulting, which developed from Hickling-Johnston Ltd, a strategy and organization consultancy acquired in 1984 that now provides a range of consulting services

- William M Mercer Companies, founded in 1945, which is Canada's largest employee benefits and compensation consulting firm
- National Economic Research Associates, which provides economic consulting.

Towers Perrin

Towers Perrin was formerly known as Towers Perrin Tillinghast and before that as Towers Perrin Foster & Crosby.

Like William M Mercer Companies, Towers Perrin is a major international pay and benefits consultancy. From this base it has moved into human resource management consultancy. Its position in the UK consultancy market in this area was enhanced when it acquired the small, niche and relatively new firm of Kinsley Lord, a change management firm, in 1995. Also like William M Mercer Companies, this company has activities in insurance: its Tillinghast division is a specialist insurance and risk management consultancy.

Management consultancy institutions

The management consultancy profession is represented by two associations:

- the Management Consultancies Association (MCA), which represents consultancy firms
- the Institute of Management Consultants (IMC), which represents individuals.

The Management Consultancies Association (MCA)

The MCA was founded in 1956. The principal founding fathers of the MCA were the heads of PA Consultants, as it was then known, and P-E Consultants.

The MCA currently has 34 members, of whom the newest is IBM Consulting Group. Most of these are UK-owned consultancies. Except for Kepner Tregoe, the US strategy consultancies are not members of the MCA. About half its members are large consultancies, while the remainder are small- to medium-sized firms, including some niche firms such as Hay Management Consultants Ltd and Marketing Improvements PLC.

Membership is open to all firms of consultants established in the UK 'who have achieved a good reputation for their work and are capable of sustaining a high-quality service.' The criteria for membership is that 'in general, member firms must have been in practice in the UK as management consultants for at least 5 years, employ on a full-time basis no less than 15 consulting staff, with its 3 senior principals having at least 10 years' management consultancy experience of which 5 must have been with the firm.'

The MCA adds, 'To demonstrate adequate levels of experience and supervision, 25 per cent of consulting staff must have been with the firm for 5 years and, to show stability, the average length of service within the firm of the whole consulting staff must be at least 3 years. 90 per cent of the consulting staff in the firm must hold degrees or equivalent qualifications and within the firm there must be a documented and established programme of training covering both new entrants and existing staff.'

The Institute of Management Consultants (IMC)

The IMC, which was founded in 1962, represents individual consultants. It has about 3450 members, of whom about a quarter are working for large consultancy firms or as internal consultants in a major company. The majority of members are working either for themselves or for a small consultancy firm.

The IMC has four grades of membership:

- affiliate
- associate
- member
- fellow.

Affiliate members are usually junior or part-time consultants or they are recent MBA graduates or are staff at a university or business school. A fellow of the IMC has to have shown that 'they are engaged in the independent full-time practice of management consultancy at the time of application, and have been in such practice for a continuous period of not less than five years.' They also have to have been a full member for not less than five years.

The IMC has introduced the qualification of Certified Management Consultant (CMC), which it hopes will become an accepted benchmark of professional competence. To become a CMC, an individual has to have a degree or an equivalent recognized professional qualification and be a practising management consultant with five years' full-time consultancy experience – unless the individual is a member of an IMC-recognized training practice, in which case only three years are required. IMC recognized training practices include PA Consulting

Group, Coopers & Lybrand, Hay Management Consultants, Price Waterhouse, IBM Consulting Group, Collinson Grant, BDO Stoy Hayward, Morton Hodson and Towers Perrin.

In 1996, the IMC set up an ethics helpline for its members who are concerned at some of the ethical issues that they are having to deal with – both their own and those of their clients.

Perhaps the biggest issue for the IMC is how to increase its membership. Its membership numbers have been more or less static for several years, and yet the number of consultants has been rising continually. A recent president of the IMC, Barry Curnow, has suggested that the IMC ought to be more welcoming to new, young recruits to the industry and also to the 'very experienced line managers who set up as a consultant as a second career'. (*Management Consultancy* magazine, January 1997). An unspoken problem for the IMC is the reluctance of the big consultancy firms to make membership of the IMC mandatory for their staff.

In 1997, the IMC began a lengthy re-evaluation of its role. It now intends to rebrand itself as the Institute of Management *Consultancy*, embracing a wider constituency of 'stakeholders' in the consultancy process: clients, government, business, schools, etc.

FEACO

Each national management consultancy association in Europe is a member of the European Federation of Management Consultancy Organizations, known as FEACO. FEACO has had a chequered history. In 1996, partly as a result of pressure from the UK's MCA, FEACO's activities were scaled down. Its key role now is representing Europe's management consultancy associations to the European Commission.

FEACO could well play an important role in responding to the informal proposals from the European Commission to introduce some kind of European certification for management consultants. Both the UK's MCA and IMC, would prefer to retain the current *status quo* of self-regulation. However, if European certification were introduced, then the IMC believes that its own CMC qualification could become an important element in such certification.

The future for this industry

Back in the 1960s, or even 1970s, it was patently clear what management consultancy was all about, and it was also obvious who the management consultants were. The entry of the accountancy firms blew this cosy picture apart, and then the arrival of the IT companies changed the picture once again. Those firms that were once dominant in the industry have either been overwhelmed by the newcomers or subsumed into the newer consultancy groupings.

This transformational process is continuing. By the middle of the first decade of the twenty-first century, this industry will have undergone a further massive change. There are three constituents to this.

First, Brian O'Rorke, former Executive Director of the MCA, believes that the banks will start to take an interest in this industry and will enter it through a process of acquisition. As an example, he cites Germany's Roland Berger, which is owned by Deutsche Bank.

Another development that has already begun, albeit in a small way, is that the big advertising, marketing and PR companies will move into this industry. Saatchi & Saatchi, the advertising agency, tried and failed in the 1980s, with its purchase of Hay Management Consultants. However, its failure to make something of its acquisition was caused by corporate problems unrelated to Hay Management Consultants. Since 1996, two advertising agencies – Euro RSCG and D'Arcy Massius Wynne Williams – have signalled their intention to move into management consultancy. They will be followed by others, for the very simple reason that, if they don't, they will lose forever a significant amount of marketing and advertising work.

Third, another new entrant is likely to be the big telecommunications companies. BT and MCI are already putting together plans to undertake work in the IT consultancy sector. Telecommunications companies such as BT have very strong technical resources – they are also starting to use these resources to advise companies how to structure their work in a much more efficient manner. BT is already helping companies to introduce virtual work systems into their organizations. By the year 2000, BT is likely to be a significant human resource management consultant. So the old paradigms of consultancy will disappear. Management consultancy has become an extremely pervasive industry.

References

'Andersen's Androids', *The Economist*, 4 May 1996

Byrne, JA, and McWilliams, G (1993), 'The McKinsey mystique', *Business Week*, 20 September

'Current Trends in Management Consultancy', *Management Consultancy* magazine report, VNU Business Publications, 1995

Datamonitor (1996), *Management Consultancy in Europe*, FT Financial Publishing, London

Greiner, L, and Metzger, R (1983) *Consulting to Management*, Prentice-Hall, New Jersey

Hammer, M and Champy, J (1993) *Re-engineering the Corporation*, Nicholas Brealey, London

Hyman, S (1961) *An Introduction to Management Consultancy*, Heinemann, London

O'Rorke, B (1997) Management Consultancy supplement, *Financial Times*, 19 June

Porter, M (1985) *Competitive Advantage: Creating and sustaining superior performance*, The Free Press, New York

Tisdall, P (1982) *Agents of Change: The development and practice of management consultancy*, Heinemann, London

2

Professionalism and ethics

Paul Lynch

Professionalism

One of the first questions to occur when contemplating the idea of professionalism is, 'What does it mean, this word, "professionalism"?' One common understanding of the word 'professional' is as a contrast to the term 'amateur'. There is a tacit, widespread understanding that we should not expect as much from an amateur as we would from a professional. Expressed another way, an amateur practises until they can do something right, while a professional practises until they cannot do it wrongly.

The London-based college named after Sir Thomas Gresham has sponsored free public lectures since 1597 in London. In the last half of the 1980s, Gresham College invited Professor Jack Mahoney, SJ MA DD FRSA, to present a series of lectures seeking to reinterpret the role of business in society. One of his lectures, delivered in 1989, considered the question of professionalism and its origins (Mahoney, 1989). He contrasted the idea of a career with that of a profession and argued that the two are not necessarily synonymous. It is 28 years since Alvin Toffler wrote of the 'Age of Transience' in his book, *Future Shock* (1970). He popularized the notion there that the 'half life' of a graduate may be ten years or so, meaning that any new graduate will find that half of his new and hard-earned knowledge will be obsolete in ten years. In this day of portable pensions, and the increasingly persuasive idea of the 'third career', there is no great surprise in this idea of accelerated lifestyles and experiences. Rather, there is probably general agreement that a career in one of the professions may not necessarily be the way ahead for ambitious young people. The body of professional knowledge will be modified and changed as society changes, and as fresh and innovative demands are made of the profession.

Another view suggests that the idea of professing teaching, medicine or the law, embodies the understanding of service to others. As Mahoney says (1989), 'the Latin word *profiteri* means literally to speak out, or to make a statement, or further to give an undertaking to others'. Mahoney goes on to quote Gaylord Noyce, an American writer who affirms that 'accepting a professional role is unavoidably a promise-making act'.

These considerations also find echoes in the medieval professing of monks, nuns and other clergy, who gave up marriage, family life and business to be of service to others. Notwithstanding the social changes that have taken place – in particular the move from employment in manufacturing to that in service industries – it may be that, with a reduced commitment to religious ideals in today's society, there has been a change in the notion of service to others. There is much talk of service levels and customer charters, but it appears to me that anecdotal evidence supports the idea that there is widespread dissatisfaction with service.

Perhaps we should, in the words of another American writer, Norman Bellah (1985), 'reappraise the ethical meaning of professionalism, seeing it in terms not only of professional skill but of the moral contributions that professionals make to a complex society'. In this area, codes of professional conduct can help professions to make transparent what they are trying to achieve, and publicize the standards of personal behaviour expected of such professionals.

If these arguments are accepted, then the professional spirit of contributing to the community goes beyond the idea of a job or of a career and takes on a social dimension, accepting a wider role in society. In Roman times, Cicero put it this way: 'The good of the people is the chief law'. This would widen the professionals' horizons beyond self-regarding preoccupation with social status and remuneration.

It seems clear that, in the UK, there is a preference for self-regulation, but if business, and the professions that serve it, fail to respond and meet rising expectations, then society will surely seek to impose restrictions. One example of such a restriction, is the responsibility of professional advisers to report to the authorities the suspicion or knowledge that money a client is handling is the result of dealing in drugs. It is in their own interests that professions focus on the spirit and behaviour of individual members as an indispensable condition for the ethical conduct of their profession. Such a focus is often embodied in self-regulatory codes of professional conduct members of the body are expected to adhere to, failing which sanctions may be imposed on errant members. This can help to win public confidence and assist the professional bodies to legitimize their control over the profession in the absence of statutory regulation.

Another important part of professionalism is the commitment to 'continuing professional development'. How can an individual claim to be a professional if they do not maintain their currency? All the more so now that we see Toffler's prophecy of the obsolescence of current knowledge manifesting itself wherever we look.

Management consultancy

There are some who would argue that using the terms 'professionalism' and 'ethics' with management consultancy creates an oxymoron. They go on to quote the old and dog-eared story about the management consultant who borrows your watch, tells you the time and then disappears into the distance with his fees for the job – and your watch! George Bernard Shaw opined that 'All professions are conspiracies against the laity'. That is a charge all professionals, not just management consultants, strive to counter, and so greater transparency and accountability are encouraged wherever possible.

The incursion of foreign management consultants into the UK market in the 1950s resulted in much unfavourable publicity for their 'un-British' ways of finding clients. These criticisms extended to the way these consultants and their UK counterparts conducted their business. Much of that criticism persists to the present day. A government report in 1995 by the Cabinet Office Efficiency Unit appeared at first sight to condemn government departments for making extensive use of management consultants at great cost to the taxpayer and failing to gain savings to justify the costs of hiring the consultants. However, the media failed to grasp the added value argument, namely that of transferring scarce skills at short notice to clients. The media also failed to acknowledge the costs to society of failing to bring in new government systems and procedures on time and within budget. Indeed, the report said, that 'it is difficult to do good work for a bad client, and it is difficult to do bad work for a good client!' Subsequent media coverage was muted when these arguments became more widely understood.

Yet the old myths still abound, and in June 1997 a TV news presenter asserted during discussion that there are no qualifications and no codes of ethics for management consultants – errors that could have easily been avoided by simply making a telephone call to either the

Management Consultancies Association (MCA) or the Institute of Management Consultants (IMC).

The 'complex society' of Bellah and the pace of change in society have meant that such generalistic views have become outdated, and often refer to only a minority of management consultants. While there will always be rogues who make a practice of duping clients, in my personal experience these are outnumbered by the many management consultants who take pride in delivering an outstanding service to their clients.

Consultants who display integrity often belong to a larger body. Such bodies may be one of the major consultancy/accountancy firms that lay down their own standards. These standards have the added bonus of being self-serving in that they help to build the confidence of clients and encourage a steady flow of work from them. The large firm may also be a member of MCA, which, at the time of writing, represents 34 large management consultancy firms and has a code of conduct to which member firms must subscribe. Individuals, whether employed by a firm, large or small, or in practice on their own, may be members of the IMC, which has a code of professional conduct, ethical guidelines, and requires an annual commitment to continuing professional development. Failure to observe these codes can result in sanctions being applied against the offending member. Unfortunately, if the subject of a complaint is not a member of either of these bodies, then little can be done as the profession is not regulated by statute.

Both the IMC's and MCA's codes focus on the clients. They have served these bodies and their members well up to now, but the time may be approaching when it will be necessary to widen their scope, to cover a social dimension and other ethical 'stakeholders', particularly protecting the public interest, however difficult 'public interest' may be to define.

To some extent this social dimension has been recognized indirectly with the formation of the Guild of Management Consultants, which is seeking to become a liveried company in the City of London. To succeed, the Guild must build up a fund available for charitable works and be seen to carry out such good works. This, at least indirectly and subconsciously, seems to acknowledge the social dimension.

In 1993, James Kennedy interviewed a number of leading American management consultants and found that not more than 60 per cent regarded management consultancy as a profession. However, many of those in the management consultancy business are also practitioners of professions such as accountancy, engineering and the law. In addition there are special interest groupings for management consultancy within professional bodies, such as the Institute of Management and the Chartered Institute of Management Accountants. These links lend a sense of professionalism to management consultants by association.

Management consultancy is without doubt a business – but so is the work of professional firms. It is also a separate commercial activity from management as it requires skills and techniques to practise it. Not only must consultants understand management, they must also understand how to achieve tasks without power, using only their ability to persuade and influence the client.

A final word about the need for codes of professional conduct. In the United States, we can observe the litigation phenomenon. The rise in the volume and value of cases of professional negligence has required professional firms to take great care that they manage the risks to which they can be exposed.

> For negligence to be proved, the plaintiff must demonstrate failure to exercise all reasonable professional care in carrying out work which the firm or individual warranted, by taking on the work, that they possessed the professional skill to perform. The standard of care can be measured by reference to the quality of work reasonably to be expected from a professional firm or individual having such a skill at the time. It is further measured by reference to the purpose for which the work or advice was required.

> *(Excerpt from the presidential address of Duncan G R Ferguson, MA DipAgSci FIA, President of the Institute of Actuaries, 7 October 1996)*

Such considerations are powerful motivators when considering the need to protect a firm and manage the risk inherent in providing advice. The senior, or managing, partner cannot be everywhere and cannot control the quality of advice provided and the research each employee conducts. Instead, they must find a means of building integrity into the firm's operations.

Three examples of the sorts of dilemmas that may face management consultants follow that might be helpful at this point to clarify the challenges discussed above. The examples are from Milan Kubr's book, *Management Consulting* (1996).

Conflicts of interest

A large firm is advising a client in targeting potential third parties for takeover to enhance their strategic position in the market. The favoured target for takeover happens to be the client of another office of the same firm, where a separate team of consultants is advising the target firm on how it might improve its competitiveness.

An audit firm suggests that its client use its consulting division to deal with a specific problem identified during the course of the audit. There may be other consulting firms that could do the same job better or at less cost or without any possibility of a conflict of interest arising between the audit and consulting arms of the firm.

A consultant is carrying out an assignment strictly according to the agreed plan. However, it is almost certain that he will make no progress and his proposals will not be implemented. Thus, in such a case, the temptation would be not to put much effort into it.

Becoming a certified management consultant

The internationally recognized professional qualification for individuals in management consultancy, whether employed by a large practice or self-employed, is that required to become a certified management consultant. The qualification, once achieved, stays with you when you move from one practice to another or from employed to self-employed status.

In the UK, the qualification is regulated by the IMC, and it is regulated in 23 other countries by national institutes that are members of the International Council of Management Consulting Institutes (ICMCI). A list of these bodies and the contact details for the ICMCI are given in Appendix B to this chapter.

Among other matters, to retain the certified management consultant qualification it is necessary to make an affirmation each year that you will abide by the code of professional conduct and agree to continuing professional development.

Ethical norms

Many professions publish detailed ethical rules and regulations. However, seeing these in operation, there is a tendency on the part of members of these professions to seek ways of avoiding or evading the rules. As a result, some bodies have concluded that codes of conduct need to be principle-based. This helps to avoid the need to rewrite codes and extend their application in ways that were never imagined when the codes were initially drafted. However, there is also a need to build in a process that enables a reinterpretation of the principles to cover new situations when they arise.

There was far from uniform agreement when it was suggested that management consultants should raise their sights by extending their enforceable code by means of *unenforceable* ethical guidelines. The need to define such norms became clear, however, when a group of experienced consultants responded to a simple questionnaire. The questionnaire and the responses are reproduced in Appendix C to this chapter.

The percentages reported represented the proportions of the respondents favouring each response. For example, in response to question 3, regarding the copying of the office's computer software for home use, 33 per cent of the consultants thought that this was wrong, a further 52 per cent could find some justification for doing this, while the remainder, 15 per cent, could see no reason for this being wrong, and circled the 'Acceptable' response.

The respondents were predominantly experienced older management consultants, white and male. It was thought that with such homogeneous backgrounds, there would be a large degree of convergence and agreement among such a group. Judge for yourselves what happened. While you are considering the relatively simple dilemmas posed, perhaps you would like to think about how you would have answered the questions. Note that no further information was given to the respondents, and the situations had to be judged solely on the basis of often inadequate information. (Do you ever have all the information you feel you need to arrive at a satisfactory conclusion?)

The responses showed unexpected divergences of opinion – in some cases the differences were quite large. Some of this may have been a reflection of the differing commercial pressures on large firms and their smaller counterparts. For example, the polarized responses to questions 17 and 18, regarding conflicts of interest, could be explained, perhaps, by the stands taken by members of large firms and sole practitioners respectively, the large firms turning their practices into multidisciplinary service businesses and the smaller ones tending to offer services in just one area.

After debate on these unexpected results, it was agreed that ethical guidelines should be drawn up. These were published by the IMC in 1994, and it is believed that, at the time of writing, they are unique.

Ethical guidelines

The IMC's and MCA's codes of professional conduct embody the following basic principles:

- high standards of service to the client
- independence, objectivity and integrity
- responsibility to the profession.

For a fuller explanation of these principles, see Appendices D and E to this chapter, which contain the IMC's and MCA's codes respectively.

It is my belief that the focus of ethical behaviour should be on the individuals who make up the firms, and not on the firms themselves. As a result, the emphasis of this part of the book is on individuals and the recognized body regulating individual management consultants' qualifications and behaviour in the UK, which is the IMC.

For members of the IMC and MCA, the codes of professional conduct are legally enforceable, and, assuming that a case can be proved, sanctions can be applied to any member who fails to comply. The extension of these principles into guidelines on ethical behaviour are unenforceable, but the IMC's members are expected to observe them when deciding their course of action or inaction.

Assuming that the facts are known and established, which is not always the case, then two additional principles should be considered, and these are supported by a series of testing questions. These are the principles of:

- vulnerability
- transparency.

The principle of vulnerability

This is the first principle. It identifies the extent of the risk for parties involved in a particular situation. For example, one party may be weak because of ignorance or financial capability.

The testing questions suggested in the ethical guidelines are designed to take the consultant through a self-administered process that will enable them to identify the vulnerable or weak stakeholders in the situation. ('Stakeholders' is a term that has gained currency in recent years and is used to refer to all parties who may have an interest in, or be affected by, a decision.)

The principle of transparency

This is the second principle. This is the degree to which there is openness in a situation or how much knowledge or information has been made available to stakeholders. If they are not in possession of all the relevant facts, the question should be posed, why not?

Again, the process of working through the testing questions can help individuals to develop an insight into their dilemma. By doing so, the solution may become obvious. Alternatively, the true nature of the dilemma may be revealed, and the route to a solution can then be planned based on facts.

Applying the guidelines

None of these testing questions, or other consultations, excuses an individual from responsibility. In a firm, a sense of collegiality can help. There may be a trusted colleague with whom an individual can talk over the dilemma without compromising their responsibility to the client or their position in the firm. For sole practitioners, talking with a former colleague or a trusted and informed friend can make all the difference.

For those without formal or informal support structures, the UK's IMC has established the Ethical Helpline, which offers confidential non-judgemental counselling to assist members towards managing their own solutions to such difficult challenges. The Ethical Helpline is supported by a number of experienced management consultants, who have had training in telephone counselling. Often a dilemma can arise unexpectedly, and needs to be addressed urgently. Because the Helpline is manned by experienced consultants, they can quickly gain an understanding of the situation being outlined to them and respond in an appropriate and sympathetic way. This enables members to test out their attitude without fear or risk of public censure and hopefully arrive at a suitable solution that strikes an acceptable balance between the interests of the stakeholders involved.

As a final paradoxical comment on the matter, I have heard it said 'that the true nature of a dilemma is not so much the choice between right and wrong, but the choice between two rights!'

References

Bellah, R N (1985) *Habits of the Heart: Individualism and commitment in American life*, University of California Press, Berkeley

Institute of Management Consultants (1994) *Code of Professional Conduct*, Institute of Management Consultants, London

Ferguson, D G R (1996), 'Presidential address', 7 October, Institute of Actuaries, London

Management Consultancy: A handbook for best practice

Harrison, R (1995) *Study into the Government's use of External Consultants,* HMSO, London

Kennedy, J H (1993) 'Management consulting today – a look around and a look ahead', *Consultants News,* Kennedy Publications, Fitzwilliam, NH

Kubr, M (1996) *Management Consulting: A guide to the profession* (3rd edn, revised), International Labour Office, Geneva

Mahoney, J, (1989) Business as a Profession, Gresham College Public Lecture, London

Management Consultancies Association, *Code of Professional Conduct,* Management Consultancies Association, London

Toffler, A (1970) *Future Shock,* Bantam Books Inc, New York

Appendix A: Members of the International Council of Management Consulting Institutes (ICMCI), August 1997

Australia	Institute of Management Consultants, Australia
Austria	Fachverband Unternehmensberatung Und Datenverarbeitung
Bangladesh	Institute of Management Consultants, Bangladesh
Canada	Institute of Certified Management Consultants
Denmark	Foreningen af Management Konsulenter
Finland	The Finnish Management Consultants, LJK (Lükkeenjohdon Konsultit RY)
France	Office Professionnel de Qualification des Conseils en Management (OPQCM)
Germany	Bundesverband Deutscher Unternehmensberatur (BDU e V)
Hungary	Association of Management Consultants in Hungary
India	The Institute of Management Consultants of India
Indonesia	Institute of Management Consultants, Indonesia
Ireland	Institute of Management Consultants, Ireland
Italy	Associazione Professionale Italiana Dei Consulenti Di Direzione Ed Organizzazione (APCO)
Malaysia	Institute of Management Consultants, Malaysia

Netherlands	Orde van organisatiekundigen en-adviseurs (OOA)
New Zealand	Institute of Management Consultants New Zealand Incorporated
Nigeria	Institute of Management Consultants of Nigeria
Poland	Association of Economic Consultants
Singapore	Institute of Management Consultants, Singapore
South Africa	Institute of Management Consultants, South Africa
Sweden	Swedish Association of Management Consultants
Switzerland	Association Suisse des Conseils en Organisation et Gestion (ASCO)
United Kingdom	Institute of Management Consultants, UK
United States of America	Institute of Management Consultants, USA

Full contact names and addresses of these institutes can be obtained from:

The Executive Office
International Council of Management Consulting Institutes, Inc
858 Long View Road
Burlingame
CA 94010 – 6974
United States of America

Tel: + + 415 342 2250
Fax: + + 415 344 5005
E-mail: icmci@icmci.org
Web site: http: //www.icmci.org/icmci

Appendix B: Ethics questionnaire and responses

The three choices of responses to each of the situations were:

- wrong/unacceptable
- wrong in principle, but acceptable
- acceptable.

Respondents were asked to circle the response with which they felt most comfortable.

Question No.	Situation	Wrong	Wrong but Acceptable	Acceptable
1	You move into a new flat and find that you have cable TV connected but never receive a bill. You keep watching it anyway.	33%	57%	10%
2	You have only one term to finish your degree. On a job application form, you say that you have a university degree.	100%	0%	0%
3	You have a home computer but do not have the same software that you use in the office. Your boss says it is OK to take the software home and copy it.	33%	52%	15%
4	Your son/daughter needs a paper typed for school or university. You ask your secretary to type it and make any necessary grammatical and spelling corrections.	19%	28%	53%
5	The bank makes a £100 error in your favour. You decide to let them find it.	52%	43%	5%
6	You take up a collection for a fellow worker and find that you have more money than you expected. At lunchtime you find that you don't have enough cash for lunch. You take £5 from the collection envelope knowing that it will never be missed.	96%	4%	0%
7	You call a director while they are at lunch, hoping to find the secretary who may have some information but is likely to be less suspicious about your motives.	10%	33%	57%
8	A headhunter on a cold call was told by the Director of Engineering to get off the phone – he never dealt with headhunters – no one in the company was permitted to speak to headhunters. If he, the headhunter, called again, he, the director, would institute legal action. A senior colleague overheard the headhunter and said 'Let me show you how to deal with this.' Ten minutes later he phoned the same director and said he was a university student whose professor had told him to contact one of the company's engineers, but unfortunately he had forgotten the engineer's name, and he was afraid to call the professor back. Over the next half hour, the Director proceeded to reel off the names of 150 engineers in his organization, describing them by background, experience and speciality.	62%	28%	10%
9	Your client already knows the solution that they want to the problem.	43%	14%	43%

Professionalism and ethics

10	Your client wants you to omit important information from your written report.	76%	14%	10%
11	Your client wants proprietary information that you gained while on an assignment with another client.	100%	0%	0%
12	Your client wants you to lie to his boss.	100%	0%	0%
13	You are a headhunter and a member of a client's staff wants you to recruit him.	85%	15%	0%
14	Your client wants you to invoice them for more, or less, than the actual amount involved.	85%	10%	5%
15	'When in Rome, do as the Romans do' – go native.	24%	28%	48%
16	I own a few shares in my client.	60%	0%	40%
17	My business partner, a chartered accountant, is auditor to my client.	62%	5%	33%
18	My business partner, a lawyer, is legal adviser to my client.	55%	0%	45%
19a	The Tylanol crisis. Tylanol capsules were poisoned in the Chicago area by being laced with cyanide. Johnson & Johnson had two choices: • withdraw all supplies immediately.	0%	0%	100%
19b	• assume it was an isolated incident and withdraw only in the Chicago area.	68%	10%	22%

Source: Questionnaire and responses 1992, © Christian Paul Lynch

Appendix C: Code of professional conduct of the Institute of Management Consultants (IMC) ©

The IMC is the professional and regulatory body for individual management consultants in the UK.

In recognition of their obligations to clients, to the public at large and to the profession, all members annually agree, in writing, to comply with the Institute's code of professional conduct. They also agree to undertake relevant continuing professional development activities. This distinguishes management consultants who are members of the Institute from other practitioners.

The code of professional conduct

The Institute's code of professional conduct is based on three basic principles dealing with:

- meeting the client's requirements
- integrity, independence, objectivity
- responsibility to the profession and to the Institute.

These principles are underpinned by detailed rules, which are specific injunctions, and practical notes, which either lay down conditions under which certain activities are permitted or indicate good practice and how best to observe the relevant principle or rule.

The Council of the Institute may, from time to time, issue further principles, rules or notes that will be promulgated in the Institute's publications before being incorporated into a revised edition of the code. Members are expected to abide by all such new provisions from the date of their publication.

The principles, rules and notes of the code apply not only to the members personally but also to acts carried out via a partner, co-director, employee or other agent acting on behalf of, or under the control of, the member.

Definitions used in the code

Member	A fellow, full member, associate member or affiliate of the Institute.
Client	The person, firm or organization with whom the member makes an agreement or contract for the provision of services.
Declaration	A written statement referring to and disclosing the facts relevant to the situations covered by particular rules of the code.
Independent	In a position always to express freely your own opinion without any control or influence from others outside the (consulting) organization, and without the need to consider the impact of such opinion on your own interests.
Institute	The Institute of Management Consultants.

Disciplinary action

Members are liable to disciplinary action if their conduct is found, by the Disciplinary Committee of the Institute, to be in contravention of the code or to bring discredit to the profession or to the Institute.

In accordance with the by-laws, members may be required to make a declaration in answer to enquiries from the Institute concerning their professional conduct. A member failing to make such a declaration may be found in breach of the principle to which the rule or note relates.

Professionalism and ethics

Principle 1: Meeting the client's requirements
A member shall regard the client's requirements and interests as paramount at all times.

Rules

Competence
1.1   A member will only accept work that the member is qualified to perform and in which the client can be served effectively; a member will not make any misleading claims and will provide references from other clients if requested.

Agreement on deliverables and fees
1.2   A member shall agree formally with the client the scope, nature and deliverables of the services to be provided and the basis of remuneration, in advance of commencing work; any subsequent revisions will be subject to prior discussion and agreement with the client.

Subcontracting
1.3   A member shall subcontract work only with the prior agreement of the client, and, except where otherwise agreed, will remain responsible for the performance of the work.

Confidentiality
1.4   A member will hold all information concerning the affairs of clients in the strictest confidence and will not disclose proprietary information obtained during the course of assignments.

Non-poaching
1.5   A member will not invite or encourage any employee of a client for whom the member is working to consider alternative employment, unless it is the purpose of the assignment.

Due care
1.6   A member will make certain that advice, solutions and recommendations are based on thorough, impartial consideration and analysis of all available pertinent facts and relevant experience and are realistic, practicable and clearly understood by the client.

Communication
1.7   A member will ensure that the client is kept fully informed about the progress of the assignment.
1.8   A member will encourage and take note of any feedback provided by the client on the performance of the member's services.

Respect
1.9   A member will act with courtesy and consideration towards the individuals contacted in the course of undertaking assignments.

Management Consultancy: A handbook for best practice

Principle 2: Integrity, independence, objectivity

A member shall avoid any action or situation inconsistent with the member's professional obligations or that in any way might be seen to impair the member's integrity. In formulating advice and recommendations, the member will be guided solely by the member's objective view of the client's best interests.

Rules

Disclosure

2.1   A member will disclose at the earliest opportunity any special relationships, circumstances or business interests that might influence or impair, or could be seen by the client or others to influence or impair, the member's judgement or objectivity on a particular assignment.

2.1.1 Rule 2.1 requires the prior disclosure of all relevant personal, financial or other business interests that could not be inferred from the description of the services offered. In particular this relates to:

- any directorship or controlling interest in any business in competition with the client
- financial interest in goods or services recommended or supplied to the client
- any personal relationship with any individual in the client's employ
- any personal investment in the client organization or in its parent or any subsidiary companies
- any recent or current engagements in sensitive areas of work with directly competitive clients
- any work for a third party on the opposite side of a transaction, such as bid defence, acquisitions, work for the regulator and the regulated, assessing the products of an existing client.

Conflicts of interest

2.2   A member shall not serve a client under circumstances that are inconsistent with the member's professional obligations or that in any way might be seen to impair the member's integrity; wherever a conflict or potential conflict of interest arises, the member shall, as the circumstances require, either withdraw from the assignment, remove the source of conflict or disclose and obtain the agreement of the parties concerned to the performance or continuance of the engagement.

2.2.1 It should be noted that the Institute may, depending on the circumstances, be one of the 'parties concerned'. For example, if a member is under pressure to act in a way that would bring the member into non-compliance with the code of professional conduct, in addition to any other declaration that it might be appropriate to make, the facts should be declared to the Institute.

Inducements

2.3   A member shall neither accept discounts, hospitality, commissions or gifts as an inducement to show favour to any person or body, nor attempt to obtain advantage by giving financial inducement to clients or client staff.

2.3.1   Payment for legitimate marketing activity may be made, and national laws should be respected.

Privacy of information

2.4   A member shall not use any confidential information about a client's affairs, elicited during the course of an assignment, for personal benefit or for the benefit of others outside the client organization; there shall be no insider dealing or trading as legally defined or understood.

2.5   When required or appropriate, a member will establish specific methods of working that preserve the privacy of the client's information.

Objectivity

2.6   A member will advise the client of any significant reservations the member may have about the client's expectation of benefits from an engagement.

2.7   A member will not indicate any short-term benefits at the expense of the long-term welfare of the client without advising the client of the implications.

Principle 3: Responsibility to the profession and to the Institute

A member's conduct shall at all times endeavour to enhance the standing and public recognition of the profession and the Institute.

Rules

Annual affirmation

3.1   A member will provide the Institute with annual affirmation of adherence to the code of professional conduct.

Continuing professional development

3.2   A member will comply with the Institute's requirements on continuing professional development in order to ensure that the knowledge and skills the member offers to clients are kept up to date.

3.3   A member will encourage management consultants for whom the member is responsible to maintain and advance their competence by participating in continuing professional development and to obtain membership of the Institute.

Professional obligations to others

3.4   A member shall have respect for the professional obligations and qualifications of all others with whom the member works.

3.5   A member referring a client to another management consultant will neither misrepresent the qualifications of the other management consultant, nor make any commitments for the other management consultant.

3.6   A member accepting an assignment for a client knowing that another management consultant is serving the client will ensure that any potential conflict between assignments is brought to the attention of the client.

3.7   When asked by a client to review the work of another professional, a member will exercise the objectivity, integrity and sensitivity required in all technical and advisory conclusions communicated to the client.

Fees

3.8   A member will negotiate agreements and charges for professional services only in a manner approved as being ethical and professional by the Institute.

3.8.1 Members are referred to the Institute's 'Guidelines on Charging for Management Consulting Services'.

Publicity

3.9   A member, in publicizing work or making representations to a client, shall ensure that the information given is:

- factual and relevant
- neither misleading nor unfair to others
- not otherwise discreditable to the profession.

3.9.1 Accepted methods of making experience and/or availability known include:

- publication of work (with the consent of the client)
- direct approaches to potential clients via entries in any relevant directory advertisement (in printed publication or on radio or television) or public speaking engagements. Members are referred to the Institute's 'Guidelines on the Promotion of Management Consulting Services'.

Personal conduct

3.10   A member shall be a fit and proper person to carry on the profession of management consultancy.

3.10.1 A member shall at all times be of good reputation and character. Particular matters for concern might include:

- conviction of a criminal offence or committal under bankruptcy proceedings
- censure or disciplining by a court or regulatory authority
- unethical or improper behaviour towards employees or the general public.

3.11   A member shall not wilfully give the Institute false, inaccurate, misleading or incomplete information.

Source: © Institute of Management Consultants, UK

Appendix D: Code of professional conduct of the Management Consultancies Association (MCA).

The MCA is the trade association of larger consultancy firms in the UK.

Each member shall at all times maintain the highest ethical standard in the professional work undertaken and, in matters relating to a client's affairs, act solely in the interest of the client.

It shall be regarded as unprofessional conduct for any member:

- Rule 1 to disclose, or permit to be disclosed, confidential information regarding their client's business and staff
- Rule 2 to accept work for which the consultancy is not qualified
- Rule 3 to enter into any agreement that would detract from the objectivity and impartiality of the advice given to clients, and, in particular, it would be unprofessional conduct:
  - to accept or permit any member of their staff to accept from a third party any trade commission, discount or consideration of any kind in connection with the supply of goods or services to clients
  - to supply or recommend to a client goods or services in which they have a direct or indirect financial interest without disclosing such an interest to the client
  - to pay commission or any other form of remuneration to persons not on their staff for the introduction of clients
- Rule 4 not to agree in advance on the terms of remuneration and the basis of calculation thereof
- Rule 5 to do anything likely to lower the status of management consultancy as a profession.

Any member who, in the opinion of the Council, fails to comply with the code of professional conduct is liable to suspension from membership of the Association.

It shall be the duty of the Executive Director and the right of any member of the Council or aggrieved person to lay before the Council any facts indicating that a member has failed to observe the rules laid down in the code of professional conduct.

Part 2

The consulting process

3

Consultancy in a changing world

Philip Sadler

Introduction

This chapter outlines the major environmental changes that have affected, and will continue to affect, organizations and draws out the implications of these changes for the consultancy industry.

Change brings with it new problems, the solutions to which cannot be derived from past experience. Many changes occurring simultaneously and interacting with each other give rise to complexity. The essence of consultancy lies in the twin activities of devising solutions to new problems and in resolving complicated issues. Thus, the greater the rate of change, the greater the demand for consultancy services.

The main categories of environmental change

It is common practice to use the mnemonic PEST to refer to the four main categories of change – political, economic, social and technological.

Political changes

These are occurring at every level – global, regional, national and local.

Some of the things that have affected many businesses and public-sector organizations in the past decade or so include:

- the passing of power upwards to supra-national bodies, such as the EU
- the passing of power downwards to regional government
- privatization

- deregulation in some respects, such as financial markets
- increased regulation in others, for example with regard to the environment, health and safety, and EU harmonization
- the reduction of East–West political tensions and military preparedness following the collapse of communist regimes
- diplomatic problems with foreign governments, such as those of the UK with Saudi Arabia and Malaysia
- various political (as distinct from military or economic) decisions to purchase or not to purchase such goods as military aircraft or major infrastructure projects.

In addition, business prospects can be significantly affected by the economic and social policies of the government of the day and are likely to change radically if there is a change of government.

In the 1980s and 1990s, a series of changes with very significant consequences for the consultancy industry resulted from the UK government's programme for the reform of the public services. This involved questioning almost every aspect of the established ways of doing things. Large-scale changes took place in the context of the shifting of a great deal of activity from the public to the private sector, and in making the public sector itself more responsive to market forces.

There were three main strands to the government's programme.

1 Pushing responsibility and accountability for performance closer to the point of service delivery. This involved the creation of 'Next Steps' executive agencies with enhanced managerial discretion within defined performance standards.
2 Getting close to customer needs and expectations. This included the Citizen's Charter, calling for a greater openness and a focus on improving service quality.
3 The 'Competing for Quality' initiative, which sought to test services against market criteria and, in appropriate cases, led to contracting out non-core activities.

As a consequence, the traditional way of centrally conceived and uniformly applied policies and practices has been challenged and dismantled. The customary obedience to rules is being replaced by the requirement for flexibility and innovation. Hierarchical structures are being flattened and teamworking is replacing functional departments. New performance standards are being developed.

All this activity has resulted in a much greater use of outside consultants. Consultancies have, in response to these needs, developed special competencies in dealing with the public sector. They have had to become skilled in the process of tendering for assignments and in working within the constraints of public-sector organizations where the freedom to change things is limited – sometimes because of legislation, sometimes because of culture, custom and practice.

Economic changes

It is important to distinguish between short-term or cyclical change and longer-term structural or fundamental change. This is because although short-term changes may well call for related changes on the part of organizations, they will not normally require radical shifts in strategic direction. The longer-term changes, however, will almost certainly result in the need to revise an organization's strategic thinking and, in consequence, call for more fundamental changes to be made to the organization's policies and practices.

Short-term, cyclical changes
These include such volatile elements in the economic environment as:

- the business cycle
- interest rates
- exchange rates
- property values
- inflation
- levels of taxation
- bull and bear markets in the world's stock exchanges.

The normal response to such changes on the part of business is tactical rather than strategic, with the implication that radical change can be avoided. In practice, a very severe recession or a collapse in property values may give rise to radical cost-cutting programmes, involving plant closures and redundancies. A more strategic response might involve, for example, developing products or services that are less susceptible to the business cycle, or are even counter-cyclical. Short-term changes such as these can, of course, change the assumptions underlying a consultancy project, leading to significant change in its objectives or even its curtailment.

In the modern world, periods of economic stability are rare indeed, with the result that top management spends a great deal of time and energy 'fire-fighting' as it develops tactical responses to these short-term shifts. Unfortunately, this distracts them from paying attention to the underlying trends that, in the long run, may prove a much more serious threat to the organization's continued existence.

Pascale (1991) has given us an apt analogy – the case of the boiled frog. If you put a frog in a pot of cold water and bring it – very, very slowly – to the boil, the creature will make no attempt to escape and will eventually die. This is because the change in temperature is so gradual that the frog cannot sense it. Similarly, some of the really significant changes that are taking place as we approach the twenty-first century are so gradual that they escape the notice of decision makers.

Longer-term underlying changes
Among the most important under this heading are the following.

Underlying, growth rates
Booms and recessions tend to conceal the fact that, in almost every part of the world, per capita income increases from one decade to the next. Despite the depth and duration of the recession in the UK in the 1990s, the value of UK gross domestic product, in real terms, rose by over 6 per cent between 1990 and 1995.

Long-term economic growth is significant in the developed world in terms of its impact on the structure of demand as the proportion of disposable income available for discretionary spending increases. However, it is of even greater significance in developing countries. As growth takes place in China, for example, what is potentially the world's largest market is beginning to develop very rapidly. According to Naisbitt (1994), as measured by the purchasing power parity method, China is already the world's third largest economy after the US and Japan, and, if the current momentum is maintained, it will be the largest in the world by the year 2003. More telephone lines will be installed in China in the next decade than during the whole of the twentieth century in North America.

The globalization of markets
A number of factors – such as the dismantling of many former barriers to international trade, the deregulation of financial markets, the growing convergence of consumer tastes and improvements in communications – have led to the growth of transnational business. The consequences of this are that, for many industries, the market for their products or services is now worldwide, but the rub is that there are few domestic industries that are not now faced with competition from overseas.

Kenechi Ohmae of McKinsey in his book *The Borderless World* (1990) has brilliantly set out the consequences of globalization for business strategy. The consultancy industry itself is typical in this respect. Increasing globalization has placed new demands on the consultancy world – the need to be able to communicate in different languages, work effectively in highly differing cultures and withstand the stresses associated with extensive foreign travel.

Regional economies
The EU has become a major force for change. Partly this results from efforts to create 'a level playing field' in the interests of fair and free competition between member states. Partly it is a function of the new opportunities for mergers, alliances and joint ventures. The advent, sooner or later, of a single European currency will have very considerable consequences that are very difficult to predict.

New sources of competition
In a number of industries, the *status quo* has been radically disrupted by the growth of competition from unlikely, non-traditional sources. Nowhere is this more evident than in the field of financial services. In recent years, for example, the traditional credit card-issuing companies (banks and American Express) have been challenged by such unlikely competitors as General Motors and AT&T. AT&T has moved from a standing start to become the major issuer of credit cards in America in just three years. Similarly, in Britain, Marks & Spencer is now a major source of personal finance and pension plans.

Deindustrialization
Since the 1960s (even earlier in the US), an important long-term trend in the developed economies has been the relative decline in manufacturing and the relative growth in the service sector. In the UK, for example, in 1966, the number of people employed in manufacturing, at just over 4 million, was less than 25 per cent of the number employed in the service sector – some 16.8 million. The service sector is, of course, a substantial employer of women and this, coupled with important social changes in family life, has led to the rapid growth in the numbers of women in employment alongside the decline in employment for men.

Deindustrialization reflects a number of other underlying trends:

- the industrialization of the Third World means that more and more manufacturing is taking place in countries such as Malaysia, South Korea, Brazil, Taiwan and Indonesia
- as people's standards of living rise, they tend to spend disproportionately more of their incomes on services, such as banking,

insurance, travel, and leisure pursuits, and, at the same time, industry itself makes growing use of such services as advertising, design, consultancy and facilities management.

One consequence of the growth in the service sector trend has been the opening up of a new specialist consulting activity relating to the achievement of service excellence.

Changes in the structure of economic organizations
The tightly structured, hierarchical, bureaucratic and monolithic type of large business organization that was pioneered by General Motors, and that typified major corporations up until the 1980s, is on the way out, giving way to flatter, leaner, more freewheeling structures, as typified by ABB, CNN and the IT consultancy EDS.

Downsizing and delayering have become widespread. The message for the 1990s from Jack Welch of GE was 'Think small. What we are trying relentlessly to do is to get that small company soul – and small company speed – inside our big company body.' Employment in GE was cut by over 100,000 in 11 years.

The breaking up of very large companies – as was the case for ICI and Courtaulds in the UK – has emerged as a new trend in the late 1990s that is beginning to displace 'merger mania'.

Companies have also sought to focus on what they deem to be their core business and to subcontract or outsource the non-core activities, particularly such things as transportation, catering, security, facilities management and IT.

Consultancies specializing in strategy and structure have both influenced these trends and prospered from their growth. Perhaps the leading advocate of such developments has been the American consultant-cum-guru Tom Peters, who, in his personal appearances and books such as *Liberation Management* (1992), has powerfully stated the case for banishing bureaucracy.

Another important structural trend has been the growth in the number of strategic alliances. Jordan D Lewis points out in his book *Partnership for Profit* (1990) that, at the same time as global competition is raising the standards for quality, innovation productivity and customer value, the scope for what a firm can do alone is shrinking. Using examples from such firms as IBM, Fuji, Rank Xerox, Ford, Dow Chemical, Intel, Komatsu, Sony and Apple, he goes on to show how alliance partners build trust and share key decisions, while at the same time protecting their business interests and core technology. This has been particularly marked in the automotive and airline industries, as exemplified by Ford with Mazda and Volkswagen or Rover with Honda, and British Airways with American Airlines.

The growth of the 'knowledge economy'

Economic theorists and practising managers alike have come to understand that, in the modern economy, the traditional factors of production – land, labour and capital – pale into insignificance alongside knowledge. The competitive edge of most companies and all national economies rest, in the last resort, on the ability to generate and exploit new knowledge. Today, probably the newest but most rapidly growing field for consultancy is the field of knowledge management or, as it is sometimes referred to, the management of intellectual capital.

Changes in the nature of work and employment

William Bridges in his best-selling book *Jobshift* (1996) has drawn attention to the way in which the nature of work and employment is changing. Trends already mentioned – such as deindustrialization, the growth of global competition, the flattening of organizational structures, the outsourcing of non-core activities, together with the spread of automation – have led to a sharp decline in the traditional kind of job on the assembly line, in the mines, docks or transport industry, and to the disappearance of large numbers of middle management jobs. One result of this has been a mass migration of middle managers into the consulting industry – often as sole practitioners or in small partnerships. Another has been the growth of opportunities for consultancy firms in the field of outsourcing, particularly with respect to IT. A third consequence has been the growth in the number of small firms and the related development of smaller enterprise advisory services as a specialist consulting field. This trend is particularly strong in the United States, where *Fortune* 500 companies now account for only 10 per cent of the American economy, down from 20 per cent in 1970. Over half of the USA's exports are created by firms with fewer than 20 employees. The same is true of Germany.

The implications

If we pause and consider the implications of these longer-term trends for one UK company – Rolls Royce PLC – we can see how, sooner or later, they will necessitate strategic change. Long-term economic growth will determine the rate of growth in the world demand for air travel, and differential growth rates will determine which nations will be the major purchasers of aircraft engines.

Who, in the 1960s, would have predicted that Singapore and Hong Kong would now be major world players in the airline industry?

China's future development is an obvious market to go for in the longer-term, but there will be some surprise entrants also.

The industry is already a global one with three major players: GE, Pratt and Whitney, and Rolls-Royce. Already joint ventures and strategic alliances are being formed. The future will see growing involvement in the industry on the part of Japanese and German companies. Mergers are not beyond possibility.

Given the cost pressures and political influences, another issue facing the company is the question of where to locate any expansion of its manufacturing activities. Would having plants in Japan or the US increase the company's chances of having its products chosen by national airlines in those countries? Are there countries where the level of skill in the workforce would meet Rolls-Royce's exacting quality requirements, but with significantly lower labour costs than in the UK?

On the one hand, none of the above issues has necessarily to be resolved within a short timescale. On the other hand, if the company ignored them, its own long-term future might be in danger.

The scope for consultancy advice in relation to these issues arises in a number of ways. Specialists in the aviation world could be called in to advise on future trends in the demand for aircraft engines. Consultants of a different kind could be involved in due diligence investigations prior to acquisitions or joint ventures. A firm with strong experience of developing manufacturing plants on greenfield sites could advise on establishing new manufacturing capacity overseas.

Social changes

These take various forms. One aspect of social change is changes in people's attitudes, values and beliefs. Long-term changes in Western countries over the past two or three decades include:

- a much greater emphasis on health and safety – with the result that huge changes have been forced on such industries as tobacco, food manufacturing and retailing, motor vehicle manufacturing, construction and civil engineering
- a steadily growing concern for the environment – in this area, public pressure and lobbying, by such bodies as Greenpeace and Friends of the Earth, has led to a mass of new legislation, and the major industries that have had to adjust include the oil industry, the chemical industry, electricity generation, motor vehicle manufacturing and fishing; a whole new field of consulting practice has grown out of these developments

- a growing demand, increasingly backed by legislation, on the part of women and members of ethnic minorities, for equality of treatment and equality of opportunity
- changing attitudes to authority – people in positions of authority, such as teachers, managers, even policemen, increasingly find that their decisions are challenged, that compliance cannot be assumed (managing change in industry calls for winning people's hearts and minds rather than giving orders) – those in charge have to learn how to lead instead of the traditional 'command and control' approach – and trends of this kind have led to a growth in demand for consultants with the skills of process facilitation and the development of interpersonal skills.

Changing social values and attitudes affect people's lifestyles and, hence, such things as their purchasing habits and patterns of television viewing. Tracking such changes is, therefore, of considerable importance to business and particularly to companies manufacturing fast-moving consumer goods or providing mass services, such as package holidays.

In the UK, one method employed by Synergy Consulting to do just this involves dividing the population into three broad groups:

- the inner directed
- the outer directed
- the sustenance driven.

For most of the last 20 years – not just in the UK, but in most of the Western world – the first two groups have been growing while the sustenance group has been declining.

These three groups can be further subdivided into seven social groups, as follows:

- self-explorers – expected to grow over the next few years
- experimentalists – expected to increase (with more women joining this group) in the long-term but presently decreasing
- conspicuous consumers – tends to grow in times of economic health, so the numbers in this group were stagnant in the early 1980s but are now growing
- belongers – there has been a gradual long-term decline in numbers, but these vary in response to economic cycles
- social resisters – continuing long-term decline as members age and their value set becomes less appropriate for tomorrow's world
- survivors – increased sharply between 1992 and 1996; now static, but has been forecasted to decline in the future
- aimless – very gradual long-term decline of numbers.

A second aspect of social change is the effect it has had on social institutions. In the majority of societies, the most fundamental social institution is the family, and it is at the level of family life that some of the most profound social changes have been taking place. The increase in the divorce rate, the decline of parental authority, the growth in the number of single-parent families and the separation of older people from their families have created enormous challenges for the public sector, particularly education and the social services.

A notable feature of UK society in recent years has been the growth and professionalization of the voluntary sector. This has led to a considerable volume of consultancy work, and several of the larger firms now have divisions specializing in assignments for charities.

Other changes in this area include those in the role and power of trade unions, the rise of the transnational organization and the decline of traditional religion.

There have also been profound changes in the third aspect of social change, the social structure – particularly the age structure. The full implications of an ageing society have yet to be grasped in most developed countries, particularly in terms of its impact on pensions and the provision of health care.

The fourth area of social change is that of patterns of behaviour. Demand for goods and services is very much a function of people's lifestyles. As discretionary incomes rise, people become more conscious of the quality of life and patterns of spending change. The demand for low-calorie, low-fat diets increases, and the consumption of 'unhealthy' products goes into decline; people spend more and more on leisure activities, second holidays become much more common, and more and more people become involved in keeping fit. Unfortunately, it is also the case that crime rates – particularly crimes involving violence – continue to grow. Thus, the already huge cost to industry of theft, fraud and sheer vandalism is likely to increase in the years ahead, giving rise to a greater demand for consultancy in respect of security.

Technological changes

We tend to think of technology as essentially to do with hardware. However, the essence of technology is *applied knowledge,* and this can take the form of 'software', by which I mean not simply computer programmes, but know-how of many kinds.

Using the term in this way, there are all sorts of technological changes occurring today.

- New processes for manufacturing goods or delivering services. Into this group come not only new forms of 'hardware', such as automation equipment in a factory or automatic cash dispensers in retail banking, but also new 'soft' technologies such as the Just-in-Time (JIT) method of inventory control, which are more to do with systems and procedures than with machinery. This latter type of change has led to considerable growth in the demand for consultancy as firms seek to achieve world-class standards in productivity and quality by means of a combination of new plant and machinery, increased automation, Just-in-Time management of stocks and work in progress and overall improvements in workflow. This field has given rise to a series of generic approaches, such as Total Quality Management (TQM), business process re-engineering and lean production.

- New thinking in the field of management itself. Consulting firms such as The Boston Consulting Group, Hay Management Consultants, McKinsey & Co and others have themselves played a leading part in developing the 'technology' of management, creating tools and techniques for analysing company performance, formulating strategy, designing organizational structures and creating effective remuneration systems. Other influences have included the 'gurus' of the business schools and models derived from the conspicuous success achieved by some Japanese companies. This is a dynamic and rapidly developing field in which new techniques flow thick and fast. Richard Pascale in *Managing on the Edge* (1991) charts the change in management tools since the 1960s (when T-groups, brainstorming, Theory X and Theory Y, the Managerial Grid and decision trees were current) through to the 1990s (value chains, scenario planning, activity-based costing (ABC), etc).

- New products and significantly improved products resulting from advances in technology and/or science in such diverse fields as electronics, pharmaceuticals, materials, food processing and aeronautics. In recent years, the list includes compact discs, mobile phones, digital TV, virtual reality, a whole range of new ethical drugs and low-cost personal computers. Consultants with strong marketing expertise are often involved in designing programmes for new product launches.

- Developments in the technology for processing and transmitting information. This is the domain of information technology (IT), which combines computers, telecommunications technologies and television. These developments are to do with both hardware and software and have consequences for all organizations, large or small.

They are proceeding at incredible speed, such that today's solutions rapidly become obsolete. Once valued primarily as a means of reducing costs and raising productivity, IT will increasingly play a strategic role. The Internet, operating on a global scale, and the Intranet, providing a new framework for corporate communications and data retrieval, are still both in their infancy. It is also increasingly apparent that changing IT without thinking through related changes in organizational structure and process design is unlikely to yield satisfactory results. IT developments have led to huge growth in the demand for consultancy services, including very large outsourcing contracts, and there are many firms that now specialize in this type of work. At the same time, the consultancy firms have had to learn how to adapt IT to fit into their own operations.

• Developments stemming from breakthroughs in the biological sciences, such as the identification of genes, genetic patenting and cloning. The implications of such new technologies for business have yet to work themselves out, but are likely to lead to the creation of whole new industries and open up yet new fields for specialist advice.

Turbulent environments

The word 'turbulent' has come to be used to describe an environment characterized both by several changes occurring rapidly and simultaneously and by a situation such that only the most optimistic see the possibility of a return to a more stable environment in the foreseeable future. Such a turbulent environment has been experienced by IBM.

Past	Present
• Few customers.	• Millions of customers.
• Traditional competition.	• Thousands of competitors.
• Predictable technological change.	• Exploding rate of change.
• Hardware-dominated.	• Software/systems/solutions.
• Direct sales force.	• Business partners/alliances.
• One set of terms.	• Many ways of doing business.

The impact of all this change on the once invulnerable giant corporation is now well known – financial losses on a massive scale, downsizing and loss of its position as one of America's most admired companies in the annual *Fortune* survey. IBM is now fighting back and facing the need for continuous and fundamental change if it is to recover its previous pre-eminence in its field.

Conclusion

The speed with which the business environment is changing carries with it a number of implications for the consultancy industry.

- To remain effective, consultants need to be fully aware of the major trends and able to assess the impact of these on the strategic positions of their clients.
- Consultants must develop considerable competence in the field of change management if they are to be of real value to their clients. Successful implementation in today's climate calls for great sensitivity to the various causes of resistance to change, sensitivity of a kind that comes with considerable experience of change management in a range of situations.
- They must also develop other skills in such diverse fields as IT, working across cultures, using psychometric tools and survey research methods.
- Finally, the consulting firm itself must adapt to new environmental pressures and opportunities.

References

Bridges, W (1996) *Jobshift*, Nicholas Brealey, London
Lewis, J D (1990) *Partnership for Profit*, The Free Press, New York
Naisbitt, J (1994) *Global Paradox*, Nicholas Brealey, London
Ohmae, K (1990) *The Borderless World*, Collins, London
Pascale, R T (1991) *Managing on the Edge*, Penguin Books, London
Peters, T (1992) *Liberation Management*, Macmillan, London

4

The client–consultant relationship

John Mulligan and Paul Barber

Introduction

We see consultancy as both a science and an art. Consultancy as a science provides knowledge, models to enhance understanding, diagnostic and measurement tools. Consultancy as an art is a relational process, an expression of belief and values, and an act of emotional exploration within the bounds of a social relationship. The art and the science of consultancy represent its yin and yang nature.

Yin – consultant as artist	Yang – consultant as scientist
• Soft focus.	• Hard focus.
• Inner world-directed.	• Outer world-directed.
• Explores through experience.	• Applies theories.
• Attuned to feelings and intuitions.	• Attuned to thoughts and senses.
• Attends to the relational dance.	• Attends to boundaries and rules.
• Concerned with being.	• Concerned with doing.
• Expresses and creates.	• Diagnoses and tabulates.

We all know of consultancies and consultants who fall into the above categories. Neither stance is right nor wrong, they just hold a different position, and both stances need each other. Too much yin, and we have loads of meaningful experience and social interaction, but nothing gets done and no critical reflection on practice occurs. Too much yang, and systems come before people, we 'do' a lot, but quantity takes over from quality as we perform ever more mechanically. Better a consultant holds the middle ground and draws from each end of the continuum as necessary.

The client–consultant relationship

Though this chapter offers maps to orientate you over the terrain of consultancy, it is primarily concerned with the relational dance of the client and consultant, how this develops over time, the various features that influence it and how excellence in relationships can add value and quality to consultancy. In this way, we veer towards the softer yin position, while keeping a healthy dialogue with the hard-edged stance of the yang.

Having trained consultants for a number of years, we are only too aware of how the client–consultant relationship, though the primary medium of communication in consultancy, has a tendency to be forgotten or taken for granted rather than developed or explored. Placing the relationship in the background rather than to the fore in consultancy is a grave error for when clients voice satisfaction or dissatisfaction, their comments regularly have a tendency to cluster around the client–consultant relationship. In this context, the relationship is the major tool and grease of the consultancy function.

Within the scope of this chapter, we attempt to focus on the client–consultant relationship in relation to the purchase of a professional service, the transfer of learning and the facilitation of change this entails. The viewpoint we share concentrates on the personalized, relational field that develops between the consultant and client – the micro level of human interaction rather than macro level of the organizational contract. Our attention to relationship here will need to be related to the focus on task – the business of the consultancy (as covered in Chapter 5). Our focus, though primarily on external consultation, makes reference to internal consultants.

Within this scenario, we invite you to examine the nature and purpose of the client–consultant relationship, broad methodologies that highlight the purpose and function of this relationship and the various explicit and covert, ghost and shadow roles that the consultant and client enact, such as the expert, an extra pair of hands, collaborator, representative, commissioner and so on.

The nature and purpose of the consultancy relationship

At its simplest, the purpose and nature of a relationship can be inferred from the way in which it is generated. The client needs help with something they are unable to do or choose not to do for themselves, and the consultant offers assistance and expertise in one form or another in response to this need. In classic terms, the consultant is there to identify, clarify and meet the needs of the client, usually in the form of helping them solve a particular problem. Would that it were so simple. However, it does provide some indication of the core nature of the relationship, namely, providing a service, usually in the form of a paid contract, while, increasingly, entailing a transfer of knowledge and skills. The seeking and giving of a professional service provides the backdrop against which the relationship exists – it is its *raison d'être*, and we would do well not to forget this fact, despite the many forms the relationship takes. As the relationship makes effective intervention possible, so it needs considerable care and attention.

The dimensions of relationships

In any social relationship three dimensions of relationships are at play (Greenson, 1967):

- *the contractual relationship* a level of social agreement where a working allegiance and firm boundaries and rules of engagement are formed
- *the idealized relationship* an imaginary level of engagement where each person transfers in prior learning and desires and proceeds to act these out, such as when parent–child interactions flower or friends each seek what they need or wish from each other without being aware or able to articulate or communicate it to themselves or others
- *the authentic relationship* a level over and above the contractual and personalized or dramatized one, where you witness yourself, come clean at the very least to yourself and, where appropriate, share your true stance with others.

Interestingly, although the contractual relationship seems to be to the fore in most consultants' awareness, the idealized relationship is the one we – as teachers of consultants – see most often acted out, with the consultant holding forth from the position of parent/expert. When we come to analyse what makes for a successful client–consultant relationship, looking at those that have stood the test of time, we often find a high degree of authenticity flavours the interaction.

The expertise offered and the approach used

The nature of the expertise the consultant offers or the client requires significantly influences and shapes the relationship. Management consulting requires expertise of many kinds – economic, financial, marketing, IT, people management, organizational development and so on.

The client–consultant relationship

The expertise possessed by consultants may focus primarily on task or process. Task-centred consultants tend to focus on the task or the problem and minimize the people and relationships aspects. Economic, financial and IT consulting comes more from the task end of the spectrum – the yang region or 'what' needs to be done. Process-centred consultants, however, generally tend to focus more on people and their relationships and have a tendency, by and large, to leave the task or problem to the client to solve with some facilitative help – the yin region or 'how' things are done. The approach of the Tavistock Clinic in London is an example of the latter approach, the consultant facilitating insight rather than providing technological expertise. However, an exception, business process consultation – or 're-engineering' as it is also called – although focused primarily on process – 'how' the business is enacted – is less focused on the people dimension.

A problem with this commonplace distinction occurs when 'the task' or the problem is 'the process', whether this is defined in people, business or technical terms. 'Process' has several meanings. For example, Schein (1969), in the context of organizational development, uses this word to refer to relational processes or interactions that take place between people; Hammer and Stanton (1996), in the context of re-engineering the business, use the word process to refer to a series of tasks that constitute the way business is carried out. IT uses 'process' in another, yet related, way, meaning tasks can be automated, computerized or 'processed'. Consultants therefore need to define their terms if they are to be understood correctly.

All the above are closely related to, or overlap with, management consultancy, so it may be useful to use the terms 'problem-centred' and 'people-centred' consultancy to denote the differences between the two generic approaches to management consulting. It is, of course, becoming increasingly necessary for consultants to be adept at both problem and people dimensions of their work and to demonstrate both task and process expertise.

How does the relationship actually start?

How the relationship starts can have a significant impact on its development. The client–consultant relationship can often begin before face-to-face contact, especially at the level of the idealized relationship. Consultants may also be imposed from either within or without the organization. Such imposition will influence the relationship and may generate relational difficulties before consultancy work even begins.

69

Internal consultants already have knowledge of the problem and a relationship with management by virtue of being part of the same organization. This may be advantageous in terms of knowing the organizational culture and the management problems that exist, but can hamper openness or limit credibility – depending on previous experience and interaction within the 'organizational family'. The convenience and lesser expense of an internal consultant may likewise facilitate the relationship.

External consultants have the advantage of being seen as a relatively neutral resource, unless they have been imposed, and have the added credibility of their expertise and track record, which is why, presumably, they were invited in the first place. Clients often find it easier to share a problem with an outsider, but it can be a disadvantage not to have personal experience of the culture and an insight into the business of the organization. It may therefore take longer to build an effective consulting relationship. Third-party referrals may ease the entry difficulties by establishing credibility more quickly.

From the clients' point of view, the relationship may be further complicated by the practice, often within larger consultancies, of having a client services director or contracting agent who is someone other than the person who delivers the work. The client will usually want to know and meet the consultants who will be actively engaged in the delivery. This is especially important where the initial relationship is sustained at an institution to institution level. Ensuring that the psychological or relationship contract occurs between the real client – those with ownership of the problem – and the consultants charged with responsibility and delivery is crucial, but this relationship is best integrated in the wider field of both consultant and client systems.

Who is the client?

The answer to this question may seem simple, especially for novices, but it can be quite complicated and, if not clarified early on in the relationship, can have a detrimental effect on the effectiveness of the intervention. The answer will provide the basis for more in-depth exploration, as outlined under the heading Orientation below.

● Do you regard the person who contacts you initially as being the client?
● If so, what about the stakeholders – the people who require or have a vested interest in the outcome of the consultancy; those who might be brought in to help plan the intervention?

- Might the sponsors – those who are going to champion or fund the consultancy or the people who own the problem, those who will have to do the learning or changing – need to be considered?
- Would you also need to include the subordinates or superiors of the latter in your client system?

It is often the case that you do not have one client but several clients or categories of client and that 'the client' is often a group or an organization – not just individuals. This throws up the considerable question 'who are you engaging with?' and has a major impact on the mode and style of communication you choose.

Cockman, *et al.* (1992) credit Revans with the suggestion that three key groups of people be included in your client system:

- those who know
- those who care
- those who can.

'Those who know' about the problem, and those who know of sources of help, may include superiors, human resources staff or even client customers if necessary. 'Those who care' could include those who may be suffering as a result of the problem or shortcoming, such as those in positions of responsibility, personnel and training, sponsors or even shareholders. 'Those who can' should include those who can do something about the problem – budget holders, those with line management authority, those with enabling resources and the work groups and individuals who will accomplish the required changes. An effective consultant needs to listen to the dialogue of all three.

Phases of the client–consultant relationship

Preparing for contact

Needless to say, preparing for the initial face-to-face interaction improves the chances of success. That said, it is surprising the number of first meetings that get off on the wrong foot because of failure to prepare adequately. Being informed about the state of the client's business and operating environment will be of benefit, or even essential, depending on the type of consultancy offered. Some initial research in trade magazines, journals and published documentation and, of course, good use of your networks and the grapevine, will give considerable advantage in framing the information and request you are about to receive from

71

your client. It will also show the client your willingness and commitment to getting to know them and understanding their work.

When the contact results from the consultant's search for new business, the consultant will need to be prepared to address the validity of what they have offered in their marketing process. They will need to demonstrate their track record, how their mission or values will be delivered and that they have the interests and needs of the client as their primary motive, rather than just being a commercial driver.

If the consultancy work has been initiated by a potential client, the consultant may need to show an ability to relate to the painful shortcomings of the client's struggles and help them understand their position, while illustrating how the consultants expertise might be of value to them. A multitude of motives may prevail. The client may be motivated by a desire for competitive advantage or want to improve productivity; be experiencing pain or difficulty, but be unable to define what the problem is; or else they may be adept at defining the problem and want to focus more on how the consultant might work on it. In this context, the approach may be a 'shopping expedition' to discover what the various consultancies have to offer or a focused and informed approach based on previous knowledge of what the consultant can do. Each will require a different kind of response from the consultant.

The initial contact may come from a third party, perhaps the owner, a more senior executive to a subordinate, a friend or peer within or outside of the business. Whenever a third party introduces a consultant, they are initially seen as part of their introducer's world and this may help or hinder the first meeting. Recommendations from trusted colleagues often count the most, but whether the consultant is experienced as an imposition or a welcome source of assistance, the form of introduction is often best acknowledged and dealt with early in the relationship so that the trust-building process necessary for effective consultancy is not impeded or ignored.

First meetings can serve different purposes. They can be briefings about a tender, presentations of a tender response or an exploratory meeting about the problem that has been contracted by the consultant as the beginning of the engagement itself. Each will require different kinds of preparation.

Consideration will also need to be given in advance to who should be present at the meeting, given its nature and purpose. Schein (1969), using process consultation as an example, suggests that someone high enough in the organization to have influence, someone in favour and with experience of using consultants, someone who can help identify and clarify the problem, someone familiar with behavioural science and process consultancy, are the kinds of people he would like present at a first meeting. He recommends not having anyone who may be hostile in early meetings. Other styles of consulting will have their own requirements and preferences.

Once the client and consultant have made it to the stage of face-to-face contact, then other influences exert their effects. As in all relationships, the client–consultant one journeys through various phases. In the interests of encouraging reflection, a framework of four phases is offered for consideration (Peplau, 1969; Barber, 1997):

- orientation
- identification
- exploration
- resolution.

Read these sections critically. They are not meant to provide an answer, but rather, to stimulate you towards making a map of your own. (See also Chapter 5.)

Orientation

In the spring of the relationship, the client and consultant meet as strangers, orientate to each other's world views and begin to form a bond. Without this bond, the working allegiance fails to form and the relationship progresses no further. When bonding is successful, however, the client and consultant start to negotiate and refine their respective roles.

Critical to the bonding process and the development of rapport is the match between the communication styles of the client and consultant. Consultants will tend to have their own jargon, and the client will have ways of communicating aligned to the culture of their organization, business, racial and national background and so on. Attention to how these communication styles can be matched and aligned will greatly facilitate bonding and mutual understanding. Handy (1989) suggests how we might communicate with different types of organizational cultures, while Laborde (1984) shows how neuro-linguistic programming can enhance personal communication. Marginalization of one another's communication styles is a common cause of failure in consulting projects and relationships.

The orientation process for the consultant will include checking who the 'real' client is (see under Who is the client? above), their position and status, the degree of openness of the client, their willingness and readiness to explore relevant issues, experience of using consultants, misconceptions of what is on offer, clarity of their brief and so on. For the client, it may include, among other issues, congruence, awareness of needs and or brief, trustworthiness and competence, potential for dependency or collaboration (as gleaned from the early signs), consultants' communication skills – their sensitivity to feelings, dilemmas, vulnerabilities and so on.

In sound relationships, each player, at this stage, will have noted their reactions to the other, checked out their concerns, laid their stereotypical reactions aside and moved towards sharing a portion of their store of authenticity. Can you work with the client's values, attitudes and perception of their problem? What emotional reaction in you does the client stimulate – excitement, anxiety, revulsion, compassion? It will be important to pay attention to such early feelings and intuitions when deciding whether or not to accept the work. Respect, congruence, empathy and unconditional positive regard were regarded by C Rogers (1983) as the basis for a healthy helping relationship. Without authenticity, the relationship stays superficial and gamey and will tend to crack as the tensions of the consulting process impact on it.

During this formative phase, the character of the relationship is mainly person-centred, as the client and consultant consciously and unconsciously set about establishing rapport and start to negotiate 'rules of engagement'. The key relationship issue at this point is inclusion. There may be fears for the client about letting a stranger into their system at a time when it is vulnerable, and a need to be protective as well as to grow or change. For the consultant, there will be concerns about gaining access and being allowed in.

Identification

Should the orientation phase prove successful, the relationship moves into its summer season – a time when trust is developing and the client and consultant are able to work together to identify what are considered to be the problem areas desirous of attention.

In this phase, the client educates the consultant about the organizational world they work within, and the consultant educates the client about the possible purposes and tasks of consultancy. In this way each clarifies the perceptions and expectations of the other, notes the values and history that lend light and shade to the definition of the situation and relationship they are in and, in the process, develop further trust. At this time, strategies both for the task and the relationship are considered and the way forward is planned.

In the diagnostic phase of consulting, besides trying to understand how the client's problem and the consultant's expertise might marry, there is an underlying relationship agenda beginning to take form at an implicit and an explicit level. This is to do with how both will engage in the work together and the nature of the relationship that will contain, facilitate and deliver the service. We believe it is best to make this as explicit as possible. Here are some core questions to ask at this stage.

- Will the consultancy be done 'to' or 'with' the client as well as 'for' them?
- Will the consultation be carried out autocratically, cooperatively or be self-directed (with the guidance of the consultant)?
- How will both parties participate and what roles and responsibilities will each contract into?
- What will be delegated?
- What access is allowed or denied?

Underlying assumptions of both client and consultant can be surfaced by asking the above questions, and the answers given will illuminate both the dynamics of the relationship and a portion of the desired outcomes of the consultancy. For example, many consultants see the desired dynamic as akin to the doctor–patient relationship. A doctor knows and diagnoses what is wrong with the client, tells them, prescribes a remedy and hopefully relieves the symptoms or cures the disease. The assumption here is that the client has little to contribute to the resolution of their problem, besides giving a description of the symptoms and taking the medicine. With this approach, the result is that the problem is solved, but the transfer of skills and learning is minimal and the client is dependent on the doctor indefinitely.

Other consultants prefer the relationship to be akin to one between cooperative enquirers in an active research process. Here the consultant is a collaborative enquirer with some advanced capacity to enquire and engages with the client as a peer in an action research process to identify the problem, then generate, implement and evaluate solutions. The assumption here is that the client has much to contribute to resolving their own problems and the capacity to do so with some facilitative assistance. Results include a solution to the problem, plus the capacity to identify, enquire into and find a resolution for their own or joint problems and a greater capacity for autonomy and interdependence.

At this point, we have begun on the contractual level of engagement in the relationship as well as an exploration of the problem. Relationship issues of power and control tend to surface strongly at this time. Is the client willing to influence and be influenced by the consultant and vice versa? Efforts to strategically position themselves to best effect will tend to characterize the relationship behaviour of the respective parties. A key underlying question is 'Can or will our respective needs be met?'

The orientation stage is akin to Tuckman's (1965) 'forming' stage of group development. This stage can sometimes become quite stormy, as consultant and client jockey for position and strive to meet their needs. The willingness of both parties to be authentic and strive, despite the sometimes stormy atmosphere, is a sign of a healthy relationship and will result in agreement on enabling norms for the relationship and task.

Exploration

Having harvested awareness and gleaned a sound understanding of the contract, the relationship moves into a mature performative phase where consultant and client implement their chosen strategy, modify this in light of systemic feedback and decide future steps as they engage in repeating cycles of planning, action and reflection on what unfolds. Ideally, from a relational stance, both take active and responsible roles, explore the thoughts, feelings and intuitions that arise from the information and experience they acquire until a successful strategy is produced and problems are resolved.

During this phase, the relationship is strategy-centred as themes are developed, supports put in place, a pathway chosen and cycles of experiential experiments are enacted. This action research approach may relate to the diagnostic and implementation phases depending on the type of consulting approach being used.

What is critical, however, is that if the relationship has progressed through the storming and norming stages (Tuckman, 1965) to become a robust container for the consulting task, the client and consultant will have developed a trust in one another and be willing to take the risks entailed in making swift progress towards their common goal. They will now, if this stage is successful, achieve a respect for each other's strengths and weaknesses, a capacity to accommodate diversity and conflict, and have developed a robust and compassionate relationship. This period will be characterized by 'the relationship in action'. This performative stage of the relationship is further elaborated on below under Interventions and roles.

Resolution

With successful completion of the original contract behind them, the client and consultant enter the winter of their relationship – a time when they take stock and prepare for withdrawal, one from the other. At this point, the outcomes of the consultancy are evaluated as attention is directed to completing the consultancy process and terminating the present relationship. Future follow-up may be reviewed, issues relating to endings and unfinished business explored. In this phase, the relationship is especially quality-centred, as client and consultant debrief, covering insight, new learning and the completion of a meaningful relationship.

For some modes of consulting this will relate to reporting and helping the client to assimilate the findings of their work, while, for others, it may mean attending to other aspects of the client field that have been uncovered during the earlier phases of the consultancy and perhaps contracting a further piece of work. Ending or terminating a piece of work often does not mean terminating the relationship so much as changing the form of contact and contract.

Reporting may be a complicated and difficult process if the client has not been involved in the collection and interpretation of the data, especially if you leave it until the end of the engagement. Considerable care will therefore need to be taken to prepare the client for findings and ensure their readiness to receive them. This is especially true where the findings materially and psychologically affect individuals in their work environment. It is usually good practice to inform such people of the results personally and give them time to take on board the implications of the findings, as well as ensuring that support is in place before news gets to them on the grapevine.

It is more common nowadays – even with the more traditional approaches to consulting – to feed the results piecemeal to the client, gain their buy-in and develop understanding long before the final report is handed to them. With the more participative approaches to consulting, this is much easier because the client usually collaborates in the sense making and generation of interpretations and conclusions.

Disengaging will also entail keeping the doors open for possible future business and establishing mutually supportive networks. Debriefing the client and clearing up any unfinished business in the relationship needs to be structured into the disengagement process. It is important to include a relational aspect to any evaluation, so that relational learning, and its implications for future practice, can be carried forward on both sides. It is worth keeping in touch on an occasional basis once the task has been finished as it is not unusual for such relationships to foster ongoing friendships or collaborative networks.

Summary of the four phases of a client–consultant relationship:

Phases	Issues	Nature
Orientation	Forming a working allegiance	Client-centred
	Adapting to each other's world	
	Developing trust	
	Negotiating rules of engagement	
Identification	Clarifying problems	Problem-centred
	Raising strategies	
	Understanding the contextual frame	
	Bonding in partnership	
Exploration	Implementing chosen strategies	Strategy-centred
	Modifying and experimenting	
	Enacting mutually supportive roles	
	Deepening understanding	
Resolution	Evaluating outcomes	Quality-centred
	Completing consultation	
	Reviewing follow-up	
	Debriefing for insight	

Interventions and roles

Models of intervention

Specific forms or models of consultancy tend to have prescribed or recommended modes of intervention, based on their own implicit or explicit views of what the client–consultant relationship ought to be like. Some examples of these include client-centred consultancy, process consultancy, coaching, business process re-engineering, structural change, problem solving, action research, product development, market research and so on.

It would be worthwhile selecting key models to give some illustrations of what various kinds of interventions might look like, together with the kinds of relationships with the clients that they generate. Given the limitations of space in this chapter, we will examine some key roles common to many of the approaches used in the light of Heron's (1990) generic six category analysis of behavioural interventions that can be associated with a helper working with a client.

The client–consultant relationship

Authoritative interventions are:

- *prescriptive* directing, advising, recommending, suggesting, requesting
- *informative* telling, interpreting, demonstrating, giving feedback
- *confronting* contradict, disagree, ask challenging questions, raise awareness.

Facilitative interventions are:

- *cathartic* releasing tension, physically stretching, inviting expression of feeling, using humour
- *catalytic* using self-discovery structures, open/closed questioning, reflecting, summarizing
- *supportive* valuing, affirming, appreciating, expressing concern, welcoming.

Some general guidance for each type of role is suggested below. Let us not forget, however, that different forms of consulting relationship, as distinct from behavioural interventions, can be illuminated by viewing them through different lenses, for example psychodynamics, transactional analysis, Gestalt, process-oriented psychology and several others. Not only does this have the value of highlighting the similarities and differences between the different approaches, it also provides the consultant with a basis for reflection on their personal practice and for critical reflection on the suitability of the approach or model of consulting for a particular task or client.

In exploring roles, we will examine various commonplace identities along a continuum from directive to non-directive, expert-led to client-centred, and raise for discussion the question of how such roles might impact the client–consultant relationship. Some interventions are more appropriate and relevant for some roles than others. For example, advocate, technical expert and trainer roles would fit more comfortably with the directive end of the continuum, whereas the reflector, counsellor, facilitator roles would be found more often at the client-centred end (Lippitt and Lippitt, 1986).

Consultant and client roles

Many consultants – often the good ones, we think – have an ongoing identity crisis. Are they experts, counsellors, salespeople, trainers or what? Being an effective consultant requires that you have a fluid identity, or even several different identities or roles, and the capacity to flow seamlessly from one to the other. Multiple roles or identities, while essential for good consultancy, are also a hazard if managed badly and can lead to considerable confusion and conflict in the relationship between client and consultant. For example, if one day you are negotiating hard over fees and the contract and the next you are acting as facilitator or counsellor to the same person, the potential for transference or interference of one relationship dynamic with the other in an unhelpful way is immense.

There are so many consultant roles worth surfacing and exploring that it would be impossible to do them justice in this short chapter, so here we shall concentrate on just a few consultant roles, but we forget at our peril that the client is also likely to be the bearer of multiple roles, such as commissioner, problem-bearer, contractor, sponsor, manager, subordinate and so on. As consultants, we do well to identify the roles of people within our client system early on.

Possible consultant roles include guide, mentor, friend, trouble-shooter, shadow consultant, problem-solver, evaluator, confidant, project manager, systems analyst, role model, guru, designer/innovator, report writer, critical reflector and so on. Here we will focus on a few of the key roles consultants commonly engage in, highlight the kinds of relationship dynamics they might generate and the kinds of interventions that tend to be associated with them.

Technical expert
The 'expert' role is one of adding value by exhibiting knowledge and a high level of competence in an area of expertise. Often this will entail doing something on behalf of the client, such as designing a new system, training staff in a new skill, acting as a trouble-shooter in areas beyond the client's current expertise or where it is more economic to hire it in from outside. This entails the consultant taking on responsibility and accountability for resolving the problem. While the initial brief may be prepared by the client, they will be dependent on the expert for advice and guidance. Little collaboration is involved, other than the client facilitating and monitoring the actions of the expert.

The consultant's expertise may relate to either content or process, and when the consultant is hired for, or speaking from, this role, they are expected to speak authoritatively and will commonly use prescriptive, informative and occasionally confronting interventions. Failing to speak authoritatively and give advice, guidance and direction may leave the client confused and floundering. Overuse of the authoritative mode, however, may overpower or demoralize the client, induce inappropriate dependency and, on occasion, induce resistance or even antagonism.

The expert role needs to be used in the full knowledge that the client is free to avail themselves of or reject advice or guidance, and such advice is best given with a view to eventually enabling autonomy in the client system. That is, you are authoritative with a view to the client becoming authoritative for themselves.

Problems often arise when the expert is so focused on the 'expert task' that they fail to take account of the impact of their consulting on people affected by their work, perhaps due to limited awareness of, or sensitivity to, the people dimension of change. Acquiring this ability, or intentionally working with someone who has it, will greatly improve the assimilation of the expert's contribution into the client system.

Counsellor

This role is becoming more common in the repertoire of the consultant, especially for those focusing on people issues. Depending on the approach, the role may focus on releasing the inherent potential of the individual or helping the client solve their problems and meet their needs. The relationship can often be problematical in that consultants using this role can often experience conflict about who the real client is, and may feel torn between the expressed needs of the client and those of the contracting manager. Maintaining appropriate boundaries, both in contracting and practice, is crucial to building the necessary trust with the client – more so, if you are an internal consultant. For example, confidentiality associated with this role needs to be maintained if the organization or sponsor desire feedback about the client's progress.

For the most part, counselling is person-centred – that is, the person undergoing the counselling will expect help in working through their problems and challenges. It will tend strongly towards the facilitative end of the intervention spectrum and client self-direction. Interventions will be primarily supportive, catalytic and cathartic, though spiced with occasional authoritative interventions – especially at a process level as necessary. It is easy to create client dependency in such cases, especially in a relatively (from a personal point of view) unsupportive organization, so care needs to be taken with disengagement and endings.

Advocate

Some believe the consultant should retain a neutral stance and not become an advocate or source of influence. We believe that this is impossible to do even if you wanted to, and that the best we can do is be aware of, and able to articulate, our own values and biases so the client will be in a better position to choose whether or not to be influenced by them. Being a process advocate is often seen as more acceptable these days than a product or solution advocate. Many consultants are hired for their know-how, which is needed to help clients generate their own solutions. Being an advocate of particular solutions carries with it heavy ethical responsibilities (see Chapter 2), especially if you have a vested interest in a particular solution.

Advocacy is also sometimes necessary to support and strengthen people within the organization, and the consultant will need to be acquainted with a range of influencing strategies and behaviours. Prescriptive and informative interventions – the use of devil's advocacy, questioning and other challenging interventions – can be influential when operated from a position of expertise, while developing rapport, common vision and empathizing with feelings and needs are powerful facilitative interventions when there is need to influence. We have found that supportive interventions – from a declared value position and guided by the client's needs – are the most powerful and ethical mode of influencing, especially in the context of a collaborative relationship.

Coach/educator

This role has become central to all forms of consultancy that have change within and via people as part or the whole of their aims. Transfer of learning and expertise from consultant to client has become one of the key benchmarks of successful consulting and this is crucial if inappropriate dependency on the consultant is to be avoided. The coach or trainer role is notorious for generating troublesome transference of earlier schooling experiences, such that an unfortunate use of academic rank and privilege by educators has resulted. For many people, low self-esteem, resistance to authority and anxiety about personal exposure and vulnerability often accompany learning.

The core expertise of this role has shifted from teaching to learning. While the role still entails some 'chalk and talk' skills, it is essential that expertise in learning processes – especially experiential, on the job and now organizational learning – is possessed in large measure. Besides the capacity to identify learning opportunities and design learning processes, the role demands extraordinary fluency right across the six categories of intervention mentioned earlier in this chapter, in both authoritative and facilitative modes, and an advanced capacity for mutuality in relationships, such as that suggested by Rogers (1990) and

The client–consultant relationship

Buber (1970). People rarely learn from people who do not value them or show them respect, empathy and compassion.

Researcher

The role of researcher has often been reduced to one of fact finding and diagnosis. This idea has been reinforced by the common practice of consultants generating data and solutions, but not being involved in their practical implementation. The researcher role may therefore often be construed as an impractical one. However, developments in research over the past 20 years – especially in the areas of action-oriented, cooperative and participative enquiry – offer the possibility of research activity that is not only practical, but more amenable to both consultant and client. These forms of research engage both the consultant and client in a collaborative relationship aimed at generating the focus of research, gathering data, making sense of it, implementing solutions and evaluating them in successive cycles of action and research.

Because of the collaborative nature of the relationship, there is much greater ownership and effective implementation in action research than in more traditional forms, where the researcher gathers and makes sense of the data, presents it back and leaves implementation to the client. Building research competence and maintaining the collaborative relationship over the course of the research is complicated (Heron, 1996; Reason, 1988). Early on, interventions will tend to be prescriptive with regard to the research process and facilitative with regard to content. Later, as research competence is developed and a peer learning community established, consultant interventions will be predominantly supportive and catalytic.

Facilitator

Often called a 'process specialist' in the behavioural sciences, this role is concerned mostly with interpersonal, intergroup and organizational dynamics, and the collective learning and change that is entailed. In this role, unlike the expert role, the consultant never takes on responsibility for the client's problem. Here the consultant facilitates the client's emerging understanding of their own problems and difficulties and strengthens their ability to respond creatively and effectively to them. The assumption, as with all facilitative interventions, is that the client has the capacity or potential to resolve their own problems if this can be liberated and supported. The relationship is essentially collaborative, with responsibility for the problem lying explicitly with the client.

The facilitator's role is primarily catalytical, though they may use the full range of interventions. Schein (1969) describes process consulting as 'a set of activities on the part of the consultant which help the client perceive, understand, and act upon the process events which occur in the client's environment'. Key to the success of this approach – as it is to that of the researcher role described above – is the transfer from consultant to client of the methods and values that enable the client system to diagnose and remedy its own problems. Like the counsellor and educator roles, considerable rapport, trust, empathy and openness are necessary on both sides for this role to function effectively.

It is easy for the consultant – who may have spent years developing such transparency by means of personal development and in group interaction – to be unaware of and even abuse their expertise and privilege in these areas. They may have forgotten how frightening or threatening it is to have hidden agendas and group norms surfaced and fail to be sufficiently supportive to either the dominant or marginalized parts of the client system. Good boundary keeping, courage, compassion and humility will be very much in demand if the consultant is to relate well in this role.

Conclusion

As with all working relationships, they need maintenance to stay healthy. It is very easy to get lost in the task or the problem and not devote sufficient time to ensuring that the relationship remains vibrant and alive. Most change occurs via people, and they have their own personal needs that must be fulfilled. The consultancy project and workare part of their lives, although the tendency is to see the people as part of the consultancy project and thus forget the broader backdrop of their humanity and the impact the project might have on them. Time must be built in to review how the *relationship* is going – not just the *task*. There will be a need to plan small wins to keep spirits up and build morale, time for celebration and relaxation, time for nurturance and energizing, to make the best use of the ebb and flow of people's energy and motivation.

References

Barber, P (1997) 'The client therapist relationship: an action research approach', *British Gestalt Journal*, 6, 1
Buber, M (1970) *I and Thou*, Charles Scribner's Sons, New York
Cockman, P, *et al.* (1992) *Client-centred Consulting*, McGraw-Hill, Maidenhead

Greenson, R (1967) *The Technique and Practice of Psychoanalysis*, International University Press, New York

Hammer, M and Stanton, S (1996) *The Re-engineering Revolution Handbook*, HarperCollins, London

Handy, C (1989) *The Gods of Management*, Pan, London

Heron, J (1990) *Helping the Client*, Sage, London

Heron, J (1996) *Co-operative Inquiry*, Sage, London

Laborde, G (1984) *Influencing with Integrity*, Syntony Publishing, Palo Alto, CA.

Lippitt, G and Lippitt, R (1986) *The Consulting Process in Action*, University Associates, CA.

Peplau, H E (1969) 'Psychotherapeutic strategies', *Perspectives in Psychiatric Care*, **6**; pp. 264–78

Reason, P (1988) *Human Inquiry in Action*, Sage, London

Rogers, C (1983) *Freedom to Learn for the 80s*, C E Merrill Publishing, Columbus, OH

Schein E (1969) *Process Consultation: Its role in organizational development*, Addison-Wesley, Mass.

Tuckman, B W (1965) 'Developmental sequence in small groups', *Psychological Bulletin*, **63**, 6; 384–99

5

The entry phase

David Hussey

Introduction

This chapter describes the entry phase, looking at it from two viewpoints; that of the client and that of the consultancy.

The term 'consultancy' is used to mean the business, and should be interpreted to mean the lone practitioner as well as a firm. The word 'consultant(s)' is used to describe the professional resource or resources that will represent the consultancy during the entry phase or work on the contract that may result. For the lone practitioner, the 'resource' and the 'business' may appear to be inseparable, but the conceptual split is still worth making.

Without an entry phase there can be no consulting assignment. This chapter explores what the entry phase is and its purpose, and will examine the various stages that are involved. Particular attention will be paid to the proposal.

What is the entry phase?

By the 'entry phase' is meant the period between the invitation to discuss a possible assignment with a client and the award of a contract to the selected consultancy. Kubr (1996), holds that 'Entry is very much a matching exercise. The client wants to be sure that he is dealing with the right consultant, and the consultant needs to be convinced that he is the right person, or that his firm is the right consulting organization, to address the problems of this particular client.' Although the consultancy will not win every assignment, the way in which the firm behaves during this phase is also important in building relations with the potential client as it may enhance the reputation of the firm or result in being asked to bid for a future assignment.

What causes a client to invite a consultancy to discuss an assignment is beyond the scope of this chapter, although it is worth noting that all successful consultancies have a high element of repeat business with existing clients, and often relationships are already well established. In this chapter, the assumption will be that the consultancy is dealing with an invitation from a potential client with whom it has not previously worked as, using just a little common sense, the actions described can be modified accordingly when there is already a relationship with a client. However, the first rule is never to be complacent, as a good relationship and past excellent work never guarantee that a new assignment will not be offered to another firm.

The starting point may be a telephone call, a letter or sometimes an invitation to pre-qualify to go onto a bid list. This last is more typical of government and EU contracts than commercial ones, although some private-sector organizations do also use this approach. The bid process for public-sector work is often highly formalized: once on the tender list the consultancy may be faced with a lengthy tender document, and contact with the client may be restricted or channelled through a specific person. Despite all the paperwork, it may be harder to identify real needs from such a process than from the somewhat less formal methods used by most private-sector organizations. This is because, at the initial meeting, the amount of detail provided by a private-sector client may vary from very little to a carefully documented description of the issue, containing many of the facts that the consultancy will need to complete a proposal.

The purposes of the entry phase

The entry phase has a number of very specific purposes, and the lists below examine these from the perspectives of the client and the consultancy. The consultancy that can think through the purpose from the client's perspective as well as its own is more likely to be successful than one that views things from its own perspective only.

The purposes from the consultancy's perspective	The purposes from the client's perspective
• Gaining economic benefit from the assignment.	• Gaining economic benefits from the results of the intervention.

- Understanding the real problem or issue the client faces.
- Making sure that the firm has the competence to deliver a good result.
- Convincing the client that this firm is the one to choose.

- Signing a legally binding contract that results in fees being paid.
- Enhancing the reputation of the firm even if the bid is not won.

- Matching the consultancy's view with its own understanding.
- Understanding the capabilities of the consultancy firm.
- Being convinced that this consultancy firm is the best and will deliver the expected value.

- Signing a legally binding contract that will result in the benefits being delivered.
- Reinforcing the belief that appropriate firms were chosen to bid.

The objectives of the entry phase are driven by an economic imperative for both client and consultant (although occasionally the client's motivation may be political or the aggrandizement of an individual rather than the success of the organization). We can summarize the objectives as:

- understanding
- relationship building/selling
- contractual.

All are important.

Understanding

Part of the process of matching client to consultant is the development of a common understanding of the problem or issue the client faces. Sometimes this may be relatively easy and clear, and the issue is not what to do but how to do it. Other assignments may be very complicated. The client may either not have all the information needed to ensure that the matter is defined or may misinterpret some of the information, or else words may be used in a different way by client and consultant so that what appears on the surface to be clear is, in fact, obscure. However, without a good understanding of the problem, the consultant cannot clarify the role the consultancy should play, will be unable to assess the skills needed for the assignment, cannot estimate the costs of the assignment and will be hard put to convince the client that their firm is the best one to do the job. Even if the assignment is given to the firm, by some miracle, problems will emerge later, and both the client and the consultant may be damaged.

Relationship building/selling

The award of the assignment marks the end of the entry phase. During the whole of the intervening period, the consultancy should be building a professional relationship with the client. There is a selling element here that is usually more effective if it is subtle. High-pressure selling is often resented, although, to a degree, this is a cultural matter. However, during this whole process, the firm should be emphasizing its values, approaches and competences. Relationships may be built up from the chemistry between individuals, the ideas that may be given to the client in discussion and the demonstration of a genuine interest in the client.

Although it is not unknown for a client to approach only one consultancy, it is always wise to assume that competitors have also been asked to bid. Therefore, the task is to convince the client that the firm is capable of delivering the value that is sought, and will also do this better than anyone else. At the same time, benefits should not be oversold, because all the chickens will come home to roost if the assignment is won.

Contractual

During the entry phase, both client and consultant are working towards a form of contract that will specify what the consultant will do and how and when the client will pay for these services. Overselling the benefits of an assignment can have legal implications over and above the damage to client relationships and reputation.

A contract does not have to be in writing to be binding, and most consultancies will have started some work for a well-known client on the strength of a telephone call or handshake. It is prudent, however, even with valued and trusted clients, to follow-up a verbal contract with a letter confirming the arrangement.

Generally, the entry phase ends with some form of written contract. For simple matters, a letter may be adequate, but anything complicated should have a proposal drawn up that is agreed by both parties. If there is no contract at the end of the entry phase, there is no assignment. There may be some benefit, in that the client may be impressed with the firm and call them in later for something else, but generally the entry phase is costly to the consultancy in both professional time and out-ofpocket expenses, so the aim should be either to drop out very early if the assignment is not right for the firm or to do everything ethically to ensure that your firm wins.

The stages of the entry phase

The four broad stages of the entry phase are listed below, as well as some of the skills that are required during each phase. These skills are additional to the particular expertise the consultancy has to bring to bear to deal with the issue the client faces, and any additional requirements that are specific to the consultancy's approach (what is sometimes termed the 'service concept': see Heskett, 1986; Normann, 1991) or that project the image the consultancy wishes to demonstrate.

Stages	Skills needed
1 Agreeing the brief and its scope.	• Active listening.
	• Effective questioning.
	• Business understanding.
	• Conceptualization of vague situations.
	• Ability to relate to the client.
	• Professional selling.
	• Clarifying.
	• Problem-solving skills.
	• Creative thinking.
	• Negotiating (sometimes).
2 Planning the project.	• Conceptualizing.
	• Structuring.
	• Understanding consultancy's resources and capabilities.
	• Project management.
3 Preparing the proposal.	• Scoping.
	• Estimating time and costs.
	• Proposal writing.
	• Contract law.
4 Presenting the proposal.	• Presentation skills.

The list of skills will be extended in particular circumstances. Business understanding might have to be reinforced by understanding of government administration for public-sector assignments, say. If the client is in a different country or requires work to be done in other countries, intercultural differences may become important. The purpose of the list above is not to illustrate every possible skill that may be brought to bear, but to make the point that a complicated bundle of skills is needed, which should be considered in relation to the potential client.

Agreeing the brief and its scope

As we have already seen, this is a key objective of the entry phase. Usually there is an initial meeting with a potential client, during which the client explains the requirements as they are perceived and the consultancy confirms that it is both competent and willing to take the discussions further.

The consultancy should prepare for this meeting by finding out as much as possible about the organization and its industries and relating this to whatever details were given in the invitation to the meeting. As far as possible, the consultancy should ensure that the person or persons who attend the meeting on its behalf have the knowledge and skills to respond to the client's needs and that they have a good knowledge of the capabilities of all other areas of the firm. Do not try to be too clever in this meeting – by dropping into the conversation irrelevant extracts from press reports or the annual report merely to demonstrate that you have done some preparation, for example. This always comes across as contrived. Instead, use the information you have to help you frame questions or interpret answers.

The meeting should be used not only to find out as much as possible about the problem or issue the client faces, but also to obtain information that will help the firm to respond in an appropriate way. A minimal checklist of things the consultant should try to find out from the meeting is given below.

- Who will make the decision about whether or not to accept the proposals?
- Who else may influence the decision?
- What process does the client intend to use to make the selection?
- When are the proposals required by?
- How many other firms have been asked to bid?
- What are the names of the competitors?
- How is the client organized?
- What is the problem or issue as defined by the client?
- Why is the matter important?
- Why are consultants needed?

- Have any initiatives already been taken by the client to resolve the problem or issue?
- What is the scale of the project (the numbers of managers and other employees in the area of the problem, location of activities, number of locations and so on)?
- What benefits is the client hoping for from the initiative?
- Are there any reports or documentation that will shed more light on the matter?
- What is the client's timetable for the completion of the assignment?
- What resources will the client provide?
- Can the organization confirm that the consultancy will be allowed access to all information and to managers and employees at all levels?
- Are there any constraints that the client may impose that need to be defined?
- What experience has the client gained in working with consultants?
- Is there a common view of the broad range of prices for consultancy assignments?

Part of the purpose of the initial meeting is for the consultancy to give such details as may be relevant about its own capabilities. Examples of similar assignments may be given (without breaching client confidentiality) and the client may also ask for references. However, what will convince the client to ask the firm to prepare proposals is the grasp that the firm has of their issue, the way in which questions are asked and the ideas that the consultant may give during the interview. At this stage, the client will be more impressed with questions that show that the consultancy has an awareness of the complexity of the issue than with superficial solutions and glib comments. The client will want to understand the values and philosophy of the firm. Both client and consultant, although with very different agendas, are trying to build confidence and the beginning of a professional relationship.

The variety of assignments for which consultancy help may be sought is immense. Some situations are relatively straightforward, and it is possible to prepare proposals with little more information than can be gained from this first meeting. Others may be so complicated that even a series of discussions with managers would not bring a full understanding of the problem. There is considerable risk to both consultancy and client in rushing into a programme of consultancy work where there is no shared understanding. The consultancy has to decide how much time should be given free (to do all the investigatory work before proposals can be made) or whether there are other ways in which it is possible to deal with uncertainty.

In the 1960s, the consultancy solution offered was often to carry out a survey – sometimes charged at half the normal prices – to enable enough information to be collected to properly define the issue and potential solutions. This may create some problems for the client, particularly when they are trying to compare the bids of several rival consultancies, although it may be very easy to suggest this (and charge it at the normal rate) to a client where there is already a strong relationship of trust.

An alternative is to build the investigatory work into the proposal, but with a review step once the issue has been clarified, when the validity of the consultant's original ideas will be tested, and any changes to price and expected results notified (see later, under Preparing the proposal, below). It makes sense for both client and consultant to have a cancellation opt out at this stage, if things are markedly different from the expectations.

There may be ethical reasons for a consultancy not wishing to bid for an assignment (see Chapter 2). Examples are if the firm has a conflict of interests, in which case it should terminate the discussions as soon as this becomes apparent, if it is not convinced that it has the expertise to do the job or if it believes that there is something unethical about the way the client wants it to behave. It is also legitimate to decline to bid for commercial reasons, such as a belief that the client is not serious, if the chances of winning are thought to be slim or when it is believed that the approach the client demands will not yield anything useful to the client.

Planning the project

Although the project should not be overplanned at this stage – after all, the consultancy may not win it – enough has to be done to determine how the issue would be tackled, the skill requirements needed, the availability of the right people and the amount of professional time that would be needed. This requires conceptualizing the assignment, structuring the solution into stages of work and preparing some time/task analysis, such as a Gantt chart.

This stage is essential prior to the preparation of the proposal as it enables the consultancy to check whether or not it will be able to satisfy the client's needs, to be aware of any resourcing problems and its solution to them and to have a labour requirements analysis, which will aid the pricing of the proposal. The conceptualization of the problem may reveal issues that had not previously been expected, and will convince the consultancy that it can (or cannot) offer a result that will give the client satisfaction. The end result of this phase is a decision to decline to bid or to move on to the proposal stage.

Preparing the proposal

The proposal has to fulfil all the purposes of the entry phase, in particular:

- specify the objectives for and the approach to the assignment, based on an agreed understanding of the problem
- be a persuasive selling document
- be the basis of a legally binding contract.

The first of these is the foundation for the other two. The second should be constrained by the professionalism of the consultancy and, if this is not enough, by an awareness of the third – that promises are legally binding.

The following are the kinds of headings that might be included in a proposal.

1	The problem (described in the context of the client's business situation, strategy and competitive position)
2	The anticipated benefits of the assignment
2.1	The methods and approaches the consultancy will use
2.2	The results that are expected from these approaches
3	The experience and staffing of the consultancy
3.1	Experience and capability of the firm
3.2	Professional staffing
4	Standard terms and conditions
4.1	Professional fees and expenses
4.2	Billing arrangements
4.3	Standard terms and conditions

Appendix 1: Resumés of the key professionals who would work on the assignment
Appendix 2: Client list and examples of relevant assignments
Appendix 3: Technical explanations (of methods, techniques, etc)

Individual firms may take different approaches, in order to reinforce their own values and visions, and to differentiate themselves from competitors. It is also necessary to make changes to the headings so that the proposal will fit a given assignment. For example, the development of a highly tailored training programme, the design of an information system, the analysis of strategic prospects, the psychological testing of managers, the re-engineering of a business, and a retainer arrangement to give regular advice to top management on an ongoing basis are all examples of consultancy assignments where the proposal's headings would be different to those given above. The latter, because the issues and problems are unspecified and the arrangements are open-ended, would not fit the suggested format very well. All that is required in this case is a letter setting out how the arrangement will work and how the client will be charged. The others are all more complicated and may require an expansion of the headings or the insertion of subheadings. However, if the above list is used as a starting point, common sense and the policy of the consultancy will point up any changes that are needed.

Note that the headings above may be irrelevant in cases of public-sector proposals, where the format for proposals is set by the buyer, and any variation can mean disqualification. Next, let us look at each of the headings in further detail.

The problem

Enough has already been said to show why this is important. Thus, this section of a proposal should summarize the position, cross-reference to any key client documents and set out the objectives of the consultancy assignment. Putting this information into the proposal means that it is all in one place and if there is an error of perception by the consultancy, it is obvious and can be dealt with before things progress any further. Clients also sometimes try to change the direction or scope of an assignment while it is in progress, and it is useful to be able to make it clear that any additional work will be subject to charges over and above those in the contract.

The anticipated benefits of the assignment

The methods and approaches the consultancy will use
The wording of this heading may be changed to fit better with the client situation, but the heart of the section remains the same. It is what the consultancy intends to do to provide the solutions that are needed.

The client will normally expect to be told a great deal about the way the task will be tackled, the approaches and methods the consultancy will use and how the consultancy intends to interface with the client. In

95

complicated assignments, a flow chart should be provided to show the tasks that have to be undertaken and the time required to tackle each. The points at which reviews will be held with the client should also be made clear.

Because the variety of possible assignments is so large, it is not sensible to be more specific about the detailed content of this section of a proposal. However, the objectives that lie behind what is included are likely to be similar in all assignments. These are as follows.

- *Helping the client to confirm that there is a fit with the consultancy* This requires that this section of the proposal be thought about from the customer's viewpoint, that enough detail is given for a decision to be made and that the relationship of the actions planned to the customer's problem or issue are explained. The business need of the customer should be reflected in the writing, and the tone of the section should make it clear how the actions planned will aid this.

- *Making an intangible product appear tangible* Chapter 9 covers the marketing issues for management consultancy firms. Kotler (1994) argues that ' . . . the service provider's task is to "manage the evidence", to "tangibilize the intangible"', and the way the proposal makes the actions specific is a part of this process. The more vague the proposal is, the less tangible the service will appear to be.

- *Removing uncertainty* Intangibility brings uncertainty. Buyers are tempted to take the action that makes them feel more secure. Things such as the image of the consultancy firm and the past experience of the buyer will affect the degree of uncertainty and, therefore, any risk the buyer may feel they are taking. This section of the proposal should be written to provide as much comfort to the buyer as possible, without puffing. Often the lesser-known firm can steal the business from under the noses of the large, high-profile firms because thought has been given in this and subsequent sections of the proposal to the reduction of buyer's risk.

- *Helping the client you are in contact with to influence others in the firm* Even by the proposal stage, the consultant may not have met everyone in the client's organization who will influence the purchase decision. Kotler (1994) lists six buying roles exercised by various people in the organization: users, influencers, deciders, approvers, buyers and gatekeepers. More people may read the proposal than the consultant knows. It is of value to write the proposal so that it is clear to the unknown faces as well as the known, so even if verbal agreement appears to have been reached over the approach the consultancy will take, it should still be spelt out in detail for those inside the client's organization who may not have an intimate knowledge of the consultancy or even their own situation.

- *Differentiating the firm* This section of the proposal will also position the consultancy as a differentiated provider or as the purveyor of a commodity service, which can affect both whether or not the assignment is won and the price the client is willing to pay. Obviously, if there is nothing unique about the consultancy's approach, there is nothing to be said here, but often there are differences of method that can ensure that the result delivered is more likely to fit the client's needs than would another consultancy not using these methods.

The results that are expected from these approaches
An alternative heading for this section might be 'the business case', as this is what the section should provide. It should show very clearly what the client's organization would get for its money, and why the proposal will solve the problem the client had in the first place. Although the 'deliverables', such as the reports the firm will prepare, should be specified, this alone is not a justification for the assignment. Because the range of possible assignments is so wide, the way in which a business case is made will vary. The consultancy may, for example, be able to give a quantified estimate of the cost saving that would be likely to be achieved from installing a Just-in-Time manufacturing system, but may not be commissioned to do more than make an assessment of a particular acquisition candidate and therefore cannot argue the bottom line impact should the acquisition take place. However, even in the second example, it is possible to specify what the client will obtain from the assignment. There is a caution to add here: in a contract, what is promised must be delivered, so it is prudent not to make irresponsible statements and to be up-front with the client where there is uncertainty about what will be gained. In the JIT example, it may be more prudent to quote an expected range of cost savings rather than one figure, and to add the caution 'provided the recommendations are followed in full'.

The experience and staffing of the consultancy

Experience and capability of the firm
The aim of this section is to convince the client that the consultancy has the capability to do what it will promise later in the proposal. Lengthy descriptions of past assignments are best kept to an appendix, although it is often valuable to give some broad examples of the types of work the

consultancy has done that are of relevance to the client. It is easy to be trapped into generalities in this section, such as 'our consultants have extensive international experience'. It is far better to tailor what is said about the consultancy's capability to the requirements of the assignment and any concerns that the client may have. It may be much more reassuring to state that the firm's policy is to use the team named in the proposal, barring events over which the firm has no control, such as illness or resignation. This may answer a concern that many clients have, that the resumés listed in proposals often have nothing to do with the team that actually turns up to do the work. If the client has a concern over the way an assignment is handled, this can also be tackled in this section.

So, although what is stated should be factual and accurate, it is also tailored to helping the client to recognize the capabilities that will be brought to the specific situation. In fact, it is possible to go one stage further. Hussey (1995) describes an extensive study of competitors and how this was used to change the way his consultancy wrote proposals:

> We redesigned our basic approach to proposal writing, so that our strengths in so far as they were appropriate to the assignment were presented in such a way as to invite the client to probe to see whether other bidders also possessed them. Our research had shown significant areas where we knew that the competitors likely to be asked to bid did not possess similar strengths.

Without in any way mentioning or denigrating competitors, this approach established the importance to the fit with the client's needs of certain aspects of the consultancy's capability and so reduced the attractiveness of the bids of those competitors who could not match the fit.

Professional staffing

Brief details of the professional team that would work on the assignment should be given, with more detailed resumés appearing in an appendix. Remember that the resumés are not a CV for employment and so should summarize relevant experience rather than giving a blow-by-blow account of every job held and every assignment fulfilled. The people are key in any professional assignment, and every effort should be made to demonstrate that the firm has the human resources that match the needs of the client. When possible, the key person or people should have met the client before the proposal is prepared and should play a part in the preparation of the proposal and its presentation to the client (subject to practical limitations, such as when the assignment requires a very large number of consultants).

Standard terms and conditions

Professional fees and expenses

One of the crunch points for the proposal is what the client will be charged. Contracts may be fixed price or flexible (time-based, retainer arrangements or staged, with possible revisions as each stage is completed). How the price is determined is dealt with in Chapters 9 and 10, but the important thing is that there should be absolute clarity about this in the proposal. A complicated way of setting out charges may confuse the client and make it difficult for competing bids to be compared.

Points that require specific consideration include any charges, such as travel expenses, that will be made in addition to fees, whether these are at cost or subject to an administrative charge before being passed on, how price increases will be handled on assignments where the start is delayed or that are intended to stretch over several years and the addition of VAT (or other similar taxes required by law). On most assignments, VAT is a relatively simple issue, but it can become complicated when the work is being done with an organization in another European VAT area or when work is undertaken in the consultancy's home country for an organization in another country. Consult the accountants.

Some of these issues require definitions of terms and these should be cross-referenced to the Standard terms and conditions section at the end of this part of the proposal.

Billing arrangements

The way in which the client will be invoiced and the time allowed for payment should be set out clearly. Failure to say anything could mean that the consultancy can demand no payment until the assignment is completed, which could have severe cash flow implications. Clauses here might include ones concerning advance payments, stage payments and the number of days' grace given before the bill is considered overdue.

Standard terms and conditions

It would, of course, be possible to put all the definitions in the text of the proposal, but this could make it harder to read. The purpose of the standard terms section is to ensure that there is genuine understanding of what the contract means, and for the consultancy it is a bid to have its own definitions and terms accepted rather than those of the client (sometimes a client will set standard terms as part of its contract procedure, although these will rarely cover everything that is important in the assignment). Here are some examples.

- Which law? For contracts entered into between British organizations, the presumption is that English law applies. However, what if a British consultancy wins a contract with a Hungarian client? Ensuring that the law used is English law is clearly in the interests of the consultancy.
- What is a day? We all know, but do we? When a proposal says that a client will be charged so much per consultant day, or pro rata for less than a full day, what does this mean? If a consultant spends 12 hours with a client on 1 day, does that generate a charge of 1 consultant day, 1½ days or something else? The consultancy knows its internal definitions, but the client has to know them, too, as they may be different to those of other consultancies.
- What are expenses? Is the client clear about what may or may not be charged? What about the grey areas in a fixed-price contract when the consultancy buys a report (expense) that could have been consulted in a library (consultancy time)?
- Under what circumstances may a contract be cancelled by either party and, then, what cancellation charges are due? Setting this out in advance, when neither party is contemplating cancellation, can make life much easier later.
- What rights does the client have to use material supplied by the consultancy after the assignment has ended? This may be straightforward when the end product is a report, but what if proprietary psychological testing instruments were used during the assignment or material was written for a course that incorporated the consultancy's intellectual property?
- Confirmation that the consultancy will maintain confidentiality, unless authorized by the client to make disclosures, is very valuable.
- Excusing either party from performance as a result of acts of God can be a sensible precaution.
- The consultancy may gain relief from non-performance if specific requirements from the client are not met. Generally, a client's failure to cooperate is more likely to increase costs or delay performance than to totally frustrate an assignment, so a defined mechanism for charging for these costs or avoiding delays can be helpful.

The legal implications of a contract

Some of the less exciting parts of the proposal discussed above relate to the legal implications and, earlier, attention was drawn to the contractual aspects of the entry phase as a whole, and the proposal in particular.

The entry phase

It is very easy to forget, in the excitement of winning an assignment, that a proposal is also a binding contract between the consultancy and the client. At the point where a contract is awarded, there is a belief by the client that the consultancy will do certain things within the specified time in order to achieve the agreed result, and by the consultancy that the client will provide whatever facilities have been agreed and will pay invoices on time.

However, if the client's organization does not receive what is set out in the proposal, it has the right to demand what was specified and can legitimately refuse to pay either all or part of the fees and expenses and, in certain circumstances, claim damages.

If the consultancy has performed as per the proposal, it has the right to insist on payment and may enforce that obligation through the courts.

It makes sense to ensure that proposals clarify any points on which a dispute can arise, partly to protect both parties from misunderstanding and partly so that both parties are able to enforce their rights under the contract. The legal remedies for enforcing payment of an unpaid invoice are much simpler when the client has not disputed the bill. If the bill is disputed, on grounds that what was promised has not been delivered or that no bill is due, this issue may have to be settled by arbitration (if the contract provides for this) or through the courts.

Cancellations of contracts also occur and many consultancies have faced situations where a client's circumstances have changed (perhaps the manager who commissioned the work has been replaced or the client has been acquired by another company). Sometimes these are handled by the client in a very cavalier manner, with cancellation taking place without warning (and, in very occasional cases, without bothering to tell the consultancy) and quite regardless of the commitments the consultancy has made to do the work. This may happen before work starts or at any point afterwards.

When one party cancels a contract, the other party is entitled to compensation that puts it in the same position as if the contract had been performed. This does not mean that the consultancy can sit back, do nothing and expect to receive full fees when a client cancels a contract. First, the injured party has a duty to minimize the loss and will be required to demonstrate, should the case go to court, that every action was taken to find alternative work for the consultants who should have been performing the work. Second, the payment that can be gained is related to loss of profits, which will only be the value of the assignment if the work had to be performed in the next few weeks. The courts have upheld the claim that the loss is almost equal to revenue when the consultancy cannot take action to reduce staff in the period and so has to carry the salary and overhead costs, as well as lose profit. Considerable store is put by the courts in cancellation or contract variation situations on contemporaneous records, such as diary entries, letters and file notes that record discussions, the fact that meetings or telephone conversations took place and what was agreed. Sometimes the client may argue that there never was a contract, in which case evidence that there was may be critical, which is why there may be weaknesses in relying on verbal acceptances without some form of written follow-up.

The emphasis on the rights of both parties does not mean that either will wish to sue the other or that it makes economic sense so to do. Court action is costly and one party will always lose. Usually both parties move into litigation only after their legal advisers have said there is a good chance of winning, but they cannot both be right. Sometimes it is a game of bluff and a settlement can be negotiated in place of legal action. The consultancy also has to consider the client relationship and the longer-term consequences of pursuing an action. Where the client relationship is strong, it is likely that any disputes will be settled by discussion, with perhaps a measure of give and take on either side.

Because the contract is legally binding, the consultancy should be careful to avoid any misrepresentation at every stage of the entry phase. The immediate response to this thought is 'of course we would not do this', but the fact is that consultancies have been known to let enthusiasm get the better of judgement and sail very close to the wind when claiming expertise in an area or past experience of it. A firm that enforces ethical standards of behaviour would avoid this trap.

Presenting the proposal

The consultancy's motivation is to turn every proposal into a contract, although this cannot happen in every situation. Although some clients choose on price rather than quality, and this may be particularly so when they are working to an internal budget limit, in theory at least most are seeking a cost-effective solution to their problem or issue.

The span of prices and differences in approaches in a competitive situation may be very large. Hussey (1988) provides a case study of how one client chose a supplier from competitive bids from seven firms or business schools. The range of prices quoted varied from £141,330 to £435,950, and every supplier suggested a different approach. The assignment did not go to the cheapest contender. Surprisingly, three of the suppliers put in bids that ignored one of the major requirements specified in what was a comprehensive briefing paper.

Typically, in a competitive bid, some consultancies may be eliminated when the proposals are received. Others may be invited to make presentations to the client and to discuss the proposal in some depth.

The initiative passes from the consultancy to the client when the proposal is lodged. It is useful for the consultancy to keep in touch with the client in a gentle way during this period, but without hustling. A telephone call to check that the proposal has been received, and an enquiry as to whether or not any more information would help the client shows that the firm is interested in the client and the assignment without being overly pushy.

A presentation is often required even when the client has either eliminated the other bidders or never invited any others in the first place. It can also be part of a 'beauty contest', with several firms being invited, sometimes in the same week or even on the same day, to make a presentation. (Beauty contests may also be held in a pre-qualifying process.)

A small consultancy can find it particularly difficult to be available on the dates given by the client for a beauty contest as often they are set by the client, who may have considerable problems bringing together the internal team that will make the decision and so they cannot be flexible. Thus, the date is often given to the consultancy in a 'take it or leave it' way, which can be very difficult when the key people required to go are committed to other clients. Although clients will try to be accommodating, within their own tight constraints they may only be able to shift the time on the chosen day.

See the checklist on p. 87 to help you prepare adequately for attending a beauty contest and make an effective presentation.

What to find out in advance

- What the client's expectations from the presentation are.
- Whether or not a formal presentation is wanted.
- The time allowed for a formal presentation and for discussion.
- Who will be there and what their interests are.
- Which other firms have been asked to present.
- What the batting order is for presentations.

The presentation

- Prepare the presentation carefully.
- Rehearse the presentation so you can keep strictly to the time allowed.

- Make the presentation client-centred, stressing what is important to them.
- Do not always follow the proposal literally: keep to key points and change the order to suit the situation.
- Make sure all visual aids are of a high quality.
- Decide who is to attend and the role of each.
- Build in flexibility.
- Encourage discussion.
- Try not to bore them – yours may be the umpteenth presentation they have seen that day.

There may be an element of negotiation at the presentation stage. For example, a client may like the approach in general, but find the price too high and so will want to know what savings might result if part of the task were handled slightly differently.

Finally, win or lose, use the bid opportunity as a chance to learn. Speak to the client if you win to find out why your organization was preferred to the others (but do not appear to be surprised!) and if you lose, ask the client, without appearing to criticize their decision or trying to alter it, what the reasons were for their choice and where your bid was lacking. Apart from improvements that may come from this analysis, it can build a relationship with the client and is a good way of gaining information about competitors.

References

Heskett, J L (1986) *Managing in the Service Economy*, Harvard Business School, Boston

Hussey, D E (1988) *Management Training and Corporate Strategy*, Pergamon Press, Oxford

Hussey, D E (1995) 'Competitor analysis: A case history,' in D E Hussey ed, *Rethinking Strategic Management*, John Wiley, Chichester

Kotler, P (1994) *Marketing Management: Analysis, Planning, Implementation, and Control* (8th edn, Prentice-Hall, Englewood Cliffs, NJ

Kubr, M (1996) *Management Consulting: A guide to the profession*, (3rd edn, revised), International Labour Office, Geneva

Normann, R (1991) *Service Management: Strategy and leadership in service businesses*, (2nd edn), John Wiley, Chichester

6

Data collection and diagnosis

Clive Rassam

Introduction

This chapter looks at one of the central parts of a consultancy assignment: the collection of information and the resulting diagnosis. It discusses the need for a strategic and routine analysis of the organization's activities, looks at the customary requirement for a reframing of the client's problems and issues and then moves on to the diagnostic phase. Finally, it points out the need to be familiar with some of the basic concepts of social science research methodology.

Analysis

Before you start to collect information, you need to decide what you are seeking to find out and, therefore, what kind of data you require. Otherwise you can end up with a mass of information that is of no practical use. Calvert Markham, a consultant, trainer and writer, makes the point that, 'it can be easy to embark on a highly structured programme of data collection without reflecting what the data is to be used for', adding that, in such cases, the information will have 'failed to address the important issues' (Markham, 1991).

You therefore need a framework or, as Markham suggests, a 'model of performance' that will enable you to decide just what sort of data you will need. This entails two kinds of analysis. First, an analysis of a strategic nature in order to assess the organization's main activities, its objectives and the environment within which these processes are being undertaken and, second, a routine analysis to examine the organization from a day-to-day operational point of view.

Strategic analysis

The diagnosis of a company's problems must first begin with a general strategic analysis. The purpose of this analysis is to get a broad view of the company so as to identify as quickly and efficiently as possible 'where the shoe pinches' before engaging in more detailed survey work. The aim is also to initiate a strategic process in the company and to identify possible areas where competitiveness and profitability can be improved.

European Handbook of Management Consultancy, 1996

Strategic analysis should investigate the following *(European Handbook of Management Consultancy,* 1996):

- the core business purpose of the organization
- the business units
- the strategic position of the organization as a whole and that of the business units, examining strengths, weaknesses and competition, both current and possible
- the strategic potential of the organization and the business units (this should include a financial analysis, plus an assessment of product lifecycles).

A key part of this analysis should involve, as Porter (1985) explains, an examination of the competitive position and structure of the industry in which the company is operating, the forces that are impacting the company and its competitors and all the possible sources of competitive advantage that lie within the company.

Porter's five competitive forces that determine an industry's profitability need to be considered (these are explained later on in this chapter). How well is the company responding to these forces in comparison with its competitors? How far is the relative significance of these forces changing, maybe as a result of the emergence of new competition or new substitute products or services? How is the industry being shaped by its constituent players, by new entrants and by technology?

Other significant factors that Porter identifies include:

- the proportion of product value that companies are able to capture for themselves
- how the supply/demand balance affects the industry's pricing and profits.

What kind of strategy is the company pursuing? Is it based on cost advantage or differentiation or is it grounded on focusing on a particular niche market? Is the strategy still relevant or is it becoming threatened by new competition or new technology? Has the company's strategy been consistent?

It is also important to consider how far the company might be able to influence the forces that are impacting the industry, but this needs to be put into a long-term perspective. Short-term gains by one company can sometimes lead to instability in the industry, encouraging new competition that, ultimately, is detrimental to the company that initiated the change.

Within the company itself, there will be many sources of competitive advantage. These will be found along the value chain – that is, the separate activities involved in designing, making, marketing and delivering the product (see under Diagnostic techniques, later in this chapter).

Routine analysis

No matter how good the strategic position of an organization is, this can be held back by deficiencies in its routine operations. The operational analysis should principally cover activity and information analysis. 'Activities' in this context means 'a group of logically related decisions made and actions carried out to manage products, services or resources' (*European Handbook of Management Consultancy*, 1996).

It is usually impossible to do a complete activity analysis of the whole organization because of the amount of time that this would take, so a number of activities have to be chosen. Which activities are selected to be analysed will be determined by the conclusions of the strategic analysis.

One technique that is useful here is value chain analysis, which 'illustrates the company's overall, customer-perceived value creation, with emphasis on the work that has to be done to produce, market and deliver/support the products and services offered' (*European Handbook of Management Consultancy*, 1996).

The aim of the information analysis is to examine the information flows 'among the activities in the identified value chain' (*European Handbook of Management Consultancy*, 1996). The information analysis may well highlight a number of problems. It will show which activities are 'information-intensive' and it will enable you to compare the organization's value chain with its structure. Thus, it will draw attention to those activities where the organizational linkages are weak and highlight where routine operations are least effective.

Analysis of the organizational perspective

The strategic analysis should be supported by a judgement about the organization, its structure and its corporate health. Thus, the consultant could pose the following questions.

- Does the organization have a flexible or a fixed structure?
- Are the lines of communication clear and working well or are there problems in communication?
- Are the organization's mission statements and core business objectives understood and recognized or are they seen in a negative way?
- Have there been recent changes of emphasis in the organization or sudden shifts in aims or power struggles?
- Does the organization's history cast a shadow or a light over its present activities?

Functional strategic analysis

The organization's principal functions also need to be analysed in terms of their strategy. The strategy for each of the following functions needs to be examined and reviewed:

- financial
- marketing
- human resources
- IT.

The consultant therefore needs to ask what are the objectives that the financial managers are trying to achieve? What are the corporate aims in terms of working capital and liquidity management? Are there any particular external pressures that are determining the strategy? To what extent is the financial strategy working?

To analyse the marketing strategy, the consultant needs to ask the following kinds of questions. Is the strategy product-oriented, production-oriented or market-oriented? How far are the organization's products going towards satisfying customer demand, to what extent are they mutually supportive and can they be modified to solve customer and market problems? Is the company seeking to be a market leader or follower? What are the weak links in the marketing strategy?

What kind of human resource management strategy does the organization have and how well does it match the overall corporate needs of the organization? What are the inputs into this strategy and at what level in the hierarchy is policy set? To what extent has the organization's human resource management strategy hindered or helped the organization? What are the organization's information needs and how well are these met by the current IT strategy? 'General management often finds it more difficult to evaluate the performance of the IT function than that of any other aspect of business' (Kubr, 1996). IT is also often a source of conflict in an organization – because the systems are not delivering the kind of information that is wanted, in the right format and at the right time – so the way in which the IT function formulates policy usually needs to be looked at.

What to do next

These modes of analysis will then prompt the consultant to reconsider the situation that the organization is in. This is a time for reflection. Markham (1991) makes the point that consultants are too ready to make snap judgements based on their initial information. His advice for the early stage is 'don't just do something, sit there and think!'

Reframing the brief

The initial analysis frequently leads to a re-examination of what the assignment should focus on. This can be an awkward time for the consultant, especially if the client has very fixed views about what needs to be done or what the main problems are. You, as a consultant with an outside view, will see things differently. The series of analyses described above will have brought to light many pieces of information that the client has either overlooked, underestimated or maybe ignored.

Greiner and Metzger (1983) recall an assignment that was ostensibly about helping a client to decentralize, 'only to find after several interviews that a lack of capable general managers would prevent decentralization'. So, the problem was redefined as 'one of designing a program to develop managers for a decentralized organization'. Greiner and Metzger add that the redefinition of a brief will often lengthen the assignment, so the extra cost and time involved need to be negotiated carefully.

Data collection

The nature of the assignment will determine the kind of data that is required. This is usually either internal or external data. The aim should be to collect a certain number of objective facts, but these will be coloured by additional, subjective facts and interpretations. Depending on the assignment, the subjective information can be as important – sometimes more so – than the objective, verifiable data.

The choice as to which kind of data to collect should not only be influenced by the obvious business considerations of the client's organization, but also by other cultural and political factors intrinsic to the organization. For example, the views of certain individuals or departments, although not ostensibly germane to the assignment, may need to be consulted. This is where the consultant has to show tact, discretion and intuition. Thus, the data-collection process has to be discussed closely with the client, but this does not mean that the client should determine the entire remit of the data-gathering activity. If a client is reluctant to pursue certain lines of enquiry, this needs to be explained and defended. Also, bear in mind that the data required and the method of gathering it will develop and change as more information appears and as the initial analyses are modified.

Internal data

For sources of internal business data, the consultant has recourse to:

- company accounts
- business plans and budgets
- technical and sales records
- personnel records
- records concerning key suppliers and customers.

These records should enable the consultant to make assessments regarding the organization's sales and financial performance. The organization's financial health can be judged by using various ratios, such as the equity ratio, debt ratio, stock to sales ratio, return on capital, rate of return on equity, profit as a percentage of turnover and operating margin. The information elicited from these ratios can then be used to make further assessments about the organization.

As IT is such an important aspect of an organization's activities, it is also useful to collect information about the organization's IT system. For example, how the system operates, what its objectives are and so on, as well as how the system is perceived by its users. The data collected should therefore combine written and interview-based information.

Some assignments will require human resource data, such as personnel turnover, employee attitudes, corporate culture and so on. Such information can be acquired by means of questionnaires, surveys and interviews as well as by looking through company records.

External data

The consultant will also need to obtain external data concerning shareholders, suppliers, customers, markets and public image. Among other pieces of salient information, it is important to find out the following:

- who the major shareholders are and how the organization is perceived by the financial community (assuming it is a public company)
- who the organization's main suppliers are and what their financial status is and their position in the market
- who the organization's principal customers are and how they perceive the organization
- how large the organization's market is, how fast it is growing and in what ways it is developing and what threats there are to it
- what the organization's market position is in its various markets and on what factors this is based – price, quality, range of technologies or service, geographical position, historical links and so on.

Sources of such information include market research from such publishers as Jordan, Euromonitor, Key Note, and Mintel, stockbrokers' reports, trade journals and newspapers. Most of this information can now be sourced on-line, too. Some of this information can also be used for benchmarking the performance of the organization against that of its competitors. A detailed benchmarking analysis will show where an organization is falling behind its competitors in terms of productivity, efficiency and quality.

Choosing data collection methods

Consultants have four recognized ways of collecting information:

- reading reports and documents
- interviewing people individually and in groups
- sampling people's experiences and attitudes by means of questionnaires
- observation.

Each of these methods has its merits.

Reading reports and documents

If they are factually accurate, reports and documents are likely to provide the basic building blocks for data gathering. Their disadvantage is that they will have been written for a specific audience, will assume certain kinds of knowledge and will leave out issues that did not appear to be important, but which may be important to the consultant reading them.

Interviews

Interviewing is a popular means of obtaining information as it allows personal contact, reveals significant subjective issues in the organization and makes those interviewed feel that they are contributing to the outcome of the assignment. However, the process is time-consuming and requires careful construction.

Questionnaires

These are less time-intensive than interviewing, enable comparisons to be made and can be analysed more easily than can interviews. However, questionnaires have disadvantages, too. People may misinterpet some questions, they may be constrained not to tell all that they know and feel for fear of being discovered and so give the answers that they think are required. Also, the questionnaire leaves very little room for supplementaries.

Observation

As a data-gathering technique, observation is used almost unconsciously by most consultants. This kind of first-hand information can be useful, but its usefulness is likely to be qualified by two factors:

- the consultant might only notice what they are looking for
- the consultant's very presence – like that of royalty – will alter the behaviour of those around them.

However, observation will still reveal details about an organization, and it is in the details that some of the larger issues can manifest themselves.

Establishing the issues

Once the data has been collected, it will be clearer what the main issues for diagnosis are. Usually a cluster of issues will present themselves. These may show that there is a discrepancy between the organization's goals and its competences or between its objectives and its financial performance. They may suggest that the organization is pursuing strategies that have now become contradictory.

The data so far collected may not all point in the same direction. The diagnosis will clarify what is happenning.

Diagnosis

'More is at stake during the diagnostic phase than gaining an understanding of the problem', according to Greiner and Metzger (1983). They explain, 'The perceptive consultant will also need to assess how ready the client is for change. Brilliant solutions will be ignored or rejected if the client's employees are devoted to the status quo.'

Greiner and Metzger also make the point that the client's problem is unlikely to have a single or simple cause, so they offer three cautions.

1 'Suspend early judgement on problems or solutions.' In particular, maintain detachment from the client's problems in order to retain your objectivity.
2 'Look behind every tree.' What they mean is that part of the answer to a problem will come from unlikely sources.
3 'Don't believe the client's diagnosis.' Neither should a consultant accept the diagnosis of a client's employees. The reason is that people rarely see themselves as part of the problem that is being talked about.

At the start of the diagnostic phase, it is easy to feel overwhelmed by the amount of data that you have. Greiner and Metzger (1983) make four useful points in this respect.

1 'Distinguish between symptoms and causes.' Much of what you will have been told will be symptoms and not causes. Acquire further detail on what you have been told if need be, but your task is to search for causes.
2 'Recognize the principle of multicausality.' Most problems, and indeed most opportunities, have several causes.

3 Recognize 'the interrelationships between causal factors'. Thus, the fact that an IT system is not working effectively may have more to do with changes in corporate strategy, in suppliers and in certain managers' changed needs than with there being anything inherently wrong with the IT system. The causes that have been responsible for the breakdown of the system are related.

4 Understand 'the law of interdependence'. There is often a sound reason for bad management and organizational practices. Therefore, before you recommend a change from an outmoded or inefficient way of operating, you may need to ask why that practice grew up in the first place and address that issue.

In other words, you need to ask how has the present set of circumstances been created? Arthur Turner wrote in the *Harvard Business Review* (1982):

> Competent diagnosis requires more than an examination of the external environment, the technology and economics of the business and the behaviour of non-managerial members of the organization. The consultant must also ask why executives made certain choices that now appear to be mistakes or ignored certain factors that now seem important.

Diagnostic techniques

To help them make a diagnosis, consultants have a number of tried and tested techniques at their disposal. There are many more, but 14 of the most commonly used techniques are described below. The first seven are particularly suitable for dealing with macro questions, such as corporate strategy and marketing, while the second seven are helpful in examining the detail of issues.

Five competitive forces

In his book *Competitive Advantage* (1985), Michael Porter identified 'five competitive forces that determine industry profitability'. These are (see also Figure 6.1)

- competition in the industry
- potential entrants
- substitutes
- suppliers
- buyers.

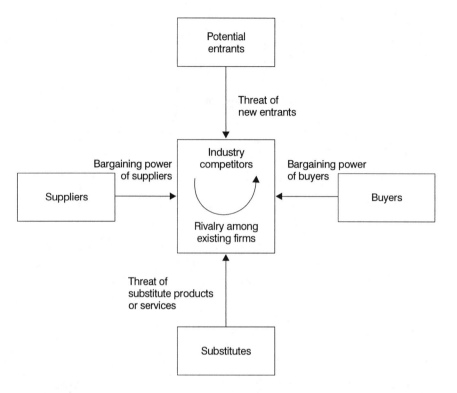

Figure 6.1: The five competitive forces that determine industry profitability

These competitive forces are critical, says Porter, because they influence the prices, costs and required investment of firms in a given industry. The strength of the five forces varies from industry to industry, and their collective strength will determine the profitability of firms in that industry. Companies can gain a competitive edge if they can cope with these five forces better than their rivals. He adds that companies can adopt one of three competitive strategies:

- cost leadership – being a low-cost leader
- differentiation – uniqueness
- focus – niche market-driven.

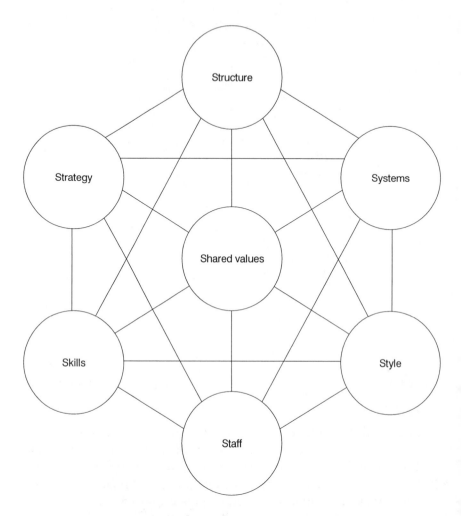

Figure 6.2 The McKinsey 7-S Framework

The McKinsey 7-S framework was developed by McKinsey in the early 1980s as a way of analysing high-performance organizations. It was used as a basis for the research for Tom Peters and Robert Waterman's book, *In Search of Excellence* (1982).

The seven variables (shown in Figure 6.2) constitute an independent reinforcing network. Peters and Waterman explain that the framework 'has as much or more to do with the way things work (or don't) around your companies as the formal structures and strategies do,' and they

Data collection and diagnosis

assert that, 'four years' experience throughout the world has borne out our hunch that the framework would help immeasurably in forcing explicit thought about not only the hardware – strategy and structure – but also about the software of organization – style, systems, staff (people), skills, and shared values.' For management consultants, this framework is a way of seeing how the 'hard' and the 'soft' issues in an organization interact.

Value chain analysis

Value chain analysis is a way of describing the activities within and around an organization that is then used to identify potential sources of a company's economic advantages, and thereby make an assessment of its competitive strengths.

Value chain analysis, originated by Porter (1985), derives from value analysis, an accounting tool developed in the 1950s. Value analysis was designed to show the value-added components in a company's manufacturing process. Porter took the concept a stage further by linking all an organization's separate operations and then assigning a value to each activity.

Each activity is analysed in terms of its cost drivers and its relationship to other activities, then the company's cost position is assessed in relation to those of its competitors. Porter explains, 'A firm gains competitive advantage by performing these strategically important activities more

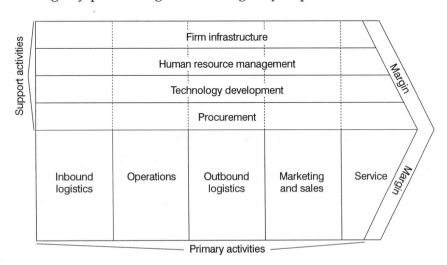

Figure 6.3 The generic value chain

117

cheaply or better than its competitors', adding,'differences among competitor value chains are a key source of competitive advantage'.

Benchmarking

Benchmarking is a method of improving performance by identifying and implementing best practice. It is based on making comparisons between the performance of the company – its products and processes – and the performance of its best competitors.

Some of the first companies to use benchmarking were in the motor manufacturing and steel industries, where fierce Japanese competition forced them to rethink their whole manufacturing processes.

The best kind of benchmarking not only makes comparisons with a company's competitors in its own industry, but also seeks to make comparisons with best practice in other industries.

The Boston matrix

The Boston matrix – named after The Boston Consulting Group, which devised it – is a method of classifying a company's activities according to market share, profitability and growth potential.

The Boston matrix is one of the most widely used strategic analysis tech-

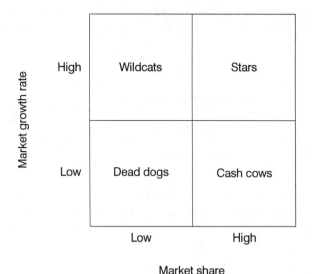

Figure 6.4 The Boston matrix

niques. It divides business activities into four categories:

- stars – activities that have high market share and high market growth
- cash cows – activities that have low market growth, but high market share
- wildcats – activities that have high market growth, but low market share
- dead dogs – activities that have low market share and low market growth.

This kind of diagnosis can help to identify areas for product development and areas that are ripe for withdrawal. The matrix will also show which are the high-risk areas.

PIMS

PIMS – which stands for profit impact of market strategy – is a computer-based model 'using marketing and financial data to determine the characteristics of a successful business in a given industry' (Greiner and Metzger, 1983).

Strategy evaluation

The various strategies that could be opted for need to be evaluated. This can be done in a number of ways:

- ranking options against key factors in the organization's environment, its resources and its shareholders' expectations
- drawing decision trees, whereby options are eliminated according to several criteria
- scenario planning, where available options are matched to different scenarios and the optimum one is chosen
- simulation, where the organization's business system is modelled using a computer and then assessed within various models of its competitive environment.

Activity-based costing (ABC)

Activity-based costing 'increases the accuracy of cost information by more precisely allocating overhead and other indirect costs to products or customer segments' (Rigby, 1997). Whereas traditional accounting systems distribute indirect costs using bases such as direct labour hours, machine hours or material hours, 'ABC allocates overhead and other indirect costs by activity.'

Carrying out an ABC analysis involves determining key activities that are performed, the cost drivers for each activity, the group overhead and other indirect costs by activity using identified drivers, collecting data on each activity and then assigning costs to products based on activity usage. An ABC analysis can be used to reprice products, reduce costs and improve new product design.

The Delphi technique

The Delphi technique is used to solve major problems or questions and for the purposes of planning. It is both a diagnostic tool and a data-collection method.

In essence, it is based on asking experts inside or outside an organization, or both, a series of fundamental questions, maybe relating to an industry or sector or a technology.

As Markham (1991) explains, this technique consists of three staged actions:

1 'establish the major responses to an initial open-ended question'
2 'determine the relative weighting of these responses'
3 'establish the reasons for experts' views which are significantly different from the norm'.

The answers are usually assessed quantitatively, but they can also be judged qualitatively.

Group process model

Like the Delphi technique, this model is both diagnostic and informational in its intent. It can be argued that it takes the Delphi technique one stage further by the use of a group of people examining various issues. There are many types of this model. For example, Greiner and Metzger (1983) cite the Mason-Mitroff dialectic model, which is based on the use of 'questionnaires and discussions to map out the diverse assumptions and opinions made by senior managers toward a variety of stakeholders in their environment.'

There are two major differences between this dialectic technique and the Delphi model. The dialectic mode of analysis is based on group discussion, whereas Delphi questionnaires are answered individually and in secret. The analytical process resulting from a dialectic model is more structured and is conducted in a group meeting, whereas with the Delphi technique, the consultants make the diagnosis themselves.

Another mode of group-based diagnosis is the brainstorming session, which is much more open-ended than the dialectic approach.

Group-based diagnosis needs to be facilitated by an experienced consultant with an understanding of group dynamics, and it is not applicable in every circumstance. Most consultants would say that it is not suitable where there are deep personal or organizational conflicts.

The Pareto principle

The Pareto principle can be applied to a great number of problems. It is based on the observation of an Italian economist, Pareto, that 80 per cent of the elements of a given set of circumstances are generally due to 20 per cent of the causes of those elements. The Pareto principle is also used more loosely to denote that a small number of factors, inputs, occurrences and so on will usually have a disproportionate effect on an eventual outcome.

The financial performances of many businesses bear out this principle – the majority of a company's profits are often derived from a small percentage of its turnover. Thus, in a consultancy assignment, it can often be the case that a relatively small number of factors are responsible for a large part of a problem.

Paired comparisons

Pairing different elements of the same data so as to rank them in importance is another way of diagnosing what is a significant issue and what is not. This method enables the consultant to screen out the trivial and highlight underlying difficulties.

Force field analysis

Force field analysis was developed by Kurt Lewin as part of his field theory of organizational change. Lewin stated that, in any organization, there are two sets of forces in operation:

- those forces that are driving change
- those forces that are restraining it.

121

If the two forces are of equal strength, then the organization is in equilibrium.

When a consultant is proposing change (or maybe diagnosing why change has not already happened when it should have done) using this approach, they would weigh up the balance of forces in the organization and ask why the forces of change are being held back.

Critical incident

The critical incident technique focuses on critical events as a way of explaining deep underlying problems and issues. Whether questionnaires or interviews are adopted as the main data-gathering technique, the overriding aim is to find out the key occurrences that have triggered major events.

Sometimes these critical events are widely known in an organization, but sometimes they lie hidden unconsciously in people's experiences.

Research methodology

A good management consultant is aware of the value and pitfalls of various research methods. In particular, the consultant needs to understand what the mediating factors are that will make their efforts successful or otherwise.

First, two broad points need to be made.

- The consultant needs to be self-aware and recognize their own intellectual and professional assumptions about management issues. These natural, instinctive, habitual assumptions can be quite powerful – all the more so if the consultant is unconscious of them.
- The consultant also needs to be conscious of their own impact on the organization. Just by being there or by asking questions the consultant will change behaviours in the organization. Markham (1991) cites the Hawthorne studies conducted in the USA in the 1930s by industrial psychologist Elton Mayo, who showed that people's behaviours are affected by the very fact that they are being observed.

Some of the research methodology issues have been ably covered by Chris Argyris, in his seminal work *Intervention Theory and Method* (1970). Argyris reminds his readers of 'the unintended consequences of rigorous research.' He points out that a group of external researchers in an organization will be seen as a separate social system. As such, they may arouse suspicion and fear and may generate deception and non-cooperation.

Citing another leading organization theorist, Warren Bennis, Argyris also points out that the researchers' spirit of enquiry may well be anathema to the culture of the organization they are studying. This means that a programme of interviews or questionnaires may not yield as much 'truth' as the researchers expect.

Argyris also has another very telling concern. He asks:

Can a researcher conduct an exploratory study without a hypothesis? Every act of perception is a selective decision-making process which usually contains many hypotheses which should be made explicit. As employees have pointed out, they can tell that the researcher doing exploratory research has one or more hypotheses by the way he asks questions and takes notes.

However, it may not be wise in a consultancy assignment to make a hypothesis explicit. A degree of concealment may be necessary in order to prevent the respondent from prejudging the intention of the questioner.

A core part of a consultant's research will involve interviews, questionnaires and surveys. These techniques require structured approaches. The design of a questionnaire is likely to be influenced by the criteria to be used to evaluate it. The questionnaire design should also take account of social and professional differences among those being surveyed. Therefore, the words that are used in it should be such that they are interpreted in the same way by different people. The questionnaire should also show clarity, objectivity and openness to new ideas.

A useful guide to research methodologies used in the social sciences is the Open University's Social Science Third Level Course, *Research Methods*, Block 3A, *Research*, and, Block 3B, *Design*.

Conclusion

Although we have delineated analysis, data collection and diagnosis as if they were three distinct categories, in practice they overlap. Indeed, some consultants argue, for example, that data collection and data analysis are really one activity – largely on the grounds that you need to know what information you are looking for before you seek it. There is clearly a range of views on this subject. However, what consultants do agree on is that getting this phase, early on in an assignment, right is essential – it shapes everything that follows.

References

Argyris, C (1970) *Intervention Theory and Method: A behavioural science view*; Addison-Wesley, Mass.

Block, P (1978) *Flawless Consulting*, Pfeiffer, San Diego

Greiner, R and Metzger, L (1983) *Consulting to Management*, Prentice-Hall, Englewood Cliffs, NJ

Kubr, M (1996) *Management Consulting: A guide to the profession* (3rd edn, revised), International Labour Office, Geneva

Markham, C (1991) *Practical Management Consultancy*, Institute of Chartered Accountants, London

Oppenheim, A N (1976) *Questionnaire Design and Attitude Measurement*, Heinemann, London

Peters T and Waterman, R (1982) *In Search of Excellence*, Harper & Row, New York

Porter, M (1985) *Competitive Advantage: Creating and sustaining superior performance*, The Free Press, New York

Rigby, D K (1997) *Management Tools and Techniques: An executive's guide*, Bain and Co, Boston

Turner, A (1982) *Harvard Business Review*, September/October

European Handbook of Management Consultancy (1996) Oak Tree Press, Dublin

7

Presenting advice and solutions

Clive Rassam

Introduction

This chapter looks at how to formulate and present recommendations, whether they are in the form of advice or solutions. No matter what the assignment is or what kind of relationship the consultant has with the client, there comes a time when diagnosis must give way to advice and recommendations. The advice might be given orally on a one-to-one basis or by means of a presentation or report. The advice or recommendation might be given in stages – especially if the assignment is lengthy – or at the end. Whatever the circumstances, the consultant needs to weigh up the options that lie before the client, be aware of likely resistance to proposals and present their case with clarity and sensitivity to the client's situation.

Back to basics

In formulating advice and recommendations, it is a good idea to briefly reconsider the original brief. Surrounded by piles of data, facts, figures and interview notes, consultants can sometimes lose sight of their original purpose. At this stage, the consultant should pose the following questions.

- What am I trying to achieve for this client?
- What have been the core issues or problems for this client?
- Are there particular circumstances, internal or external to the client, that have changed since the assignment began? (For example, have there been any new appointments to the board, have any competi-

tors shifted their strategy or launched new products and services, have the economic forecasts for the industry or for the economy changed?)

- Of all the issues facing the client, which ones are the most critical?
- What are the priorities for the client?
- What are the timescales of change – that is, how much time does the client's organization have for the change to take place?
- How will the proposed changes improve the organization's profitability?

Consider your role

Block (1981) says that consultants broadly adopt one of three roles:

- the expert
- the pair of hands
- the collaborator.

The consultant as expert is the initiator, the repository of knowledge and is seen as the primary problem-solver. The client is offloading a problem onto the consultant.

Where the consultant is a pair of hands, the client retains much of the initiative and, in effect, the consultant's task is to provide answers to a prescribed set of problems or issues.

When the consultant is working in a more collaborative way with the client, 'problem-solving becomes a joint undertaking, with equal attention to both the technical issues and the human interactions involved in dealing with the technical issues' (Block, 1981). The consultant does not solve problems for the manager, but, instead, they apply their special skills to help the manager to solve them.

So, the consultant can play the role of boffin or outsourced employee or catalyst. In reality, the consultant's role may change and move between these three dimensions.

There is also a further role – a comparatively new one – of the consultant as a risk-taker. This occurs in some of the big IT assignments where the consultancy and the client share some of the financial risks and benefits of the project.

The role that the consultant has taken on during the assignment will shape the client's expectations and, therefore, should influence how the consultant formulates the recommendations.

Where the role has been collaborative, the client will already have contributed much to the diagnosis and may well have some favoured solutions. However, where the consultant has been perceived as the expert, the client is likely to expect a stronger lead from the consultant, though this does not mean that the client will automatically accept what the consultant says. So, before you present your advice or recommendations, consider what your role is in the client–consultant relationship.

List the options

An important part of the consultant's role is to outline the range of options that are open to the client. The client needs to understand that they have a series of choices and that each one will have its merits, its costs and maybe its risks. The financial benefits will also vary with each option.

In setting out these options, the consultant should consider the following characteristics of the client organization:

- its immediate needs
- its long-term requirements
- its skills and competences
- its financial health
- its internal politics
- its capacity for change
- its financial requirements and aspirations.

All these characteristics will have a bearing on the options for change. They will determine what the options should be, and they will strongly influence whether or not the consultant's recommendations are ultimately acted on. Where a consultant's report and recommendations are not taken up by the client, it is usually because they have foundered on one or more of the characteristics or factors listed above.

There will be arguments that favour radical solutions and there will be others that lean towards incremental ones. It is unlikely that all the data or diagnosis will point in the same direction, so the skill of the consultant lies in how they evaluate the different possibilities. Technical, financial, market-driven and human resource criteria may need to be used to assess each option.

Four other considerations should illuminate the proposed alternatives:

- coherence
- realism
- practicality
- relevance to the future.

127

Considerations to note when weighing up the options

Coherence
Is a proposed course of action intrinsically coherent – that is, do all its elements fit well together? If not, what can be done to make them do so?

Realism
Does the course of action address the real needs of the client? Greiner and Metzger (1983) argue that a high number of consultancy studies 'define the problem one way and then implement a solution that fits only a pet idea of the consultant or the client.' The recommendations should match the original problem. Off-the-shelf solutions are not always appropriate.

Practicality
Is the proposal competely feasible, and, if not, what changes would have to be made in order to make it so? What practical financial difference will the proposal make?

Relevance to the future
Does the course of action take into account future scenarios? In other words, do the recommendations look beyond the immediate future, beyond the fulfilment of the recommendations? If not, then their benefits might be short-lived.

Involve the client

It is important to involve the client in formulating your recommendations. If the client has played an active role in this process, it will contribute to the recommendations' authority and ultimate effectiveness. If the client has not been involved in the process of reaching solutions, they are less likely to feel a commitment to them. There is little 'ownership' of the recommendations.

Thus, the client should be involved in critiquing the options that the consultant has drawn up. The client will have views on which options look the most profitable, and they are likely to have additional ideas that can be added to the consultant's list. Even if the client has up until now taken a somewhat detached role during the assignment or if they have not had the time to be more active in it, now is the moment to involve them.

Ideally, the client will be able to provide a small team of people to work with the consultant and examine each option. Feasibility studies may be needed to cost the options. The process of assessing possible lines of action and planning the means of implementation can be used to prepare senior management for the changes that are needed.

However, this stage of the assignment is politically very sensitive. The consultant and client might decide to restrict details of initial proposals to a very select few – to people who can be expected to support them. On the other hand, they might prefer to 'leak' some of the proposals in order to test opinion in the organization.

The consultant's discussions with the client at this point might lead to another stage in the process of making recommendations. Rather than simply accept or reject the consultant's proposals in their entirety, the client might conclude that some of the proposals need to be amended in some way, especially if the client's strategy has shifted or if the organization has altered. Also, the very recommendations themselves might throw up new opportunities for the client's organization that, if acted upon, could have implications for some of the proposals. So, what is needed now is a meeting involving some of the client's staff and the consultant at which the original recommendations, plus new ideas, can be discussed so as to arrive at an agreed solution.

Create solutions

A good consultant empowers their clients by helping them to gain new insights into themselves and their organization. Enabling a client to contribute to their own solutions is part of this process. Thus, before making the final recommendations, the consultant might want to 'facilitate' an options review meeting. Sometimes this facilitative role is exercised jointly by the consultant and the client. If this meeting is to be fruitful, the consultant should bear in mind the following considerations.

- Set aside enough time for the meeting, possibly a whole day.
- Each person attending the meeting should be well briefed with the necessary facts and figures.
- The consultant should come up with an agenda that is flexible. One technique is to split the agenda into three parts
  – idea creation
  – idea evaluation
  – practical consequences.
- In the idea creation stage, it is important to encourage any new suggestions and concepts, no matter how unusual or unconventional they may appear to be. Even ambiguous, slightly fuzzy ideas can be valuable, because they may contain the seed of something useful

later on. Also, ideas that initially seem impractical may turn out to be feasible.

- The consultant should not only be facilitating the contributions of others, but, at appropriate times, also pose questions and ideas of their own.
- The purpose of the idea evaluation stage is to search for a number of ideas that require further investigation and analysis. However, it is important to split the resulting critiques into objective and subjective assessments, for some ideas will appear to be inadequate from a subjective point of view, but right from an objective one. The consultant can play a valuable role here by quietly challenging some of the criticisms of unorthodox ideas.
- In the third stage, the chosen ideas are taken forward in a more practical way. For example, a proposed new product that has survived the test of evaluation might require a new distribution route or it might require some changes to the client's manufacturing process. Thus, a broad outline of the practical consequences of the new ideas should be worked out now.

This stage should lead to a set of agreed solutions, which can then form the basis of the consultant's report.

Report writing

Report writing is not something that comes easily to most consultants or to most managers. It is a skill that has to be acquired and nurtured with experience. According to consultant, trainer and writer Calvert Markham (1991), report writing is the one aspect of consultancy that new consultants find most difficult.

There are essentially three kinds of consultant report:

- interim reports
- discussion reports
- end-of-assignment reports.

This section focuses on the final report with its conclusions and recommendations.

Make sure it is needed

Markham makes the point that, before considering writing a report, you should ask yourself 'is this report really necessary?' In his view a report is needed if:

- there is something to report
- you want to set out the progress that has been made during the assignment
- a progress report is needed in order to stimulate more thinking and discussion on an issue
- an assignment is coming to an end.

Markham wisely advocates writing a report only if it is essential. He gives two main reasons for this. First, clients are busy people and they usually prefer to receive information face-to-face rather than in report form. Second, too much report writing by the consultant not only takes up the consultant's time, it can also put up a barrier between the consultant and the client.

Structure it

A consultant's report needs to be well-structured and well thought out. First, a good structure and a well-reasoned set of arguments leads to clarity, which means that it will be read and understood. Second, the better the structure and more cogent the arguments, the more the report will be proof against criticism.

In structuring the report, remember that the client may still have reservations about the changes that are being proposed, and remember, too, that, for most of its readers, much of the information contained in it will be new.

One way in which to write the report is to adopt the following seven-step plan.

1 *Begin with an executive summary* Highlight the initial issues and recommendations in no more than two pages.
2 *Outline the original terms of reference* Remind readers of why you were called in – this puts what follows in perspective.
3 *Summarize the data collected* Show that every avenue of investigation has been explored and that the data collected has been objective and carefully considered.
4 *Set out your findings* Explain your assessment of the information that you gathered. In writing this section, be aware of the political sensitivity of some of the material, especially if some of it is based on unattributable sources. Be careful in your use of quotations as long-serving members of an organization can usually guess who the author of an anonymous quotation is.

5 *Make your recommendations clear* Set out clearly, and in a focused way, what needs to be done. Show what the benefits of proceeding with the recommendations are, especially the financial advantages, and also point out the risks if the recommendations are only partly or not acted on.

Both the short- and the long-term financial benefits should be spelt out clearly. Commercial benefits, such as increased market share, the ability to provide a wider range of products and services, the possibility for cost or price reductions and so on should be spelt out.

It is also extremely important to set out the timeframe within which the changes should be made, both from a commercial point of view and in terms of the time that will be needed to make the necessary changes within the organization.

6 *Show the implications* There are likely to be many implications flowing from the proposed changes and these should be spelt out. If some of them are awkward, then show how the associated problems could be ameliorated. Be positive.

7 *Conclude with appendices* You cannot include all your material in the main body of the report. Some of the supporting material in the form of figures and diagrams will have to be gathered at the back of the report. The appendices are also the place where you should explain the methodologies that you have used, such as the kind of survey and analytical techniques you chose.

Begin each chapter of the report with a one-page summary of one-line points. Within each chapter, give each major point its own headline. In each chapter, too, take special care with the first one or two paragraphs, so that they show how your mind has been thinking. In this way, the reader will want to read the rest of what you have to say.

Culture and language

In writing the report you need to take great account of the culture of the client organization. This means two things. First, understanding and showing a recognition of the way the organization has evolved, the way it routinely operates now and the manner in which it expresses its values and beliefs. Second, using words in such a way that they reflect and match the language of the organization. For example, an organization that is highly action-oriented should be addressed in terms that stress activity rather than reflection. By all means introduce into the report concepts and ways of thinking that are new to the organization, but, if they are to be accepted, they should not be too way out, unless you have very good reasons for going out on a limb.

It is also important to use the client's own language and to reflect this back to the client. Neuro-linguistic programming (NLP) is a useful technique here. NLP has been described as the science of communication, with yourself as well as with others, and also as the art and science of personal excellence.

An excellent guide to NLP is Dr Harry Alder's *NLP for Managers* (1996). Part of the book looks at 'some of ways in which we differ, in thought and behaviour, and at the many filters that make our mental maps mutually hard to understand' when we are communicating. NLP helps you to understand 'where the other person is coming from', which is 'vital in establishing the rapport upon which successful communication depends'. He adds that NLP 'is a more effective basis for achieving your outcome than the most sophisticated communication system or carefully rehearsed presentation.'

Simplicity

Keep what you have to say simple, but not simplistic. Remember that you are writing for your client and not for fellow consultants, so there is no need to show off your knowledge, use impressive jargon or make your remarks unduly complicated. You may feel that the ideas that you have are complicated and subject to qualifications, and you will be right, but simplicity is still attainable. You can do this by setting out the core points strongly, and then following these with qualifying points listed separately and in logical order.

Another reason for keeping your message simple is that it compels you to think simply yourself – that is, in a focused way. If you find it difficult to write or say what you want simply, it can often mean that you do not actually know what you want to say.

The use of graphic material

Using graphs, bar charts and diagrams will enliven your report and break up the text. Also, using material that is graphically dramatic will mean that your report is remembered. Graphic material should be original, distinctive and imaginative.

Giving presentations

Making presentations is a routine part of most consultants' lives. They make presentations when bidding for business, delivering a progress report during an assignment and then when concluding the assignment. A lot can depend on these presentations. As Markham (1991) points out, 'The importance of presentations to a management consultant is that his (or her) business success can depend on how well they are done.'

This section concentrates on presentations that are made at the end of an assignment.

The format

The format of the presentation will depend on the size of the audience. The smaller the audience, the more informal the presentation can be, with fewer visual aids and with more time left for questions and open discussion. The larger the audience, the more structured the presentation needs to be.

The length and content

Almost every speaker addressing an audience speaks for too long. When was the last time you saw a public speaker stick to their allotted time? A major reason for this is that most of us completely underestimate how long it will take to say what we have to say. We forget that we will have to pause between major segments of our talk, that we will have to adjust our delivery according to the behaviour of the audience and, most important of all, we tend to forget that the technology of the audio-visual apparatus will interrupt our flow. Therefore, try to ration what you set out to say.

The content of your presentation should be clear and logically structured. It is useful to kick off with an illustrated outline and then to proceed from there. Balancing the amount of time you devote to analysis, findings and recommendations will depend on circumstances, but, generally speaking, it is a mistake to wax too long on the analysis and findings at the expense of your recommendations as it is the recommendations that your audience will be most concerned about.

In preparing the content of your presentation, remember that it should take account of the different constituencies in your audience.

You will be talking to a group of individuals who will have different professional views and priorities.

Visual aids

Knowing how to use visual aids is an art few speakers really master. Whatever you wish to illustrate should complement what you are saying and not distract from it. The visual message should be clear, straightforward and uncluttered. There is a tendency to put far too much material on one slide. If your illustration involves a complicated diagram, consider how you will interpret it. Expecting the audience to do the interpretation for you wastes time and is self-defeating because the audience might miss a significant point in the few seconds they have to see the slide.

Remember that visual aids are not only useful as a means of supporting your message, but also as a way of pacing your presentation. If you want to add some humour to your talk, then a slide is often a good way to do this.

The venue

You will not always get the chance to influence the choice of venue. When you do, try to select a location that will be neutral to the audience and possibly away from the site of the organization.

Preparation

There are two kinds of preparation: rehearsal and preparing the scene of the presentation. At the very least, read through the presentation material before delivering it and, if possible, do a trial run. Experience will tell you that your rehearsal time turns out to be less than the actual presentation time, so, if the time it takes you to do your rehearsal is the same as the time you have for the presentation, then you have too much material. Cut it down.

On the day of the presentation, it is useful to ensure that all the equipment needed is in place and that it works satisfactorily. You want a suitable space to put your notes, which should be easily accessible to you and well lit. Also, decide where you are going to stand in relation to the audience, which should be where you can read your notes easily, operate the audio-visual equipment effectively and speak at the same time.

Put yourself in the place of the audience, too – they need to be able to see you easily, hear you distinctly and read your audio-visuals without straining. Too many presentations are spoiled because these dynamics are not addressed.

Conclusion

The findings and recommendations you make will look different to the client than the way they will look to you. Consultants sometimes overlook this. To the client, the consultant's report is something that they and their colleagues will have to live with, whereas to the consultant it is just another report. Therefore, don't belabour the client organization's mistakes and weaknesses – in their hearts they know these already.

Do not put overly sensitive information into the report, especially the kind that a competitor would like to see, because even the most confidential of reports can find its way into the hands of a rival. To avoid such problems, agree the final draft with your client.

Above all, put yourself in your client's shoes. Your recommendations should start from where the client is now. They should be practical, encouraging and uplifting.

References

Alder, H (1996) *NLP for Managers*, Piatkus, London
Block, P (1981) *Flawless Consulting*, Pfeiffer, San Diego
Greiner, L and Metzger, R (1983) *Consulting to Management*, Prentice-Hall, Englewood Cliffs, NJ
Markham, C (1991) *Practical Management Consultancy*, Institute of Chartered Accountants, London

8

Implementation

Nick Obolensky

Introduction

Implementation is key. Without implementation, the most elegant consulting solution is of little value. Even though the consultant may not be involved in implementation, any worth their salt will be concerned with this issue.

Over the past three decades, the growth of management consultancy has been matched by unease about the value that it brings to business. Part of this is due to the fact that, too often, consultants focus on the formulation of great and worthy recommendations, but take little heed of the implementation issues the client will face long after the consultant has gone.

Implementation is generally a difficult area and no panaceas exist, but there is little to beat experience. This is especially so in this field where credibility with a client will depend on the ability to demonstrate achievement of implementation as well as the ability to empathize. At the end of the day, it is people who get things done – and people are often irrational and hard to fathom. Those adept at implementation are also adept at dealing with a variety of people, and such skills are rarely learnt from books. So, with implementation, the more you do, the more you learn.

This chapter, therefore, is designed to give an overview of the issues that you may need to think about when considering implementation. It is in four main parts, with each part posing a question, which is then explored. The questions and the areas they concern are given in brief below.

- *What is implementation?*
  Here we consider the definition and 'domain' of implementation.

Unlike other consulting domains, it is fraught with irrationality and behavioural issues that more typically rest with psychologists than consultants.

- *Why do recommendations fail to be implemented?*
  One way of dealing with the issues that implementation brings is to have an acute awareness of some of the more common pitfalls that await the consultant's recommendations. Such awareness will enable the consultant to at least ask the right questions and prepare the ground for a more fruitful outcome than would otherwise be the case.
- *What typical 'techniques' exist to aid implementation?*
  Although panaceas are lacking, a variety of techniques can be used to help.
- *What is the consultant's role and what skills are required?*
  As consultants enter the domain of implementation, they will find the need for a whole set of skills that others concerned with pure formulation/recommendation do not need.

At the end of this chapter, you will find a checklist. Whether or not you intend to be involved in implementation, this checklist is designed to ensure that your input to a client adds the best value and does not, like so many consultant interventions, gather dust in some far-flung forgotten corporate filing cabinet.

What is implementation?

'Implementation' is the noun derived from the verb 'to implement', which can mean to fulfil, to carry out, to execute or, rarer, to supply with implements. It is a Middle English word with roots in the Latin verb *implere*, which means to fill up or fulfil. Within the dictionary definition is the implicit assumption that something is empty (usually the situation) and something is used to fill it (usually the recommendation). And for a recommendation to exist, something happens before implementation, which is usually formulation. And here the fundamental distinction lies. Formulation is often based on rational, objective facts and analysis, which is a domain within which consultants traditionally operate and assist their clients. Alternatively, implementation is about people, and people are not fully rational. Thus, a recommendation (which is born from formulation, the world of rationality) is put into the world of people (who are often irrational). Implementation is the process of

Implementation

doing this and, thus, the domain of implementation is very different to that of formulation.

Why do recommendations fail to be implemented?

The implementation of recommendations can fail due to a whole host of reasons. The list below contains a brief consideration of the most common reasons. Typically, however, 'the reason' will be a mix of reasons rather than just one. A skilled implementation consultant will be aware of the risks. By asking intelligent and well-timed questions, the consultant will be able to surface these risks, which means they can be dealt with.

The quality of the formulation was weak – what and how?

The quality of the formulation will, to some degree, affect the quality of implementation. There are three pitfalls in formulation:

- weak analysis and too narrow or subjective an opinion – the 'what' is poorly defined
- focusing on wants, not needs
- no detailed plan or consideration of consequences – the 'how' is not detailed enough.

Weak analysis and too narrow or subjective an opinion
If the formulation is based on weak analysis and too narrow or subjective an opinion, it may contain factual errors that will impede implementation. A typical scenario is the formulation of recommendations that have a wide impact, but are based exclusively on the views of the top and middle managers. The views and opinions of external stakeholders (such as customers and suppliers) and those lower down the hierarchy are not sought or validated. Implementation fails due to the fact that the logic is flawed, and this provides easy ammunition for those who resist change.

An acid test is to ask yourself who is affected by the change, and to what degree have they been consulted? If those affected by the change have not been consulted, then the risk of implementation failure increases.

Focusing on wants, not needs
Another classic fault of formulation is that recommendations focus on client's wants, not their needs. A typical scenario could be the commis-

sioning of a strategy consulting assignment, where the client wants a new corporate strategy. However, the underlying need could relate to the fact that the team is fiercely territorial, divided and unable to gain consensus. It may also lack the skills to devise a strategy itself. The formulation of an elegant and logical strategy may well flounder as the underlying need to train and unite the team has not been addressed. Indeed, the consultants can become part of the problem rather than part of the solution.

A good question to ask is what led to the need for a consultant in the first place, as the reasons given in answer may contain the rocks on which the implementation will flounder. The 'five whys' is a good technique here: ask 'Why?' to each response/answer five times to get five levels down into the detail.

No detailed plan or consideration of consequences
During formulation, people spend too much time on what needs to be done and too little time on how it can be done. The failure here is that no detailed plan or consideration of consequences is taken into account. Formulation looks at the 'what' 90 per cent of the time and at the 'how' only 10 per cent of the time. And the rocks that can make implementation flounder are 90 per cent of how things are done and 10 per cent of what is done. The classic situation is that the time taken to define what needs to be done eats up the patience for action and so once the clarity is achieved, the implementation begins. However, because no clear plan has been developed and agreed, and because the consequences of the implementation have not been fathomed, implementation soon flounders. Therefore the action planning (and all that entails) slips between the two stools of formulation and implementation, which results in the former being a waste of time, the latter being a disaster and all those involved feeling disappointed and frustrated.

Formulation is important, both in the way it is done and what it includes. However, be wary. Analysis and planning, if taken to excess, can lead to paralysis! So, it is balance of these factors that is needed within the formulation if the risks of implementation are to be lessened.

Unclear/unconvincing reason for the change – why?

During formulation, as we have seen, much time is spent on looking at 'what' needs to be done and, if it is well thought out, the 'how'. However, the changes to be implemented will involve others who may not have been involved in the formulation. Even if they have been, the formulation may well have been done without building a clear case for change. Not building a clear case for change is a common mistake.

Another common mistake is to build a case for change that is convincing for those who build it, but not for the wider target audience. When people ask why they need to implement a recommendation, do not expect them to be overly motivated by a vague 'To increase shareholder value' as the reason.

The best-formulated plans usually think through, in detail, the consequences of not implementing the recommendations. In other words, both the 'gain' of the implementation and the 'pain' of the non-implementation are clearly articulated in a way that appeals to the emotions of those involved in the implementation. It is no coincidence that the successful implementation of changes, which have resulted in quantum improvements, have usually been preceded by some sort of a crisis.

So, check that a clear, compelling case for change has been made before implementation begins, one that will appeal to the instincts of those to be involved and that includes both the 'gain' of the recommendation and the 'pain' of non-implementation. One way to work out how to do this is to fill in the boxes in a pain/gain matrix, as shown in Figure 8.1.

In the four possible scenarios shown in Figure 8.1, only one is where success lies – the other 75 per cent breed failure. So, the odds of failure in this specific area alone are stacked against success! Reading

Figure 8.1 Pain/gain matrix

through this list of reasons for failure, you can begin to understand why implementation is not easy and why, for example, the majority of 'change' programmes fail to deliver.

The politics and power consequences have been misunderstood

We all hear about 'corporate politics' and, in the consulting field (especially in those firms that major on formulation/recommendation services), we pride ourselves on being able to 'ride above the fray', retaining a dignified, professional and unbiased stance. And for those inside the company, talking about such issues openly is often too 'political'. So, they remain unresolved and, sadly, this all too often is a cause of failure. Such issues lie below the waterline, out of site, like sharp rocks ready to rip the bottom out of the implementation of an unsuspecting recommendation happily steaming through the seemingly calm corporate waters above.

Again, this issue is best handled during the formulation phase, rather than it being left to the implementation phase. A starting point is to understand who, initially, will be seen as 'winners' and who will be seen as 'losers'. Resistance to the implementation of a change often comes from people who think they have something to lose if the recommendations go ahead. Unless such people are identified, and a specific plan made to ensure that their perceived loss is managed in a positive way, then the risk of failure increases.

Within the formulation stage, if the human consequences of what the recommendations bring are not taken into full account, then implementation will be even harder. Do not mistake this issue for appeasement – it is not about being 'nice', it is about being effective.

Psychological aspects of the change have been ignored

Implementation invariably means change. Here I will briefly summarize the two typical reactions to change that, if ignored, can lead to implementation failure.

If change is imposed, the reaction typically moves from one of shock, to denial, anger, depression and then realization and acceptance. The secret is to allow this to happen, rather than to deny it. Many implementation problems arise as those seeking to impose change react clumsily to what they think is an unnatural reaction (such as denial and anger).

Another aspect of the same issue is the typical experience of those implementing recommendations. Many go from a feeling of 'uninformed optimism' to one of 'informed pessimism', especially when the implementation gets tough. They then reach the 'check-out zone' where they typically 'cop out' by either absenting themselves physically or by going through the motions. Implementation falters and then fails as a result. The visible support from top management for those who are charged with the implementation is a simple remedy to this, but sadly it is often lacking.

Insufficient support processes in place

Implementing new recommendations invariably means changing something, either by replacing it or by supplementing it. All too often this calls for new skills and resources as well as implementation know-how. Often, because the focus is on 'getting it done', this is ignored. A typical issue, which does not get sufficient attention, is the training in the new skills that are needed. Many implementation processes depend on project teams. These are often cobbled together and then told to get on with it in an 'empowering' way, but the empowerment falls short of giving people the right training, such as in project management. There are few people who have been in a project team who understand what a critical path is, for example. Another area of training not typically seen is team dynamics. Implementation often depends on the successful functioning of teams, yet many receive little or no training. Again, implementation falters as the team dynamics get in the way of the implementation.

Another aspect is the communication and measurement processes needed to control implementation. Implementation projects are launched, but often there is no measurement, both of how the implementation is going and what is being achieved. Objectives are not 'SMART'– which stands for specific, measurable, achievable, results-oriented, time deadlined – and the trade-offs between time, cost and quality are not managed. Thus, resources are incorrectly allocated, the implementation has a negative knock-on effect on the day-to-day running of the business, and progress stalls and then quietly flops.

Inflexibility

The flip side of inadequate planning is detailed planning, planning that is so detailed any flexibility is ruled out from the start. This can lead to implementation failure. Any recommendation is predicated on assumption. However, making a detailed plan and then sticking to it no matter what assumes a static world within which the constancy is the assumptions on which the plan is based. This is manifestly not a sensible way to go about implementation. Many assumptions on which the implementation plan is based will, sooner or later, change. Given the pace of change in the last part of the twentieth century and the early part of the twenty-first, it is likely that assumptions will change quickly. The world is not as static as it was.

Thus, a successful implementation strategy has to be adaptable or else inflexibility will lead to failure. Although the 'what' can be fixed, there has to be flexibility in the 'how'. One way to ensure this is to do some contingency or scenario planning when planning implementation. Such an exercise will 'plan in' flexibility, as well as exercise those responsible for implementation in thinking flexibly. The latter is probably more important than the former as many a scenario has yet to conform fully to reality!

Mistaking compliance for commitment

In order for implementation to 'stick', those involved need to believe in it. This belief has, necessarily, to be emotional, based on a rational, logical framework of understanding. In other words, it is not enough simply to get intellectual agreement during implementation. For it to stick, you need to get emotional belief. Without that, it is hard for people to commit. Those who agree but do not believe will often comply, but, as time goes on, compliance may not necessarily lead to commitment, and so the implementation comes unstuck. And in organizations that have an overbearing 'hire and fire' type of culture, the compliance may even be based on fear rather than agreement. As the implementation unfolds, not many measure this aspect of commitment and so the changes do not stick and the desired results are not achieved.

For implementation to succeed, you need to appeal to both the intellect, to get rationally based agreement, and the emotions, to get deeply held commitment. The sounder and more logical is the formulation of the 'what', the better the chances of intellectual agreement. The sounder and more thorough is work done on the 'why' and the 'how', the better the chances of gaining belief. One without the other can lead to dangerous situations, as expressed in Figure 8.2.

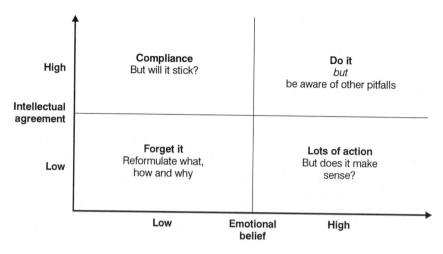

Implementation

High	**Compliance** But will it stick?	**Do it** *but* be aware of other pitfalls
Low	**Forget it** Reformulate what, how and why	**Lots of action** But does it make sense?

Intellectual agreement

Low   Emotional belief   High

Figure 8.2 Balancing belief and commitment

Change does not fit with culture and character

Every organization has its own unique culture and there are many ways of defining and mapping culture and individual character. I link culture with character because the characters within an organization will shape its culture. When implementation of a recommendation is undertaken, failure often occurs because the cultural aspects of a company are not taken into account.

For example, implementing a highly systematic process in a, to date, decentralized and entrepreneurial sales team is unlikely to succeed, unless part of the process allows experimentation. You need to implement in a way that is sympathetic to the current culture, rather than one that condemns it.

Another example would be of a managing director who is very empowering and new to the organization. He would be likely to be frustrated when he tried to introduce changes involving people taking more responsibility in an organization that hitherto has been top down and very centralized. In such an organization, people would not be ready to take responsibility too quickly and, thus, the changes would need to be gradual to take into account the cultural dimensions.

At the end of the day, implementation is driven and delivered by people. The more tools and techniques you have to map culture and character types, the better armed you can be when implementing. They will provide you with insights that will enable you to be more aware of the organizational nuances that are often ignored, yet are crucial to success.

Summary of some common reasons for failure of implementation

When an implementation fails it is not usually due to just one of the above, but often to a mix. The trick, for those who wish to become masters of implementation, is to be acutely aware of what is happening, so as to anticipate better the pitfalls.

The reasons for failure detailed above are common, but there are many others. Some are rare (such as a natural disaster interrupting a carefully laid corporate implementation plan) or tragic (such as the death of a key member of the implementation team). Those listed above should come as no surprise – many of you, I am sure, will have gone through an experience of failed implementation. Looking back on your own experiences, I would be surprised if you have not lived through some or all of the points. Relive those experiences, as they will mean more to you, and drive the lessons home better, than any words you can find in a book!

What typical 'techniques' exist to aid implementation?

So far we have covered what defines implementation and why it often fails. Now we shall look at some ideas for how to avoid the pitfalls or how to go around them when they occur. Many books have been written on how to achieve successful implementation, so here I will only give a brief overview of some of the more common tools and techniques. They vary in theme, but all of them aim to achieve one, or a mix, of the following:

- gain ownership and commitment
- ensure quality and accountability
- remain flexible and adaptable
- encourage learning and development.

Let us look at each of these areas in more detail and at what tools and techniques exist to help achieve them.

Gain ownership and commitment

Ownership and commitment are key to successful, sustained implementation. Without them, implementation quickly crumbles. It is difficult, if not impossible, to 'build ownership' without allowing those who need to 'own' recommendations and implementation create part of it for themselves. In other words, if people are denied the opportunity to have an input in what is going on, do not expect them to have ownership and commitment.

A variety of techniques exist to facilitate the process of gaining ownership and commitment, including:

- communications strategies
- workshops and facilitation
- large-scale intervention techniques (such as OST and future search)
- benchmarking
- maintaining the importance of values and 'soft' issues as well as 'hard' rationality
- internal focus groups.

We shall now look at each of these in turn.

Communication strategies
Communication is the key to successful implementation, yet few implementation plans seem to include an explicit communications strategy. Those that do usually do better than those that do not. Another common mistake is that many see communication as something you 'do' to someone else. For example, the members of the management team of an organization wish to communicate their changes, but leave little, if any, time to gauge reaction by listening to the views of those they have spoken to. Communication, to be effective, has to be a two-way process – successful implementation plans include a two-way communications strategy. Such strategies should include a variety of communication methods, rather than depend overly on one (such as cascade). Ownership and commitment are built by means of open dialogue and engaging those you are communicating with in what you are saying and doing. Thus, if you want implementation to succeed, you need to plan the communication.

Workshops and facilitation
A very common tool for building ownership and gaining commitment is the workshop. Any workshop needs to be planned and its desired outcome needs to be clearly articulated. A workshop is a useful way to share recommendations, and then gain understanding by allowing attendees to work on the details and consequences themselves. Thus, a successful workshop will allow much time for attendees to discuss and create new ideas.

Those running a workshop may wish to pass on information, but they must be as ready to receive and collate the work done by attendees.

A key skill in running a successful workshop is facilitation. It is beyond the remit of this chapter to delve into this subject too far, but suffice it to say here that facilitation is a key implementation skill, too, and those who wish to excel in the consulting field of implementation should undergo facilitation training. Figure 8.3 below gives an overview of what facilitation involves.

Large-scale intervention techniques
While workshops are good with relatively few numbers, they cannot easily be used with larger numbers (say, more than 50 people). However, workshop-type interventions for larger groups do exist. Three good examples of such techniques are the open space technology (OST) technique, developed by Owen (1993), the future search technique, developed by Weisbord and Janoff (1995), and the round tables technique.

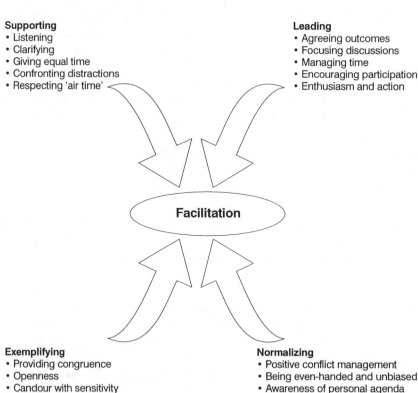

Supporting
• Listening
• Clarifying
• Giving equal time
• Confronting distractions
• Respecting 'air time'

Leading
• Agreeing outcomes
• Focusing discussions
• Managing time
• Encouraging participation
• Enthusiasm and action

Facilitation

Exemplifying
• Providing congruence
• Openness
• Candour with sensitivity
• 'Walking the talk'
• Role playing

Normalizing
• Positive conflict management
• Being even-handed and unbiased
• Awareness of personal agenda
• Use of humour
• Wearing de Bono's six hats

Figure 8.3 Key skills for facilitation

148

Implementation

OST is a technique whereby the agenda for participation is left to individuals. Following a presentation that may prime the subject for discussion, individuals are left free to form their own discussion groups. Each group has a recorder, whose responsibility it is to record the discussion. The recorders' notes are fed to a central team that summarizes the detail for the whole group. Central plenary discussion usually agrees key actions.

For involving a large number of people, this technique is quite effective, although the free-flow discussions may cloud the desired focus somewhat.

Future search is a slightly more focused and managed process. It involves 'whole system' representation, so, for example, if a company was involved there would need to be representatives from all the key groups, such as employees, managers, suppliers, customers, community and shareholders. A future search event is held over three days, during which time each participant looks at the past, present and future in order to build ownership, consensus and commitment to change.

The round tables technique focuses on engaging people in dialogue. It usually starts with a presentation by those who wish to pass on a recommendation, vision or need for change. The presentation is brief, with people sitting at round tables, listening. Each table is given three key questions (usually, 'Is this the right thing to do – what have we missed?'; 'What are the key barriers to implementation?' and 'Given the direction pursued, what should we stop doing and what should we start doing?'). The tables' discussions are summarized and fed back in a plenary session by a table moderator. This technique is valuable for quickly generating new ideas for implementation, as well as testing assumptions. If the tables are linked by a client/server laptop system, then a huge amount of data can be quickly captured. If this is managed well, literally hundreds of people at a time can be involved.

Benchmarking

One of the key barriers to implementing recommendations is that, before new recommendations are implemented, they remain hypothetical. In other words, many in the organization may find it hard to imagine that implementation is possible and beneficial. However, the chances are high that other organizations have, in fact, already implemented similar recommendations.

Benchmarking was originally used to find out what others (normally those who demonstrate best practice) have achieved. When benchmarking became common practice, it was typically used in a narrow sense, by linking measures of performance. This usually involved visiting the relevant company, finding out what measures of performance they had achieved, and then using these measures of performance to 'benchmark' one's own performance. However, such visits provide more value than just this – they enable an organization to learn not only what is possible, but also how it can be achieved.

A consultant can find it hard to persuade others what is possible. A visit to a company that has already achieved what is recommended can be a far more powerful way of building commitment. Taking managers to another company to show what is possible and how it can be implemented can build a level of commitment that is more sustainable than that based only on the intellectual argument of a consultant. The key to a successful visit is having a very clear idea of what questions you are seeking the answers to.

Maintaining the importance of values and 'soft' issues as well as 'hard'
rationality
When you are trying to build ownership and commitment, most of the efforts are based on rationality and logic. Thus, workshops and benchmark visits will typically be based on an approach that uses factual logic as a starting point. However, these should not be used to the exclusion of other 'softer' techniques. The use of values can be a powerful way to build commitment and ownership, if the necessary behaviours are identified to enable the implementation to occur. Behaviours are based on values and attitudes. Implementation of new recommendations can become easier if they are explicitly linked to the values the organization is trying to achieve.

Typically, however, the values the organization aspires to are different to those values that actually exist. Quality and flexibility, for example, may be desired, but are unlikely to exist in an organization that does not tolerate mistakes and relies on rank and authority for making decisions. An identification of current values will assist those involved in implementation to see how well the recommendations fit. If they do not fit with current values, but do fit with values to which the organization aspires, then the inclusion of the implementation of values with the implementation of recommendations will enable the linkage to behaviour on a more tangible level.

There are many ways of implementing values. The process outlined in the book *Managing by Values* by Blanchard, O'Connor and Ballard (1995) details an approach that encourages a wide involvement of people across the organization. Linking such an approach to the implementation of specific recommendations can assist in building ownership and commitment.

Internal focus groups
The use of voluntary 'diagonal slice' focus groups is another common way of building ownership and commitment. 'Diagonal slice' means drawn from across the functions and across the hierarchies – rank is left outside the room.

Focus groups can be asked to look at particular implementation issues and come up with recommendations for action. They are typically facilitated, and have a clearly defined issue to focus on, with a clear deliverable (usually a presentation for senior management or employees as a whole). They enable people to become engaged with an issue, rather than have it rammed down their necks, and as they are typically closest to the problems, they can be expected to come up with pragmatic solutions to implementation problems. One of the largest challenges of focus groups is that of managers allowing their people to participate. This needs careful handling, but if it is done well, it will allow the people in the organization to learn how to become responsible for their own time and how best to manage it.

Summary
All these techniques for building ownership and commitment have one thing in common – they strive to create opportunities for involvement. They try to build an atmosphere of creation rather than consumption. In other words, they enable people to create and build on recommendations, rather than consume them as foregone conclusions. The difference is a theatre-style meeting, where top executives exhort employees to give commitment (consumption), versus an interactive workshop with dialogue, where employees are given the chance to voice their ideas and views and these are listened to and taken on board. Treating people like mature adults gets commitment faster than treating them as ignorant and immature people.

Ensure quality and accountability

Implementation needs to be managed with a degree of quality and transparency. The more common techniques that exist to achieve this are:

- 'just do its' and 'projects'
- change teams

- communication tactics – surfacing resistance, a 'war room', naming initiatives and so on
- measurement techniques – soft into hard.

Let us briefly look at each of these.

'Just do its' and 'projects'
The implementations of recommendations fall broadly into two camps:

- 'just do its' (JDIs)
- 'projects'.

JDIs are just that – they do not require planning and coordination for their implementation. They are often known as 'quick wins' and serve a useful purpose in the implementation of cross-organizational initiatives as they breed success and credibility. The implementation of most recommendations will contain some quick wins, and these should be identified and used. However, if the implementation of cross-functional or more complicated recommendations is done in such a JDI way, quality suffers and accountability becomes blurred. When it all goes wrong, it is hard to say who did what, when and why. The most common way of implementation of such recommendations is via projects.

There are not many organizations that do not have improvement projects in hand. The secret for success here lies in ensuring that those involved are well versed in project management techniques. It is outside the scope of this chapter to detail the ins and outs of project management, and many courses exist to train people in the necessary skills. In outline, therefore, successful projects depend on the following key aspects (Obolensky, 1993).

- *Clear roles and processes* Each project should have a nominated project manager who is responsible for the delivery of the project and managing/coordinating the project team. The project should also have a 'sponsor', normally a senior executive to whom the project manager can report and go to to seek support and advice. Within the project team, each task that needs to be completed should be clearly allocated, with defined expectations of what each person needs to do. The project management process should include regular progress measurement and reporting, with reviews and milestones (that is, specific dates that can be clearly identified, with expected actions/results within the project).
- *Project definition* A project should have a clear definition that includes specific objectives, costs and benefits, deliverables, measures of success, and underlying assumptions. Objectives should be

SMART, which stands for specific, measurable, action-oriented and achievable, results-oriented, and time deadlined. Costs and benefits should be worked out in advance of the project being signed off, with an idea of what resources will be needed (and when). Deliverables should be physical, such as training materials, presentation, newly skilled individuals and so on. Measures of success – and a process by which the measurement can take place – should be defined to ensure that the planned benefits are achieved. Underlying assumptions should be explicit and monitored (if they change, the rationale of implementation may well change too). Many projects fail as a result of unclear definition. For example, a project the stated objective of which is to 'increase sales' is not one based on a SMART objective. While the *benefit* may be an increase of sales, the project's objective should be worded so that it says what, specifically, must be done to achieve such an increase. An example of such an objective would be 'To establish a trained call centre sales team by Quarter 3'.

- *Critical path action plan*   The use of a Gantt or PERT chart is necessary to monitor the different actions needed to bring the project to completion. These actions need to be planned – the plans showing which actions depend on which, who is responsible for them and how long they will take to achieve. The plan should be created by initially focusing on the various tasks that need to be achieved. By understanding the logical flow of the tasks, and how long they will take, the project manager should have a clear idea of how long overall the project will take and where the critical path lies.

- *Managing time, costs, quality*   At the end of the day, any project is going to be a trade-off between time, costs (including resources) and quality. If there is a clear understanding of what the project is trying to achieve, and the priorities have been set within time/costs/quality, then the project will have a good chance of success. No matter what time is put into the project plan, reality will more often than not do something else and the secret of a project's success is being aware and flexible enough to adapt quickly when circumstances change.

Too often, groups of people are pulled together, called a project team and given responsibility to implement something. They are rarely given project management training, and many an implementation project has failed due to that fact alone.

Change teams
Change teams, which assist the management of a variety of cross-functional implementation projects, are becoming more common.

While a project team may be focused on the explicit delivery of a single project, change teams usually have a less focused role and are used to assist the management of a variety of actions/projects across an organization. They usually report to the highest levels and have *carte blanche* to help assist implementation across the organization. They can be particularly useful as a reserve of talent to help when implementation becomes difficult. They are useful, too, as a career development opportunity as they can expand the horizons of those involved. If an organization has a number of projects it needs to implement across functional boundaries, the existence of a change team, with the responsibility to assist implementation, can greatly increase the chances of success. Such a team can help to ensure quality and reinforce accountability.

Communication tactics
We saw, under the heading Communication Strategies on page 147, that having a clear strategy for communication can help to build ownership and commitment. Communication is also key in helping to ensure quality and accountability. A variety of techniques exist to help achieve this. Clear and regular updates on progress, as well as mentioning the names of those involved reaching goals along the way can build a sense of pride and achievement. It is best to avoid hype and exaggeration and be truthful about progress. A lack of quality and accountability is often due to a lack of transparency and clarity about what is actually happening within the implementation process. A variety of communication techniques exist. Full use should be made of current media and, if necessary, new media should be introduced.

If various implementation initiatives are happening all at once, then the use of a 'war room' can also help communications and ensure transparency. This should have the outlines of what is going on pinned onto map boards on the walls so that anyone can see who is doing what and what is expected of them. The more transparent the communication, the less risk of lack of accountability. Obviously common sense needs to prevail and some projects may need to be codenamed if they are of a particularly confidential and sensitive nature.

Another technique is to give the implementation initiative a clear name and identity. This helps people to identify what is going on, who is involved and what is expected. If implementation is undertaken beneath a veil of secrecy, then do not expect a wide accountability.

Other communication tactics include regular and face-to-face meetings between senior executives, employees and those responsible for implementation. These should be open and honest and give people the opportunity to let off steam and frustration. Open and honest communication about what is going on and why can be very disarming. One should be aware that resistance to open communication is often due to people fearing open accountability and wishing to have the option of delivering lower-quality work or results for a quieter life. The more open the communication can be, the more transparent the accountability and so the higher the degree of success.

Measurement techniques – soft into hard
Management consultancy is full of measurement techniques, but many of these focus on hard and obvious issues, such as finance, production or logistics. Implementation also includes hard measures that usually relate to task deadlines, milestone achievement and implementation budgets.

However, the measurement of these alone is not enough – success will also depend on the measurement of softer issues. These can include to what extent those implementing change feel supported, how much resistance there is to it in the organization, how people feel and what their attitudes are. Measuring such things is not easy, but can be done. The technical side is relatively easy – graded responses and questionnaires can quickly turn these issues into numbers. For example, the method shown in Figure 8.4 for asking a question of project managers – using a graded response question – can be used to ask others many other similarly intangible things:

To what extent do you feel supported by senior management in what you are trying to implement?									
Not at all		Hardly		Some		Mostly		Totally	
1	2	3	4	5	6	7	8	9	10

Figure 8.4 Example of turning soft issues into hard ones

The important thing about this quantitative approach is that it is measuring perceptions, not necessarily facts. However, many issues that get in the way of implementation are perceptual. And these perceptions need to be measured to ensure both the quality of what is being done and the accountability of those doing it. Such quantitative approaches can be backed by qualitative approaches, such as a facilitated group. The key issues are how the measuring is done, how often and, more importantly, what is done with the data that has been gathered. It is pointless measuring implementation if there is no feedback loop or follow-up. As it is perceptions that are being measured, such follow-up needs to be done in a supportive and positive way, rather than in a penalizing and negative way. Without measurement, quality and accountability is hard, if not impossible, to achieve.

Summary
Ensuring quality and accountability depends on sound and carefully planned implementation processes. Thus, in planning implementation, it is not enough to consider only the 'what' – the 'how' must also be planned.

Remain flexible and adaptable

When implementation efforts fail to go according to plan (and most will), you have three basic choices to keep things moving forwards:

- do nothing
- change how you do it
- change what you want.

Do nothing
First, get a feel of why things have not gone according to plan. Many issues may have got in the way. The natural tendency will be to rush in and sort things out. However, before you do that, think through the option and opportunity of doing nothing. Many problems have a habit of sorting themselves out. Although such an approach may run counter to Anglo-Saxon management style, if the problems are small then sometimes it is better to conserve energy, time and money for the bigger problems that may be to come.

Change how you do it
There are three basic levers to pull:

- time
- cost
- quality.

Time can be looked at within a critical path model. However, a delay may be unacceptable. The next possibility could be to add extra cost by using more resources – either money or people. Finally, an option is to trade quality. Instead of a 100 per cent solution, perhaps the 80 per cent solution will do. In striving for 100 per cent, the additional 20 per cent could, in true Pareto style, cost 80 per cent in terms of effort – is it worth it? And if the quality concerned is the quality of life of those involved (as is so often the case), then you need to ask why people are struggling to keep up with an unrealistic plan and is the pain of implementing the plan in this way more than it has to be? The danger is that the pain of implementation begins to outweigh the aggregate of the pain of the *status quo* and the gain of success. In such cases, implementation will falter and is more likely to fail altogether.

Once the trade-offs of time, costs and quality are considered and decisions made, it will be necessary to replan and redocument. The danger if this is not done is that people will lose sight of what is going on and why, and implementation will then falter due to complexity and lack of clarity.

Change what you want
The final option is to check that what is being implemented is actually needed. With the best will in the world, objective factors on which key assumptions are based may make implementation in its original decided form meaningless. Making such decisions is a hard and brave thing to do. However, when they are made they are usually for the best. Scenario planning during the planning stage will often help the decision-making process as you can 'game play' what should happen if key assumptions subsequently turn out to be false or they are changed.

Summary
Before any of these options is pursued, however, it is best to obtain a real feel as to what is happening. Regular transparent measurement helps, as does a sympathetic ear. Before evaluating options, it is better to seek to understand than to judge, and a consultant can play a key role in facilitating such understanding and counter the natural tendency of those involved to let emotion run away with them.

Encourage learning and development

Thus far, we have considered implementation and its relationship to formulation, and seen how these two can be best linked. We have also considered implementation in its own right, both the pitfalls and techniques that help it to be succesful. However, there is another aspect of implementation we need to consider – that of learning. For organizations of today and the future, learning is key. The opportunity that implementing recommendations gives is that of helping to foster a culture of learning and (necessary for learning) exploration. This can be enhanced by:

- team learning
- use of an academy
- use of JIT training
- attitude to failure.

Team learning

The work involved in implementation projects is typically carried out by teams. The members of such teams often come together from across the organization and may not typically work together in their day-to-day jobs. Thus, they will have the opportunity to learn about other areas of the organization. They may well also be using different skills to those they normally use and, again, this increases the learning. When the team disbands, after the implementation has been delivered, the organization can capture the learning that has taken place by means of a formal review of what the team has learned. This will enable future implementation teams to build on the learning, as well as avoid the mistakes that the earlier teams had to work through.

Use of an academy

Many large implementation programmes involve inculcating large amounts of new skills and attitudes. Establishing an organizational academy can enhance this process. Implementation of new improvements can be linked to the learning undertaken in the academy. In this type of scenario, implementation and learning become blurred into a single activity or, more accurately, a whole series of different activities linked by means of a single theme of improvement. In this type of organization, implementation becomes a way of life, rather than an activity designed to bring in recommendations when they occur.

Use of JIT training

In many cases, the establishment of an academy will not make sense. However, training often enhances the quality of what is being implemented. The use of Just-in-Time (JIT) training is a particularly effective way of achieving this. If, for example, you have an implementation team that needs project management training, instead of sending them on a general project management training course, it may be more effective to give them training while they are actually drawing up their plan for the project. The use of training applied to the actual implementation task in hand both increases the quality of the implementation as well as the quality of the learning.

Attitude to failure

As discussed under Remain flexible and adaptable, above, many implementation plans do not survive contact with reality. Many would see this as failure, and those involved may even be penalized. However, such an attitude creates a climate of fear and a low level of risk taking, which has the effect of the implementation becoming, at best, pedestrian and, at worst, ineffective or even destructive. Equally, people may fail due to incompetence and inability; they may be in a position where they do not have the skills needed to succeed.

If implementation is linked to learning, failure is quickly identified rather than being left to do damage. It is seen as an opportunity to learn, improve and adapt. Personal failure then results in coaching rather than castigation. If personal failure persists, however, it will be clear that the person is in a role that does not suit their abilities and they can be moved to a more suitable situation.

Many implementation efforts fail because when failure occurs it is typically ignored, and the situation is left to decline to a stage where the whole implementation effort fails overall. However, if failure is picked up early in a positive way, as an opportunity to learn, adapt and improve, the implementation effort will be more flexible and so more likely to succeed.

Summary

Linking implementation to learning is a very useful technique for avoiding the typical pitfalls implementation efforts can fall into. It does involve effort, but once that is done, the benefits to the organization are often in addition to the benefits the implementation is bringing into effect.

What is the consultant's role and what skills are required?

Up to this point, we have talked about implementation in isolation, with a few exceptions, from the role of the consultant. Here, though, we shall look at the role of an implementation consultant and the skills needed.

The consultant's role

A consultant who is involved in implementation will play a different role to that of a consultant involved purely in formulation. They will need to dance the paradox between being an external, uninvolved adviser and internal, involved catalyst. They will need to remain unbiased and maintain their integrity and yet, at the same time, become involved in the typical political behaviour in an effort to help the organization through the implementation maze. Their role will be a mix – with differing emphases on the various elements, depending on the circumstance – of the following.

- *Adviser*   An implementation consultant will need to give advice and guidance. However, unlike the formulation consultant, this advice will concentrate on the 'how' rather than the 'what'. Having said that, as the 'how' unravels, new opportunities, they will need to have a sound awareness of the 'what' so as to further the opportunities facing the organization.
- *Educator*   Implementation consultancy is as much about skills transference as anything else. They will need to be able to pass on their skills to others within the organization to enable them to improve the quality of implementation. Implementation invariably needs to include training for new skills and processes, and the consultant will need to have a good understanding of the various ways that training can be delivered, even if they will not be delivering the training themselves.
- *Coach*   This is different to the role of educator. It is a role delivered to individuals, coaching and mentoring them. During implementation, people will feel the need to offload frustrations, seek guidance on their interpersonal issues and advice on behaviours and perceptions. They may welcome an independent person to seek advice and encouragement from. While the implementation in hand may be just routine to the consultant, it may be a new experience to those within the organization. A few well-placed words of encouragement to individuals can help things move along. In addition to this type of coaching, there may also be the need to coach in more technical areas, such as project management.
- *Leader*   At times, it may be necessary for the consultant to take a lead and encourage others to keep moving forwards. Taking a lead is different to taking control, as leadership is as much about inspiration and enablement as anything else. In the early stages, the consultant will

Implementation

need to inspire and enable those around him who, because they lack the experience, feel less confident about their ability to implement.

It is the mix of these roles, and the times they are used, that makes for a skilful implementation consultant. Timing is down to catching the nuances of the situation, and nuances can best be interpreted by an experienced consultant. Underlying these roles, however, are some technical skills, an overview of which now follows.

The skills required

The range of skills and competences that make for a successful implementation consultant is wide, as there will be a need for sound technical ability coupled with the need for superb interpersonal skills.

It is beyond the scope of this chapter to detail every individual skill here, but, in outline, they can be broadly categorized as follows:

- formulation skills
- process skills
- educational skills
- people skills
- leadership skills.

Let us look at each of these in more detail.

Formulation skills
This group of skills enables a consultant to understand a situation quickly, what the options are and which option it is best to pursue. This is important in implementation as situations change, decisions need to be made quickly and they need to be based on sound and rational logic rather than emotional and perhaps misguided belief. The types of techniques that are of particular importance are situational analysis, criteria selection and scoring (using weightings if necessary) for prioritization, decision tree analysis and Pareto analysis. These techniques, among others, help a consultant formulate the options for action.

Process skills
These range from being able to facilitate workshops (either small or large ones, like OST – see page 148), to managing projects, managing a collection of projects within a programme and being able to map a process. They all have one thing in common: they are designed to get

the best from people when they are working in groups or teams. Some of them require technical skills, such as project management and process mapping. Some require 'showman' skills, such as are involved when running a large-scale intervention workshop using an approach like OST. All of them require a degree of confidence and competence.

Educational skills

Delivering training requires a whole host of educational skills. These include being able to identify training needs, design training courses and deliver them. As skills transference is key to an implementation consultant's job, if they are unable to transfer skills in both a formal (such as on a training course) and an informal way (say, in on-the-job training), they will not add as much value as a client needs. Coupled with this is the ability to identify different learning styles and preferences of individuals and match them in a personal way. The implementation consultant's apex of skill in this area is being able to train others to be trainers (for example, run 'train the trainer' courses).

People skills

Implementation is achieved by people – an obvious statement, but one frequently forgotten in this high-tech, jargon-rich age. An implementation consultant will need a range of 'people' skills to enable them to do their work. These can be broken down into two broad categories: interpersonal and intrapersonal. Interpersonal skills will include listening, verbal and visual communications skills and the ability to empathize with others. Intrapersonal skills will include a good understanding of psychology and the various psychometrics that exist (such as Myers-Briggs, Belbin and so on), teambuilding techniques and resolution of conflicts.

Leadership skills

Leadership is concerned with two things:

- achieving tasks
- developing people/relationships.

Put together, leadership becomes the art of getting things done through other people. Many leadership styles and theories exist. A useful one for the implementation consultant is Hersey and Blanchard's (1977) situational leadership model, which plots four different styles against the two axes of people and relationships and tasks and objectives. Applied to the role of consultancy, their matrix could be drawn as shown in Figure 8.5.

Implementation needs to strike a balance between people and tasks. The role of the consultant is to ensure that these are in balance and, depending on the situation, they will need to modify their behaviour as necessary. Along each of the two axes in Figure 8.5 are all kinds of different skills, some of which have already been alluded to earlier in this chapter. A possible breakdown of the skills required for leadership in implementation is shown in Figure 8.6.

Many of the skills mentioned in Figure 8.6 are self-evident, but perhaps one requires some explanation – 'use of humour'. Implementation is hard and can be fraught. The ability to see the humorous side of a situation can be a great blessing. While others internal to the organization may feel constrained, a consultant can, perhaps, see a lighter side of what is happening. Passing that on, relieving the tension and introducing some humour can be very cathartic!

Summary

As can be seen, the role and necessary skills of an implementation consultant are wide and varied. This is due to the fact that, of all the areas of management, implementing new recommendations can be the hardest thing to achieve. Those who position themselves as being able to help management in this will therefore need to be widely skilled and competent.

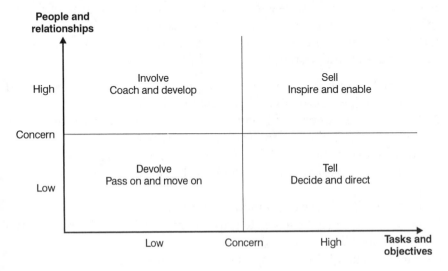

Figure 8.5 Situational leadership styles matrix

163

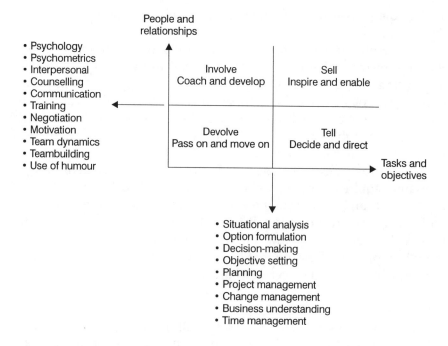

People and
relationships

- Psychology
- Psychometrics
- Interpersonal
- Counselling
- Communication
- Training
- Negotiation
- Motivation
- Team dynamics
- Teambuilding
- Use of humour

Involve	Sell
Coach and develop	Inspire and enable
Devolve	Tell
Pass on and move on	Decide and direct

Tasks and
objectives

- Situational analysis
- Option formulation
- Decision-making
- Objective setting
- Planning
- Project management
- Change management
- Business understanding
- Time management

Figure 8.6 Implementation leadership – the underlying skills required

A checklist for consultants

There are very few panaceas and quick fixes within the area of implementation, so I offer the following checklist as a starting point of enquiry for the consultant rather than a definitive, cast-iron guarantee that, if the questions are highly scored, success follows!

1 To what extent are the recommendations to be implemented based on rational, well-researched and analysed objective facts?
2 Is there agreement and belief among those involved in the implementation that the recommendations are the right ones?
3 To what extent have the underlying needs of the organization been addressed? Why was the recommendation formulated in the first place?
4 How detailed is the implementation plan?
5 How much were those key to implementation involved in the initial formulation?
6 Has the pain of the *status quo* been clearly identified?
7 Has the gain of implementation been clearly identified?

8 Have both the pain and gain been made meaningful in a personal way (not so much 'decrease share price' as 'loss of job')?
9 Have those who may 'lose out' been identified, and is there a plan to help them?
10 Is there a clear and consistent communication plan and has a variety of methods been included?
11 Have the various options for implementation been considered and clear priorities been assigned?
12 Does the implementation plan include elements to build ownership and commitment?
13 Is there a clear degree of accountability?
14 Do those within the implementation process have the right implementation skills (such as project management)?
15 If implementation projects exist, do they have quality project plans with clear definitions, critical paths and deliverables?
16 Is there a transparent and regular process of measuring progress and results?
17 Is there a clear process of follow-up to the measurements of progress?
18 Are the assumptions on which the original recommendations are based checked regularly?
19 Is the learning of those involved in the implementation process being captured for others to learn?
20 Are those who are supporting the effort correctly skilled and experienced or are the blind leading the blind?

These questions can be scored or simply used for discussion. Remember, they are a starting point, not a destination!

Summary

Implementation cannot really be learnt from a book – experience is the best way of learning. I hope that this chapter has given you a taste of what the domain of implementation is like and that, in your consulting career, you have the opportunity to work with a client in an implementation team. Of all the consulting experiences, being part of a successful implementation team, and playing a key role within that team, has to be one of the most satisfying that the profession can offer.

References

Blanchard, K H, O'Connor, M, and Ballard, J (1995) *Managing by Values,* Berrett-Koehler, San Francisco

Hersey, P, Blanchard, K H and Johnson, D E (1977) *Management of Organizational Behaviour: Utilizing human resources* (3rd edn), Prentice-Hall, London

Obolensky, N (1993) *Practical Business Re-engineering: Tools and techniques for achieving effective change,* Kogan Page, London

Owen, H (1993) *Open Space Technology: A user's guide,* Abbott, Potomac, Md.

Weisbord, M, and Janoff, S (1995) *Future Search: An action guide,* Berrett-Koehler, San Francisco

Part 3

Managing the business of management consultancy

9

Consultancy marketing strategies and tactics

Martin Pollecoff

Introduction

In the past, many successful consultancies and even some of *The Times'* top 100 companies launched themselves on an instinctive reaction to some envisioned opportunity. However, for every great company that has been launched on a hunch there are hundreds of failed businesses that some excited entrepreneur once saw as the key to their future fortunes. And there are hundreds more businesses that neither flourish nor fail.

The purpose of working on a strategy, and the aspiration of this chapter, is to consider how to move from that sweet hunch – 'I think my new consultancy would be a winner' – to the stage where you are certain where you will concentrate your efforts. If you are already part of an established consultancy, you can use the proven marketing methodologies featured in this chapter to help you make, confident, informed decisions as to what you will be offering your clients, and why they will be pleased to buy your services as opposed to those of your rivals.

Marketing and some important definitions

Like theologians arguing over the true rankings of the hosts of seraphim, people like to debate the difference between strategy and tactics. For the purposes of this chapter, which is essentially practical, 'strategy' means what we are going to do to be successful, and 'tactics', how we are going to do it.

Most consultants would agree that the success of any professional service company depends on being able to understand the clients' point of view – the issues they have in their industries, in their companies and in their own roles. I would like to refer to this approach as marketing, but the problem is that the word 'marketing' suffers from a surfeit of definitions because it is used for several separate ideas. Marketing is a way of looking at doing business (which we will call the 'marketing concept'), promotional activity and a location.

The marketing concept involves meeting three logical requirements, which are that:

- decisions about what your business should do are based on your clients' needs and wants
- you select the best way to meet the needs of your clients and prospective clients
- your organization's performance objectives are achieved by meeting clients' needs in a way that satisfies (and, hopefully, delights) them.

Although today the idea of running a 'customer-oriented' company is hardly new or radical, it is important to see this marketing concept set against the two other approaches from which it has developed.

- In a *production-oriented* company you create the product or service that you are good at creating and then you hope that clients will also like what you are offering.
- In a *sales-oriented* company, the gap between what you offer and what the customer really would like to have is bridged with the charm and charisma of the salesperson.
- In the *marketing-oriented* company, the consultant enters the client's domain to learn all there is to know about the client's fears and desires and then uses that information to design and supply the service.

Although marketing will never eliminate the need for selling, it is a movement towards being able to create a product or service that fits the client so it will sell itself.

Marketing has also become a function or a tactic. For example, the British Institute of Marketing defines marketing as 'the management process responsible for identifying anticipating and satisfying customer requirements profitably'.

Note that this functional approach means that, instead of marketing being a way of looking at business, it becomes someone's job or a special department that has the responsibility of understanding the customer on behalf of everyone else and somehow has to make the rest of the company conform to the customer's expectations.

No wonder that, in their 1994 report *Marketing at the Cross Roads*, Coopers & Lybrand's survey of marketing in 100 blue chip companies, the first criticism was 'Marketing departments undertake an ill-defined mixture of activities which could often be delegated to other functions or dispensed with altogether'.

Second on the list of criticisms from these companies was 'Marketing departments have been over-indulged, lacking both the defined responsibilities and accountability which characterize most other functions'.

As mentioned earlier, the word 'marketing' is also used for a location. An office where young people produce advertisements, exhibitions, posters and all the other gee-gaws of promotion. Again, marketing offices are not usually integrated into the rest of the company. They have their own culture (normally more glamorous than the dominant culture) and that adds to the suspicion that people not in the marketing department have towards the marketers.

As the Coopers & Lybrand report takes pains to point out, although the *function* of marketing has lately fallen into disrepute, the *philosophy* of marketing is still the single most important underlying concept behind strategic planning. However, this research-based approach, which is the very strength of the marketing concept, is also its Achilles' heel. If every consultant were to go out and survey their clients and prospective clients to find out what they need and simply supply that service, then:

- offerings from rival consultancies would be very similar
- clients would be leading their consultants, not the other way round.

It follows, therefore, that client surveys and research from the marketplace are simply the foundations on which you can build a service.

Thus, the marketing concept is a safe starting point, but, if you are to provide a service that gives your clients a competitive advantage, it is your duty to use your research and study to stay ahead of the client, to be there with guidance when they encounter the issues that you know will be an inevitable part of their project. In this way, the client outsources their research and development function to the consultancy because, in the consultant's specialist field, the client relies on the consultant's know-how to keep them competitive.

It is similar to the process of buying software, which is simply another form of know-how. When you are choosing software, you are looking for a provider who will not only give you the best current software, but also provide you with regular upgrades.

You do not have to be in what Maister (1997) describes as 'that sector of the consultancy market that deals in Brain Surgery' to value the competitive nature of 'know-how'. Even if you are doing a straightforward task of implementation, it is imperative that you invest time in researching the best way in which to do that implementation.

Direct marketing

Management consultants are involved in business-to-business marketing. You are seldom, if ever, going to have to market your services to consumers – the general public.

The number of members of the general public who could and would use a specialized consultancy's services is relatively few: but then, you do not need a lot of business clients to be successful.

It really does not matter if people in the street know about you or your consultancy or not. What does matter is that people who could use your service know about you, and, in this sense, as consultants, we are in the business of direct marketing. Drayton Bird (1996), one of the world's most experienced marketers, defines direct marketing as being, 'any advertising activity which creates and exploits a direct relationship between you and your customer as an individual'.

The purpose of direct marketing is to isolate your prospects and customers as individuals and build a continuing relationship with them – to their greater benefit and your greater profit. You are therefore out to find, win, retain and grow clients.

The advantages of direct marketing

You are treating your clients as individuals
By isolating your prospects as individuals, you can find out what makes them tick and use the knowledge you gain about them to help you select the ones you feel confident you can serve and ignore those who are less likely to want to work with you. To do that, you need to understand and calculate the likely income you could gain from each prospective client and likelihood (and the cost) of being able to win that business. You can only decide which individuals to invest in if you have detailed knowledge of your prospective and existing clients.

You are in control
With direct marketing you are in control. You can test your message, you can change it for each person you are addressing. You can contact your

prospects at times you think will be likely to elicit the best response. If you record every communication and its response on your database, you also then have the data that is necessary to make good decisions and you can learn from each campaign or promotion.

When I first started teaching direct marketing, I would have said that by testing campaigns you could predict the response to them. In business-to-business marketing today, however, things are moving so fast that by the time you have collected and analysed your response data, the market has changed. Thus, although traditionally it has been seen as a way to certainty and predictability, this is less true now.

You cut down on risk

Investment analysts record both the downturns and the peaks in the performance of their investments. Consultants, however, are naturally success-oriented and so record their wins efficiently, but tend to gloss over uncomfortable failures. For instance, if a consultancy wins one out of every three pieces of work it pitches for, the one win will tend to be discussed and the lessons learned there disseminated at meetings or over drinks. The two losing pitches also involved an investment in terms of money, time and goodwill, yet they will be brushed beneath the carpet. However, to make the most of that investment, you need to find out exactly why you did not win and make sure that the lessons learnt there are incorporated into your planning for future pitches.

I have observed two ways in which the reasons behind being turned down can be found out. Either a director can call up any prospect who says 'No' or a special unit can be set up to track wins and losses. What should not happen is that the consultants involved in pitches that have not been successful do this.

If you are willing to put aside issues of failure and success and simply record what happened on each campaign and on each pitch, then you will improve your strike rate and cut down on the risk inherent in future investments (Reicheld, 1996).

An 11-step planning programme

Its useful to have a formalized process of planning and so, for the purposes of this chapter, I have adapted a planning methodology from Drayton Bird's book *Common Sense Direct Marketing* (1996; see Figure 9.1). I chose this particular model because it is efficient and leads quickly from visionary heights to what you have to do on a day-to-day basis to get results.

1   Business mission

2   Business objectives

3   Marketing objectives

4   Marketing strategy

5   Communications objectives

6   Communications strategy

7   Advertising objectives

8   Advertising strategy

9   Creative strategy

10 Media strategy

11 Contact strategy

(Adapted courtesy of Drayton Bird, attributed to Rod Wright)

Figure 9.1 An 11-step hierarchy of marketing thinking

A word of warning about emotion and the process of planning

Business planning is not a remote, academic activity – especially if it is your own career you are planning; the process is emotionally and politically fraught. You may discover that your great idea is not so good or, even more difficult, that your boss' or client's vision for the future is a disaster waiting to happen.

To produce a plan that is both achievable and inspirational is difficult because this is the stage where the icy waves of reality begin to temper the fires of vision. Good marketers are aware of this and the high emotional content of the whole process. When working with clients, they tend to operate a bit like painters, starting with rough outlines and then working in the fine details. Take a tip from them and start with 'broad brush strokes' of the idea you want to create. Run quickly through the whole process. Have fun with the ideas and where you can see problems developing, try to create alternative paths. In your first sweep you will certainly not have all the information you need to make decisions. List the data you need to collect and prepare yourself for round two. Keep doing this until you have all the information you need to make realistic decisions. If such information is not available, make decisions but be aware of where you have had to make assumptions.

Step 1: Business mission

The first step in planning your marketing strategy is to decide what kind of consultancy services you will be offering. This should arise naturally out of your existing business experience. If you have spent 20 years as a marketing director in the finance industry, then you would probably be better off choosing to consult on advertising or PR or marketing for financial companies than be a production consultant in the pharmaceutical industry, which may be an uphill struggle.

However, you are not your title. Perhaps during your time as a marketing director you acted as a personal adviser to the MD or CEO, perhaps you oversaw the opening of the Singapore venture or carried out a feasibility report on the emerging market in China for credit cards. You may then consider, for instance, offering your services as an executive coach or as an expert on the Chinese credit card market.

Most marketing theory was developed for products, so it is easy to forget in planning a consultancy that, unlike a product, you have a choice as to where you wish to make your contribution. Consultancy is a business, but it is also a professional service and, as such, it is inherently personal.

The consultant sells their own skills and knowledge, but these attributes come bundled together with the consultant's personality, interests, values, creativity and will. It is these human extras that create differentiation between consultants. These are the qualifications that you will use to set you apart from your competition. Thus, despite talk of the 'commoditization' of consultancy, the reality is that a consultancy project will only be as good as the person or team implementing it. Whether a client uses the world's largest practice or a local two-person firm, it is the skills, experience and attitude of the consultants doing the job that make the difference.

When you have done your research and are faced with sheets of facts about your market, its growth potential and your competitors, it is easy to believe that the marketplace creates work. It does not. It is the will of the consultant that creates it. My point here is that 'people marketing' is not cut and dried. A consultant is not a product. The individual chooses where they want to work and how they want to work. As Tom Peters states in *The Pursuit of Wow!* (1995), 'Do what turns you on, not what the statistics say'. He then uses contrarian thinking to offer this advice: 'Go where the Hot Spots aren't'. Further down the page he continues, 'In slugabed industries, slugabed competitors seem to dominate – and leave gaping holes for agile, turned-on folks to slip into.'

If, like most people, you have any doubt as to where your talents lie, ask your peers and, better still, ask your clients. It is enough to state what service you would like to offer. Marketing is an iterative process between you and your marketplace and clarity comes with time.

The competition
Once you have decided what service you wish to offer, find out more about your competition. In marketing terms, competition is a good thing. This is because if you have no competition, you will be educating the marketplace in your new service. You will not only have to be able to sell your service, you will also have to explain what it is and how to use it. That is a very expensive and time-consuming activity.

Keep a file on every one of your competitors. Where possible, read their accounts, study their strengths and their weaknesses. However, never, when you are selling, talk badly of them. This sort of behaviour will make you appear small.

Use your competitors as a benchmark. Ask your PR company to maintain a press search on your competition. In this way you will know what they are doing and your PR company will have some benchmark to use to challenge the results they find out about.

Here are some of the questions you should ask yourself when comparing your own firm with the competition.

- Who are they? Who are the people who founded the business and who is running it now?
- What is their consulting philosophy (do they have special matrices they use or a view of the market)?
- What is their organizational culture like?
- What is their image in clients' circles?
- What lessons can be drawn from their growth patterns?
- What are their core competences?
- Where are they heading? What is their vision?
- Who are their clients (your prospects)?
- What are their terms of business?

● How can we use this information to provide a different service that offers more value. (The point of collecting competitor information is not to ape your rivals' work, but to create ways of working that will push your company ahead of them.)

A test of your marketing strategy is this: can you explain your consultancy's points of difference? Can your staff? The acid test is can your clients explain the differences?

Step 2: Business objectives

In March 1997, The Management Consultancy Information Service surveyed 95 UK-based management consultancies, ranging in size from sole practitioners to major international practices.

Part of the survey showed that the average mean daily fee rate is £875, up 17 per cent from the figure given in their 1995 survey. In the highly detailed report of the survey, they record that consultants surveyed charged between £200 and £3000 a day, with the differences arising from factors such as the size of the firm, geographical location, specialization and, of course, the background and seniority of the various consultants.

These sorts of figures look very lucrative, but when you are working out your potential turnover, it would be a mistake to believe that you will be involved in revenue-generating work five days a week. The reality is that consultants sell their services, do unpaid work, may spend a year on one project and then emerge from it to find that they have nothing lined up at the present. You may be involved in the internal management of the company. Hopefully you will also be involved in a continuous education programme or some *pro bono* work. Thus, the daily rate is only a guide to the kinds of annual revenues you can expect.

Some consultancies prefer to work on a 'contingency' basis, which means a fee plus an extra reward based on results. Using this system, you may choose to cut your daily rate and take a bonus on successful completion. Alternatively, you may be able to estimate the value you are adding to the client's project and take a percentage of that or simply a cut of the increased revenue.

My only caution regarding this idea is that the work consultants do usually has a pay-back over several years, so it is wise to build in a reward for years two and three, when the real returns are likely to begin. The question here is are you willing to take the same risks you are asking your client to take, and are you willing to ask for a share of their rewards?

Again, as you start to work out your business objectives in terms of turnover and where you want to be in five years' time, you can use these figures as a rough guide to how many staff you will be able to provide.

Marketing planning is a creative act, perhaps you have an idea that you might want to expand into continental Europe or open up in China. Use this stage of the planning process to pose lots of 'What if?' questions. It is only by working out the costs of such creative ideas that they can be exposed to reality and you can make informed decisions as to what resources you need to make it all happen.

Step 3: Marketing objectives

Your marketing objectives are the issues you want to deal with year by year. For instance, in year 1, you may have three objectives:

- to protect and grow your current client base
- to identify and win three new clients with contracts worth £100,000 each for delivery in year 1 (in sales planning it is important to be precise about when the sale has to be made in order to deliver the revenue you need when you need it)
- you may decide to set up an effective sales and marketing infrastructure or invest time and money in creating a fascinating new service or products that will project you ahead of your rivals (Kleiner, 1996).

Old clients versus new clients
In any business it is far less expensive to sell your goods or services to a friend than it is to attract and win over people you do not know. The marketing costs in proportion to the amount of business you are attracting are much lower with old clients. In fact, according to a speaker from Ernst & Young consultants at a lecture I attended, it costs between 5 and 25 times as much to attract new customers as it does to sell to an existing customer.

With a new client, the costs of marketing and learning how to work with that client are so high that initial engagements are seldom profitable. Also, the more complicated the project the higher the ratio of input to revenue generated. Indeed, one of the consultants stated that to sell their auditing services to someone they did not know was about 25 times as expensive as it was to gain a repeat order from a client they were already auditing.

It is this reality that caused Harvard marketing Professor Theodore Levitt in his book *The Marketing Imagination* (1983) to help redefine the nature of doing business when he said that the aim of a business is not to make a profit but to win and retain clients. It is fine having revenue goals and profit goals, but Levitt's definition gives you a stronger guide to action. To grow a successful business, find, win, retain and grow profitable clients. Profits come from these actions.

Why bother with new clients?
You need a steady stream of new clients because, however good you are at selling in 'that next piece of work' to your existing client, all projects and assignments come to an end. Consultants are dispensable. Plus, new clients bring with them new problems and learning situations and with these you can develop new solutions, expanding the range of skills you can offer clients. And, of course, new clients, if well managed, grow into very profitable old clients.

The emphasis you place on acquiring new clients will depend on the maturity of your practice and your marketing strategy.

Step 4: Marketing strategy

This depends on your business objectives. Do you want to be number one – the country's largest, best-known consultancy in your specialization?

If that is your strategy, what are your tactics? How are you going to usurp your competition? Will you use a low-price strategy to undercut them or will you go for high margins and added value – sell on quality and service rather than price? Do you have some method of delivery that will change the way in which your clients perceive consultancy? Will you go into partnership with your clients to outsource the function on which you advise? There are many ways to achieve your goals.

Step 5: Communications objectives

A useful model to bear in mind when considering your communication objectives is Murray Rapheal's 'ladder of loyalty', shown in Figure 9.2.

In this model, Murray Rapheal divides the marketplace up according to the strength of their relationship with your firm.

At the bottom of the ladder are 'suspects'. These are the people you believe may be able to use your services.

Next up the ladder are 'prospects' – people you have identified who could definitely use your services. In fact, they may presently be your competitors' clients.

Figure 9.2 The ladder of loyalty

The next big step is to turn these prospects into 'customers' – a term he uses for people who have used you once already.

On rung four are 'clients' who are those decision-makers who will naturally call you when they have a need for your type of service. They may, however, also ask others to pitch for the work.

At the top of the ladder are 'advocates'. These are people who love what you do. They want to tell their friends about your services. These are the clients who naturally bring you referrals.

The ladder of loyalty is a useful model for that distillation process we have of finding, winning, keeping and growing clients. A common mistake is to invest in communicating to prospects or suspects and neglect communication with your customers, clients and advocates. There seems to be an assumption that people we are working with do not need to be sold to, but the opposite is true. Clients need constant reassurance that they have made the right choice. And as we shall see below, clients are also your best prospects.

Step 6: Communications strategy

Your communications strategy is a list of things you are going to do to enable you to communicate to the people in your marketplace when you want to. A good communications strategy puts you in control.

If you are starting your consultancy from scratch, then a sensible strategy is to begin compiling a database of customers and prospects so that you can begin to build relationships with the people in your marketplace. Database building is a lifetime's task, but there is nothing complicated about it. A marketing database is just an electronic system that helps you manage your relationships.

In your personal life, you may use an address book and a diary to help you manage your relationships. The address book gives you the names and locations of people you know and people you may need to know – a plumber, a florist someone has recommended. The diary gives you details that help you manage that relationship – when you will meet, when to send cards and so on. Notice how, with time, those relationships change. People you may have spoken to every day last year you may not have spoken to at all this year.

In seminars I have spoken at, delegates normally reckon to run 100 to 150 relationships successfully using these methods. The task of automating this human process into a database for work merely enables you to handle many more. In database marketing, our aim is to manage one-to-one relationships by the thousand or the hundred thousand. And it is your database that will put the power behind your marketing, for however brilliant the letter you write, however exciting your offer, however persuasive you are, if you are communicating to the wrong person, you are not likely to make a sale.

Having said that, for the past six years I have been part of a team that produces a newsletter on the subject of customer management in the call centre. Our broadsheet is called *The Dog & Bone* and every two months it goes to 15,000 prospects and customers. Of the many enquiries brought in by *The Dog*, 50 per cent come from people who are not on our database. If you send out useful information, recipients tend to pass it around.

The reason that it is so difficult to maintain an accurate database is that the marketplace is never stationary. It helps to think of your marketplace as something like an escalator. People getting on, staying on for a while and getting off at the other end. Allow for changes to 30 per cent of your database over a period of 12 months – that is people changing their titles, locations or jobs. As the database is guiding your marketing, if

30 per cent of it is incorrect, then 30 per cent of your marketing budget is going to be wasted. That is why it is recommended that you use telephone researchers to clean your database every six months.

Step 7: Advertising objectives

What do you want your advertising to achieve? Remember that advertising in this case means all your sales communications and, I could argue, all your other communications as well.

- You want your clients to know that you are specialists and that you have specialized and valuable information that is at the disposal of your clients – simply by becoming your clients, they gain a competitive advantage.
- You want them to know that you are not in the business of undercutting others. Rather, you charge high-end fees because of the value you provide.
- You want them to know that you are human beings, not just a collection of suits. What is more, you consider that they are important people. You are there to serve. Perhaps you want them to know that you care about other things aside from business and are involved in the larger community?
- What you want them to do is build a relationship with you. If they are prospects, you want them to become 'customers', and if they are clients, you want them to grow to become advocates of your work.

Step 8: Advertising strategy

Once you have your messages clear, everybody in your firm understands these messages and what you are trying to create, then you are in a strong position to create clarity in the marketplace by ensuring that these messages are included and reflected in everything you do. For instance, in the early days of the Merchants Group (when it was called Programmes Limited), feedback from our market survey showed that Programmes was considered very professional, but we lacked warmth and hospitality. From then on, every marketing communication that went out for the next three years had on it the phrase 'Please come and visit our offices where, over a working lunch or our famed coffee, we can discuss . . .' Although this 'working lunch' line became a bit of an in-joke, it was efforts like this that laid to rest a rather formidable reputation.

Consultancy marketing strategies and tactics

Some of the ways in which you can promote your consultancy

For a consultancy, there are several well-proven ways of promotion. I will list them here in order of merit. That is to say, we will start with those activities that have proved to show the greatest returns and work our way down to those with the lowest returns – those items that are interesting rather than vital.

Research

If you were a chef, your research would start with your stockpot – the source of many other dishes. Earlier in the chapter I stated that it is the role of the consultancy to help their clients gain and sustain a competitive advantage, at least in the areas you are working on. To do that, you need information – the consultant's stockpot. You need to know about the industry. You need to know about global trends and how they will affect your specialized areas of expertise. You want to know what advances have been made by others that you can use. You want to know what is working and what is not working in other firms.

This is also what your clients want to know. By choosing to be your clients, they gain the know-how that helps them stay ahead.

Run workshops

Here is where you can start dipping into your research stockpot to create workshops where delegates can gain information that they could not get elsewhere. I am mentioning workshops rather than seminars because it is important to make these events intimate and interactive. Plan for no more than 20 delegates. Do not leave relationship building to chance. Make sure that four or five of your own consultants are there and each one has targeted the clients they will be working with. Follow each short speech with a round table discussion led by one of your team. Brief them well to run round table discussions with the delegates.

By charging for the workshops, you force yourself to give value and you gain the revenue you need to advertise to sell places. The fact that people have paid for a workshop makes them more likely to turn up, but you will still have some 'No shows' however much you charge. I recommend a policy of guaranteeing to return the fees of any delegates who are less than delighted. If someone has taken the time to listen to what you have to say and does not feel they have received value, it is much better that they tell their colleagues that you were boring and you gave them their money back rather than them feeling you ripped them off.

I have proof that this is so: one dissatisfied delegate who was refunded his £200 workshop fee came back a week later and signed up for £150,000 worth of consultancy.

When you advertise the workshops, you are also advertising your specialist skills. For every person who buys a ticket to your workshop, hundreds more notice the name of your consultancy and what you do. Right now they may not be in the market for your services, but when they are, they know who to turn to.

People who are considering using your services will be drawn to test the waters by spending time at your workshops. Often it takes time before a prospect buys from you. Clients take as much trouble finding the right consultancy as consultants do finding clients. During this preliminary courtship time, they may have come to many of your workshops.

Write articles for trade magazines
To find out what magazines there are in your specialist field, consult *British Rates and Data* (BRAD), which is available in most reference libraries. Compile a list of those magazines that you and your clients are likely to read. Approach the editors of your chosen magazines with articles that are of topical interest and also feature solutions that your company provides.

Speak, too, to the editors of American business magazines and journals. Explain your area of expertise and offer to supply them with information on the UK scene. I mention America because its magazines and journals are often read in the UK. There is no reason for you not to supply the same story you are writing for the UK market (with a few adaptations) to similar magazines throughout the world.

Editors and their readers like 'how to' articles, which provide the reader with know-how they can use, such as 'A step by step guide to . . .' Again, use your stockpot of research to do this.

There is a widespread fear in the industry about giving away know-how as it is feared that your competition will learn something and copy you. In reality, if competitors do copy your work, they will be right where you want them to be – behind you. Giving yesterday's secrets to your rivals is a great way to encourage yourself to move on.

To make the most of this work, your articles can be reprinted to be handed out at seminars or sent to clients.

Maister (1997) recommends setting targets for articles, say one per professional per year. If you do this, it is best that you employ a journalist to work with your consultants because they are consultants not writers, and without help they cannot be expected to create good, interesting material.

Speak at conferences

Your purpose in making a speech should be to address the two or three people in the audience who are ready right now to use your service. What you really want is for them to come up to you afterwards and ask you about it. All marketing is about courtship and one of the ways you can encourage delegates to approach you is to promise copies of your slides or some other vital piece of information to those people who want to give you their business card.

The trick to public speaking is, of course, to have something interesting and relevant to say. Here, again, you can rely on your research stockpot for material.

Most speakers are mundane. They do an OK job of putting across information, but, if you wanted data, you could get that from a book. Delegates come to a conference looking for more of a human touch. The best speakers, therefore, are human and entertaining. You feel you would want to work with that person. Their world view is exciting and charming.

If you are inexperienced at public speaking, find someone whose work in front of an audience you admire and ask them to train you.

To get yourself started on the conference circuit, collect all those conference invitations that arrive in the post. Write to the organizers and tell them about your work and the subjects you like to speak on. Normally the conference organizers pay your expenses, and, if you are one of the top speakers, you may also command a fee. Everything is negotiable.

Set clear boundaries for the distances you will travel and the subjects you want to speak on. It is flattering to be invited to Singapore to give your wisdom, but if you are not interested in business in the Pacific rim, then the conference would have a low priority.

Start a newsletter or magazine

One of the problems marketers have is that you never know when someone in your market is ready to buy your type of service. You can identify the decision-makers in your marketplace, but what you do not know is when they will be in the market for your services. Sometimes a company's needs change so fast that a need suddenly arises. You need to keep reminding your clients and prospects that you exist so they will turn to you first, but such continuity of communication is difficult to achieve normally without being annoying. Publishing a magazine, however, allows you to write regularly to those on your database.

The downside of magazines and journals is that the quality tends to drop after issue one, so only start one if you can ensure a continuous flow of interesting articles. It is best to use an outside publishing house to do this as your consultants will simply not have the time to do this properly.

Brief the publishing house on your advertising strategy, which should be mirrored in every story. Use the newsletter to make heroes of your clients. Write about them and make sure that the articles that feature their stories are circulated in their company. Also, use the newsletter to sell your own workshops and surveys, making sure that people can respond to such items. Putting your phone number on the back is not enough. Many people do not like calling in response to advertisements – they prefer to write – so always make sure you include a reply coupon on the back page. Designers hate coupons and tend to leave them out whenever possible, but marketers know that simply adding a coupon to an advertisement will boost results by around 20 per cent.

Create dining clubs
Part of the pleasure of working with a particular consultancy can be the entrée it gives you to a new social/business world. Forming your own dining club allows both clients and prospects to meet their peers and your consultants in an informal manner.

A useful way in which to organize a dining club evening is to choose a subject for discussion and invite an expert guest speaker to get the ball rolling. Then, each person round the table gives their view for a minute or two.

PR
Over the past ten years, the functions offered by a public relations company have expanded to include strategy and marketing. To begin with, find a company that will help you gain editorial space in the press or appearances on television or radio. They should also provide you with a press cutting service, to enable you to track your own coverage.

The main block to them doing their job well is a lack of publishable stories that are interesting to the public and therefore to the press. Here is where you can use your research and your surveys. Stories about public companies are automatically valuable because shareholders are always attentive to their investments. Unfortunately, stories about privately owned companies do not have the same priority with journalists.

Over the years, I have noticed that even national press coverage brings very little in the way of solid enquiries, so try to make sure that you are offering something in the articles. For instance, in financial terms, it is better to have an article on your new research survey (which is for sale) than a profile of one of your consultants. People are really polite and will normally contact you only when they are invited to do so, and most newspaper articles do not invite a response.

Another part of PR is the winning of awards. In my time with the Merchants Group, we won 41 national and international awards – many more than our competitors. This is not simply because the Merchants Group is a good company, but because we took award-winning seriously and gained expertise in how to win. If you are considering entering for awards, contact the organizers and find out what they are looking for, ask to see examples of work that has won in previous years.

The publicity around awards does tend to bring in work, but, perhaps more importantly, awards do wonders for staff and client morale. In the long term, collecting awards demonstrates that your company is established and recognized for the standard of its work.

Direct mail

The reason I prefer newsletters to direct mail as a means of promoting a consultancy is that direct mail tends to be sporadic when you should be aiming to build a continuous relationship with the individuals in your marketplace. Use direct mail when you have something important to offer.

When discussing direct mail, clients always ask for response rates or what they refer to as 'industry standard response rates'. There is no such thing. If you make a 'soft' offer like 'A *free* Harrods hamper when you visit our office', you will get a high response rate. A 'hard' offer like 'please do not call us unless you are determined to increase your revenues and have a million to spend on consultancy this year' will produce a lower response rate. The real issue is the cost of the mailing versus its returns over a period of time.

In advertising, there is a lot of talk about creating the right image for the public, but the reality is that you will know how popular your message is by the response you get and the revenues you generate – anything else is just a consolation prize.

In 1923, Claude Hopkins, then the world's highest-paid copywriter made the following assertion:

> To understand advertising or to learn even its rudiments one must start with the right conception. Advertising is salesmanship. Its principles are

the principles of salesmanship. Successes and failures in both lines are due to like causes, thus every advertising question should be answered by the salesman's standards.

Treat it as a salesman. Force it to justify itself. Compare it with the other salesmen. Figure its costs and results, accept no excuses which good salesmen do not make. Then you will not go far wrong.

Let me emphasize that point: the only purpose of advertising is to make sales. It is profitable or unprofitable according to its actual sales.

Use the telephone

I think it was *The Times* that ran that great headline – 'The most powerful business tool in the world is sitting on your desk'. And it is true – nobody interrupts a meeting or gets out of the bath to answer their mail or check out a TV commercial, but they will do so for a telephone call.

Precisely because it is so powerful, you have to use it with care. Cold calling has long been a salesperson's standby, but do not cold call a prospect without first working out something you want to give them. Do not cold call to ask them for something.

Let me give you an example. In 1981, I worked with a recruitment agency called the Work Programme. We were slaving away, cold calling, pleading for vacancies. Then we changed tactics. Each morning, each caller would be issued with the details of our most highly qualified secretary. We would then cold call saying, 'Mr Prospect, I have someone who has just come on to our books. She's tri-lingual has a maths first from Cambridge, types 120 words a minute, takes shorthand and can fly a jet. We thought you might be interested in having someone like this work for you.' Our prospect would normally decline the offer of superwoman, but would then happily talk about what help he actually needed.

Use the telephone to gather data on your clients and prospects. You may be surprised at the amount of detail a good researcher can gain over the telephone. In fact, each phone call you make has four valuable products.

- The prospect who says yes or no to your offer. Very few cold calls end in a yes. Those may be your bull's-eyes, but if you simply count the yeses you will find it has been an expensive exercise. The no's are also important, though, because you can save money by taking that prospect off your list.
- Valuable PR. You will find that people remember your call, especially when you have been warm and enthusiastic. Even if they say no, they should have enjoyed talking to you.

- The person who tells you that they cannot use your service right now, but would be interested in finding out more in June, say, when, for instance, they are considering opening an office in Beijing.
- Research. Always use each call to gather information you need, even if it is to check the spelling of someone's name.

Use the Internet

'The Internet is not a selling medium it is a communication medium, and an educational medium, and a support medium'. These words are from the introduction to *Strategic Internet Marketing* by Tom Vassos (1996).

A good Internet site should be like Disneyland – plenty to do and always something new to keep you coming back. Its real advantage is the fact that it is global – many of the responses you will get will be from outside of your territory.

Maintaining a good site is an expensive labour of love. If you position yourself as a leading IT consultancy, clients may expect you to have a great site. However, whatever type of consultancy you are in, it is a good idea to simply put up one page on the Web, explaining who you are, how to use you and giving your e-mail address as well as your phone number.

You can also use the Internet as an intranet. Allow your clients to dial up with their own password and find out what is happening on their projects.

Corporate hospitality

There are plenty of companies that organize and offer corporate hospitality events. However, they seem to organize the same events for everyone – the opera, Goodwood, Wimbledon, Silverstone. The question is, how do you use corporate hospitality to differentiate your company? Personally, I have always been more honoured by an invitation to a firm's staff functions than I have being invited to the opera. Practices eager to ally themselves with 'excellence in the Arts' often display their own lack of imagination.

Ask yourself what it is that your clients get from being with you that they cannot get anywhere else. This is an important point and one that it is vital to define.

Work for free

Sometimes you may spot an opportunity in someone's company that they are not aware of. They have not commissioned the work because they are not aware of the potential that you can see. At this point, you may offer to do the initial scoping of the project for free, with the understanding that, if your hunch is right, you will get the contract.

Do work that is socially important

Of course business is socially important, but there are certain community issues that affect the quality of life for everyone. Major issues such as drugs, unemployment, crime, homelessness and so on need the best brains on the case. If you feel you have a contribution to make, do it, because, apart from the satisfaction involved, you will also gain valuable publicity.

Advertise

Some consultancies choose to advertise in trade journals. If you have a new service or a service you want to introduce to a new market, then it may be a good idea to have your name 'out there'. If the offer in your advertisement is generous enough, it may be an inexpensive way of building your database.

Use advertisements to sell reports and workshops. Always include a telephone number and a coupon.

As mentioned before, art directors do not like coupons, considering them vulgar, but when a coupon will improve the response rate by at least 20 per cent, it pays to ignore the finer sensibilities of your creative team.

For consultancies, direct mail and newsletters seem to produce higher returns than do off-the-page advertisements. This is because they are more proactive and can be accurately targeted on your prospects. A good place to advertise, however, is in the in-house magazines of your clients. Take space to thank them and congratulate them on successes.

Produce brochures

I have put brochures at the bottom of the list because they are the one item that new management insists on, but are the least likely to bring in revenue.

A good brochure is hideously expensive and a political nightmare. They are invariably created by committee, which is the worst possible way of creating communications. I have yet to see one that is not out of date by the time it has been completed.

A way round this is to create one-off brochures for each important pitch. Using laser printing techniques, you can customize the information in each brochure for every decision-maker in the client company.

These are impressive and their effect can be measured in terms of revenue won.

It is possible to exist for years without a corporate brochure. Instead, print off good case histories and service sheets detailing each service you offer.

The only good thing about brochures is that creating one can be used as a way of bringing the whole company into the discussion of 'what we do here'.

Steps 9 and 10: Creative and media strategies

By 'creative strategy' I mean deciding on the tone in which you wish your story to be told.

A word of advice on creative work in relation to consultancies: it does not work to brag about your abilities. The trick is to *demonstrate* your genius rather than *proclaim* it. A classic way of doing this is to feature client testimonials and have them talk about their work with you.

Work out your creative and media strategies simultaneously. The 'media strategy' is what are we going to do when and where. Thus, when you are going to book an advertisement, it helps you decide which journal to choose to advertise in.

Here is a simple first draft of a marketing plan covering six months.

January Launch newsletter to invite clients to the workshop in March.
February Follow-up newsletter to prospects *re* workshop with phone shot to non-respondents at the end of the month.
March Begin survey on 'The medium-term effects of business process re-engineering'. Work with PR firm to interest quality national in an exclusive on the report. Book guest speakers for June workshop. Newsletter No. 2: pre-sell the report on business process re-engineering.
April PR blitz on survey findings, put advertisement in *Utilities Now* selling the report and May workshop on the report.
May Workshop on the BPR report.
June Mailshot to selected clients and prospects to invite them to one of six dinners. Newsletter No. 3 out advertising workshop in September (this is the repeat of January's workshop). Database cleaning begins.

Use a year planner when you are drawing up such a strategy. Remember that, in order to get revenues in month 12, you probably have to get that lead or enquiry in month 6. Because of this time lag, I recommend that your marketing planning is signed off halfway through the year. If you wait for the year plans to be completed in January, then you will be too late to bring in work for the first quarter.

How to allocate your budget
It is a surprise to me that few consultancies track the success or otherwise of their marketing spend. Some spend fortunes on sponsorship, yet are unable to tell you how much income they have gained from that investment. Others will send out sporadic mailshots and buy advertising space whenever work seems to be drying up. However, it is only when you track the results of your promotions that you get a clear picture of the return on your investment and gain the intelligence necessary to make wise investment decisions in the future.

Step 11: Contact strategy

Before we look at how to plan how and when to contact prospects and clients, I thought it would be helpful to look at the results of some interesting research in this area.

Through your client's eyes
In 1994, I witnessed a series of focus groups in which the Merchants Group invited marketing directors and brand managers to talk on the subjects of how they felt about their jobs, their careers and, incidentally, when and how they came to choose and use consultants.
   The following important findings emerged from the discussions.

- Interviewees thought in terms of keeping their present roles for no more than two years. (Some spoke of leaping 'over the wall' into consultancy.)
- As a result, they were only interested in results that could be created within this two-year window.
- They were all from large public companies. They measured their success in terms of increased revenues – they felt that profit was 'out of their hands'.
- They chose consultants from the group of people they already knew or used those firms that had bothered to stay in touch.
- They did not read all the direct mail they received, but they did remember those people who had taken the trouble to find out about them and do something different.
- Although they all had budgets and year plans, the need to hire a consultant could come up at a moment's notice, particularly if a chair-

man or CEO came up with some new idea. It was impossible to predict when they would need specialized consultancy skills. When they did need a consultant, they tended to shortlist someone they had used before or someone who had recently come to their attention.

- They wanted consultants to delegate problems to and so did not appreciate receiving phone calls telling them of more problems for which no solutions were offered.
- When the contract worked, they wanted the consultancy to remember that it was the client who initiated the work. (Some consultants tend to take all the credit for something working.)
- They liked to work with consultancies big enough to take the blame and pay up if the project does not work. (This follows the IT adage 'You never get fired for buying IBM'.)

It is important to remember that your client is answerable to the Board. If the client works with one of the large consultancies and the project does not work, the Board will be sympathetic and help change consultancies. If, however, the client has employed someone they met at the golf club who is from a tiny practice, then they have no one to blame and they risk their own job for lack of judgement.

Developing a strategy
Most consultancies use a key account strategy. If you have a database of 10,000 names from 1000 companies, you cannot possibly contact them all personally. You therefore take out maybe 12 companies that you choose to be your key accounts, and these are the ones you will deal with personally. These are the ones to which you will give the most attention. Key account strategies allow you to concentrate your consultants' selling time where you consider it will gain the best results.

There are two types of costs in marketing:

- people's time
- money.

More general direct marketing simply costs money. For example, I could write a letter today and use a mailing house to help me mail out 50,000 copies of the letter. Within a few days, I will have contacted 50,000 people, and in just another week, I will have their replies. Now all that takes is money.

A key account strategy costs time and money. It means personal involvement on the part of your consultants, it involves phone calls, lunches, research, meetings, conferences with colleagues on the account and so on.

Despite the expense, you should have a key account strategy and a non-key account strategy. This is because the majority of the costs involved in doing a mailshot or any printed promotion are in the origination of the first package. The costs are in the copywriting, artwork and printing. If you are going to print 1000 copies for your key accounts, why not print 10,000 copies and send them to all the names on your database. For the 9000 extra, all you are paying is the price of the printing and postage. These incremental costs are low and are easily repaid by the extra returns that will be generated as a result.

There are two ways of choosing which are going to be your key accounts. The first is by scientific research, sorting the accounts by how similar they are to other accounts with proven yields. The second way is to allow consultants to form a wish list of the six accounts they would most like to work with.

Consultants make their own luck and, as it is the motivation of the consultant that will make it happen, I always prefer the second methodology.

The allocation of budgets

I have emphasized that marketing is about making investment decisions. One of those decisions involves asking the question 'How much do I spend on attracting new clients versus courting my existing clients?' Because of the confusion about what marketing is and what it should be doing that I mentioned at the beginning of this chapter, most marketing spend is put where it has the least effect – that is, the generation of new business. It is often assumed (mistakenly) that existing clients are being taken care of, nurtured and sold to.

A sensible investment decision is to allocate the majority of your budget to where you know it will have the most effect – courting existing clients. If I were to give a rough rule of thumb, it would be to allocate:

- 60 per cent of the budget to growing existing clients
- 15–20 per cent to research (the stockpot of your marketing)
- the remaining 15–20 per cent to generating new business.

Obviously, if you are starting a new consultancy, the percentages will be different.

However, be warned, the marketing budget is often used by those in the finance department as a reserve fund that can be raided in a crisis, especially in the last quarter of the year. This, in turn, creates sales and revenue problems in the first quarter of the next year. Experienced marketers understand this and create their own contingency plans (Broadbent, 1989).

Making it happen

Continuous marketing – that is, research and communication – is an integral part of the health of any consultancy. If you only communicate sporadically – when it looks like you need new business – then you will create problems. Work will falter, then you will be tempted to lower your fees or to take on second-rate work simply because it is there.

As the whole point of marketing planning is to have you create a consultancy that works the way you want it to, it is imperative to follow-up the planning with continuous and consistent action.

Or, as those marketers at Nike say, 'Just do it.'

References

Behr, E T (1997) *The Tao of Sales: The easy way to sell in tough times*, Element Books, Dorset

Bird, D (1996) *Common Sense Direct Marketing*, Kogan Page, London

Broadbent, S (1989) *The Advertising Budget: The advertisers' guide to budget determination*, Institute of Practitioners in Advertising and McGraw-Hill, Maidenhead

Coopers & Lybrand (1994) *Marketing at the Cross Roads: A survey of marketing in 100 blue chip companies*, Coopers & Lybrand, London

Essinger, J (1994) *Starting a High-income Consultancy*, Pitman, London

Kleiner, A (1996) *The Age of Heretics: Heroes, outlaws, and the forerunners of corporate change*, Currency Doubleday, New York

Levitt, T (1986) *The Marketing Imagination*, The Free Press, New York

McCormack, M (1988) *McCormack on Negotiating*, Century, London

Maister, D H (1997) *Managing the Professional Service Company*, First Free Press Paperbacks, New York

Ogilvy, D (1995) *Ogilvy on Advertising*, Prion, London

Peters, T (1995) *The Pursuit of Wow!*, Macmillan, London

Rapp, S and Collins, T (1995) *Beyond Maximarketing: The new power of caring and daring*, McGraw-Hill, New York

Reicheld, F (1996) 'Learning from customer defection', in *Harvard Business Review*, March/April

Reis, A and Trout, J (1994) *The 22 Immutable Laws of Marketing*, HarperCollins, London

Reis, A and Rivkin, S (1995) *New Positioning: The latest on the world's No. 1 business strategy*, McGraw-Hill, New York

Vassos, T (1996) *Strategic Internet Marketing*, Que, Indianapolis

10

Finance and control issues

John Kind

Introduction

This chapter is arranged in four sections. The first describes, briefly, the underlying economics of the management consulting industry and the financial performance of the individual firms within it. The second explains, with practical illustrations, the economic characteristics of consultancy businesses and the factors that determine financial success or failure, while the third focuses on financial planning and budgeting. The fourth section, project management, is devoted to the theme of 'excellence in execution' – the approaches and techniques that enable all the initiatives presented and approved in the budget to be implemented on time and with the agreed resources.

The basic economics of management consulting

Management consulting is a global business. According to Wooldridge (1997), the combined worldwide revenues of the 25 largest firms were nearly £15 billion in 1996. At least ten of the firms, including Andersen Consulting, McKinsey & Co and Coopers & Lybrand, disclosed revenue figures well in excess of £500 million. In the UK, the total consultancy market is worth about £2 billion. Two-thirds of the revenue comes from the ten largest firms, of which six are also major accountancy and audit practices. It is difficult to assess the performance of these businesses because, as private firms, their financial results are not fully disclosed. However, one vital statistic – revenue per consultant (a measure of the productivity of professional staff) – can be calculated from published information. On a worldwide basis, illustrative figures of these revenues are as shown in Table 10.1.

Table 10.1 Revenue per consultant *(Management Consultant International,* June 1996, and June/July 1997)

Consultancies	1995 £000s	1996 £000s
McKinsey & Co	284	303
The Boston Consulting Group	253	235
Arthur D Little	224	194
Coopers & Lybrand	93	101
Andersen Consulting	80	86

As the data makes clear, the financial performance of the more broadly based firms, such as Andersen Consulting, is less impressive than the results achieved by the strategy specialists, such as McKinsey & Co.

The American Association of Management Consultancy Firms (Acme), reported that, in 1995, revenue per consultant for the 80 firms participating in their survey averaged £119,000. The average profit per partner (perhaps the most important indicator of all because it is a measure of the owners' return on investment) was £76,000. According to Acme, net profit expressed as a proportion of fees was 20 per cent in the US, but only 12 per cent in Europe.

The economic characteristics of consultancy businesses

Having looked at the overall economic performance consultancies achieve, we now turn our attention to the financial and control issues that individual firms need to consider. For the purposes of illustration, the activities of Expert Limited (EL) will be looked at in some detail. It is involved in providing IT advice and offers business process re-engineering services to a number of major clients.

There are 32 professional staff, of whom 4 are partners (or directors). They are the owners, the most senior executives in the business. There are 8 managing consultants, while the remainder (20) are more junior consultants who are expected to spend most of their time working on specific assignments. This time is 'chargeable' to clients at the agreed daily or hourly rate. The consulting staff rely heavily on eight 'support' staff – the secretaries, a financial controller, a small number of assistants and the printing and publishing department.

EL's profit and loss account (or income statement) for the year ended 31 December 1997 is shown in Figure 10.1.

Let us now look at the notes.

Note 1: Revenue

Revenue is based on:
- the number of fee-earning days each grade of professional staff has worked during the year – a measure that is often referred to as utilization
- the appropriate daily or hourly charge-out rate for each consultant.

Expert Limited

Profit and loss account for the year ended 31 December 1997

	£000s	£000s
Revenue (see Note 1)		2860
Salaries (see Note 2)	(1354)	
Other operating costs, such as office rent, utility costs (water and electricity) and marketing and sales promotion.	(956)	
Total costs		(2310)
Operating profit		550

Figure 10.1 Example of a profit and loss account

198

Finance and control issues

Here is an example of how these figures can be set out.

		Weeks	Days
Utilization			
Total available time		52	260
Less	– annual leave	(4)	(20)
	– public holidays	(2)	(10)
	– sickness	(1)	(5)
Available time		45	225
Chargeable time			
	– Partners	18	90
	– Managing consultants	25	125
	– Consultants	30	150
Utilization rate (chargeable time expressed as a percentage of the available time)			
	– Partners	40%	
	– Managing consultants	55%	
	– Consultants	65%	

The average utilization rate for EL as a whole was (18 + 25 + 30 weeks), divided by (3 x 45 weeks). The '3' refers to the 3 categories of staff – partners, managing consultants and consultants. The answer is 54 per cent.

Different fee rates are charged to clients according to the seniority, expertise and experience of the consultant. *Management Consultant International* (March 1997) reported that the average daily billing rates for partners, managing or senior consultants and consultants in Europe were £1000, £700 and £600 respectively. Applying these figures to EL, we arrive at the following figures for the revenue these different groups generated.

	£000s
Partners	
(4 x 90 days x £1000)	360
Managing consultants	
(8 x 125 days x £700)	700
Consultants	
(20 x 150 days x £600)	1800
Total	2860

The overall allocation of chargeable time for EL is as follows.

	Chargeable time – days	*Proportion of time*
Partners (4 x 90 days)	360	8%
Managing consultants (8 x 125 days)	1000	23%
Consultants (20 x 150 days)	3000	69%
Totals	4360	100%

Note 2: Salaries

Using Acme European figures for each grade of staff, the annual salaries (including social security and pension costs) for EL were as follows.

	£000s
Partners (4 x £72,500)	290
Managing consultants (8 x £38,000)	304
Consultants (20 x £30,000)	600
Total for professional staff	1194
Support staff (8 x £20,000)	160
Overall total	1,354

The figures in EL's 1997 profit and loss account highlight some extremely important points for management consultancies.

First, the four most senior staff (the partners) produce only 13 per cent of EL's total revenue (£360,000 divided by £2.86 million). The non-partner staff produce the remaining 87 per cent of the total revenue. This is referred to as the leverage effect – the ratio of non-partner staff to the partner group. In the case of EL, it is 7: 1 (28 professional staff, 4 partners).

Leverage is crucial to the satisfactory economic performance of EL. It produces 'profit per partner' of £137,500 (operating profit of £550,000 divided by 4). Maister (1993) calls this the equivalent of return on equity. The 'equity' is the expertise and resources provided by the partners, as well as the capabilities offered by the other 'non-partner' professional staff.

To achieve the appropriate leverage means ensuring that the staffing mix for a project is optimal. For EL and for every 100 hours of chargeable time, there should be a partner for 8 hours, a managing consultant for 23 hours and a consultant for 69 hours.

Finance and control issues

If the leverage ratio falls from, say, 7: 1 to 6.4: 1 because the number of partners increases by 1 (from 4 to 5) following the promotion of a managing consultant, the effect will be to reduce the profit per partner by nearly 25 per cent. This can be explained as follows:

- revenue will increase by £2500 (£90,000 for the extra partner, offset by £87,500 for 1 less managing consultant)
- salaries will increase by £34,500 (£72,500, the salary of a partner, less £38,000, the salary of a managing consultant)
- operating profit will fall by £32,500 (£34,500 salaries less £2,500 revenue) so that the profit per partner will fall from £137,500 (£550,000 divided by 4) to £103,600 (£550,000 less £32,500 = £518,000 divided by 5).

Second, the staffing mix needs to be monitored extremely carefully – in particular, the extent to which the more senior staff such as the partners and managing consultants, are spending more time on chargeable client work and the more junior staff (the consultants) less time.

Assume, for example, that EL produces the following utilization profile.

	Actual %	Estimated %
Partners (4)	45	40
Managing consultants (8)	65	55
Consultants (20)	55	65

Then, revenue will be as follows.

	£000s
Partners (£360,000 x $^{45}/_{40}$)	405
Managing consultants (£700,000 x $^{65}/_{55}$)	827
Consultants (£1.8m x $^{55}/_{65}$)	1523
Total	2755

EL's revenue has fallen by £105,000 (nearly 4 per cent) from £2.86 million to £2.755 million. Costs, however, are unchanged. This means that the shortfall in revenue has directly affected profitability. Operating profit has fallen from £550,000 to £445,000, a reduction of 19 per cent. Profit per partner has dropped from £137,500 to £111,250 (nearly 20 per cent).

We have mentioned that profit per partner or director is the most important indicator of profitability. We have highlighted, too, the leverage effect and the influence of the staffing mix. We now need to consider the interrelationships between these factors in a more formal way. This can be done by using the following profitability formula:

$$\frac{\text{Operating profit}}{\text{Partners}} = \frac{\text{Operating profit}}{\text{Revenue or fee income}} \times \frac{\text{Revenue}}{\text{Staff}} \times \frac{\text{Staff}}{\text{Partners}}$$

| Profit per partner | Profit margin | Staff productivity | Leverage ratio |

In the case of EL, the figures are:

$$\frac{\pounds550,000}{\text{4 partners}} = \frac{\pounds550,000}{\pounds2,860,000} \times \frac{\pounds2,860,000}{28} \times \frac{28}{4}$$

$$\pounds137,500 = 19.23\% \times \pounds102,143 \times 7$$

There is a danger of placing too much emphasis on profit margins. It is quite possible for a relatively low-margin practice to be more profitable on a 'profit per partner' basis than a higher-margin one. For example, Niche Limited is in a lower margin range of activities than EL (with a 10 per cent rather than a 19.2 per cent margin). However, its leverage is higher – it has 9 professional staff per partner rather than 7. As a consequence, its profit per partner is 45 per cent higher than EL's at £200,000. Niche's profitability formula, which is shown below, demonstrates how this is achieved.

$$\frac{\text{Profit}}{\text{Partners}} = \frac{\text{Profit}}{\text{Fees}} \times \frac{\text{Fees}}{\text{Staff}} \times \frac{\text{Staff}}{\text{Partners}}$$

$$\frac{\pounds800,000}{4} = \frac{\pounds800,000}{\pounds8m} \times \frac{\pounds8m}{36} \times \frac{36}{4}$$

$$\pounds200,000 = 10\% \times \pounds222,222 \times 9$$

The profit per partner of £200,000 is significantly influenced by staff productivity (£222,222 of fees for each consultant) and the leverage ratio of 9:4. Even if the profit margin falls to 7 per cent, Niche's profit per partner will still be equal to EL's. One of the practical consequences of all of this is that, with high productivity and high leverage, a consultancy firm can afford to spend more on business development and training to sustain its competitive position. A virtuous circle develops so that high efficiency supports high investment, which supports even higher efficiency.

Productivity

We have defined productivity as fees or revenue divided by staff numbers (excluding partners). It can also be calculated as follows:

$$\frac{\text{Fees or revenue}}{\text{Staff}} = \frac{\text{Fees}}{\text{Chargeable days}} \times \frac{\text{Chargeable days}}{\text{Staff}}$$

$$= \text{Daily charge-out rate} \times \text{Utilization}$$

In the case of EL the figures would be:

$$\frac{£2.5m}{28} = \frac{£2.5m}{4000} \times \frac{4000}{28}$$

$$\begin{array}{lll}
£89,285 & = & £625 \times 142.85 \\
\text{(approximately)} & & \text{(average daily charge-out rate)} \quad \text{(chargeable days per consultant, per year)}
\end{array}$$

Note that the revenue figure used was the total, £2.86 million, less the £360,000 generated by the 4 partners – £2.5 million. The calculation for the number of chargeable days is 4360 less the 360 attributable to the partners.

Cost structure

EL's profit and loss account indicates that salaries account for nearly 60 per cent of its costs. Over a period of several months, these costs are likely to be fixed until decisions are made to reduce staff numbers if the outlook for consultancy work deteriorates. This means that EL is 'volume sensitive – profitability is significantly influenced by its utilization rate. This is shown in Table 10.2 and Figure 10.2.

Table 10.2 The influence of the utilization rate on EL's profitability

Year ended 31 December 1997	
Utilization rate	*Operating profit (loss)*
(chargeable days ÷ total	
available days x 100)	*£000s*
70%	1397
60%	868
54% (current performance)	550
45%	73
40%	(192)

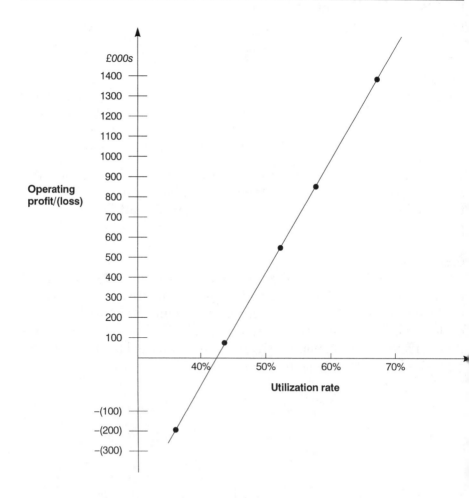

Figure 10.2 The relationship between EL's profitability and utilization rates

204

The steep gradient of the line in Figure 10.2 demonstrates how small changes in utilization have a more than proportionate impact on profitability. This is a direct consequence of EL's inflexible cost structure (at least in the short-term). It is a characteristic that is evident in management consultancies more generally. For example, a 10 per cent reduction in activity (utilization falling from 60 to 54 per cent) results in a profit reduction of nearly 37 per cent (from £868,000 to £550,000). By contrast, relatively small improvements in utilization – say, from 45 to 54 per cent (an increase in activity of 20 per cent) – produce enormous improvements in profitability (from £73,000 to £555,000).

Critical mass
Another very important point is critical mass. This means having enough resources, especially staff, to meet the volume of client work and generate enough revenue to cover costs and earn a satisfactory profit.

Let us imagine for a moment that EL is facing a substantial reduction in its workload. As a consequence, it is considering reducing its professional staff from, say, 32 to 25. One partner may be asked to leave along with 3 managing consultants and 3 consultants. What are the potential consequences of this?

• First, annual revenue will fall by £622,500 or 22 per cent (1 partner, £90,000; 3 managing consultants, £262,000; 3 consultants, £270,000).

• Second, annual staff costs will fall by £276,500, excluding the possibility of redundancy costs (1 partner, £72,500; 3 managing consultants, £114,000; 3 consultants, £90,000).

• Third, the other operating costs, such as office rent (at least in the short-term, over a period of months) will remain unchanged. Even if steps are taken to reduce them – such as subletting surplus office space – it will take time before the benefits materialize.

The revised financial scenario for EL if it went ahead with this plan would be as follows.

	£000s
Annual revenue	
(£2.86m less £622,500)	2237.5
Operating costs	
Salaries (£1.35m less £276,500)	(1073.5)
Other operating costs (unchanged)	(956.0)
Operating profit	208.0

This means that a reduction in professional staff from 32 to 25 (22 per cent) produces an operating profit that is 62 per cent (£550,000 to £208,000) lower. This would make EL even more vulnerable to utilization rate changes. For example, if utilization was 54 per cent for the reduced number of consultants, this would produce an operating profit of £208,000. However, a slight fall in utilization from 54 to 49 per cent would produce only a break-even result. Even if utilization increased to 60 per cent (from 54 per cent), the new operating profit would be only £452,000, rather than the £868,000 it can make with the present staff numbers.

The overall message as far as cost reduction is concerned is that, as this inevitably involves professional staff, revenue-generating capacity will be adversely affected. The remaining staff will need to operate at extremely high utilization levels for the firm to be as profitable as it was with higher staff numbers. In the case of EL, for example, a utilization rate of 70 per cent would need to be achieved by 25 professional staff to produce an operating profit of £868,000. Before the staff reduction, it only had to reach a 60 per cent rate. And, of course, achieving an overall utilization rate of 70 per cent is significantly more difficult than achieving one of 60 per cent.

One of the ways this problem can be solved – apart from making significant reductions in non-staff operating costs – is to use associates. They are consultants who are only used by EL when there is enough work to justify it. It is the consultancy version of outsourcing and, because the consultants are not employees of the firm, they are a variable rather than a fixed cost. As a result, EL's profitability will be improved by the extent to which the charge-out rate used for associates exceeds their cost. Consultancies will seek to earn a margin of at least 35 to 40 per cent, so if the daily charge-out rate is £600, then the associate's cost to EL should not be more than about £390.

Project profitability

So far, our attention has been devoted to EL's finances as a whole. However, we now need to turn to pricing and costing considerations for individual projects. In particular, how much should a client be charged and what resources will EL need?

Let us take an example. EL has just been asked to submit a proposal for a new IT advisory project. The first step is to estimate the time that will be required for each grade of consulting staff. The revenue information is as follows.

Finance and control issues

	Estimated no. of days	Daily fee rate	Fees chargeable to the client
		£	£
Partner	10	1000	10,000
Managing consultant	25	700	17,500
Consultant	75	600	45,000
Total	110		72,500

The figure of £72,500 is included in the proposal as EL's fee estimate. The second step is to estimate the costs attributable to the project.

	Days	Salary costs	Support staff and other operating costs
		£	£
Partner	10	8,050	
Managing consultant	25	7,600	
Consultant	75	15,000	
Total	110	30,650	28,160

Regarding the total salary costs, this is the sum of the following:

- for the partner, 90 days of total chargeable time at a salary cost of £72,500, which is equal to £805 per day, and 10 days times £805 equals £8,050
- for the managing consultant, 125 days of total chargeable time at a salary cost of £38,000, which is equal to £304 per day, and 25 days times £304 equals £7,600
- for the consultant, 150 days of total chargeable time at a salary cost of £30,000, which is equal to £200 per day, and 75 days times £200 equals £15,000.

The total for support staff and other operating costs was arrived at in the following way:

- support staff and other operating costs (sometimes referred to as indirect costs) for EL are £160,000 and £956,000 respectively, giving a total of £1,116,000
- for the year as a whole, EL expects 4360 days of chargeable time
- the daily cost of support staff and other operating costs is, therefore £256

- for this project, the indirect costs are £256 x 110 days, which equals £28,160.

The attributable costs for the project are salaries of £30,650, plus £28,160 of indirect costs, giving an overall total of £58,810.

The third step is to calculate the estimated 'profit' for the project, which is done as follows:

	£
Revenue	72,500
Attributable costs	(58,810)
Project 'profit'	13,690

If EL's proposal is accepted and work on the new project starts, then usually progress can be monitored every month. This is done by looking at the timesheets completed at weekly, fortnightly or monthly intervals by all consulting staff. The timesheets enable EL to assess how many days are being spent on specific projects and compare these actual figures with the original estimates. To the extent that more time is being spent than budgeted, the profitability of the project will suffer, unless the additional days can be charged to the client.

For EL's proposal, the original estimate is that the fees of £72,500 will be 123 per cent of the project costs of £58,810. This is sometimes referred to as the 'recovery rate'. It is the principal measure of project profitability.

If more time is spent on the project than estimated so that a partner, for example, spends 13 days rather than the 10 days budgeted, the recovery rate will fall. The fees of £72,500 will now be offset by costs of £61,225 (£58,810 plus 3 extra partner days at £805 per day). This is equivalent to a recovery rate of 118 per cent.

Sometimes it will be appropriate for EL to accept an assignment even if its estimated level of profitability is insufficient to cover all the costs involved. For example, although a consultant's budgeted daily fee rate is £600 (their daily employment costs are £200), it would be acceptable to charge a client, say, £400. That would cover the consultant's direct costs. This is referred to as contribution or marginal cost pricing. However, it can be extremely dangerous if it is applied indiscriminately. Only the consultant's salary costs will be recovered rather than all EL's costs plus a satisfactory profit margin.

With the economic and financial background to EL's activities in place, we now turn our attention to financial planning and control.

Financial planning and control

It is true to say that planning and control are essential for any business, not just management consultancies. The mechanism for ensuring that they happen, in practice, is the budget. This is simply a plan – a statement of intent, expressed in numerical terms, both financial and non-financial – that covers a specified period of time, usually a year. However, it may well be broken down into shorter periods, such as calendar months.

Having a budget means that actual performance during a particular period can be compared to the budgeted performance. Control is, therefore, exercised by specifying the objectives for the budget period, preparing a detailed set of budgeted figures to support them and reporting current performance against the set of expected outcomes. Increasingly, a budget is regarded as a management or 'performance' contract. It is a formal commitment to achieving a set of results. The budget is the budget, so it is not normally changed within its duration.

The benefits of budgeting are as follows.

- EL can plan its future. This means, for example, that the effects of changes such as increasing (or decreasing) utilization levels, extra staff numbers and higher fee rates can be explicitly taken into account. It means that options can be compared and resources allocated, taking into consideration such matters as using consultants on a full- or a part-time basis, leasing or purchasing equipment, renting extra office space or providing facilities that will enable professional staff to work from home. Finally, it means that responsibilities can be assigned to individual EL executives by breaking down the overall budget into its constituent elements, possibly on a departmental or business sector basis.
- Activities can be controlled. As we have seen, this means that a variance analysis can be carried out. This is a review of the actual results against the budgeted results to discern differences in order to focus management attention on what needs to be done to restore EL to its budgeted path.
- EL's performance can be improved. This can be done by concentrating on what are sometimes called the key performance indicators (KPIs). These are the business equivalents of blood pressure and pulse rate. In the case of EL, it means looking at such measures as fee rates, utilization levels, profit per partner and revenues for each consultant. By directing attention to the KPIs, the economic issues facing

EL can be more quickly identified. For example, a decline in utilization levels during the first quarter of its financial year might indicate that insufficient attention is being devoted to business development or that the success rate with new business proposals has fallen. As a consequence, work is not being won to the extent required in order to meet the budgeted new business objectives. If this trend continues it may have repercussions for EL's existing staffing levels.

Preparing a budget

There are some extremely important points to consider in the preparation of a budget.

First, it is essential to understand last year's results. In the case of EL, the KPIs for the year ended 31 December 1997 are:

- revenue or fees per consultant, £102,143
- profit per partner, £137,500
- leverage ratio (the ratio of non-partner consulting staff to partners), 7:1
- utilization rate, 54 per cent
- average daily billing rate, £655
- operating profit, expressed as a percentage of fees (the profit margin or operating margin), 19.2 per cent.

This is the basis on which budget discussions for the 1998 financial year can start.

Second, there must be a wide-ranging debate to agree the objectives for 1998 and to orchestrate it in a way that stimulates a strong element of personal commitment. The partners are responsible for different aspects of EL's business. In the first instance, they should involve their own staff in the budget discussions that are relevant to their work so that, at the end of the process, everyone should accept responsibility for achieving specific budgeted objectives.

The objectives do need to be realistic, but a strong element of performance improvement is necessary so that EL's competitiveness can be sustained. For example, it might be agreed that the budgeted utilization rate in 1998 be set at 60 per cent rather than the 54 per cent achieved in 1997. The profit per partner might be projected at £148,000 – an increase of 8 per cent over that of 1997. All of this means that a comprehensive financial model (spreadsheet) should be prepared for EL so that specific assumptions about the budgeted KPIs for 1998 can be used and the implications can be calculated. Other assumptions, such as the number of consulting staff and the projected increase in revenues, can also be included in the budget discussions.

Being clear about the assumptions is also important because, as the financial year proceeds, differences between the actual results and the budgeted ones are bound to appear. The more senior executives in EL will be called on to explain why they have materialized. Their task will be made easier if they are conversant with the assumptions. For example, if it is assumed that, say, five new consultants will join the firm during 1998 at regular intervals during the year, then the budgeted increase in salaries will be evenly spread across the 12-month period. However, if all the new consultants are actually recruited in the first quarter, salary costs will be much higher than anticipated in the early part of 1998. The difference between what was budgeted and what would happen in that circumstance could be explained and justified by reference to the underlying recruitment assumption.

An increase in the overall utilization rate from 54 per cent to 60 per cent means that, if this target is met, the number of chargeable days will increase from 4360 in 1997 to 4845 in 1998. What consequences will this have for the expected utilization rates of the partners, managing consultants and consultants? The financial model should provide the answers. Also, the projected increase in the profit per partner of 8 per cent might well affect the level of salary increases that can be contemplated, especially if the number of consultants is expected to go up to meet the anticipated rise in the workload.

The financial model will enable a comprehensive sensitivity analysis to be carried out. This simply means being able to answer the 'What if?' question many times so that the consequences of changes in one or a number of variables can be worked out in advance before final decisions are made.

Controlling the business

Once the overall budget has been agreed, and the new budget period starts, EL's activities need to be controlled or monitored. This should mean the following two things happen.

- The differences between actual and budgeted performance are compared at regular intervals (normally monthly) during the year. In particular, the reasons for both favourable and unfavourable variances should be identified. Corrective action should then be taken to correct any undesirable differences with an estimate of the time that will be needed before any corrective action becomes effective. For example, what should be done to accelerate the recruitment programme for new consultants if resourcing is becoming a major problem? Otherwise, it may be several months before extra staff join EL.

- Regular forecasts should be prepared so that the management team can assess the significance of the variances by their potential impact on the results for the rest of the year. These forecasts will change, of course, as the financial year proceeds. The budget is, however, the budget. It will remain unchanged as it is the benchmark against which EL's performance (and the individuals within it) will be assessed.

Project management

The market trends faced by EL suggest that a much greater emphasis is placed by clients on results, keener pricing and tangible evidence of receiving substantial 'added value'. All of these factors demand a very high standard of management of assignments in order to ensure that quality work is produced.

Many consulting assignments can be considered to be projects. Indeed, EL itself can be regarded as a large portfolio of projects of different sizes with different durations, revenues, costs, staffing and resource requirements. Effective project management is, therefore, a critical success factor if client demands are to be met and EL is to achieve its objectives.

A project such as the design, development and implementation of a computerized management information system for a client has a number of features including:

- a focus on results – what the project will have achieved when it is completed
- clearly defined beginning and end points, normally with demanding deadlines
- a multidisciplinary approach to address the wide range of client issues that are likely to be involved
- a customer – the most senior client contact, who will need to be satisfied that the project's objectives are being and have been achieved
- the management of scarce resources (finance, people and skills) in an environment of uncertainty and risk.

212

Focusing on results means focusing on what must be achieved before deciding on how to achieve it. It also means organizing the work into related activities (or milestones) and tasks, all of which are necessary to achieve the project's objectives.

Planning

Let us imagine for a moment that EL has decided to launch a new service – managing clients' IT functions on an outsourcing basis. The first step, in what is sometimes referred to as the project management cycle, is planning. This involves gathering and analysing the facts about this new project situation to ensure that clear terms of reference are agreed with the client, including recognition of the associated risks. For example, it could be decided that for a project using this new service, EL will take complete responsibility for a client's IT activities. This would include responsibility for all employees as well as the hardware and the associated hardware for an initial 2-year period for an agreed fee of £500,000.

The outline terms of reference, therefore, are clear. However, the precise objectives for EL's project need to be spelt out in more detail. For example, it could be stated that the contract will start on 1 January 1998 with annual project costs of £200,000, so that, over the whole period, EL is expecting to earn an operating profit of £100,000. The risks of such a project include the possibility that some of the staff inherited from the client's IT department will leave, with the inconvenience, cost and disruption this will cause. There is also, of course, the possibility of breakdowns of the IT equipment and programming problems with the software.

The technique to use at the start of such a project is 'milestone planning'. This involves identifying and agreeing the principal stages and the intermediate targets that will occur at each point during the project. The word 'when' is used sometimes as the prefix before the description of each milestone. For example, to reach complete agreement with a client before accepting an outsourcing contract might involve the following milestones:

- when EL has appointed an IT outsourcing project manager and a dedicated project team to assume overall responsibility for the management of the project
- when new employment contracts have been agreed by the client's staff to transfer their employment to EL
- when legal agreements have been finalized to transfer operational responsibility to EL for all the hardware and software arrangements

- when the fees for the 2-year contract period have been agreed with the client
- when insurance arrangements have been concluded for all the equipment and the associated hardware.

Finally, at this planning stage, it is important to set specific performance measures against which actual progress can be assessed as soon as EL assumes responsibility for the project. These might include:

- the frequency with which client management information reports are produced
- the expected 'downtimes' for the equipment
- response times before particular client requests are dealt with
- error rates in the information produced for the client.

Organizing

The second step in the overall management of the project is organizing. In particular, the milestones or intermediate targets identified earlier need to be linked to the more detailed project tasks. Tasks are defined as identifiable pieces of work for which one individual can be held accountable. For example, to achieve the milestone 'when the fees for the 2-year contract period have been agreed with the client', it may be necessary to complete the following tasks:

- convene a meeting of the project team
- prepare a work breakdown structure (this is explained below)
- negotiate fee proposals with the client
- prepare a formal 'fee' letter
- send the 'fee' letter to the client.

The work breakdown structure (WBS) shown in Figure 10.3 highlights the relationships between milestones and tasks. To achieve the milestone about agreeing fee levels, which we shall refer to as 'A', the five specific tasks just listed (which we shall call A1 to A5) will need to be carried out.

Different sets of tasks will be needed to achieve the other milestones. By focusing the project team on the desired results, the WBS sets out the entire work programme for the project in advance. As it is also a powerful visual device, the WBS can be used to communicate with the members of the project team, its sponsors and the rest of the organization.

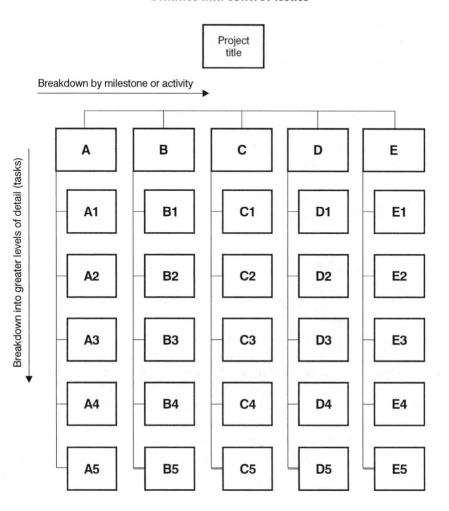

Figure 10.3 An example of a work breakdown structure

The WBS is the basis, too, for what is sometimes referred to as 'responsibility charting'. This identifies 'who' in the project team is responsible for 'what'. In practice, it means that everyone in the project will assume responsibility for the achievement of different milestones. The project manager will coordinate the efforts of the individuals who are responsible for achieving specific tasks in support of specific milestones. As soon as the WBS has been finalized, the project budget can be prepared according to the guidelines mentioned earlier in this chapter.

Although all the milestones and tasks relevant to the project will now have been identified, one remaining issue needs to be resolved – the sequence in which the tasks are completed. This is a matter of, first, agreeing the most appropriate sequence for the milestones. It will not be possible, for example, to achieve the milestone of EL's fee arrangements with the client until the milestone of employment contracts for the client's staff have been finalized.

Once the sequencing of milestones has been agreed, the ordering of the individual tasks can be resolved. The most common way of doing this is to use a bar or a Gantt chart. It shows the project drawn to a horizontal timescale with all the tasks entered and their start and end dates given. An important concept to consider when filling in such a chart is elapsed time. This is the length of time that it will take to complete a task after allowing for other priorities and interruptions. For example, it might only take a morning to prepare the formal fee letter to the client. However, if the executive responsible for writing it is away from the office for a fortnight, the elapsed time might be 11–12 working days.

Therefore, it is the elapsed time that needs to be built into the schedule.

The Gantt chart gives a comprehensive summary of project tasks and their elapsed times. However, it does not indicate what tasks are dependent on others. A budget for staff salaries in the client's IT department cannot be completed before decisions are made about the number of staff who will be transferred from the client to EL. The sequence of tasks that, if not achieved, will affect the end date of the project is called the 'critical path'. For example, a delay in agreeing EL's fees for the IT outsourcing project will lead to a delay in the project's start date.

Implementing

The third project management step is implementing the project. It is the project manager's role, supported in this by their team, to coordinate the project's activities based on the WBS, the responsibility chart and the projects budget. In short, the EL project manager is responsible for the overall organization of the project, and in particular:

- preparing the WBS so that it can be agreed with the other members of the project team to enable individual responsibilities to be assigned
- preparing the time schedules and the project's budget
- resolving conflicts and disagreements

- managing the project to meet the standards specified by the client (this may be in the form of a 'service level' agreement negotiated between the project manager and the client)
- reporting progress on the project to the client.

Controlling

The fourth and last step is controlling the project. Three aspects of control are involved. First, the monitoring of progress against the agreed project objectives. Second, taking corrective action to help ensure that the project remains on track. Third, providing feedback to individual team members about their contribution and performance. These matters relate to issues of quality and especially the reaction of the client and the extent to which they consider that the project's objectives have been achieved.

Summary

Management consultancy is a worldwide business that generates revenues of about £15 billion a year. With the exception of the strategy specialists such as McKinsey & Co, the industry is strongly influenced by the consultancy arms of the major accountancy and audit practices, such as Coopers & Lybrand.

The economics of consultancy businesses are dictated by the fact that individual firms have high fixed costs (with salaries forming the largest single item of expenditure). As a consequence, performance is highly dependent on utilization rates. Thus, even small changes will have a more than proportionate effect on the bottom line.

Revenue or fee income is derived from the number of chargeable days actually worked during the year and the daily or hourly charge-out rate that has been agreed with the client. For senior consultants in Europe, the average daily rate is in the order of £700, with the larger firms charging rather more. Consultancy practices seek to achieve an overall utilization of between 50 and 60 per cent, although the figure varies according to the seniority of the staff. Partners will be 'applied' for less than 50 per cent of the available time. Junior consultants, however, are expected to be chargeable for about two-thirds of their total working days.

Leverage is an important determinant of a firm's success. It is the ratio between the number of partners (or directors) and the number of other consultancy staff. The lower the ratio – the lower the number of partners for each staff member – the greater the profit per partner. This is the consultancy equivalent of return on equity.

On individual assignments, the staffing mix needs to be monitored carefully to ensure that the more senior consultants do not spend a disproportionate amount of time on chargeable work. If they do, it will depress profit margins and the recovery rate (the extent to which fees exceed the costs of an individual assignment), unless additional fees can be negotiated with the client. Apart from the leverage ratio and the profit margin, profit per partner is dependent on staff productivity, which is defined as the revenue generated by each consultant.

Critical mass is crucial: if firms do not have adequate resources, especially staff, to meet the volume of client work, then problems will arise. Very high levels of utilization will be required (perhaps up to 70 per cent) just to achieve modest levels of profitability. The higher levels of utilization are more difficult to achieve, which also increases the risk factor. One way to solve this problem is to use external associates on an 'as and when required' basis. They are then a variable rather than a fixed cost.

Planning and control are achieved by effective budgeting. A budget is a numerical statement of the results a business commits itself to achieve over a defined period, such as a year. It normally remains unchanged as it is increasingly regarded as a performance contract. It enables a consultancy to plan its future, control its activities and improve its performance.

Planning facilitates the comparison of options before final decisions are made. Control involves a review of actual results against the budgeted ones so that differences or variances can be highlighted as a basis for taking corrective action to restore the business to its budgeted path. Regular forecasting should also be standard practice to ensure that there are no surprises. Improvement of performance is essential to sustain competitiveness. It can be achieved by a focus on key performance indicators, such as utilization rates, fee levels and profit per partner.

The preparation of a budget requires a systematic approach, including the use of a financial model. The model will be based on assumptions, which need to be explicit. It will permit a thorough sensitivity analysis to be carried out so that answers to 'What if?'-type questions can be given.

In view of the increasing complexity of assignments and more and more demanding client expectations, effective project management is essential. Four steps are involved:

- planning
- organizing
- implementing
- controlling.

They all require dedicated attention to results – what must be achieved if the project is to be successful. The principal techniques that can be used for effective project management include milestone planning and the preparation of a work breakdown structure. Both are powerful communication devices for all members of the project team.

References

Andersen, E S, Grude, K V, Haug, T and Turner, J R (1995) *Goal Directed Project Management* (2nd edn) Kogan Page, London

Kubr, M (1996) *Management Consulting: A guide to the profession* (3rd edn, revised), International Labour Office, Geneva

Lambert, T (1997) *High-income Consulting*, Nicholas Brealey, London

Maister, D H (1993) *Managing the Professional Service Firm,* The Free Press, New York

Maister, D H (1997) *True Professionalism,* The Free Press, New York

Management Consultant International, June 1996, March 1997 and June/July 1997

The Memory Jogger (1994), GOAL/QPC, Methuen, Mass.

Wooldridge, A (1997) 'A survey of management consultancy', *The Economist,* 22 March

11

Managing human resources

David Hussey

Introduction

The aim of this chapter is to explore some of the human resource issues of a management consultancy. Although some matters are shared by all organizations, there is much that is different for knowledge-based businesses such as management consultancy. Such differences are also found in other professional service firms – consulting engineers, accountancy firms and solicitors, for example. They arise, in part, from the nature of the business itself and from the characteristics of the people who are employed in those businesses.

In management consultancy, the product delivered to the client cannot be separated from the people who deliver it. Because each client situation is different, the solution provided by the consultant will depend as much on the skills, creativity and energy of the consultant as it does on the business concept of the consultancy.

Normann (1991) provides one perspective on this with his five-component model of service management. He sees the components as being the:

- market segment
- service concept
- delivery system
- image.

Central to these four are the culture and philosophy of the firm.

The service concept 'constitutes the benefits offered to the client'. The delivery system is inseparable from the people who deliver the product, and is therefore bound up with what Normann, defines as the management of human energy, in which he distinguishes two elements. He calls the process of recruiting the 'right' people the company's 'personnel idea'. He defines this as being: '. . . the degree and type of business fit between the particular life situation and life needs of a particular group of people, and the setting or context that the company can provide for that group while pursuing its own business needs.' The second element is the human resource management approaches, such as training and career development, which make better use of the human potential within the organization.

Sveiby (1992) describes a knowledge-intensive organization as one in which the majority of employees are highly educated, and the 'product' is not standardized and involves a high degree of problem-solving skills and information manipulation: 'The four main distinguishing features of the production are: non-standardization, creativity, high dependence on individuals, and complex problem solving.'

There are logical human resource consequences that result from the nature of the business. Often, it is not only the service to the client that is dependent on the individual employee, but the whole client relationship. Management consultancies can be very vulnerable to the flight of clients on the departure of 'their' consultant from the firm. Sometimes this involves following the individual into his or her next employment: sometimes it means ceasing to use the consultancy as it is no longer seen as relevant to the client. Both can have serious implications for the firm. Some of the strategies to combat this are outside the human resource arena, but a number are directly related to the human resource strategies and resultant policies of the consultancy, and are matters of concern in this chapter.

There are issues that arise from the twin hierarchies of the project and the firm, where the expert knowledge exercised by the excellent consultant becomes a source of power that can cause conflict. What is good about the offering to the client may cause tensions that are damaging to the firm as a whole. In many firms, the value of employees who provide services that *support* the sales and fee-earning activity is underrated, and there may be a tendency to treat the non-fee earners as second-class citizens.

By the very nature of the job, management consultants are used to a high degree of independence, and may be widely dispersed. Much of the work is undertaken on the premises of clients, working to tight deadlines and so people may be dispersed, and not just in their home country, but across the world. The pattern of dispersion is constantly changing. This brings problems for those who have to manage a consultancy, and has personal implications for the consultant. The situation may be compounded by the fact that consultancy teams may include associates who are not employees or may be put together as joint projects with other firms or may even include members of the client's organization. It is a complicated kaleidoscope of shifting patterns, all of which have an impact on human resource management.

The balance of knowledge

Sveiby (1992) provides one way of looking at the personnel categories that make up a consultancy or other knowledge firm. Figure 11.1 shows two types of know-how. On the vertical axis he shows professional know-how, which is what most of us think of when we visualize a management consultant. This is the core of the consultancy, in that it is the basis of the service concept and the generator of revenue and sales. On the horizontal axis he shows managerial know-how, which,

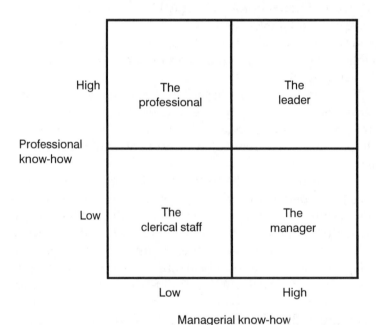

Figure 11.1 Sveiby's personnel categories (K E Sveiby (1992) 'The Know-how Company: Strategy formulation in knowledge-intensive industries', in D E Hussey (ed) *International Review of Strategic Management* (Vol 3, Wiley, Chichester, used with kind permission))

put simply, is the act of management, strategic leadership and administration.

The majority of employees in a management consultancy are what he terms professionals, for whom professional know-how is very high, but managerial know-how is low. Typically, the professional will have a greater level of expertise than their clients in a specific area of skill or knowledge, and will have a high level of education. Professionals have a great dedication to what they are doing. Some, at least in many firms, will have a worldwide reputation and will be seen by outsiders as a focus for expertise. No consultancy can operate without people of this type.

Most consultancies have some employees in the low/low box of Sveiby's matrix. These are the clerical and support staff, who perform an important and recognized function, much of it in support of the professional employees.

The bottom right-hand box is called 'the manager', with high managerial know-how, but no better than average professional skills. They are few in numbers in consultancies, although most clients have a high concentration of them. These are the people who fulfil the roles in the consultancy of accountant, human resource manager and administrator. There is often a clash between these people and the professionals, who, in many organizations, see them as non-contributors.

The final personnel category is 'the leader', who possesses both types of know-how and is thus able to relate to professionals and clients in a productive way, while possessing the managerial attributes that enable the whole firm to develop and grow.

Sveiby argues that there are too few people in know-how companies who fall into the leader category. Often, the people appointed to lead such companies are drawn from the 'professional' category, where perhaps the person with the highest fee-earning capability and the strongest client relationships, and the most respect from the peer group, is seen to be the logical choice. In fact, this can be disastrous for the long-term success of the firm, and strategy becomes the things people want to do, rather than the things they should do.

Readers may be surprised at the suggestion that management consultancies have a preponderance of people in the professional category who may be deficient in management know-how. The reason for this is specialization. In order to be highly competent in one field, such as strategic analysis, information systems, marketing, the legal aspects of human resource management – the list is endless – breadth is often sacrificed for depth. Being a superb strategist is not enough to make a person a superb managing director, as an expert at creating great marketing solutions does not automatically possess the ability to run a marketing department on a continuous basis. And if you doubt the truth of this diagnosis, look inside a few consultancies. Rarely could those with vast human resource management practices use their own organizations as examples of best practice. In only a few firms are the management information and accounting systems as good as those that clients are encouraged to follow, and superb marketing capability does not feed back to the firm itself. When an acquisition is made by a consultancy, rarely is it handled in the way that clients are advised to deal with their acquisitions. All this is avoidable, provided the right attention is given to the human resources of the firm.

One human resource challenge for management consultancies is that of ensuring there is an appropriate balance – with weightings related to the long-term strategy of the firm – between all four of the personnel categories. There is normally a good career for the person who has little interest beyond their own professional specialization, and there may be a better one for someone who has also developed more breadth. Unfortunately, personal ambition is not always related to capability.

The qualities required in a successful consultant will be discussed later, but there is another matter that should be examined first – the idea that human resource management in consultancy firms should be driven by the needs of the business.

Strategic human resource management

Sveiby (1992) states '. . . a know-how company must have a very close link between its business idea and its personnel idea, otherwise it cannot function'. Hussey (1996) defines the strategic approach:

> Business-driven means being proactive as well as reactive and playing a role in setting the strategy of the organization. It means using the strategy as the driving force for all HR policies and plans, and ensuring that this thinking becomes a philosophy that stretches to the lowest level of decisions and actions in the HR department. It means ensuring that the human factor is considered by the chief executive and other managers in all-important decisions. Above all it means that HRM must add value to the organization.

Similar sentiments will be found in Cooke (1992) and Armstrong and Long (1994).

Figure 11.2 gives a generalized framework for thinking about human resource matters in the circumstances of the specific organization. This framework is valid for all types of business and, in an expanded form (see Hussey, 1996), can be applied to each area of human resource man-

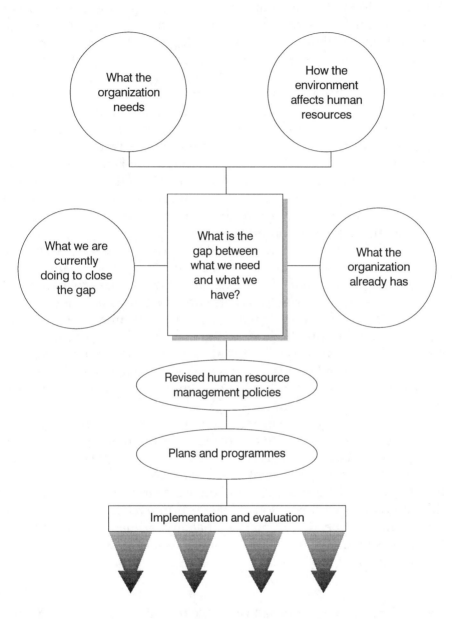

Figure 11.2 A framework for planning human resource management
D E Hussey (1996) *Business-driven Human Resource Management*,
John Wiley, Chichester. Used with kind permission.

agement activity. The main driver is what the organization needs as a result of its business ambitions, values, long-term strategy, service concept and expectations for growth or decline. These needs may be affected by events in the business environment that impact on human resource management, such as employment legislation and shifts in the patterns of supply and demand in the labour market.

From the discussion so far, it is clear that organizational needs will vary from one consultancy firm to another, not only in the areas of expertise that have to be available to enable the firm to deliver the planned services to its selected segment of the market, but also in relation to managing people in a way that establishes the culture that the firm believes to be important. The 'personnel idea' is one of the ways in which a consultancy may try to differentiate itself, and some further exploration of this can be found later in this chapter.

Unless the firm is newly established, it will already have people, systems and procedures that may or may not meet the organization's needs. Thus, as shown in Figure 11.2, next it is necessary to audit what the current state of play is, assess the gap between what is needed and what exists and review any ongoing initiatives that may be intended to close that gap. In turn, this leads to human resource management policies and strategies, detailed plans and programmes and a process of implementation and evaluation. It is evaluation that enables the firm to confirm that the effort and money expended on human resources is delivering value to the firm.

Failure to manage human resources in a business-driven way can bring a serious disadvantage to any business, but this is particularly so for a professional services organization where its people are so critical. Revenue stops instantly if clients feel that the consultants cannot deliver the promises of the consultancy, and there is no inventory of products in the warehouse that can be sold while the firm puts things right. In fact, time is the most perishable product that any business can sell, a factor that drives many of the attitudes, decisions and procedures of every consulting firm.

What does strategic human resource management really mean?

Before looking at what the strategic approach to human resource management means to those things, such as recruitment and termination, we normally associate with the human resource department, we should give some thought to the qualities required in a consultant. The view taken is that a consultant needs to be a mature person who has the skills and expertise to handle an assignment, and all these qualities would not be present in a new entrant to the profession, someone straight from university. Thus, we can start from the premise that the consultant must have expertise in something that is relevant to the firm and the client. All the personal qualities in the world are of no value to a client unless they are coupled with know-how that is appropriate to the problem or issue the firm is engaged to solve. As we have seen there is merit in the consultant having a breadth of managerial know-how for the long-term benefit of the firm. In many cases, this can also make the consultant of more value to the client, in that it enables the consultant to put their expertise into a wider context. However, all the expertise and breadth of knowledge in the world is not enough to ensure that the person is an effective consultant, so what else is needed?

Kubr (1996) gives one view of the intellectual abilities and personal qualities required in a consultant, which is as follows:

- Intellectual ability:
  - ability to learn quickly and easily
  - ability to observe, gather, select and evaluate facts
  - good judgement
  - inductive and deductive reasoning
  - ability to synthesize and generalize
  - creative imagination, original thinking.
- Ability to understand people and work with them:
  - respect for other people, tolerance
  - ability to anticipate and evaluate human reactions
  - has easy human contacts
  - ability to gain trust and respect
  - courtesy and good manners.
- Ability to communicate, persuade and motivate:
  - ability to listen
  - facility in oral and written communication
  - ability to teach and train people
  - ability to persuade and motivate.
- Intellectual and emotional maturity:
  - stability of behaviour and action
  - independence in drawing unbiased conclusions
  - ability to withstand pressures, and live with frustrations and uncertainties
  - ability to act with poise and in a calm and objective manner

- self-control in all situations
- flexibility and adaptability to changed conditions.
- Personal drive and initiative:
    - right degree of self-confidence
    - healthy ambition
    - entrepreneurial spirit
    - courage, initiative and perseverance in action.
- Ethics and integrity:
    - genuine desire to help others
    - extreme honesty
    - ability to recognize the limitation of one's competence
    - ability to admit mistakes and learn from failure.
- Physical and mental health:
    - ability to sustain the specific working and living conditions of management consultants.

A list such as this always presents some problems. First, it is a generalized view, and every firm will have some requirements that are not included in the list. There are differences, for example, between what is needed to coach a chief executive and that required when working at middle management level. Second, not all the qualities are required for every type of consultant. An example is the ability to teach and train people (under the third point), which would not be relevant for a due diligence assessment. The skills needed to design and deliver a complicated management training programme are not in the portfolio of most management consultants, but then neither are they needed for the work they actually perform.

Third, one can be critical of one or two of the statements. What is really meant by 'healthy ambition'? Perhaps 'relevant ambition' might be more appropriate, as with this phrasing there is room for specialists whose aim is to be the best in their own field, without seeking to run the organization. 'Extreme honesty' also leaves me puzzled as I always thought a person was either honest or dishonest. Apart from the obvious criteria of not fiddling the expense claims or stealing the client's property, there is another dimension that may be better termed 'openness and truthfulness in client relations'.

Subject to these reservations, the list is helpful, as is the whole chapter of the book in which it appears.

Figure 11.3 is an adaptation of one that appears in Hussey (1996) and helps to relate the concept of strategic human resource management to specific areas of policy and action in this area. The central circle

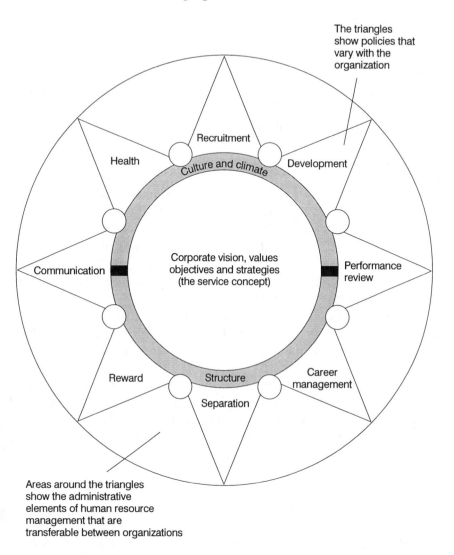

Figure 11.3 The relationship between human resource management and corporate strategy (D E Hussey (1996) *Business-driven Human Resource
Management*, John Wiley, Chichester, used with kind permission)

represents the corporate vision, values, objectives, and strategies, which
we could summarize as the service concept and delivery system
(Normann, 1991). This is ringed by the culture and climate (again with
echoes of Normann), and the structure of the organization. Neither of
these are entirely human resource management matters, but what is

done regarding this subject in the outer circle of activities will reinforce or change what happens in the two inner circles.

The outer circle carries a more subtle message. The triangles represent human resource activities, which will be discussed later in this chapter. The diagram is not meant to give a definitive list of every human resource matter and can be added to if needs be. The policies and strategies within the triangles will not be the same for all firms, and will vary with the requirements of the two inner circles. The areas around the triangles represent the many administrative tasks and procedures that could be similar in all firms, because they represent good human resource practice (these are not discussed here). The little circles between the triangles are symbolic of the fact that every element in the diagram has a two-way relationship with every other element. For example, a change in the performance management process will have an impact on the culture and climate by virtue of the behavioural changes it will trigger as it may affect how people are developed and could force a change to the reward system.

This way of thinking is appropriate whether or not the firm has an internal human resource function. Indeed, it is important for all firms. And in all firms, regardless of size, management should be in partnership with any human resource function to ensure that the right things happen. Many elements of the human resource process will not work without this partnership (for example, performance management) and, in any case, the whole subject of strategy in the area of human resource management is so important for the success of the firm that top management should retain an involvement in what is decided.

Structure and culture

A consultancy firm may be a partnership, a limited liability company or an unlimited proprietorship. Partners are not employees, but they are arguably the most critical human resource of the firm. The same level of people in a limited company are employees. The term 'human resources' is used to cover both groups of people, unless there are particular reasons to make a distinction. However, the form and distribution of ownership has an impact on the culture and the way the firm conducts its internal affairs.

In the second ring in Figure 11.3 is structure, which should be related to the service concept, delivery system and long-term strategy of the firm. In most consultancies, there are two structures:

- the one that provides the framework for business and personal development and day-to-day management
- the other is permanently changing and is related to the management of the assignment.

For much of their time, a consultant may be working directly for an assignment manager (terms for this role vary from firm to firm), and when an assignment is completed, that person may be switched to a different manager for the next project. Indeed, some consultants who are working on overlapping or parallel assignments may find themselves coming under more than one assignment manager during the same time period. In some consultancies, level in the formal structure may be forgotten and so a person may work on an assignment under someone who is their junior for the period of involvement in the project.

Typically, the formal structure involves grouping people into practice areas, which are often also profit centres. However, the product offered to a client may involve several practice areas, and the behaviour of those involved and the culture that allows this cooperation is strongly affected by non-human resource systems, such as internal transfer prices, and the way the score card of a profit centre is calculated (see Chapter 10). Practice areas may be chosen on the basis of a discipline (such as strategy, marketing or human resources), an industry (such as automotive, construction) or a type of situation (such as due diligence or privatization). There may be a form of matrix management that covers all of these headings. In some firms, a group of practices may be clustered into a business area, for example.

The structure may also be affected by the service concept. Some firms have a high element of proprietary intellectual material in what they offer (an example may be methods of psychological assessment). The structure of such firms is likely to include functions to research, develop and maintain this material, something that would not be needed in a firm with no such proprietary methods.

Another aspect of structure is the number of levels. Kubr (1996) takes a traditional large firm as his model and suggests a five-level structure:

1 junior consultants – used for recruitment direct from university
2 operating consultants, who do most of the consulting work
3 supervising consultants – manage assignments and provide experienced consulting help when needed
4 junior partners – marketing, maintain client relationships, oversee assignments and management responsibilities
5 senior partners – management of the firm.

It is perhaps symbolic of partnership culture rather than business need that Kubr includes the president or managing director within the senior level, and does not see this as a separate level.

This sort of structure may fit certain types of consultancies, particularly those that are heavily task consultancy oriented and, give or take a level or two, there are many firms that fit this pattern. There are also many that do not. There are consultancies that, because of the level of the organization at which they work or because of the type of activity (process consulting or knowledge transfer methods), have a bias to more senior people and most consulting work is done at the higher levels. There are some organizations that are completely flat, where the partners do all the work, because of the level at which they operate.

Structure is closely related to the firm's ideas about personnel.

Culture and climate are partly caused by how the top people in the consultancy manage the business, and partly by the structure and internal systems of the firm. The intended culture and the actual culture are not always the same because the way the whole organization behaves and the attitudes they display are affected by actions rather than words. The human resource actions in the outer ring of Figure 11.3 may drive the culture in the intended way or turn top management utterances into empty phrases. There is a tangible feel to the culture in different consulting firms, that, on the surface, appear to have similar businesses and structures.

The service concept will affect culture as a result of the way the firm has to operate to provide the desired service, and the types of people needed to deliver it. However, it is also possible for the service concept to be frustrated by an inappropriate culture. Culture change is beyond the scope of this chapter, but further information can be found in a number of books, of which Bate (1994), Sadler (1995) and Carnall (1997) are examples.

Policies and strategies

Recruitment

The 'personnel idea' is seen very clearly in the recruitment policy of the firm. Although some consultancy firms recruit graduates with a degree direct from university, with the idea of moving them from Kubr's level 1 to level 2 after an intensive period of induction and training, others make a higher degree a basic requirement, with a preference for either the MBA or a specialization, such as psychology, which relates directly to the skill areas they need.

Another firm might prefer more experienced people who have management experience as well as good functional expertise, and would normally recruit into Kubr's level 3. With this strategy, the people taken on at this level might be somewhat older than those in what appears to be an equivalent level in other companies.

Most firms are unlikely ever to recruit into the higher two levels, but, again, this is a rule that is broken when the growth of the firm or expansion into new areas brings more needs than can be met from within the organization.

It is likely that the new MSc in management consultancy, from the Management Consultancy Business School will increasingly be seen as the most appropriate qualification for a consultant, at whatever level.

Because consultancies may be very different in their service concept and delivery system, it cannot always be assumed that someone with consultancy experience elsewhere will fit the requirements of another firm. The skills needed to work with top management in a knowledge transfer form of consulting with an emphasis on implementation are very different to the traditional task consulting, and someone with deep experience of one may be inappropriate for the other.

The recruitment selection process is important for any firm as people who do not fit the 'personnel idea' can cause damage to the firm, and may have to leave the organization before any return has been gained from the recruitment and training costs. Personality tests and assessment centres are used by some firms to improve the fit of the person with their role.

Not all human resource needs are filled by employment. Many firms have stringers, or associates, who work as needed, either to provide a specialism that the firm needs only rarely or to meet peaks in workload. Flexibility of human resources can contribute to economic success, provided care is taken regarding quality and associates maintain the values and principles of the firm.

It is possible to operate a consultancy that is a virtual company and has no employees. The largest I know of is headquartered in Switzerland and has about 25 senior people, most of whom have worked together in the past, who are domiciled in several different countries. All are former full-time business school professors, and they work at senior level. None is an employee.

Development

Getting the right type of people is only the first human resource issue. To release their full potential, people must be helped to develop. This is important for all levels, and essential for those firms recruiting new graduates who have intelligence and potential, but who initially possess neither a relevant specialism nor have any consulting skills. The development strategy should, as with other aspects of the human resource mix, be related to the organizational needs. Guidance on how to do this may be found in Nilsson (1987), Hussey (1988 and 1996) and Bolt (1989).

Although development will include formal training programmes (the coverage of which may include functional skills, the values and procedures of the firm, consulting skills and interpersonal skills needed for the internal running of the firm, such as team building), internal courses are only part of what is available. Internal projects, coaching and on-the-job training are valuable methods for trying to meet the needs of a particular firm. Sponsorship for higher degrees and professional qualifications may be used to develop breadth or take a specialism to a more advanced level of capability. In addition, the culture of the organization can motivate people to continually work on their own personal development and improvement.

One dilemma facing all firms is how to improve the specialist skills of a senior consultant, who may already be world class. Some responsibility for keeping up to date falls on the individual and is part of their own professional approach. The firm may develop strategies to aid this process. It may encourage writing and research or set up internal forums to develop new ideas. McKinsey is very good at this (Coyne and Subramaniam, 1997, give one example involving 60 people, while another led to the classic *In Search of Excellence* by Tom Peters and Robert Waterman, 1982). The outcomes of such efforts do more than just continue the development process; they may lead to new products, enhance the image of the firm and be instrumental in making key people want to remain with the firm.

More than any other organizations, consultancies are well positioned to become learning companies, and to apply the principles of continuous improvement. Mayo and Lank (1994) give this definition: 'A learning organization harnesses the full brainpower, knowledge and experience available to it, in order to evolve continually for the benefit of all its stakeholders'. All organizations learn by accident, but only the learning organization learns by a deliberate business process.

The many situations those in the consultancy are exposed to offer opportunities to see issues from many different perspectives. However, a learning organization is as much a matter of culture as intention, and the processes and climate in many firms prevent this great potential asset from being exploited to the full.

Performance management

Basic processes of performance measurement are no different to those in general use. The criteria against which people are judged should be related very carefully to what the firm wants to achieve, so that the message is driven into behaviour. Conflicts can arise, when the short-term economic imperative is allowed to override longer-term issues. What can become dominant in looking at performance is the fees or sales attributed to the person, while other aspects of required behaviour are treated as being unimportant.

The economics of the business give an emphasis to maximizing the time that is paid for by clients, the ability to manage fixed-price assignments within the budgeted time and mix grades of labour, and, for more senior people, to press for the securing of an appropriate volume and profitability of assignments and the eventual conversion of these to sales and cash inflow.

The way these performance criteria are set and measured can cause dysfunctional behaviour. For example, although the chances of gaining business may be better if a team approach is used, performance expectations based on personal success may cause an individual to shut out colleagues. This can reduce the bid success rate and, worse still, see the rise in fortune of the selfish person, compared to the one who may act as a catalyst in bringing more work to the business, but who involves other people and appears on the score sheet to be less successful. The second person may, in fact, be doing more for the success of the business than the first, but may not be perceived in this way.

The review process should also allow for the fact that a consultant will work under many different people during the course of a review period. Therefore, a performance review by the manager in the formal structure that does not include information from the assignment managers may be deficient.

Career management

Career management is one of the weapons a consultancy can use to increase the retention rate of its employees. Most firms establish clear criteria for the promotion of staff to the next grade and, in most firms, progression is based on merit, which is another reason for ensuring that the performance management system enables the right judgements to be made.

Many firms have formal procedures for considering promotion, and the move to junior partnership (or equivalent in a limited company) may involve the use of assessment centres and a selection panel. Many employees see this as a key career point and may leave the firm if they do not receive promotion at the time they expect it, which can mean that good people are lost. In many partnerships, there is a wide divide between those who have made it and those who have not and this can make good people feel a failure.

In fact, a consultancy offers more flexibility for promotion than many other businesses, as long as the numbers of people at each level can produce an appropriate economic return. This is dependent partly on the capacity of the market and partly on the skills of the individuals to gain and fulfil business in that market.

Although there is a correlation between seniority and internal management roles, it is also possible to have a two-stream concept, which means that people of high professional competence and standing can move to the higher levels without having to take on internal management tasks. Their role might be to earn very high levels of fees and develop intellectual concepts rather than manage the business. This option is closely related to the strategies of the business.

Many consultancies have fewer levels than Kubr's five-level model quoted earlier, which means that career management expectations are different. For example, the broader development of the person can be the most important aspect of career development. Salary expectations can be met by broad banding salary scales.

Separation

Separation may occur as a result of failure to perform, retirement, redundancy or resignation, and a consultancy will need policies for all these eventualities. There are also policy decisions to be made that are directly related to the business. Should the firm have an 'up or out' policy, which means that people are expected to leave if they are not offered a promotion at the appropriate time. The argument is that only the top-quality people remain with the firm, and there are no smouldering fires of resentment from people who have been passed over (there are, of course, employment law issues to consider with such a policy). However, another firm that has a flatter structure and employs more senior people, may find that stability and continuity are the most important criteria in terms of achieving its business aims and that lack of promotion should not be a bar to continued employment.

Amicable separation is important to a consultancy for other commercial reasons. Former employees often move out of the industry and many become buyers of consultancy services themselves. They also talk of the firm with love or hatred, contributing to its image in the marketplace. The separation strategy should therefore consider ways of assisting those the company wishes to leave, other than on grounds of appalling performance or dishonesty, to move into a new career.

Reward and remuneration

The reward strategy has to do at least three jobs for the firm:

- it has to enable the firm to attract the people it needs in the right quality and numbers
- it has to be robust enough to retain the people the firm wants to keep
- it has to stimulate the sort of behaviour the firm wants to encourage.

Attractiveness is related to the reward levels of like-for-like consulting firms, and what is paid by other organizations for particular specializations at a similar level. The MCA publishes an annual salary survey of its members. This is useful, but does not take into account the differences in employment policy already discussed, which affect the age and experience of people who, on the surface, are at the same level. Also, the survey does not cover all aspects of reward policy, so, although the survey is helpful in many ways, it is often more useful for a firm to do its own survey of firms that are similar in nature.

The reward and remuneration policy should cover salary levels, fringe benefits, bonuses, profit sharing and opportunities to share in ownership. It also requires setting the basis on which salaries are regularly reviewed. In many firms increases are entirely on merit.

Communication

It is impossible to become a learning organization without communication. The content, style and frequency of communication can do much to develop a shared culture, and manage the expectations of all human resources. Intelligent people also like to be trusted with confidential information about the progress of the firm, and to feel a part of its successes and failures. Divisions between partners and others can be enlarged if only the partners are fully aware of what is happening.

Health

Management consultancy can be very demanding of its human resources, and there are pressures that drive people to spend more and more of their personal evening and weekend time working for the firm, either to catch up on the routine tasks, meet a deadline or, more frequently, put uncharged time into a project because the budget was wrongly set in the first place. There is the pressure of continually changing relationships – with colleagues, clients and associates – the feeling of confusion that has to be overcome at the start of each assignment and the ambiguity of many situations throughout an assignment. There may be long absences away from home (and from the political centre of the firm). Add to this a fear that there may be no next assignment for the consultant to work on, which means utilization percentages may fall and bring with them the fear of consultants losing their jobs, and you have a recipe for stress and illness. It should be remembered that one major source of stress is conflict between work and home, and that a person who is spending too much time working probably has the balance wrong and will be caused stress because spouse and children are neglected.

Perhaps this is what a firm wants, according to the philosophy that if it is too hot, get out of the kitchen. Longer-term thinking would suggest that it may be more appropriate to give people help in dealing with stress, look on someone who is always working weekends and evenings as displaying weakness rather than strength and establish a caring attitude to people.

In the case of Walker versus Northumberland County Council, a successful claim was established against an employer for work-related stress. Damages were estimated at £200,000, plus costs, pending the outcome of the appeal. In fact, it did not reach the appeal stage and was settled out of court for £175,000 (see Page, 1996, who reported that some 500 other cases were in the pipeline awaiting settlement).

Like it or not, stress-related illness is an issue for employers, and a human resource strategy should include measures to prevent it.

References

Armstrong, M and Long, P (1994) *The Reality of Strategic HRM*, Institute of Personnel and Development, London

Bate, P (1994) *Strategies for Cultural Change*, Butterworth-Heinemann, Oxford

Bolt, J E (1989) *Executive Development: A strategy for corporate competitiveness*, Harper Business, New York

Carnall, C A (ed) (1997) *Strategic Change,* Butterworth-Heinemann, Oxford

Cooke, R (1992) 'Human resource strategies for business success', in M Armstrong (ed), *Strategies for Human Resource Management: A total business approach*, Kogan Page, London

Coyne, K P and Subramaniam, S (1997) 'Bringing discipline to strategy', *McKinsey Quarterly 1996*, 4

Hussey, D E (1988) *Management Training and Corporate Strategy*, Pergamon Press, Oxford

Hussey, D E (1996) *Business-driven Human Resource Management*, John Wiley, Chichester

Kubr, M (1996) *Management Consulting: A guide to the profession* (3rd edn, revised) International Labour Office, Geneva

Mayo, A and Lank E (1994) *The Power of Learning: A guide to gaining competitive advantage*, Institute of Personnel and Development, London

Nilsson, W P (1987) *Achieving Strategic Goals Through Executive Development*, Addison-Wesley, Reading, Mass.

Normann, R (1991) *Service Management* (2nd edn), John Wiley, Chichester

Page, T (1996) 'Work-related stress', *Croner HRM Professionals Briefing*, 18, 4 June

Peters, T J and Waterman R H (1982) *In Search of Excellence*, Harper & Row, New York

Sadler, P (ed) (1995) *Strategic Change*, Pergamon Press, Oxford

Sveiby, K E (1992) 'The know-how company: Strategy formulation in knowledge-intensive industries', in D E Hussey (ed), *International Review of Strategic Management*, (vol 3), John Wiley, Chichester

Part 4

Change management

12

Managing organizational change

Philip Sadler

Introduction

In recent years, companies have increasingly sought the help of consultants when preparing for and implementing organizational change. This chapter outlines the main issues consultants need to be aware of when they are involved in organizational change programmes.

Incremental and transformational change

There are broadly two types of organizational change. The first kind can be described as *incremental* change. The second kind of organizational change has been described as *organizational transformation,* or *radical change.*

Incremental change

Incremental change becomes necessary from time to time in all organizations if they are to adapt to changing circumstances. It can be occasioned simply by growth, by diversification involving new products and new markets, by the introduction of new technology, by the need to respond to new sources of competition or to grasp new business opportunities afforded by deregulation. It may simply be the result of a feeling that it is time to shuffle the pack.

Incremental change can involve a wide range of decisions and actions - redefining people's roles, creating new ones, regrouping activities, changing reporting relationships, introducing new systems and procedures, modifying or abandoning existing ones, for example. Ideally, following such changes, things improve – there is, say, higher productivity, improved customer service, growth in market share, successful penetration of new markets and so on. These improvements, however, are often short-lived.

The objective of incremental change is limited: to adapt or modify an existing organization with a given culture so as to make it more effective in achieving its goals, but not alter its fundamental characteristics. For example, if the organization possesses certain characteristics that, taken together, could justify its being described as bureaucratic, the purpose of reorganizing is to make it a more efficient kind of bureaucracy, not to transform it into something quite different.

Transformational change

With transformational or radical change, the purpose is clearly to transform the organization into a radically different form from that which previously existed. Although many of the actions and decisions affecting structure and systems used in implementing incremental change – such as changes in roles, groupings, and relationships – will also be used to implement transformational change, they will tend to be more fundamental and far-reaching in nature. In particular, however, organizational transformation will always involve bringing about changes in values, attitudes and beliefs – the elements of corporate culture. Failure to bring about real and lasting cultural change will doom to failure any attempt to achieve transformational change.

It is this second type of change that will be focused on here and which presents the greater challenge to the external consultant. It is often the case that consultants are brought in by management to assist with incremental change, but, after the initial diagnostic and fact-finding stage, it becomes apparent that more radical actions are needed.

Recognizing the need – triggers for change

The most commonly recognized signal of a need for radical change is an acute crisis, signalled by financial losses, a significant fall in market share or severe quality problems. In the case of the UK's car industry, poor financial performance was compounded by a reputation for poor quality, chronic industrial relations problems and intensifying international competition. Initially, it was believed that improvements in communications, suggestion schemes, recruitment and training would be enough to turn performance around. The error in this thinking was subsequently realized and, in the case of the Rover group, for example, an employee attitude survey conducted in 1986 showed that the whole company's system of procedures, practices and management style need to change. Thus, the Rover Total Quality Improvement Programme was launched in 1987.

It requires great vision and courage to see the need for organizational transformation and to try to bring it about in advance of a serious crisis, financial or otherwise.

In *Making it Happen*, John Harvey-Jones, (1989) account of his successful chairmanship of ICI, he argues that, while it is true that it is very difficult to lead change 'against the grain' of the feelings of the people in a business, it is dangerous to wait until a situation has become sufficiently serious as to build up a powerful head of steam in favour of change. In his view, the art of leadership is to judge the pace of change in people's attitudes and instigate change before everyone is so frustrated and dissatisfied that they are 'boiling for revolution'. The dissatisfactions that provide the leverage for change arise when people realize that their livelihoods are threatened by the superior performance of other nations, other companies or other individuals. Harvey-Jones points out wisely that such dissatisfaction with the status quo can only develop in conditions of openness and the full disclosure of information. People who work for organizations such as ICI, where the account books are open and where every employee knows how well or how badly the company is doing, are much quicker, in his view, to recognize the need for change than people in organizations that keep them in the dark on such matters. It is often a key task for consultants to persuade managers in traditionally managed firms to disclose information that has, hitherto, been regarded as privileged and to be kept confidential

An approach used by many companies to create a climate receptive to the idea of change is to send teams of shop stewards and managers to see the competition for themselves and by visiting plants in Japan, Germany and the United States, truly understand, for perhaps the first time, the strength of the competition facing the company. Harvey-Jones expresses the problem well when he says that the job of leadership is to persuade people that sticking with the status quo is actually more dangerous than launching into the unknown.

The growing recognition of the role of people factors in business performance

One thing above all else has led to the focusing of attention on radical organizational change as the means of achieving world-class standards of competitiveness: this is the growing acceptance of the belief that it is clearly with people that the competitive edge will be found in the case of most industries. We now understand that the really successful businesses of the twenty-first century will be those that can attract, retain and motivate employees to use their full talents in the interests of the firm.

The economic drivers and the formulae for approaching external markets are well understood by the major companies and, consequently, in future diversity in strategy will be more likely to take the form of differences in organization structure and culture, than has been the case in the past.

In the car industry, for example, it has become accepted that, in an industry replete with highly competent fast followers, reliance on product features can provide only a short-term advantage. In the longer term, the competitive position of the company depends on its reputation for superior quality, both in product and service, and on its flexibility and willingness to learn and adapt quickly. These factors are to be achieved by building commitment to delivering extraordinary customer satisfaction and total quality via personal development, line manager leadership and the involvement and recognition of individual employees. Yet, just a decade or so ago, the conventional wisdom in this business was that the route to survival lay primarily in increased automation, product rationalization and taking a tough line with the unions!

This change in priorities, reflected in many other businesses large and small, has resulted in a new, more strategic role for the personnel function – increasingly referred to as human resource management (HRM). The response of the consultancy industry has been to build its competence and expertise in the field of HRM at the expense of the traditional disciplines of production engineering, work measurement and cost accounting.

Typical change objectives

The most common organizational change objective in the UK in recent years has been to achieve radical improvement in standards of quality of product and customer service. Other objectives include:

- achieving a more competitive cost base
- building greater flexibility or capacity for innovation
- adjusting to market pressures subsequent to privatization, or moving to trust status in the National Health Service
- reorganization and the merging of corporate cultures following a major acquisition
- continuous improvement – the creation of a 'learning organization'.

The actual changes that take place can be grouped under the headings of:

- structural changes
- new systems and processes
- cultural changes.

Structural changes

These include:

- flatter structures – removing layers of management
- the creation of highly autonomous, multiskilled work teams
- the introduction of more project-based work groups
- changes in the role of the first line manager or supervisor
- greater delegation – pushing decision-making closer to the shopfloor or the customer interface (often referred to as 'empowering')
- introduction of quality circles
- smaller organizational units
- breaking down functional barriers, creating internal profit centres.

New systems and processes

Among the most common are the following:

- seeking ISO 9000 (BS 5750) accreditation for the achievement of quality standards
- Just-in-Time inventory control
- statistical quality control
- single-status personnel policies and practices
- flexible, performance-related payments systems
- employee share ownership schemes
- regular employee attitude surveys
- continuous monitoring of customer satisfaction and service levels.

Cultural changes

These include the following programmes:

- development statements of mission, vision and values.
- training focused on changing values and attitudes, such as achieving a commitment to total quality
- teambuilding processes
- relaunching corporate identity.

Figure 12.1 illustrates the interdependence of these three aspects of organization. BP uses the analogy of a three-legged stool – if one leg is weak, the whole thing collapses.

Some of the issues involved in changing organizational culture

To change corporate culture involves persuading people to abandon their existing beliefs and values, and the behaviours that stem from them, so as to adopt new ones.

The first practical difficulty that arises is that of identifying the principal characteristics of the existing culture. The process of understanding and gaining insight into the existing culture can be aided by using one of the standard and properly validated inventories or questionnaires that a number of consultants have developed to measure characteristics of corporate culture. These offer the advantage of being able to benchmark the culture against those of other, comparable firms that have used the same instruments. The weakness of this approach is that the information obtained in this way tends to be more superficial, less rich than material from other sources, such as interviews and group discussions, and study of the company's history.

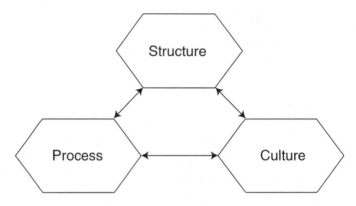

Figure 12.1 The three-legged stool

Managing organizational change

In most organizations that have been in existence for more than one or two decades, a culture will have developed in an unplanned, unconscious way as a consequence of the interactions between a whole series of factors. In the United Kingdom, for example, the culture of organizations will be influenced, *inter alia*, by the following:

- the geographical roots of the corporation – in the City of London, the North of England, the Scottish lowlands, the Welsh valleys and so on
- the sources of recruitment of élites – whether or not the organization has a tradition of graduate entry or, as in the case of the police, there is a tradition of promotion from the ranks or of the top people tending to be recruited from a particular social class or from the services
- the nature of the organization's basic activity – whether or not the work is dangerous or dirty, calls for brain or brawn, women can do it as well as or better than men, it is intellectually demanding or is highly creative
- what the business conditions have been during the organization's formative years – whether there has been fierce competition or cosy monopoly, exposure to market forces or cocooning within the public sector, operating in stable markets or in ones subject to sharp fluctuations in demand and fashion
- what the organization's record of achievement has been in the past – whether or not it can it look back on a great and glorious past, whether it has been growing or contracting.

Many large organizations that came into being in the early years of the twentieth century in Britain grew up in conditions that have left permanent traces in their cultures. These conditions included:

- a particularly rigid social class structure in the community, characterized by a considerable status gap between those who, however skilled, worked principally with their hands (blue collar workers) and those who, even at the low skill level of the clerical worker, worked with their brains (white collar workers)
- a highly protected home market, supplemented by Commonwealth preference, which made it possible to evade intense competition via a combination of cartels at home and/or protection overseas
- a strong tradition of mistrust of professionals and respect for the gifted amateur.
- ascription of low status to a career in industry or in the engineering professions relative to careers in other professions (law, medicine), in higher education, the civil service, the City or the Church

- a social context in which women were expected to concentrate their lives and energies on the home, so occupational roles were almost exclusively confined to being secretaries, nurses, shop assistants, mill girls or assembly workers in light industry
- a world in which consumers were expected to be (and usually were) relatively easily satisfied, to complain about quality or service was regarded as a sign of a bad upbringing and a chronic inability to satisfy potential demand was intensified by acute shortages in two world wars, breeding a 'take it or leave it' attitude.

The cultural features of many organizations that developed during this period included:

- complacency bordering on arrogance – 'We belong to a great and powerful organization with an unbroken record of prosperity and with products that are household names. What could we possibly learn from outside sources?'
- conservatism – 'The methods that have brought us success in the past will stand us in good stead for the future'
- production orientation – 'Marketing is just another word for selling, and salesmen – commercial travellers – are not gentlemen'
- concern for status and seniority – the company car, private reserved parking space, membership of the senior dining room, one's own secretary – these were the greatest prizes to be won
- a secretive, closed climate in which information was seen as a source of power and control, under no circumstances to be widely shared, so that even the most trivial communications passed in sealed envelopes marked 'confidential'
- tolerance of incompetence, particularly on the part of 'loyal' long-serving and senior members of the organization, such that there was little effort made to manage performance or to deal with problems such as alcoholism
- lack of sophistication in human resource management – shop floor workers were still thought of as 'hands' – and if motivation was considered at all, it was assumed that only financial incentives were likely to be effective, personnel policies supported the blue collar/white collar status divide and fluctuations in business conditions were dealt with by laying off workers paid by the hour during periods of slack demand
- the steady growth of routine practices and procedures to cover every eventuality led to a tendency to treat the rules as ends in themselves

rather than as means to an end – the phrase 'It's more than my job's worth' was heard frequently

- women rarely got on in such organizations: 'Their place is in the home.'

It was the development of stagnant bureaucratic cultures closely resembling what has just been described above that contributed to the decline of much of British industry and its loss of international competitiveness during the 1960s and 1970s. These characteristics were particularly strong in the motor vehicle manufacturing sector of industry, the larger textile and clothing manufacturers, shipbuilding and the large, old-established financial services companies.

Today, in the new climate of global competition, set in a more egalitarian society and one in which women increasingly enjoy equality of opportunity, in a world in which the customer is king and in the context of a growing recognition of the vital role of industry in the life of the nation, new, more appropriate cultures are being shaped. The old values are being scrapped, and new ones put in their place.

This is happening in organizations that have carried out an objective and searching appraisal of their existing culture and found it wanting. In most instances where this has occurred, two factors have been present. The first, as mentioned earlier, is a real sense of crisis – a genuine and widespread fear that the organization's future survival can no longer be taken for granted. The second is the arrival on the scene of a visionary or transformational leader – a John Harvey-Jones, Colin Marshall, John Egan, Lee Iacocca (Chrysler) or Jack Welch (GE) – a person with the ability not only to develop a vision of the organization's future, but also to communicate it to others and inspire them with it.

Managing culture change – key success factors

We now have enough examples of success and relative failure to be able to draw some useful lessons. For culture change to be achieved successfully, a number of requirements need to be met.

Vision

The desired future organization needs to be specified in the form of a 'vision'. To be fully effective, the vision must be clear, easily understood, challenging yet realistic and inspiring.

It helps if it can be expressed pithily in a phrase that is easily remembered – for example, 'The world's favourite airline' (BA), 'A 21st century chemical company – today' (ICI), 'Extraordinary customer satisfaction' (Rover Group), 'Quality, service, cleanliness, value' (McDonald's).

It also helps if the vision is developed in such a way that a wide range of people in the organization contribute to it and, thus, develop a sense of ownership of it.

In one small organization, employing some 300 people, it was seen as important to achieve two objectives. First, that the organization's mission should be capable of being expressed concisely in a few words, such that both employees and customers could quickly grasp its essence. Second, that all employees should develop a deeper understanding of the mission and a sense of ownership of it.

It was decided, therefore, to set up a competition in which staff were invited to enter phrases that they felt expressed the core mission. Entries were anonymous and the prize for the winning entry was a flight for two on Concorde. The prize was sufficiently attractive to motivate virtually every employee to participate – and for them to involve their families, too, in many cases. The motivation of all those who submitted entries was reinforced by presenting them with a Concorde model as a gift for their children or other young relations.

Objectivity

The existing culture must be objectively analysed and assessed so as to identify those aspects that need to be changed to arrive at the desired future organization.

In carrying out this diagnostic exercise, surveys of employees' opinions and attitudes can be supplemented by complementary information from surveys of customers and suppliers or the public at large.

It is at this stage that companies really do need the assistance of outside consultants whose fresh insight, objectivity and absence of vested interest in the status quo may be helpful in reaching valid conclusions. Ed Schein, in his account of his own experience as a culture change consultant (Schein, 1992), provides an excellent role model for this type of consultancy. Schein describes how he uncovers what he calls the 'levels of culture', which are as follows.

- **Artefacts** These include all the things one sees, hears and feels when encountering a new group with an unfamiliar culture. Examples are the physical architecture, language in use, technology, products, organization's style as reflected in clothing, manner of address and

252

displays of emotion, published statements of values, rituals and cere-monies. This heading also covers the visible behaviour of the mem-bers of the organization and the organizational processes they have developed. Schein says of the artefacts that they are 'easy to observe and very difficult to decipher'.

- **Espoused values** These are the things that people say they believe in, the assumptions that they are conscious of making. Knowing what they are makes it possible to predict what people will say in a given situation, but not necessarily what they will do. Where there are con-tradictions between the espoused values and actual behaviour, it is necessary to dig deeper and try to understand the basic underlying assumptions.
- **Basic assumptions** These are the beliefs that have come to be so taken for granted that people would regard any alternative way of thinking inconceivable. An example would be the commonly held assumption in the past that anyone in a position of authority in industry would be masculine in gender. Such deeply held assump-tions or mindsets are scarcely ever confronted or debated and are, in consequence, very difficult to change.

Willingness to change

A state of readiness to change must be created. If the organization is in deep crisis, such that its very survival is threatened, this state of readi-ness may exist spontaneously. (It is dangerous, however, to assume this is the case. Many British companies in recent years have gone to the wall with their complacency unshaken and their outdated organizational practices unaltered.)

The implementation of organizational change

The process of implementing change, and doing so in such a way that it sticks, is one that calls for intense, persistent and dedicated effort in the context of close collaboration between company personnel and external consultants.

The actual business of redrawing organizational charts, rewriting job descriptions, drawing up a new incentive scheme or redesigning the performance appraisal forms is a relatively small, albeit vital, part of the process. The greater part lies in bringing about changes in people's actual behaviour and in the values, beliefs and attitudes that underlie that behaviour.

The following are some of the most commonly used implementation techniques.

Direct, face-to-face communication

This should involve, where feasible, the entire workforce, but in groups of a manageable size at a time so as to facilitate an exchange of viewpoints and provide opportunities for feedback.

Role modelling

Leadership is important in role modelling as top management sets an example by behaving in ways that are consistent with the standards and behaviours that the new organization seeks to reinforce. Such phrases as 'putting customers first' come to life if the top team are seen to be doing so themselves.

Written communications

A whole arsenal of newsletters, posters, stickers, badges and so on – all carrying the messages associated with organizational change – help to reinforce motivation to implement the changes.

Human resource policies

Appropriate policies support the desired changes. These can include:

- revised performance criteria and methods of performance appraisal
- revised remuneration systems
- special schemes for rewarding and recognizing appropriate behaviours.

Investment in training

There will almost always need to be a very substantial investment in training – not simply to impart new skills, but to influence attitudes and values.

The programme of organizational change that resulted in the remarkable transformation in performance at British Airways was largely driven by massive investment in training at every level, starting with top management.

Managing organizational change

The use of symbolism

John Harvey-Jones tells how, on becoming Chairman of ICI, he moved Board meetings from the imposing boardroom to his own office. The boardroom had been designed in an earlier era so as to emphasize the power of the chairman. Harvey-Jones, however, wanted the ICI Board to operate more as a 'band of brothers', with free and uninhibited discussion and with people able to get up, walk around, pour themselves a cup of coffee, draw on flip charts and generally feel relaxed and unrestricted. Under the new arrangement, the Board members, instead of facing each other across a huge and impressive table, sat in conference chairs with small, adjustable side tables to take their papers. They sat, more often than not, in shirt sleeves and there were no fixed places. In this way the new Chairman symbolized a radical change in management style.

The importance of symbolism lies in the way it provides a clear message of a break with the past. Such actions as moving to open-plan offices, abolishing reserved parking places, moving to single-status catering arrangements or abolishing such traditional job titles as foreman or supervisor can have a disproportionately positive impact on creating a climate that is receptive to change.

Resistance to change

Top management tends to see organizational change in its strategic context. Rank and file employees, however, are most likely to be aware of its impact on important aspects of their working lives.

Some resistance to change is almost always unavoidable, but its strength can be minimized by careful advance planning, which involves thinking about such issues as who will be affected by the proposed changes – directly and indirectly – from their point of view, what aspects of their working lives will be affected, who should communicate information about change, when and by what means, and what management style is to be used.

The politics of organizational change

The legitimate power of the Board of directors, appointed by the shareholders, is not the sole power base in a complicated organization. In the process of discussing organizational change, it is important for the consultant to be politically astute and identify potential powerful sources of resistance.

Common sources of power include:

- organized labour
- expertise, knowledge or talent
- charismatic leadership
- exercising control over key resources
- the organization's traditional beliefs and values.

Any one, or indeed all, of these power sources can be used as the base from which resistance to organizational change is waged. It is a great mistake to believe that such powerful counterforces can be ignored and that the backing of the Board of directors will be sufficient in itself to ensure a successful programme of implementing change. Potential sources of resistance of this kind must be identified in advance and, if possible, their commitment to the proposed changes secured. Where this is not possible a power struggle will inevitably follow – a struggle that the Board must win without the kind of compromise that will jeopardize the objectives of the change programme. If necessary, powerful individuals must be moved from their positions of power in the process.

Where to begin

With the foregoing principles in mind, and given top-level awareness of the urgent need for organizational change, it is clear that an action plan is needed, setting out the steps to be taken in sequence, an overall timetable and the allocation of responsibility.

Undoubtedly, the most difficult aspect of devising such a plan is deciding where to start – that is, choosing the right kind of intervention that will get things moving. Among the many points of departure companies have adopted in recent programmes of organizational change, the following are the most common.

- **Conducting a survey among employees** that focuses on the issues facing the business, its strengths and weaknesses, and is so designed as to point to clear priorities for action. The results can then be fed back to employees with the message, 'This is your diagnosis of what is wrong with the organization and what needs to be done – let us work together to take the needed remedial action.'
- **Carry out a series of presentations or 'roadshows'** at which, over time, representatives of top management meet with large numbers of the workforce (ideally with all employees), present their views of the current situation, outline a vision for the future and seek to enthuse the audience to 'buy into' the vision and become motivated to bring it about.

- **Set up a series of cross-disciplinary or cross-divisional task forces** to investigate aspects of the company's operations and report back with recommendations for change.
- **Pick an issue** (the most common ones in recent years have been quality of product or standard of customer service) and focus energy on this using a wide range of tactics, such as ISO 9000 accreditation, quality circles, customer surveys and so on.
- **Develop and publish a mission statement,** consulting widely across the organization in the process.

There are many other possibilities. There is no one way of getting started that will guarantee success. As with so many aspects of decision making at the highest level, it is a question of judgement rather than of seeking for a formula to apply. Much will depend on the degree of urgency involved, the size of the organization, the extent to which the workforce is dispersed over many sites, the extent to which the current organization is one of strong traditions deeply rooted in the past, and the involvement or otherwise of strong trade unions.

It is vital to bear in mind that organizational change is not an intellectual process concerned with the design of ever more complicated and elegant organization structures. It is to do with the human side of enterprise and is essentially about changing people's attitudes, feelings and – above all else – their behaviour. Where the organization has a strong and well-developed personnel or human resource management function – one that is represented at Board level – the process of managing change will often involve a natural partnership and close working relationship between the chief executive, as the leader of change, and the personnel or human resources director, as its leading organizer and facilitator. It is, of course, vital to its success that the human resources expertise available to the company should be fully exploited. Equally, there must be balance as problems can arise if the programme is seen as being 'owned' by personnel rather than by the line. For this reason, it is important that other executive directors in line positions should be allocated clear and responsible roles in the management of the change process and that they are clearly seen to be strongly identified with it. Also, it is very important for the external consultant to be clear about who the client is.

Evaluating the change

It is essential to establish a system for evaluating the extent to which change is actually taking place. This can be done in two ways. First, by monitoring shifts in attitudes, beliefs and values. The starting point for many programmes for culture change is a survey to measure attitudes and beliefs of employees and/or customers. These surveys can be invaluable tools in arriving at an objective diagnosis of pre-existing strengths and weaknesses. Their value is further enhanced if they are repeated at intervals, so as to measure the shifts that have taken place – both the shifts in the values and beliefs of employees, and the perceptions of the behaviour of employees on the part of customers.

A second approach is to evaluate success in terms of results. For example, British Airways set out to achieve – by changing its culture – the goal of becoming 'the world's favourite airline'. It was able to measure and feed back to employees the progress made in approaching this goal by reporting the company's position in various league tables compiled by the travel industry media. Of even greater significance, however, was BA's rapid emergence as the world's most profitable major airline.

Summary

The lessons derived from attempts to bring about radical organizational change in British industry are now beginning to become clear. They can be summarized as follows:

- in most instances radical change – transformation – will be required, and simply tinkering with the system will get you nowhere
- it is difficult to create a climate receptive to change in advance of a serious crisis, but this is what leaders must do; the task calls for both vision and courage
- there has been a growing acceptance of the key role of 'people' factors in achieving lasting competitive advantage, so the main thrust of organizational change programmes is now the bringing about of changed attitudes and behaviour on the part of people, which, in turn, has led to a more strategic role for human resource management.

Organizations are made up of three components: structure, systems and procedures, and culture. Of these, the most difficult area in which to effect real and lasting change is culture. Yet without significant culture change, it is unlikely that changes in structure and systems will do much to transform an organization's performance.

The typical objectives of organizational change in recent years have been to improve quality and service, bringing about radical reductions in cost, improved flexibility and capacity for innovation and a climate of continuous improvement. There now exists a very substantial 'menu' of structural devices, new systems and procedures, and ways of producing culture change. Sometimes companies have been unduly influenced by fads and fashion in selecting appropriate strategies. It is very important to be selective and to match strategies carefully to objectives.

To be successful in achieving culture change, many elements are involved, including:

- a clear, widely shared vision and sense of direction
- an objective analysis of the strengths and weaknesses of the existing organization and the identification of needed changes
- the creation of a climate receptive to change
- intense, persistent effort during the implementation process
- a substantial investment in training
- the use of symbolism
- the anticipation and overcoming of resistance to change, including the choice of management style
- understanding the 'politics' of change.

Many things can go wrong. Perhaps the most important pitfalls are, on the one hand, to look for the 'quick fix' and, on the other, to expect people to wait indefinitely to see some tangible results from their efforts and sacrifices. It does take a very long time to change corporate culture and achieve lasting organizational change. It is futile to assume that it can be accomplished in one year, or even two or three. After seven years of sustained effort at British Airways, Sir Colin Marshall, in an address to the Royal Society of Arts (Colin Marshall, 1991) said, 'I think that we have started to achieve true culture change'. At the same time, enthusiasm and motivation need to be sustained by a sense of achievement over a shorter time-scale that this. In planning change, therefore, it is important to establish a series of intermediate targets, or 'milestones', at reasonably frequent intervals so that measurable results can be seen to be forthcoming.

The final lesson is that the successful direction of organizational change calls for outstanding qualities of leadership. The managerial competencies of analysis, rational decision making, planning and scheduling of changes and the like are, of course, both necessary and important, but by themselves they are not sufficient. People will only put their hearts and minds behind major efforts to change things if they are emotionally involved and feel a real sense of mission and purpose.

The securing of such commitment and involvement is the leader's unique contribution.

References

Atkinson, Philip (1997) *Creating Culture Change* Rushmere Wynne, Leighton Buzzard

Coulson-Thomas, Colin (1992) *Transforming the Company*, Kogan Page, London

Harvey-Jones, John (1989) *Making it Happen*, Fontana, London.

Marshall, C, (1991) 'Culture Change: No Science But Considerable Art', *RSA Journal*, January.

Pettigrew, Andrew, and Whipp, Richard (1993) *Managing Change for Competitive Success*, Blackwell Business, Oxford

Sadler, Philip (1996) *Managing Change*, Kogan Page, London

Schein, E (1992) *Organizational Culture and Leadership* (second edition), Jossey-Bass, San Francisco.

13

The role of the management consultant in the change management process

Bill Critchley

Introduction

The role of the change agent is itself changing. In this chapter I intend to trace this change and conclude with my current thinking, based on recent experience of the nature of this role. It is neither an easy nor a comfortable one, but it is intellectually and emotionally challenging. In this work, as I am redefining it, we sometimes make a real difference, which is extremely satisfying, and sometimes we don't. It is, however, difficult to know at the time whether or not we are being useful, which is a problem in the face of the prevailing expectation that we evaluate each step in the change process and contract for specific outcomes before we have even begun.

I think there are three major shifts taking place in our role that are intimately connected with changing perspectives on change itself. The first is from the notion of *intervention* to that of *participation*. 'Intervention' implies that we intervene as neutral outsiders in an organization, with an objective to change something from x to y by virtue of series of planned steps.

Recent discoveries in quantum physics – that an observer changed what they observed in the act of observing it – have forced us to rethink our role as objective and impartial observers. We, in fact, 'participate' in an organization, bringing our own beliefs and prejudices with us and affecting the organization by our very presence.

It is interesting that although this rethink has recently been catalysed by the scientific community, the challenge has been around for some time, coming from thinkers in fields such as systems theory and ecology (Bateson, 1972), but has largely gone unheeded.

The second shift is closely related to the first and it is the shift from a *positivist* perspective on social systems – which assumes that they have some intrinsic realities, such as hierarchy, structure, rules, to be 'built' and shaped – to a *relational* view – which assumes that organizations are social constructions that are co-created.

The fact that, since Taylor, we have conceived of organizations as machines has misled us into the belief that they are what they are. The recent rush to 'delayer', which has deconstructed the old pyramidal bureaucracies, has lead us to the realization that they are what we make them (at least, to some extent!)

The third, related, shift is from what Gordon Lawrence (1994) suggests is the politics of *salvation*, to the politics of *revelation*. This is politics in the sense of influence. Consultants have traditionally been brought in to solve a problem the client is unable to solve or to provide some expertise the organization lacks. The expectation is that the consultant leads the organization 'out of the wilderness' into 'the promised land'. This implies a role for the consultant of highlighting current problems and defining a better future, and the means required to achieve it, by means of a rational planning process that assembles and connects the right parts and the right intelligence. The implication is of active intervention and passive response, and of preconceived solutions and accompanying methodologies.

It is difficult to let go of the underlying Cartesian assumptions that lead us to this view of organizations as malfunctioning machines that may be restored to regularity by applying clockwork logic. However, the 'politics of revelation' allows us to let go of an image of ourselves as crusaders or saviours and become participants and designers of opportunities for people to discover the organizational issues for themselves, to make their own meaning and discover possible solutions. What is there that is implicitly known, in our past and our present, but has not surfaced? What thoughts are in search of a thinker, thoughts as yet unvoiced?

How may we bring in new possibilities, new voices, new mixes and generate information that unsettles, rather than confirms, via dialogue and experimentation? In a world of distributed power, of networks and loose affiliations, influence has to be claimed; it is not given.

The nature of objectives in a change process

In talking about the role of a consultant in a change process, we are making an assumption that the role is a purposive one. This may appear obvious, but it is not always so. The roles we play in the unfolding events in our lives mainly become apparent retrospectively. Harold Macmillan, British Prime Minister from 1957–63, once famously observed that the problem with politics is that it is frequently overtaken by events, and so it is with organizational life.

Organizational outcomes are the result of an unfolding encounter between intention and chance, although consultants often speak about 'managing change' in a way that suggests we have much more control over events than we possibly can have. Claims that we can help clients fix on detailed long-term change objectives in a fast-moving and complicated environment are simply no longer sustainable, and the offer of a deterministic, managed (and usually expensive) programme of long-term change is misleading and probably unethical.

So, we have a paradox. On the one hand we know that the future is unpredictable – and so the outcomes of a change programme are equally unpredictable – and yet to initiate change without some sense of purpose or objective is unthinkable. One of the first roles we need to adopt in a change process is to think through this difficult dilemma with our client, recognizing that it is as difficult for us as it is for them. I make this last point because it is very easy to intimidate and shame clients by asking them 'good' questions. We ask them 'What are your objectives? 'What are you trying to achieve?', and they stutter for a while and smile apologetically, suggesting 'You've got us there – we really ought to know that, but we're struggling, as you can see'. They think they are supposed to know because they have bought into the idea that managers are supposed to set objectives, allocate resources, monitor, control and evaluate outcomes and, broadly speaking, have some answers.

This is fine when operating in conditions that are fairly close to certainty – that is, in the short term when it is reasonably easy to see what needs to be done, such as enlarge the customer base, reduce working capital or improve product line profitability (although these are not necessarily easy to do). This is what Ralph Stacey refers to as 'ordinary management' (Stacey, 1993). However, in today's complicated organizations, other types of issues – which are often paradoxical and outside anyone's previous experience, such as the pressure to 'globalize', the requirement to innovate in response to shortening product life cycles or the expectation that companies serve the often conflicting interests of multiple stakeholders – require 'extraordinary' management. Our role is to help managers and others think through their roles, particularly in relation to the 'leadership' of change.

The notion of objectives is inadequate for this purpose – it is both too specific and too simplistic. I think it is more helpful to think in terms of *intention* or *direction*. 'Intention' combines a sense of will with a recognition that intention shapes and is shaped by unfolding outcomes. It implies purpose with flexibility and responsiveness. 'Direction' connotes a sense of purposeful exploration. I like the analogy attributed to Tom Peters, of going, for example, 'broadly west'. The direction is understood, but the terrain to be crossed remains to be explored.

I recently worked with a client in the financial services sector who believed that the 15 or so specialist service areas, which he found himself responsible for as a result of a reorganization in his company, could combine in some way to establish a more powerful presence in the market. He defined his intention as to 'provide an integrated service'. This was met with much groaning and cynicism from the professional managers in each service area. My role was to support him in sustaining his broad intention, while persuading him to explore with his managers alternative ways of interpreting it. In the event, his managers suggested a new integrated product and marketing initiative that would be supplied and resourced by a number of the professional service areas, while allowing them to simultaneously retain their separate operations.

Thus, I think our role at this early stage is sometimes to work with the individual leader, but preferably with the leadership team as a whole, to release them from the notion of defining the 'change objectives', and work with them to articulate their sense of purpose or direction sufficiently to go to the next phase – that is, of sharing, testing and developing this with a wider population.

For similar reasons, many clients are uneasy about calling in consultants until they have defined the 'terms of reference', and, of course, purchasing departments and procedures often reinforce this cultural pressure to define desired outcomes and objectives. This forces them into firming up the terms of an assignment or naming 'the problem' far too soon. The real problem is that because of the inherent uncertainty and complexity involved in working with change, managers often do not know what to do and how to act in such conditions, and this what they need help with. I will come back to this later in the chapter.

264

Diagnosis

The 'expert' role

Traditionally, a consultant's starting point would be to interview large numbers of an organization's staff, probably using some diagnostic template, to elicit data, that the consultant would then sort, categorize, and develop, inevitably with some interpretation, into a diagnosis. How this would be used would depend on the underlying 'model' of consulting being used.

'Expert' consultants would write the diagnosis in a form of report that would be well presented, usually including recommendations for action. When the role is one of an 'expert', the required skills are mainly analytical and presentational. Analytical skills are more than merely those of collecting and ordering data, as a consultant needs to have some understanding of how organizations typically work and, hence, have some ready hypotheses about how to make sense of the data. Typically, they will only interview a small sample of the population so they will need the ability to infer and to intuit as well as to analyse. Good diagnoses will be informed by a systemic perspective – that is, an ability to see the whole from the parts. Effective presentations will also have this capacity, to convey a bigger picture than the members of the organization have so far seen for themselves.

However, this role is less often adopted these days as it assumes the consultant can know more about the business and organization than the client. The 'expert' approach tends to leave the members of the organization feeling like passive recipients rather than active participants, at best admiring the consultants' insight and ability to get to the issues and put them across, at worst feeling exploited, in the sense that they see their own insights purloined and repackaged as if they were the consultants'. The former response usually gives rise to the expectation that the consultants, having diagnosed the problem so skilfully, will be skilful at fixing it, while the latter tends to evoke cynicism and suspicion of the consultants' motives.

The 'facilitator' role

This role derives from an alternative model of change that comes from the school of 'organization development'. This is based on Kurt Lewin's (1952) notion of an organization as a 'force field', held in a state of equilibrium by opposing forces, respectively for and against change. This concept is easy to relate to if we reflect on our experience of companies where market forces appear to be pushing in a new direction, while the existing operational practices, procedures and culture act as restraints and managers are lined up variously on one side of the change fence or the other, depending on how they perceive change affecting their interests. (This is not intended to be a cynical comment – it seems to me unreasonable to expect people to act against their perceived self-interest, but what *is* reasonable is for people to be willing to reconsider their perception of their interest. For example, a director in a local authority does not immediately see a change in role from being a powerful line manager to becoming an executive director of the borough with strategic responsibilities for a portfolio of activities as being attractive. However, the perceived loss may give way in the long run to a sense of influence and interest in a broader range of the borough's affairs.)

The logic of the organization development model is that equilibrium must first be 'unfrozen' before change can take place, by reducing the 'resistances' to change and supporting and 'leveraging' the forces for change. The overall sequence of events is 'unfreeze – change – refreeze'.

There are some crucial differences between this role and that of the 'expert'. Particularly, a consultant with an organization development perspective focuses on the potential of the organization to 'resist' change and sees this resistance in terms of 'natural' human resistance to change, which, if unattended to, may overturn the logic of the business imperative.

First of all, the diagnosis – which is usually carried out by means of a series of individual and group interviews – pays explicit attention to relational processes, the nature of communication, decision making, group dynamics, intergroup dynamics and place of feelings in these processes. In fact, the very word 'process' is often used to refer to relational processes as opposed to the 'tasks' that the organization needs to perform. Such a consultant assumes from the outset that the members of the organization will be primarily responsible for creating and implementing the change agenda. The consultant's job, therefore, is to build readiness for change, open up communication channels and mobilize the capacity for 'managing change'.

Here, the diagnostic data is used to create some initial discomfort with the status quo. It is usually 'fed back' to a group or groups of people, and the very fact that it raises to awareness and makes explicit relational issues and group dynamics is itself unusual, challenging and anxiety provoking. An organization development consultant seeks to raise levels of anxiety sufficiently to disturb the equilibrium and create readiness for change, while supporting and encouraging organization members to become proactive in the service of necessary change. The phases of a consulting process typically cover: gaining entry, agreeing a contract, data collection and diagnosis, feedback, action planning, implementation and evaluation.

Organization development consultancy is essentially humanistic in nature. The role that derives from it is generally described as a 'facilitative' one, in that the consultant seeks to facilitate a process of change rather than prescribe it. It requires an understanding of organizations as 'open systems' – that is, being internally interconnected, so that a change in one part will have effects in other parts, sustaining dynamic equilibrium with their environment (Miller and Rice, 1967) – of group dynamics, inter-group dynamics (boundary management) and socio-technical interfaces. Organization development consultants require, as a core skill, high-level interpersonal skills.

The practice of organization development had its heyday in the late 1960s and 1970s. It is comparatively rare these days to find assignments labelled as 'organization development' assignments, but many of its phases naturally form part of a change consultant's approach, and the role of facilitator has been widely adopted by most change consultants. At its worst, it overemphasizes interpersonal and group process, alienates some managers who are not prepared for the extent of personal exposure that it sometimes calls for and creates a separation between task and process that is unhelpful. At its best, it creates a wide sense of involvement in, and responsibility for, the change process and develops greater emotional literacy and interpersonal competence within client organizations.

An emerging view of the role of the change consultant

Both the 'expert' model of change and the 'organization development' model, though apparently very different, are informed by a similar assumption about organizations and, hence, about change. It is that they are equilibrium systems and, for change to take place, there needs to be a shift from one state of equilibrium to another.

The expert assumes that the force of logical argument will prevail, while the organization development consultant assumes that some manipulation of the social and psychological forces will be required in order to pave the way for change. As Patricia Shaw puts it (1997)

For a long time now, the classical OD focus on diagnosing the equilibrium dynamics of an organization has seemed to make sense, sustaining current functioning by seeking to align the various subsystems or attempting to unfreeze, move and refreeze the system at a new equilibrium ... However, underlying this focus there is an unquestioned assumption that a system can be moved from one dynamic equilibrium to another, by the prior intention of the legitimate system. It is assumed that the existing organizational dynamic came into being through some central purpose, however participatively arrived at, and can be changed in the same way.

Many of the current programmatic approaches to change – epitomized by 'business process re-engineering' – derive from these fundamental assumptions about organizations and change.

As indicated at the beginning of this chapter, there is an emerging view of organizations as complicated, adaptive systems that are essentially non-linear in nature and in a state of permanent flux. Structures are thus temporary manifestations that, like photographs, can at best only convey a sense of the underlying movement and dynamic possibility. From this perspective, change is inherent in the system rather than a transitional state between two equilibrium states. This fundamentally challenges the notion of 'managed' change and, hence, the consultant's role as a proponent of the need to manage change.

It also challenges the conventional view that organizations are controllable, from the top or centre, via structures, procedures, prescribed sets of values and the like and so susceptible to future planning by means of the techniques of environmental scanning, forecasting, mission creation, strategic planning and so on. Ralph Stacey (1996) suggests instead that social systems can be thought of as complicated adaptive systems in which individuals and groups interact in co-evolving sense-making and action contexts, in ways that are inherently unpredictable. He further suggests that organizations are formally understood in terms of an ordered network consisting of its hierarchical structure of roles and responsibilities, its official policies and espoused ideology, which he refers to as the 'legitimate system', and informally known by means of what he refers to as the 'shadow system', that is all those informal, self-organizing networks and connections that bypass, subvert or else maintain the formal processes and procedures.

Intuitively, we can understand this idea of a formal or legitimate part of an organization, setting all the policies, rules, performance standards and so on, and an informal system, in which people politic pursue their own ends, find creative solutions, often despite the formal procedures, or ways of getting things done that short cut or bypass the rule book. We also know from our experience that what goes on in these informal networks is both collaborative and competitive, never one or the other – they are essentially messy, somewhat chaotic processes, that are formally discouraged and their existence, at least in public, is frequently denied.

What is intriguing is the proposition that they are the source of novelty in organizations and that the possibility of innovation and evolution arises in the paradox and tension of operating in both the formal and shadow systems. The very title of Richard Pascale's (1990) book – *Managing on the Edge* – captures this idea, as do the writings of other authors, including Morgan (1986) and Wheatley (1992).

To summarize, a short definition of complex systems for the sake of completeness. For those who want to pursue this perspective, the References section at the end of this chapter, (see particularly Stacey) suggests some possible reading. Otherwise, the rest of this chapter elaborates on experiences and ideas that are in wide circulation. While they are broadly informed by ideas about the nature of complexity, a detailed understanding of the theory is not required in order for them to be entirely accessible.

Complex systems are non-linear, dynamic feedback systems driven by simple feedback laws, capable of generating behaviour so complicated that the links between cause and effect, action and outcome, simply disappear in the detail of unfolding behaviour. Feedback can have either an amplifying or a dampening effect, and it is impossible to know in advance which of these two possibilities will occur. 'When a non-linear feedback system is driven away from stable equilibrium towards the equilibrium of explosive instability, it passes through a phase of bounded instability in which it displays highly complicated behaviour. There is what we might think of as a border area between stable equilibrium and unstable equilibrium, and behaviour in this area has some important characteristics. While it is unpredictable, it also displays what has been called a hidden pattern. That is, it is in permanent flux, and the implicate order emerges while the system in this phase is inherently self-organizing. In this phase, the system has the greatest capacity for innovation and regeneration.

There are two characteristics of complicated organizations that are crucial for consultants who are interested in working seriously and effectively for organizational change, and they are *self-organization* and *emergence*. Let us look at the implications of these for the role of the change consultant.

Self-organization and emergence

Before I understood a little about complexity theory, I knew from my experience of 'facilitating' management groups that, in certain conditions, if I left the group with sufficient space, they would organize themselves perfectly well to do whatever it was that needed to be done, often in a lively and creative way, usually redefining the task I had suggested to them. Conversely, I also knew that if I 'managed' or controlled the group too much, it would become comparatively quiet, and I would feel that I had to energize it to drive it forward, usually ending up with the outcome I wanted but with the group in a mood of either passive compliance or latent hostility.

When the group 'self-organized' itself, an outcome 'emerged'. The difficulty for me was that it was not what I expected, while the group members felt enlivened by the process and had a high degree of ownership of the outcome. Intuitively I knew that what had emerged was more innovative and relevant than what I had intended, even though we might be faced with some difficulties in having it accepted by other managers not present at the meeting.

I was learning to be less controlling in my consulting in order to allow the relevant issues to emerge and be worked with. I noticed that when I allowed this self-organizing process to develop, in time I could participate in the dialogue, contributing my experience and external perspective without overly influencing the process or resuming control. Now, a difficult question presents itself: How do I create the conditions in which this self-organizing can occur?

Well, in principle, I cannot be sure of manipulating the process to ensure any outcome; I do not have that kind of control, which is a difficult lesson for us all to learn. However, there are some conditions in which it is more likely to occur and I can influence these dependent on the context. Let me take two contexts in which I often find myself operating most frequently.

Facilitating events

At various points in a change process, 'off-line' events are convened. These range from forming a change steering group, taking a team away to address some particular issues (which may include how it works together), to having a large group event. In these cases, we have two broad roles, one being to design the event, and the other to facilitate it. The design provides some sense of purpose and structure, but should be as minimalist as possible to provide the necessary space mentioned above.

The role of the management consultant

Let us look at an example. A training institute with a dispersed, largely self-employed membership felt the need to get together. My first job was to help them articulate what turned out to be four purposes:

- connecting with each other
- reviewing the relationships between different departments;
- giving information from the management team
- a review of the trends in the profession of which the institute was a part.

I started by providing one hour in which people could connect with each other by forming themselves into groups of four or five and sharing their current concerns, interests, saying how connected or disconnected they felt from the organization and what support they needed. I then kept out of the way, except to sense how much enthusiasm they had for this and how much time they needed.

After about 45 minutes, I judged that they were ready to move on and asked them to move into their departmental groups. I gave them some carefully prepared questions to address and said that people could change groups if they felt affiliated to more than one department. This piece of work generated a lot of liveliness and interest, and I had to be firm in bringing it to a halt.

My purpose in giving this example is to demonstrate the significance of the design role and the importance of firmly and sensitively negotiating the 'boundaries' throughout the event. This last role requires being permanently tuned in without becoming intrusive. It is likely that there will be a microcosm of the whole in many situations. Thus, the consultant will be able to have some sense of the whole by noting the many fragments of dialogue heard. These fragments provide a view, albeit partial of the whole in flux, that enables the consultant to modify the design in response to the emergent process. This is extremely demanding, so consultants are well advised to work in pairs or more.

I also find that it is usually necessary to state clearly at the outset the purpose of each session and give a good set of briefing questions. This provides some sense of purpose and stability within which self-organizing can take place. I find that I do very little facilitating in the traditional sense, which can feel quite uncomfortable if you are at all concerned with being *seen* to add value.

On another occasion, with colleague Patricia Shaw, I was working with a newly formed division of a multinational company on a conference design and a small steering group had been unable to agree on an agenda in advance of the meeting. Given the diversity of the division, this merely reflected the reality that 6 people could not possibly know in advance what 50 people of different nationalities, dispersed across different countries, working in different functions, would want to talk about – such is the nature of complexity.

Of one thing the group felt fairly certain – that these people did need to get together. The group recalled that, at most conferences, the formal sessions – dominated by slide-based presentations in darkened rooms – were pretty turgid and of little use. What was of real value always came out of the informal exchanges and the ensuing networking. Thus, how then to create two days of informal exchanges and networking became the task of this group.

The solution was to have the people meet for lunch, hire a stimulating speaker and then leave people at their lunch tables (in groups of six or seven) to decide what they wanted to talk about over the next two days. A networking board was rigged up, and the people asked to post on it the issues they wanted to talk about, who was going to be involved in the discussions and where in the building they were going to take place. As the discussions evolved, new issues would emerge when new groups of people got together, and all we asked was that they kept the networking board up to date so that people could see what was going on and make informed choices about what to join and what to leave. We pointed out that all the decision makers were in the room and that therefore any problem or issue that arose could be progressed.

I could say much more about this example, and there are similar experiments going on elsewhere under headings such as 'future search' or 'open space' conferences. However, what I am seeking to show here is how we attempted to enable the processes of self-organization and emergence by providing the minimum of structure. The temptation in the role of 'consultant' (I would we could find a better word) is to control too much in the interests of minimizing our own anxiety and maximizing our visibility by imposing too much structure too early.

In my experience, excessive attempts to manage or control organizations reduces their capacity to be innovative, but we have been brought up to believe in the myth of managerial control. Hence, when the conditions for self-organization occur, this gives rise to both excitement and anxiety. Our role is to name and normalize these two natural responses to the ambiguity of freedom and responsibility and have a sense of the possibilities in the emerging situation. This requires some understanding of the psychodynamic processes occurring in organizational life that allow us to recognize what is going on.

Joining meetings

As part of most assignments, I negotiate to join meetings that are already established. For instance, in a London borough, my colleague Patricia Shaw and I negotiated to join five change task forces that had been set up to address such issues as devolution, communication and so on. Here we had had no prior role in designing the meeting; we simply joined these groups as they worked on their immediate business. Our work, as we saw it, was to provoke the groups to examine and question the assumptions they were working with, the structures of meanings they were creating in the organization by their actions and help them modify or reframe their role and what they were working on as their view of the context changed. This is hard and frustrating work, but it is where our impact is at its most realistic. The effect of setpiece events is much exaggerated, and I think we rely too much on them. Change is more a consequence of a myriad of low-profile actions and events rather than a few high-profile ones. Here, I think our role is to participate rather than facilitate, with a view to disturb, challenge and support people in the mess and chaos of change.

Meta change processes

I find it easier to think of my role in terms of some meta change processes that are neither linear nor sequential, but do give some sense of purpose to my role at various stages in an assignment. These are:

- enquiry
- experimentation
- integration.

All are consistent with the politics of revelation.

Enquiry

The early stages of an assignment are characterized by enquiry. The idea of enquiry seems to be less instrumental than the notion of diagnosis, and more congruent with the concept of organizations as complicated systems. Furthermore, I believe in conducting participative or collaborative enquires, as advocated by Reason and Heron (1995), which engage the members of an organization in jointly uncovering the issues to be

273

addressed. As I suggested at the beginning of this chapter, the enquiry will probably be conducted within a broad framework of intention, which will inevitably be revised in the light of what is found out.

Experimentation

What emerges from the enquiry – which is itself a form of experiment – will be a focus on change priorities, and various configurations of people will form round these issues for the purpose of taking action. Too often, these groups collapse into task forces that make recommendations rather than change initiatives that involve experiment and risk, and it is a key part of our role to encourage and support people to experiment and take risks. These change initiatives are also engaged in an enquiry process, but the emphasis is on action rather than discovery.

Integration

Integration is a phase of temporary stability, a pause during which people reflect on what they have done and what they have learnt, when some of the experiments are consolidated into the formal processes of the organization, and people take some satisfaction from what they have achieved and also rest for a while.

A case study

I was working with some colleagues for a reasonably large engineering company that had grown as a result of a series of acquisitions. It needed to respond to some of its large customers' demands that it become more integrated in its capability to respond. This was expressed in the jargon of the day as a requirement to be a 'global player', a 'virtual company'.

In this case, the natural boundaries defined by a country or a site that had previously defined the business entity, which people saw as the source of their livelihood, and for which they strove to win orders, often in competition with other members of the same company, were now seen as an impediment by an emerging group of powerful global customers. These customers threatened to withdraw their business unless this supplier 'got its act together'.

Our way of working with this organization was to start by arranging a two-day workshop for about 50 managers in order that they could hold an enquiry, through dialogue, into what becoming 'global' would entail. We had two process principles in mind. One was to create opportunities for people to start talking and addressing problems in groupings that crossed their normal country, site or national boundaries, while the other was to challenge the boundaries of their thinking, to provoke them into experimentation with innovative ways of working. For example, as engineers, they tended to tackle problems with 'project groups', defined terms of reference, clear statements of goals, milestones and methodologies. These are fine for solving problems incrementally, but did not allow for radical innovation. Their view was that the company was facing radical change and our view was that it therefore needed to learn innovative ways of working.

Out of this initial workshop a number of change initiatives formed and we worked with each one to help them define what was really important in the broad area they had chosen, what could usefully be a project and how to tackle what could not be turned into a project. The group concerned with customer service, for instance, started by defining four parameters of customer service; they then identified the processes that had the greatest impact on these parameters – what was needed to improve each of these processes – and ended up with an impossible list of projects! They then tried to prioritize the list and then finally came to realize that the final outcome of all this work would be to solve a few problems.

The question then became how to have a wider impact, how to engage everyone with the issue of customer service so that everyone started to think of what they did in terms of its impact on the four parameters. The members of this group began to get themselves invited to operations group meetings, to explain their analysis, point out some of the problem areas in specific terms to specific groups. Some groups accepted the analysis and initiated their own activities to tackle the problems and other groups were less willing to 'own' their problems, but such is organizational reality. Nevertheless, the members of the customer service group now saw themselves as leaders of a change initiative rather than members of a project team.

One member of the team was concerned that the emphasis on releasing innovative potential might diminish the importance of incremental improvement in the engineering, project-based culture. He therefore worked with one group to help them rationalize their production systems and with another to establish an efficient and effective pan-organization costing system. Organizations need to feel sufficiently secure in their ability to get things done via the formal systems before they can embrace innovation in their business processes.

Throughout this assignment, my role was to work with the Board to support them in the leadership of the change process and help them review their roles both as individuals and as a team.

This example serves to highlight the importance of maintaining both stability and creative instability in organizations and, therefore, the need to both honour and challenge 'resistance'. In working on the boundary between stability and instability, we were drawing on the principles of complexity theory.

We started with a reasonably large grouping, which we kept working in one large room (we did not have break-out rooms) in order for people to have a better sense of the 'whole' organization. Within some broad parameters, we invited them to enquire into the issues of becoming global, as opposed to giving them a diagnosis and asking them to work on the problems we had identified, and we enabled groups to form around the issues that emerged rather than attempt to assign individuals to issues (self-organization).

It is interesting to observe that senior managers did not think that the 'right' issues had been identified, but we encouraged them to let this rather messy process of self-organization unfold rather than have them impose their own change agenda, and many of the groups subsequently redefined the issue they were working on in the light of unfolding circumstances (emergence).

Finally, we realized how important it is that senior managers do join the change groups, but not as the group leader. They were thus not excluded from the process as they would have been in a 'bottom-up approach', but were able to influence it by participating in the informal processes of the organization. This is as opposed to exerting their influence via their formal leadership role, evoking compliant responses to the exercise of formal power and inhibiting the system's potential for innovative self-organization.

Choice and influence in our roles

As you read this chapter, the sense you make of it will be profoundly influenced by your own deep-rooted assumptions and habits of thought. In this concluding section I would like to draw our attention to the way in which our own assumptions influence our role and how we can interpose, perhaps unthinkingly, a particular 'problem' framework.

If, for example, you tend to see organizations in terms of politics and power, using this as our 'lens', we may choose to define the problem as the quality of leadership, believing that, ultimately, leadership has the power to bring about change, or we might focus on creating greater equality of opportunity, believing that over concentration of power is the 'problem'.

The role of the management consultant

If our lens is a 'communication' lens, we might focus on programmes of communication to 'get the change message across'. Morgan's (1986) work on the 'images' or 'metaphors' that inform our way of seeing organizations, expands on the number of ways in which we conceive of organizations and their implications for how we might approach change. Our metaphors, unexamined, lead us to focus on particular phenomena while ignoring others, and we are inclined to exaggerate their explanatory power. They also tend to structure the way in which we see relationships.

We need to be aware of our own preferred metaphors and careful in our use of them because not only can we become their prisoners, but we can use them to tyrannize others. It is, I believe, an essential part of our ethical stance as consultants that we hold our theories lightly, recognizing their partiality, contingency and temporality.

References

Bateson, G (1972) *Steps to an Ecology of Mind: Collected essays on anthropology, psychiatry, evolution and epistemology*, Aronson, London

Lawrence, W Gordon (1994) 'The Politics of Salvation and Revelation in the Practice of Consultancy' in *What makes consultancy work: understanding the dynamics*, Roasemore *et al*., (eds), South Bank University Press, London

Lewin, K (1952) *Field Theory in Social Science*, Tavistock, London.

Miller, EJ, and Rice, AK (1967) *Systems of organization: The control of task and sentient boundaries*, Tavistock, London

Morgan, G (1986) *Images of organizations*, Sage, Los Angeles, CA

Pascale, RT (1990) *Managing on the Edge: How Successful Companies use Conflict to Stay Ahead*, Viking: London

Reason, P, and Heron, J (1995) 'Co-operative Inquiry': in Harre, R, Smith, J, and Van Langenhore, L (eds), *Rethinking Psychology*, Sage, Los Angeles, CA

Shaw, P, (1997) 'Intervening in the shadow systems of organizations', Complexity and Management Centre, University of Hertfordshire, Hertford.

Wheatley, MJ (1992) *Leadership and the New Science: Learning about organization from an orderly universe*. Berrett-Koehler, San Francisco

Stacey, R (1993) *Strategic management and organizational dynamics*, Pitman, London

Stacey, R (1996) *Complexity and Creativity in Organizations*, Berrett-Koehler, San Francisco

I would like to thank my colleague, Kathryn Evans, for her help in shaping and resourcing this chapter.

Part 5

Concept and tools

14

Strategy formulation models

Nick Obolensky

Introduction

In this chapter, we will look at some of the various models that can be used to assist us in the formulation of strategy. It would be a mistake to assume that any one individual model is sufficient to meet the needs of all occasions. While the authors of such models would have us believe that this is possible, the reality is that a variety of models can be used depending on the situation. As the philosopher Herzen once said, 'There are no general solutions to individual and specific problems, only temporary expedients which must be based on an acute sense of the uniqueness of each situation and on a high degree of responsiveness to the particular needs and demands of diverse individuals and peoples.'

It is also important to note that these models do little more than assist the thinking process – they do not replace the thinking necessary for a sustainable strategy to be formulated. Some of the models are fairly static and deterministic (that is, they use a rigid structure within which to consider relevant factors) and some are dynamic and fluid (that is, they depend on human interaction and trial and error).

What is strategy?

'Strategy' comes from the ancient Greek word meaning the art of leading an army. It is traditionally the 'art of generalship', with the word general meaning both the high military rank as well as the art of having a general, high-level, overview.

The concept of strategy being applied to business first generally emerged after the Second World War in the USA. The methodology of the US forces was adapted to US industry in the late 1940s, led by people such as Robert McNamara, then President of the Ford Motor Company and later US Defense Secretary under Kennedy. The specific bridge to business strategy, according to Igor Ansoff (1965), was the 1953 publication *Theory of Games and Economic Behaviour* by von Neumann and Morgenstern, two Princeton academics. They formulated methods of resolving conflict in politics, war and business, by interpreting strategy in two ways: *pure* strategy and *grand* strategy.

Pure strategy was exemplified by a move, or series of moves, by a business in a specific area, such as product development. Grand strategy was exemplified by statistical rules against which a business could decide what pure strategies it should pursue according to the situation.

In business today, strategy traditionally answers the question, 'How can we compete in the market, and maintain an advantage?' Such a question assumes that the market is a zero sum game, that the cake is only so big and that, inevitably, there will be winners and losers. In some instances this may well be so. However, markets are fast evolving, traditional wisdoms are becoming blurred and competitive dynamics are changing to the extent that Andy Groves, the CEO of Intel, talks of 'co-opetition' (the merger of cooperation and competition). Thus, strategy also needs to answer the question, 'How can we add value to customers in a sustained way?'

Whatever the answers to such questions are, business strategy needs to be linked to both systems (including IT strategy) and structure (HR strategy). Any successful business strategy will need to ensure it has fast and efficient processes and systems, in a structure and culture that supports the overall strategy. One should also not forget that a successful business needs a successful financing strategy (such as the correct sourcing and optimum mix of debt and equity capital). So, strategy can encapsulate any issue within business.

This chapter will concentrate on the more traditional views of strategy, which are externally focused on the market environment within which the company operates. It will consider a selection of the more common tools and techniques that can be employed to help rational decision making regarding the strategic direction of a company. Any company faces options and choices in its overall strategy, and these formulation tools are designed to ensure that choices are based on rational analysis, rather than ill-informed opinion.

Types of formulation models

There are various models that can be employed to assist in the formulation of strategy. They are broadly of three types:

- matrix-based formulation models
- nmemonic letter-based formulation models
- issues/themes models.

Matrix-based formulation models

These models take two variables (such as price and quality) and, placing one on a vertical and one on a horizontal axis, make it possible to plot various options, products, companies and so on. They typically have three design characteristics.

- **Variables** These can be dependent or independent. They need to be important issues that are of relevance to the strategic situation being considered.
- **Scale** A standard two-by-two matrix would have a scale on each axis labelled 'High' and 'Low'. With two axes represented, a four-box matrix is formed. The BCG matrix (see page 293) is an example of this. Some matrices have three scales ('High', 'Medium' and 'Low'), with a nine-cell matrix being the result. The GE/McKinsey matrix (see page 292) is an example of this.
- **Plots** A variety of things can be plotted on to a matrix. Products and/or services, companies or even strategic options. These can be represented by dots or, as an enhancement, bubbles. The size and shading of bubbles can be used to show more information (see Figure 14.2).

Matrices are simple but effective ways to marshal, analyse and show information on which strategic decision making can be based. Although various 'ready made' matrices exist (some of which are considered later in this chapter) it is easy to design one specific to the situation in hand. Take, for example, the simple situation of going on holiday. The two key variables here are normally time and money and you either have a lot of each or some of varying quantities. Thus, you can see that four basic options emerge, as shown in Figure 14.1.

Using two key variables, situations can be 'mapped out' to show what the options are, as well as what the current (and possible future) situation is. This approach can also be used to map out individual units (from people to different companies) on a matrix showing, for example, a market analysis of competitors on price/quality variables. Then, you need to do some research to get the quantitative values for each plot. You can also use arrows to show units, movements. Figure 14.2 shows this done for the motor industry.

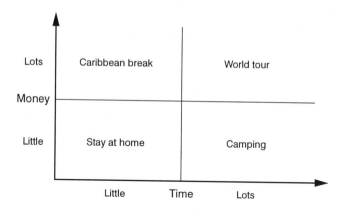

Figure 14.1 Example of a conceptual matrix

The examples shown in Figure 14.2 are purely indicative, to demonstrate what you can do. There are not many situations that you cannot translate into a matrix. The advantage of the approach is that a picture really does paint a thousand words! However, be aware that the matrix approach just gives an idea of the situation and that life is normally more complicated than a simple two-by-two matrix.

Nmemonic/letter-based formulation models

These models use a nmemonic or letters to act as a prompt under which strategic information can be gathered. The most common of these is a SWOT analysis, which stands for strengths, weaknesses, opportunities and threats (see page 303). Other examples include the five Ps (product, price, place, promotion and people) and Ohmae's three Cs (company, customer and competition) and the McKinsey 7-S framework (strategy, systems, structure, style, staff, skills and shared values), described later in this chapter.

Issue/themes models

These models are normally based on a view of strategic dynamics, so they pick out issues or themes that a strategist needs to consider. An example would be Porter's five forces (suppliers, competitors, customers, new entrants and substitute products) (see page 287).

Alternatively, the themes may focus on the process of strategy rather than the content. An example of this is Ansoff's model of strategic planning (establish objectives – establish the 'gap' between where you are

Strategy formulation models

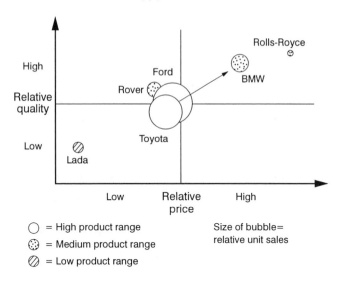

Figure 14.2 Example of a conceptual map

now and where you want to be – establish options to close the gap – select the best option; see below).

Summary

There is no point in trying to establish which one of these types of model is best or worst. In reality, a blend will be used. The effective strategist knows many of these types of model and, using their experience, applies the ones that are best to use in the unique situation of the company concerned and the context within which it operates.

Below a variety of models is considered under the headings of traditional, external, internal, financial, and hybrid approaches.

Traditional approaches

This section will look at two of the more traditional models, from Ansoff's *Corporate Strategy* and Andrew's *The Concept of Corporate Strategy* . Both Igor Ansoff and Kenneth Andrews were, in their day, strategy 'gurus'. Igor Ansoff's first leading work was published in the 1960s, while Kenneth Andrews' work first appeared in the 1970s. Ansoff's work is a fairly deterministic, 'left-brained' approach, while Andrews' is an early example of the more fluid, holistic 'right-brained' approach.

Igor Ansoff

Ansoff's work *Corporate Strategy* was published in 1965 and is generally regarded as the first to have set out a practical method for strategic decision making within a business. His 'model of strategic planning' maps out a process of decision making that starts with the highly aggregated decisions and cascades towards the more specific. Central to this process is his 'gap analysis' in which you:

- decide the set of objectives
- analyse where you are with regard to these objectives
- ascertain the gap between where you are and where you want to be
- generate the options for action that can close the gap
- select the best option according to its 'gap-reducing properties'.

Ansoff's work was years ahead in identifying the need for competitive advantage and providing a checklist against which competitors should be judged. It was also the first work to propose the concept of synergy (most simply, and memorably, described as $2 + 2 = 5$).

Kenneth Andrews

Andrews defined corporate strategy in his book *The Concept of Corporate Strategy* (1971) as being 'the pattern of decisions in a company that determines and reveals its objectives, purposes or goals, produces the principle policies and plans for achieving those goals, and defines the range of business the company is to pursue, the kind of economic and human organization it is or intends to make to its shareholders, employees, customers and communities'. He was before his time with regard to taking a holistic 'stakeholder' approach to strategy.

Andrews identified four principal strands for which strategy needs to be formulated:

- the market opportunity
- the competence and resources of the company
- the personal values and aspirations of the people involved
- obligations to society as a whole.

In formulating and evaluating a strategy, Andrews proposed asking ten key questions.

- Is the strategy identifiable and clearly understood?
- Is the strategy unique?
- Are domestic and international opportunities fully exploited?

- Is the strategy consistent with what the company is capable of?
- Are all the actions within the company consistent with the strategy?
- Is the level of risk feasible in economic and personal terms?
- Does the strategy match key managers' personal values and aspirations?
- Does the strategy deliver the desired level of contribution to society?
- Does the strategy generate organizational commitment and effort?
- Are there early indications of market responsiveness to the strategy?

As a checklist for strategy formulation, Andrews provides a sound model.

External-oriented approaches

These strategic formulation models are mainly focused on the external context within which the company operates. Michael Porter is generally acknowledged as being one of the leading contributors in this field and so three of his models, along with some other commonly used models, are described, namely the GE/McKinsey matrix, the five Cs and five Ps, the market/product expansion matrix, and the BCG growth/share matrix.

Porter's five forces

In his seminal book published in 1980, *Competitive Strategy: Techniques for analysing industries and competitors*, Porter stated, 'In any industry, whether it is domestic or international, or produces a product or service, the rules of competition are embodied in five competitive forces'. These are shown in in Figure 14.3.

The five forces are as follows:

- **New entrants** New competitors need to be analysed, and ignoring them can be dangerous. They will necessitate some competitive response, which will inevitably use resources.
- **Substitute products** The threat of substitute products, and any viable alternative to your product or service, will inevitably limit the price you can charge. In extreme cases, they can make your product completely redundant.
- **Customers** The bargaining power of customers, if strong, will reduce your ability to have high profit margins. If a company is locked into a single powerful customer, its strategic options in the short term may be limited.
- **Suppliers** The bargaining power of suppliers may limit the ability to gain supplies at a low cost, especially if they increase their prices.

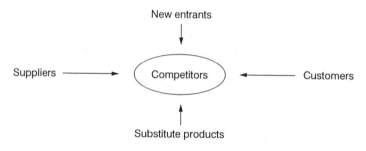

Figure 14.3 Porter's five competitive forces

- **Competitors** Competition leads to the need for investment in R&D, marketing and, possibly, price reductions. The more competitive the prices, the lower the potential margins.

These five forces determine industry profitability, and their collective strength determines the ability for a company to earn a return. The forces vary from industry to industry, and within an industry from time to time as it evolves.

Porter's three generic strategies

Another model in Porter's book *Competitive Strategy* was the notion that companies have three broad generic strategies that they can pursue:

- **differentiation** this strategy is based on the differentiation of products or services (typically in quality, features or level or service) so that customers will pay a premium to cover the higher costs involved in creating them
- **cost leadership** this strategy offers products and services at a low cost – quality and service are kept to minimum and a 'no frills' approach is followed
- **focus** this strategy targets a market segment, providing a high degree of specialization.

Porter writes that companies getting stuck in the middle – say, offering just marginal differentiation with a marginal attempt to achieve a lower cost – will result in failure. This view has been strongly challenged however and is not consistent with empirical evidence. Marks and Spencer, for example, aims at moderate rather than low cost clothing and offers goods of reasonable rather than outstanding quality.

The IMEDE HPV/LDC matrix

Building on Porter's generic strategy, the IMEDE (now IMD) business school developed a matrix that uses two of the strategies – differentiation – (called 'high perceived value' – HPV) and cost leadership (called 'low delivered cost' – LDC). The two generic ways of competing can be either by delivering 'high perceived value' (HPV) or by achieving 'low delivered cost' (LDC). In reality, most try to attain a degree of each. There is also the option to move from being an LDC operator to an HPV position while maintaining an LDC base (see Figure 14.4), which is a proactive strategy.

This, in effect, is what the Japanese car manufacturers achieved against the West's industry, entering the market at the LDC end (remember when Japanese cars were perceived as a joke?) They then invested heavily in production technology, and maintained their LDC position. They quickly took market share from others. This forced manufacturers in the West to invest in production technology and improve marketing to keep their HPV position, but achieve an LDC base. A pre-emptive strategy would have been to reduce the price of a HPV product – this, though, would call for heavy investment in production technology.

Porter's value chain model

While most externally focused strategic formulation models look at the market and customer side of the equation, this model looks at the *value chain*, or the supply chain, side of the equation. This can be of use when determining the dynamics and added value of the whole supply chain, and where the opportunities for backward or forward integration lie or

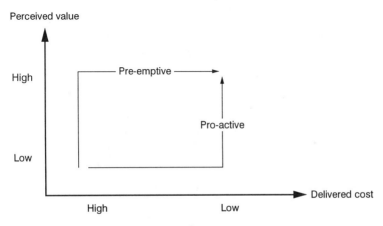

Figure 14.4 Value versus cost

for doing it better or changing the rules of the game. Put at its simplest, the price the end customer pays for a product or service is treated as 100 per cent and this is then broken down by going back along the supply chain, as shown in Figure 14.5.

Once a value chain has been constructed, it is useful to see exactly what value is added by the various parts/companies of the value chain. There are two ways in which this information can be used.

- **Do it better** This can be achieved by entering into closer relationships with suppliers and jointly exploring options to reduce lead times or costs. The savings can be used either to reduce prices (to become more competitive) or invested to increase quality.
- **Change the rules** This is what IKEA did, very effectively, in the furniture industry. It lowered the price of furniture by sourcing high-quality (but lower-cost) part-constructed furniture, going for large, edge-of-town warehouse sites and letting its customers do the final construction. The savings gained from suppliers, distribution and production were passed mostly to customers, who could purchase high-quality furniture at a lower price. Changing the rules of the game gives a company a more sustainable advantage than it would otherwise have as others often cannot respond without fundamentally changing as well. As the 'build your own' furniture segment of the market was somewhat new, in a traditionally conservative industry, not many thought it worth while responding. This gave IKEA time to carve a new niche and develop it.

The value chain approach is explained in full in Porter's book, *Competitive Advantage: Creating and sustaining superior performance* (1985).

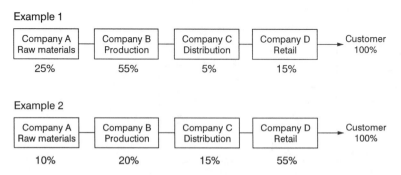

Each company's contribution in terms of percentage of value it has added can be further broken down to show the value added by each company's activities – that is, operations, marketing, administration and so on.

Figure 14.5 Value chain analysis

The GE/McKinsey shell

This technique is named after those who invented it. It is a useful tool if an organization has a number of sites or differing product sectors or businesses. As shown in Figure 14.6, six broad options emerge for consideration.

You need to 'score' a range of criteria grouped under both variables. The kinds of criteria you can use are listed below, with each variable of 'market attractiveness' and 'competitive position' split into two sub-categories.

Examples of criteria

Market attractiveness

- *Industry:*
  – absolute market size
  – growth
  – price sensitivity
  – entry barriers
  – substitution
  – competitive rivalry
  – supplier availability

- *Environment:*
  – government regulations
  – economic climate
  – currency risk
  – social trends
  – technology
  – employment
  – interest rates

Competitive position

- *Current strengths:*
  – Share of market
  – trend of share
  – profitability
  – cash flow
  – differentiation
  – relative price position

- *Sustainability:*
  – cost
  – logistics
  – marketing
  – service
  – customer image
  – technology

For simplicity, each criterion should be scored out of 3 (1 being low, 3 being high). If there is a large variation in importance between criteria, then they can be weighted to get a more even score. As long as these assumptions are reasonable, then the tool is of great indicative use, enabling elements of the organization, operating in a variety of differing locations or markets, to be plotted.

The five Cs and five Ps

The five Cs and five Ps are just checklists of things to look at and understand when considering the needs of customers, the environment in which they exist and how well their needs are matched by the organization (both in terms of products and staff) and the competition. They are useful tools when used to compare your company with the competition and the current state to the future state the organization wishes to achieve. The gap between the two states will indicate the scale of change it is necessary to achieve.

The five Cs & Ps

- context
- customers
- company
- competition
- costs

- product
- place
- price
- promotion
- people

The market/product expansion matrix

Many companies, when reviewing their strategy, seek to grow. This can be done either by expanding via new products or new markets. Using these two as variables, and a scale of old and new, a useful four-box matrix appears, as shown in Figure 14.7.

Moving into new markets with new products straight away is the riskiest, and should be avoided – the equivalent of 'Here there be dragons' on an old map!

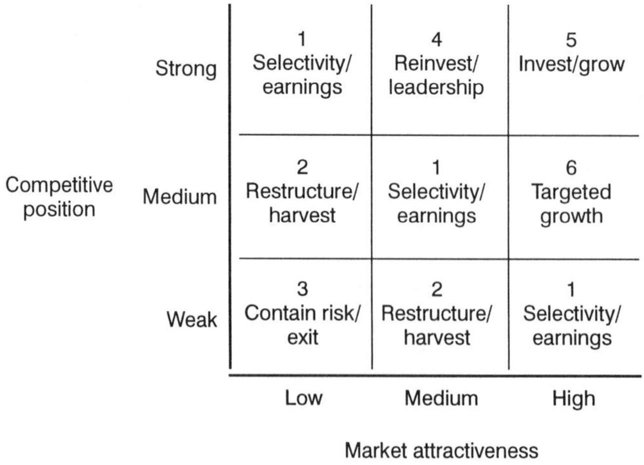

		1	4	5
	Strong	Selectivity/ earnings	Reinvest/ leadership	Invest/grow
Competitive position	Medium	2 Restructure/ harvest	1 Selectivity/ earnings	6 Targeted growth
	Weak	3 Contain risk/ exit	2 Restructure/ harvest	1 Selectivity/ earnings
		Low	Medium	High

Market attractiveness

Figure 14.6 The GE/McKinsey matrix – an analysis tool looking at an organization's competitive position versus market attractiveness

Strategy formulation models

Figure 14.7 Market versus product strategies

The BCG matrix

This matrix (shown in Figure 14.8) was invented by The Boston Consulting Group – hence, BCG – and used to assist clients to formulate strategies if they have a portfolio of businesses/investments.

The two variables used on each axis are the extent to which the market (within which the unit is operating) is growing, and the market share that unit has (compared to the other competitors). Using this matrix, you can see that it is best to 'milk' the 'cash cows' to fund the 'rising stars', review the marketing approach/strategy of the 'problem children' and restructure or sell the 'dogs' – or should you? A rigid application of this model can cause more problems than it solves.

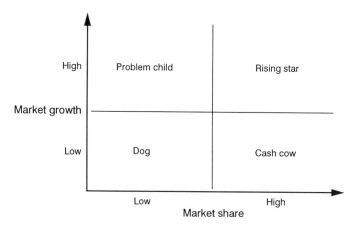

Figure 14.8 Market growth versus market share

293

The problem with this approach is that it can be too simplistic. Many difficulties are caused by the very use of the tool – not many units within an organization would like to be viewed as 'dogs', and even the 'cash cows' might have a problem with seeing all their hard-earned cash being siphoned off to feed others. In the past, some of the recommendations proposed by consultancies using this kind of approach fell foul of organizational politics.

However, this analytical tool can still help to shed an interesting light on a portfolio and is useful when used together with other tools.

Financial-oriented approaches

The financial-oriented approaches are mainly predicated on the assumption that any strategic review will generate a range of options. These options can be evaluated against financial criteria in order to select the best one in terms of its effect on shareholder value. There are quite a few theories and measures that can be used, and two of the more forward-looking ones have been selected here: Rappaport's shareholder value approach and Reimann's value-based strategic management.

Shareholder value approach (SVA)

The basic premise of SVA is fairly simple. The shareholders have invested money in assets and the true value of that investment is the future cash generated by those assets, discounted back to the present by the 'weighted average cost of capital' (WACC), to take into account the time value of money.

For those who are struggling with that last sentence (as I did when I first heard it), let's put it another way. If £100 is invested at 18 per cent to give a return of £18 in a year's time, then £118 in a year's time is worth £100 today, if we assume a cost of capital of 18 per cent. Thus, for any given corporate strategy, a net present value of the strategy can be worked out and, when compared to alternative strategies, rational decisions can be made.

This model can be particularly useful when acquisitions are involved in a strategy. It is also useful to put a monetary present value on various future strategic options. *Creating Shareholder Value* by A Rappaport (1986) gives a detailed founding in the principles and *Valuation* by McKinsey consultants T Copeland, T Koller and J Murrin (1994) also shows how the theory can be used. A succinct summary of the approach can be found in the appendix of my book *Practical Business Re-engineering* (1994).

Strategy formulation models

It is outside the scope of this book to cover all the ins and outs of SVA. However, the outline that follows should give enough of an explanation for you to be able to at least understand what the component parts of SVA are. Shareholder value is made up of four parts – three added together and one deducted – as follows:

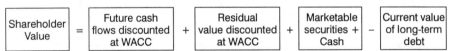

Figure 14.8 SVA analytical approach

Let's look at each one of these components in turn.

- To work out future cash flows, you'll need to decide three key things: the most reasonable yearly forecast of cash being generated by the strategy (note that profit is not cash!), the forecast period and the rate at which future cash flows should be discounted back to the present. The discount rate is derived by working out the cost of the capital of the company (which will depend on its mix and what the sources of debts and equity are).
- The residual value calculation picks up the value of the post-forecast period that is generated. After all, the business will either continue after the forecast period or an exit will be sought. There are various ways in which to calculate this, depending on what the assumptions are of what you want to do with the business at the end of the fore-cast period. You can multiply the last period's earnings by an expected profit/earnings ratio or the equity by an expected market to book ratio. This would assume an exit by the investors. Alternatively, you can assume a break-up and calculate the liquidation value (which is the most conservative approach) or that the business will continue as an ongoing concern, and turn the post-tax operational cash flow (profit after tax plus interest plus depreciation/non-cash expense) into a perpetuity. Whichever way is used, the resultant amount is discounted back to the present using the weighted average cost of capital (WACC). The most commonly used approach is to use the perpetuity method by taking the last cash flow, deducting depreciation (which was added back), and ignoring working capital and fixed asset cash flow. This assumes that the fixed assets needs after the forecast period will be met by depreciation, and that work-ing capital will come to be balanced with short-term assets matched by short-term liabilities. The resultant amount is turned into perpe-tuity by dividing it by the WACC, and then, by discounting the result

295

to the present, you have the present value (PV) of the residual value. Some people are initially uncomfortable with using a perpetuity as nothing lasts for ever. However, nearly 90 per cent of the value of a perpetuity is generated in the 15 years after the forecast period.

● The final part of the calculation is to add the marketable securities and cash of the business and deduct the liabilities to get the share-holder value approach figure.

A worked example of the whole process is shown in Figure 14.9.

As you can see, there are a lot of debatable assumptions behind this approach. It is very number oriented, and will not appeal to intuitive, 'right-brained' individuals. However, it is a very powerful tool. Its value as an approach does not lie in the absolute value figure generated but, rather, in how that figure compares to either other strategic options (calculated using the same SVA approach) or other approaches in calculating shareholder value. As such, it is a useful diagnostic tool to assist decision making when there are several ways forward.

Value-based strategic management (VSM)

VSM is similar to the SVA approach outlined above and can best be described by means of Reimann's VSM matrix. One of the variables is the net present value (NPV) generated by a particular strategy, product

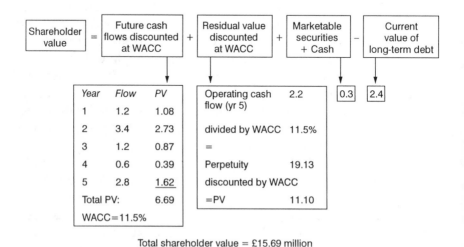

Total shareholder value = £15.69 million
Divided by 5.3 million shares = £2.96 per share

Figure 14.9 A worked example of the SVA approach

296

or part of a corporate portfolio, and the second variable is the return on investment (ROI) compared to the weighted average cost of capital (WACC). Thus, the first variable looks into the future (with the NPV result), and can be calculated using the SVA approach outlined above. The second variable looks at the current situation by comparing the ROI with the WACC. ROI is earnings divided by assets.

This matrix (see Figure 14.10) is best suited to instances when acquisitions or a variety of company options exist that need differing levels of investment.

Internal-oriented approaches

These approaches are based on the theory that the internal dynamics of the organization constitute the main consideration when formulating strategy. The examples of such approaches shown below are from some of the leading strategists, including McKinsey, Mintzberg, Hamel and Prahalad, and Cambell, Goold and Alexander.

The McKinsey 7-S framework

The 7-S framework (see Figure 14.11) is a useful checklist when checking the consistency of a proposed market strategy with the capabilities of the organization. One of the Ss is 'strategy' and, in this context, it can be taken that within the model this is the external market strategy (such as what product, place and so on). Overall, the model leans towards the

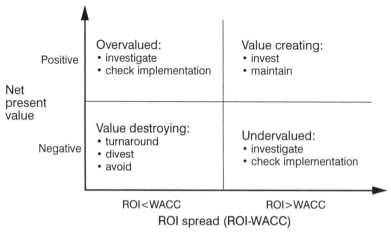

Figure 14.10 The VSM matrix

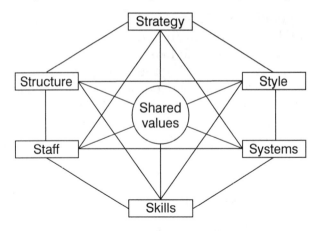

Figure 14.11 The McKinsey 7-S framework

grand strategy (that is, the all-encompassing strategy that will deliver the desired results).

The framework contains seven interactive variables that have an effect on how an organization operates and what makes it succeed or fail. An understanding of each variable, and the way that they influence each other and the overall organization, can provide some unique insights that other tools cannot.

Mintzberg's ideas on strategy creation versus planning

In his book *Mintzberg on Management* (1989), Henry Mintzberg makes a very clear distinction between *strategy creation* and *strategic planning*. Any consideration of strategy formulation should take this into account as, although models may help, it is the context within which they are used that will influence how useful they are. Mintzberg warns that if the formulation and creation of a strategy are done within a standard and (more likely) ritualistic yearly strategy planning cycle, then the chances are that the strategy that results from this process is merely an extension of what has been happening in the past, with a few minor adjustments.

Strategic planning is an analytical process, while strategy creation is a process of synthesis. So, the danger of mixing the two is that any strategy 'created' will be merely an extrapolation of existing strategies or the copying of competitor's strategies.

For Mintzberg, the real craft of strategy is that of detecting subtle discontinuities that may undermine an organization in the future. There are no techniques or programmes that can do this, save for a sharp mind, as these discontinuities are irregular and unexpected. They are therefore perceived only by minds that can understand the patterns but can also see important breaks within them. This attitude to strategy is developed further in another of Mintzberg's works, which is considered on page 301.

Competing for the future

Gary Hamel and C K Prahalad, in their book *Competing for the Future* (1994), propose a more dynamic and open-ended process for strategy formulation. They state that the strategic planning process needs to move from incremental improvements to creating new competitive space and rewriting the rules of the industry, from formulaic planning to exploratory planning, and from involvement of only executives and managers to all line staff to capture the collective wisdom of the company. For a company to begin to think this way, they propose eight questions, to be answered using a graduated scale.

- How do senior managers' points of view about the future stack up against those of the competitors? (The scale for the answer should have 'Conventional and reactive' at one end, 'Distinctive and farsighted' at the other.)
- Which issue is absorbing senior management's attention? (The scale for this should have 'Re-engineering core processes' at one end, 'Regenerating core strategies at the other.)
- Within the industry, is the organization seen as a rule taker or rule maker? (The scale should have 'Mostly a rule taker' at one end, 'Mostly a rule market' at the other.)
- What are we better at, improving operational efficiency or creating fundamentally new businesses? (The scale should have 'Operational efficiency' at one end, 'New business development' at the other.)
- What percentage of our advantage-building efforts focuses on catching up with competitors' actions versus building advantages new to the industry? (The scale should have 'Mostly catching up others' at one end, 'Mostly new to the industry' at the other.)
- To what extent has our transformation agenda been set by competitors' actions versus being set by our own unique vision of the future? (The scale should have 'Largely driven by competitors' at one end, 'Largely driven by our vision' at the other.)

- To what extent am I, as a senior manager, a maintenance engineer working on the present versus an architect working on the future? (The scale should have 'Mostly an engineer' at one end, 'Mostly hope at the other.)

Central to this approach is the identification and management of core competences and the ability to grow from internal energy.

Strategy acceptance versus quality

The models so far have been aimed at helping the quality of strategy formulation. Another aspect that needs to be taken into account is the level of acceptance the strategy enjoys. The two variables here are the extent to which the strategy is accepted and understood (is it just the Board – if at all – or does the strategy fully and clearly permeate the whole organization?) and the quality of the strategy itself (either good or bad).

If the organization has a good strategy, but poor acceptance, then there will be a need to communicate. On the other hand, a widely accepted, but poor, strategy would need to be urgently reviewed and reformulated before the whole organization happily charges over a cliff!

Every company has a strategy, if you accept that strategy is action. If the action is undirected or if the direction is known and accepted by only a few people, then the organization has a problem, as can be seen from Figure 14.12.

Depending where you are on the matrix will dictate the extent to which the organization has to rethink and involve others.

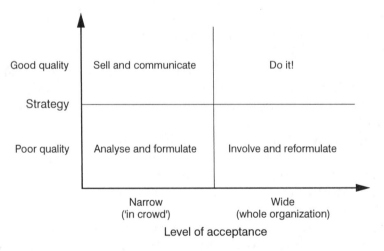

Figure 14.12 Strategic acceptance

Corporate-level strategy

In their book entitled *Corporate-level Strategy* (1994), M Goold, A Campbell and M Alexander look at the dynamics facing a company that is a multibusiness organization. Many companies having either separate trading divisions or companies focus on their own unique markets and products. The issue facing the strategy of a group is that, while each of the divisions or companies may have its own strategies, often the corporate group does not. The proclaimed strategy, if it does exist, is often nothing more than an amalgam of those of the individual units. This model of formulation suggests the need for a tight fit between the 'parent' organization and its businesses.

From their analysis of 15 successful multibusiness organizations, Goold, Campbell and Alexander identify three key essentials to successful corporate-level strategies.

- A clear insight about the role of the parent and the value it brings to each of its businesses. If the parent does not how or where it can add value for its businesses, it is unlikely to do so.
- A distinctive characteristic. The parent must have its own unique character and identity, with its own culture and personality. This needs to harmonize with the personalities of the businesses – that is, there need to be some shared values.
- The recognition that the parent will only be successful with certain kinds of businesses described as 'heartland' businesses. This focuses on the fit between the parent and the business. Do the parent's insights and behaviours fit with the opportunities and nature of the business? Does the parent have specialist skills that can add real value to the business and help it perform better?

Corporate-level strategy can be enhanced by 'parenting advantage', which creates more value in the portfolio of businesses than would be achieved by a competitor or by the businesses operating in isolation. Given the traditional discount of value assigned by capital markets to conglomerates, such an approach would typically demand a fundamental change in the basic assumptions that typically exist between a parent and its businesses.

Emergent strategies

Building on his work *Mintzberg on Management* described above, Mintzberg explored further the dynamics of strategy formulation in *The*

Rise and Fall of Strategic Planning (1994). Central to our theme of strategy formulation, Mintzberg points out three common flaws.

- The assumption that discontinuities can be predicted is the first common flaw. Most forecasting techniques tend to assume that the future will resemble the past in some way. The danger is that a false degree of reassurance is created and so strategies fall apart when events overtake them. Our passion for planning in business dates back to the 1960s when the world was far more predictable and stable than is the case today.
- Many who are involved in formulating strategy are detached from the every day workings of the organization. Thus, too often the strategic thinking is separated from the strategic 'doing', to adverse effect. Those involved in strategy formulation rely on gathering 'hard data' and the day-to-day soft (often 'anecdotal') data are ignored. It is often within this day-to-day soft data – gathered every day by those who are 'doing' – that the priceless insights exist. While hard data informs the intellect, soft data informs wisdom, and any strategy formulation process needs to ensure that it is captured and used to good effect.
- The assumption that strategy formulation can be formalized in a planning–type process. The left-brain activity of planning, by its very nature, defines and preserves categories. The right-brain activity of creativity creates categories or redefines existing ones. Overly structuring strategy formulation can close down options instead of opening them up.

Strategy formulation, as defined by Mintzberg, has the following characteristics if it is to succeed. It:

- is derived from synthesis
- is informal and visionary, not programmed or formalized
- is reliant on right-brain activity, discovery, intuition and divergent thinking
- is irregular, *ad hoc* and unexpected
- is based on managers being opportunistic and adaptive information manipulators rather than aloof conductors
- is done in times of instability, characterized by discontinuous change
- involves a variety of actors, engaged in a journey of exploration, experiment and discovery.

Thus, strategy is something that emerges rather than something that is defined. Ground-breaking strategies 'grow initially like weeds, they are not cultivated like tomatoes in a hot-house ...'. The culture and processes within an organization, on a day-to-day level, will thus be vital to ensure that the strategies formulated by means of discovery are those that can deliver success in a sustained way.

Hybrid approaches

So far we have looked at some older, traditional models of strategy formulation, models that have as a primary focus external issues and those focusing mainly on internal issues. This section will look at some hybrid approaches. These are ones that can either be applied internally or externally (such as SWOT analysis), or those that have a mix of internal and external issues (such as Ohmae's three Cs).

SWOT analysis

SWOT analysis is a good way to summarize the research of external and internal perceptions of the organization. It should be done with care as the result is perceptions (which may not be facts). However, assuming that people's perceptions are rooted in reality, it is a useful tool. It is worth using across a variety of groups so comparisons can be made. For example, comparing senior management's perceptions with those of customers in a SWOT format may show how 'in tune' the top of the organization is with its customers! Further comparisons between customers and staff perceptions may highlight internal issues as well.

Obolensky's stakeholder approach

In my book *Practical Business Re-engineering* (1994), I suggest that a successful strategy has to take into account the needs of the key stakeholders. In a business, typically these stakeholders will be customers, employees, suppliers and shareholders. I propose a process that suggests strategy formulation is about understanding the overarching vision and mission of an organization and how it will meet the needs of its stakeholders. The mission is broken down further into stakeholder goals (that is, what we need to achieve for this stakeholder in order for us to achieve our mission). These goals can be defined yet further with measures and targets and the broad initiatives and actions that will help to achieve the targets.

The dynamic is complicated and involves a process of dialogue with stakeholders (that is, strategy formulation is not something you do to them, it is something you do with them). It also starts with a clear identification of why reformulation of strategy is necessary and how such a formulation can be achieved, rather than just what strategy is necessary. This process and subsequent output can be summarized by the model shown in Figure 14.13.

Ohmae's three Cs

In his book *The Mind of the Strategies* (1982), Kenichi Ohmae suggests that any business strategy will need to take into account three main players each beginning with 'c' – as shown in Figure 14.14.

The job of a strategist is that of ensuring that superior performance can be achieved relative to the competition in the eyes of the customer, and that this matches the strengths of the corporation. The positive matching of the needs and objectives of the customer and the corporation is key for a lasting relationship. The model needs to be underpinned by an approach that is non-linear and often irrational. In Ohmae's words, 'Events in the real world do not always fit a linear model. Hence the most reliable means of dissecting a situation into its constituent parts and re-assembling them . . . is that ultimate non-linear thinking tool, the human brain'. He suggests that there are four main methods that can be used to ensure that a strategy is successful.

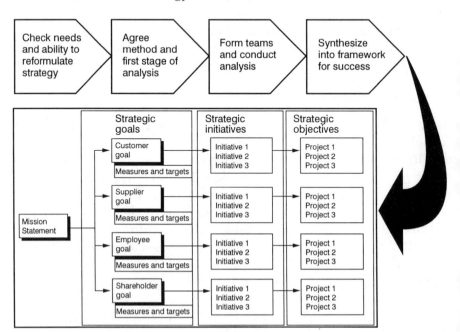

Figure 14.13 Stakeholder strategy formulation

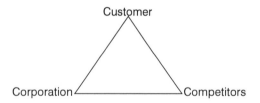

Figure 14.14 Olmae's three Cs

- Focusing on key success factors (KSFs). Knowing what your factors for success are, and then exploiting them, only makes sense when considered in light of the customer and what competitors can do.
- Focus on relative superiority. It may be that the corporation lacks significant KSFs in the eyes of customers compared to competitors. This can happen when all the competitors are seeking to compete on KSFs. Then a possible method is to exploit the differences in the competitive conditions by building a relative superiority. This could be, for example, using technology in a different way in distribution to gain advantage.
- Pursue new initiatives aggressively. Such initiatives could be to upset the current industry KSFs or change the rules of the game and introduce new KSFs.
- Make the most of 'degrees of freedom'. By this Ohmae means that innovation can be used in areas that are currently untouched by the competition.

In all four possible methods, the dynamics of the three Cs (both within and between each of them) need to be borne in mind.

Possible roles of a consultant

Consultants can be of immense use to a company formulating strategy, but they can also be a waste of time and money. The reason they can become the latter is if they do not understand the true needs of the client and, instead, only react to expressed wants. The roles they can play, and the underlying needs that are there are usually a mix of three different types of role:

- expert
- facilitator
- coach.

Expert

There are two broad levels of expertise that a good strategy consultant can draw on:

- the tools and techniques for the formulation of strategy – some of which have been outlined above
- the expertise in the process of strategy formulation itself.

The level of industry expertise can also be included in this, although this can get in the way of adding real value. If we are to believe that strategy formulation should be about actual change rather than a continuation of past assumptions, then deep industry knowledge can be a barrier. Within a company, there will be many years of knowledge to draw on, quite apart from that of outside industrial associations. Thus, it may be a strange notion, but the expertise does not have to be in the industry *per se;* it can be in the tools and process.

So, how best can the expertise be used? The underlying need could be that the client does not know how to formulate strategy. Given the pro-liferation of MBAs, this may be a rare occurrence. However, if the client does lack knowledge, they will be doubly pleased to not only be given a decent strategy, but, as important, be given the knowledge required to formulate a decent strategy in the future.

From this it can be seen that the best role for a consultant under the guise of 'expert' is that of managing the client through skills transfer-ence and passing on the skills needed (both tools and techniques or process management). Less scrupulous strategy consultants would favour the 'keep the knowledge and breed dependency approach' – avoid such temptation!

Facilitator

Many companies have the expertise they need in-house, in terms of tools and techniques, and overall process. However, given the nature of debate, a facilitator well versed in strategy can help the process run along smoothly. Here, the role is one of assisting the process, spotting obstacles before they create damage and generally overseeing the process going smoothly. Some may argue that the facilitator needs no expertise in either the industry or the tools, techniques or processes of strategy formulation. While this may be true for pure facilitation, given the nature of what is being facilitated, it is best if expertise is owned in terms of techniques and processes. If nothing else, this will enable the consultant to empathize, have meaningful conversations outside facilitated sessions and show a degree of interest.

There are some strategy formulation techniques that are gained by virtue of facilitation, such as open space technology and future search. Given these techniques often merge formulation with implementation, they have been dealt with in Chapter 8, Part I.

Coach

Many of the finest strategy formulation exercises run aground on the rocks of corporate politics. In this case, the underlying need is to sort out the political dynamics. The strategy consultant, if he is to be able to add real value, will need to deal with these dynamics in a way that ensures any formulation is followed by smooth implementation. As much of the negative attributes associated with corporate policies owe a lot to personal agendas and perceptions, coaching skills can help teams and individuals overcome their attitudes when strategy formulation gives rise to negative behaviour. If a strategy consultant is unable to help people through such barriers, then the service they are giving may well end up being an expensive waste of time for the client.

Summary

The reality is that a successful consultant in the role of delivering strategy will have expertise in the tools, techniques and the process, as well as the ability to act as both facilitator and coach. The consultant will need to act all three roles out as a mix and blend them, as required. It is the most demanding of all consultancy roles, and also one of the most rewarding!

Consultants' checklist

There follow ten key questions that can be scored out of 10 to check what the risks of the strategy formulation are.

- To what extent has the strategy been based on facts rather than merely opinions?
- To what extent have the opinions of those involved in the ultimate implementation of the strategy been taken into account?
- To what extent does the strategy break new ground in the industry?
- To what extent does the organization share the vision and overall mission that the strategy is aimed at achieving?

- How far down the line is the strategy translated into effective, measureable action?
- To what extent has the enablement of leading-edge technology been taken into account?
- To what extent is there a process within the organization to encourage emergent strategies?
- How far have the needs of the key stakeholders been taken into account (both internal and external)?
- If the organization has used consultants to help in strategy formulation before, to what extent will they need to help again in the future (the lower the need, the higher the score)?
- If the strategy has been formulated away from those involved, how much time has been spent on planning the 'how' of implementation, rather than just the 'what'?

While the above list is far from exhaustive, it will highlight some of the common pitfalls. For completeness, it should be read alongside the checklist in Chapter 8, Part I.

Summary

The strategy formulation techniques and approaches outlined in this chapter have been but tasters – there are many more. If this chapter has whetted your appetite for more knowledge, leaving you slightly frustrated that it has not supplied enough, then it has served its purpose well.

Strategy formulation is a great and fascinating art. There are many theories, some of them contradicting others. It would be a mistake to think that one or other theory was right as they are all, in their own ways, right. The secret is to know as many of them as you can, and so be the richer and more able to meet the unique and special needs of each particular client and their circumstances.

It is the application to good effect of such models that is the important part, rather than the mere knowledge of them in their own right. However, application without knowledge is ignorance and, as a consultant, unprofessional. See the References section below for a good list of books to read if you wish to study this subject in greater detail.

References

Andrews, K R (1971) *The Concept of Corporate Strategy*, Harvard Business School Press, Boston

Strategy formulation models

Ansoff, H I (1965) *Corporate Strategy,* McGraw-Hill, New York

Copeland, T, Koller, T, and Murrin, J (1994) *Valuation: Measuring and managing the value of companies,* Wiley, Chichester

Goold, M, Campbell, A, and Alexander, M (1994) *Corporate-level Strategy,* John Wiley, New York

Hamel, G, and Prahalad, C K (1994) *Competiting for the Future: Breakthrough strategies for seizing control of your industry and creating the markets of tomorrow.* Harvard Business School Press, Boston

Mintzberg, Henry (1989) *Mintzberg on Management,* The Free Press, New York; Collier Macmillan, London

Mintzberg, Henry (1994) *The Rise and Fall of Strategic Planning.* Prentice-Hall International, Englewood Cliffs, New Jersey

Obolensky, N (1994) *Practical Business Re-engineering: Tools and techniques for achieving effective change,* Kogan Page, London; Gulf, Houston

Ohmae, K (1982) *The Mind of the Strategist,* McGraw-Hill, New York

Porter, Michael (1980) *Competitive Strategy: Techniques for analysing industries and competitors,* The Free Press, New York

Porter, Michael (1985) *Competitive Advantage: Creating and sustaining superior performance,* The Free Press, New York

Rappaport, Alfred (1986) *Creating Shareholder Value: The new standard for business performance,* The Free Press, New York

Reimann, Bernard (1987) *Managing for Value: A guide to value-based strategic management,* Basil Blackwell & The Planning Forum, Ohio

15

Techniques, methods and models of consulting

David Hussey

Introduction

The aim of this chapter is to show something of the ways in which consultants develop their own product offerings from the concepts, techniques, methods and models that emerge from sources such as the universities and from the practical experience of management thinkers. Although consultants sometimes develop original concepts, more frequently their contribution is in operationalizing new developments and passing on their skills to clients. This chapter will show how detailed approaches to the application of concepts developed by others may result in the development of products and services that give added value to the client, contribute to quality standards within the firm and give a basis for differentiation. The contribution that consultants make in spreading new ideas, and providing methods to turn them from academic theory to practical advantage, is very real.

A consultancy business may be developed from an original concept and, although this is less frequent, there are numerous examples where this has happened, some of which will be discussed in this chapter.

Reference will be made to a variety of concepts, techniques, approaches and models that are commonly used in organizations and by consultants.

Different approaches to consulting

Elsewhere in this book it has been emphasized that there are many different approaches to management consulting, and these affect how knowledge is applied. Four styles of consulting are described here.

- **Task** This is the independent investigation of a problem or issue a client is facing, leading to the collection and assessment of evidence, analysis, conclusions and recommendations. This style is what springs to the minds of most people when they first think of management consultants. Assignments may be very varied, and could cover matters such as improving the manufacturing operations of a factory, examining the strategy of a multinational enterprise or giving a view on the prospects for a proposed new product.

- **Process** As its name suggests, this approach to consulting is concerned with making processes more effective rather than with problems such as where the client should build the new factory. Process consulting studies how things happen. The process consultant will be concerned with the interaction of the members of the management team, the way in which meetings are conducted and how decisions are made – and, of course, how all this can be improved to make the organization more effective. The consultant's role may be to give hands-on help to improve the process.

- **Knowledge transfer** This requires the skills of both the task and the process consultant, plus some coaching and counselling abilities. Here the consultant works with the people in the organization, transferring the methods needed for the assignment to them and helping them to interpret the results and reach decisions. Much of the detailed work will be performed by the client's own managers as part of this process. The rationale for this approach is that it results in better decisions, as the managers are helped to assess the evidence for themselves – that this involvement builds commitment – so that decisions are implemented and that the methods and techniques used become available to the organization for future problems.

- **Adviser/counsellor** This approach provides expert knowledge, on a day-to-day basis, helping managers to reach the best decision on a variety of issues as they arise. In one sense, the consultant functions as a member of the management team, with a carefully defined role. In addition to providing expertise and experience, the consultant may play a coaching role.

The style of consulting may affect how the consultancy thinks of, and uses, a particular technique or method. A task consultancy, working with a big team, will want to ensure that a methodology is in place that helps to progress the assignment and ensures that all members of the team are working together so that all parts of the mosaic of activity can be assembled. In addition, there is often value in differentiating the firm, by means of its methods, from others that rely only on the expert knowledge of the consultants and use methods that the client could find in the appropriate management textbooks.

The process consultant will often want to make use of psychometric testing techniques to obtain data about the client's managers in order to help them work more effectively. Similar techniques may be applied by a task consultant on behalf of a client, and the difference is in the purpose and use made of the results.

The knowledge transfer consultant is likely to use the same techniques and concepts as the task consultant, but also require methods that make it possible to work with managers who may have a less than expert knowledge of the subject or whose experience in its application may be limited. This might, for example, require the use of approaches to the techniques that are designed to be used in workshops and working meetings, such as workbooks that help managers to collect and interpret the information needed.

Under the adviser style, there may be less need for proprietary methods and a greater reliance instead on the depth and breadth of knowledge of an area of expertise, and wide experience of working in that area at the right level. The adviser needs to know when and where a particular technique or method may be helpful without necessarily having the expertise to apply it personally.

Building a practice on an original proprietary approach

It is not always easy to be totally original, in that a good proprietary approach may be underpinned by a variety of conceptual work and build on the general body of knowledge. So what we are talking about here is a proprietary approach that is something more than the practical application of a concept, and which promises real and different benefits to the clients that hire the consultancy. It is easy to see the attraction of this for the consultancy as well – that it is able to offer something that is uniquely the intellectual property of the firm.

There are enough firms that have taken this approach and been successful to make it worth considering, although it should also be remembered that the investment in developing and producing something that is powerful enough to build a practice on is likely to be significant. The Boston Consulting Group is one of the best-known examples of a firm that founded a substantial international reputation and business on two original concepts, which were linked to provide a powerful consultancy approach for its time. The first was its approach to portfolio analysis (see page 293), and The Boston Consulting Group terminology of dogs, cash cows and stars remains part of management vocabulary today.

In conjunction with this last technique, the firm developed the concept of the experience curve. Learning curve theory had been noted in manufacturing by others, and is the phenomenon whereby costs fall by a constant percentage every time cumulative production of an item doubles. The Boston Consulting Group did enough research to be able to extend this thinking to the total costs of the firm, enabling consultants to calculate the experience curve effect for any given company.

So, the business started with these two powerful tools for strategic decision making that fitted the strategic issues of the day at a time when little was on offer to aid the systematic analysis of strategy.

Monitor was formed by Professor Michael Porter to apply his approaches to industry and competitor analysis. However, there was a difference in that Porter's industry analysis and value chain approaches (Porter, 1980 and 1985, see pages 287–9 and 290) had been widely published and were being used by many other firms of consultants. The Boston Consulting Group, however, slowly released its methodology over a period of years, so, although the basic concept of portfolio analysis became known quite early on, many of the essential details of how to make its analysis system work only became widely known after the original technique had become outdated.

Kepner Tregoe is another well-known business that operates internationally. It was built on the back of a particular approach to problem solving. While working together at Rand, Benjamin Tregoe and Charles Kepner identified a critical need that managers had for a logical method for solving problems and making decisions. They left Rand and developed a distinctive systematic approach to problem solving, operational decision making and planning and, on the basis of this, formed their consulting firm in 1958. By 1981, they were able to claim that their techniques were used in 60 of the top 100 US companies by size, and in 400 of the largest 1,000 worldwide. They positioned their firm as the experts in the process of decision making, whereas the Boston Consulting Group, which based its business on techniques, was positioned as the experts on the content of the strategic decisions with which they were involved. Both firms are still in business today, and a number of books have been written on Kepner and Tregoe's approaches (see, for example, Kepner and Tregoe,1981).

Larry Farrell was at one time President of Kepner Tregoe. In 1983, he established his own consulting company. The initial basis of this was to introduce 'excellence' for Tom Peters to companies worldwide (see Peters and Waterman, 1982). From there he began to be concerned about how to establish an entrepreneurial spirit in large organizations. He researched the issue and developed his own concepts and processes, which are now the main activity of his firm. The company operates globally via a number of licensed associates. (Farrell, 1993, describes the broad philosophy behind his methods.)

Most consulting firms that build a business on proprietary methods move on as time passes to avoid the danger of being dependent for too long on something that could lose its value. Thus, The Boston Consulting Group today has a business that has developed new techniques and is not dependent on the success of portfolio analysis. Hay has a much broader practice than that which grew as a result of its proprietary approach to salary administration. The danger that has to be avoided is to become too hooked on the original concept, so that it is used after its sell-by date has expired, or the technique or approach is used in situations for which it is not particularly appropriate.

Operationalizing knowledge and concepts

Many popular ideas – such as core competences, the value chain, benchmarking, business process re-engineering and Total Quality Management – are often described by their originators in broad, conceptual terms. The tone of the articles and books may be persuasive and convincing, but the details of how to apply the method, concept, process or technique are lacking. This may be because the originator is interested in the ideas rather than the detail or because holding back on the detail while promoting the idea is a route to gaining consultancy invitations for the guru.

This, of course, may be one of the tactics that consulting firms use themselves. For example, for every hundred books that say what the technique of portfolio analysis is, you are lucky if you can find one that goes into any detail about how the various businesses of the organization can be plotted on the matrix. The idea is clear and the value of it is easy to see, but moving from guesswork and inspiration to a methodology that will stand up to the scrutiny of others is left to the reader.

Clients read the same newspaper articles and journals as consultants and have access to the same books. New concepts and ideas take root very quickly. Clients may develop the methodology to use the approaches themselves or turn to consultants for help. The consultants may be aware of the new ideas and want to use them in assignments for clients because it is believed that they will deliver better value to the client.

It is in this area of making things workable that consultants make the largest contribution. When a technique or method is well established, consultants may use it without contributing more than knowledge or experience. Many consultancies use recognized behavioural measurement tools in their work and most of these would involve members of the consultancy's team going through the training process, becoming licensed to use the method and thereafter buying the questionnaires from the originator. There is little incentive to invent a methodology for the application of, for example, the situational leadership concepts of Hersey and Blanchard (1969) when the authors themselves have developed everything that is needed. (Do not be put off by the date, 1969: modern material is available to apply this concept, which shows how the way in which employees should be managed is contingent on their capability and motivation.)

However, let us look at a few situations where consultants have found it necessary to develop their own ways of applying a concept, approach or technique. Although there is some overlap, it is helpful to classify the situations under the headings of audits, processes, and tools and techniques.

Audits

Everyone is familiar with accountants' audits and the fact that auditors follow careful procedures to confirm that the accounts of an organization give a true and fair representation of its results. The term is used here in a wider context, to cover situations where there is a need to assess what is happening against what should happen if a given end is to be achieved. Buckner (1993) argues, 'Non-financial audits have essentially two goals. One is to check compliance to a requirement of standard . . . The second purpose is to determine the adequacy of a product or service to satisfy the demands of customers or other key groups.'

The collection and analysis of information is part of normal activity for many consultants. The consultancy has to make a choice between relying entirely on the expertise of its consultants to decide how each assignment should be tackled and establishing a standardized approach, built around ways of undertaking the assignment that the consultancy believes are significant. Buckner includes surveys, questionnaires, focus groups, interviewing, observation and benchmarking among other techniques that may be used in the audit process. To this list might be added the analysis of hard information.

There are some types of assignments where prudence suggests the need for a carefully thought out approach, such as the firm that undertakes due diligence work, which may encompass a total performance audit of an organization. There are others where an audit offers a way of applying a concept and a method that has been given some thought becomes a sales tool, a way of building the client's confidence in what may be new thinking and a means of gaining competitive advantage.

Henry (1990) gives a partial description of the approach taken by SRI International to link technology to the corporate strategy. This has as its first step an audit: 'A technology-asset audit focuses on determining the real or perceived value that any technology node, or its individual technology links, has in the business benefit/cost chain – from raw material acquisition, to the supply of the product or service, to the customer.' The information revealed by Henry includes some models, checklists of questions and some ways of displaying the outcome.

The second step assesses the strategic implications of the technology portfolio, while the third develops a technological implementation plan – and the final one is a monitoring process. What SRI has is a method of making sense of something that otherwise would be very difficult to turn from a good idea into a practical way of benefiting the client.

Buckner provides methodologies for 13 different types of audit – leadership, culture, corporate identity, customer satisfaction, logistics, service management, productivity, information security, cost of quality, strategic alliance, technology, the environment and business strategy. These are designed for self use by organizations, and the authors include people from some of the best-known consultancies, such as PA Management Consultants, Andersen, SRI International, Arthur D Little, and AT Kearney.

Wilson (1993) provides numerous marketing audit checklists that, again, have been designed for organizations to administer themselves. In fact, there are so many questions in his book of nearly 300 pages that anyone who ever again asks a question about marketing activity is likely to be infringing his copyright!

Chapter 11, Part 3, provided a model for thinking about a strategic approach to human resource management. This is further described in Hussey (1996) and has been the basis of an approach to audit human resource management activity. This defines what information is needed and how to obtain it. It incorporates a number of checklists that show what is required – focus groups, 360° feedback questionnaires, interviews and analytical approaches to obtain the information; matrix displays and other methods – to make sense of the information.

Processes

An audit is concerned with an activity that is already happening inside the organization and, of course, may be of an existing process. Consultants are also concerned with processes that they may be hired to introduce into the organization. Attention here is focused on processes that stretch across functional boundaries, where consultants have again made a significant contribution, taking the ideas of management thinkers and turning them into something that is actionable.

There may well be an overlap between the concept of a proprietary approach to audits and to processes. However, it is only possible to audit something that exists, and consultants are often called upon to help an organization apply a process that is new to it. So, when something such as Total Quality Management (TQM) or business process re-engineering (BPR) hits the headlines and is a practice area that fits the visions and capabilities of the consultancy, there is a need to figure out how to do it.

Some firms have gone beyond this, developing their own approaches to a particular popular process. For example, the Crosby consultancy was built on the quality principles of Philip Crosby. These include a number of absolutes from which there can be no deviation (one of which is that the performance standard has to be zero defects) and 14 specific steps to quality improvement. Built around this are processes to make TQM work in an organization, and company-wide training to support the process (Crosby, 1979, 1984, 1987). Although many consultants work in the TQM field, which is probably as crowded as any, the Crosby consultancy was able to create a strong, global position based on its unique approaches.

In the 1980s, the concept of world-class manufacturing emerged, later to be extended to world-class performance. Hayes, Wheelwright and Clark (1988) defined world-class manufacturing as follows: 'Basically, this means being better than almost every company in your industry in at least one important aspect of manufacturing'. Becoming and remaining world class may involve using a number of individual approaches, processes and techniques that need to be bound together in a continuing process (for example, flexible manufacturing systems (FMS), Just-in-Time production (JIT), computer-aided design (CAD) and computer-aided manufacturing (CAM)). It is in this area that consultants move beyond the print in the textbooks to develop workable ways of introducing such processes to organizations.

In fact, it is reasonable to see many of the modern ideas of management as relating to processes rather than techniques. Creating a learning organization is seen as an important objective of many, but only happens if someone thinks through what has to be done and adapts this to the real situations of organizations. Again, the burden of doing this often falls on the consultant and it is very hard to deliver value to the client if the consultant has done no work in thinking through the processes and methods by which a learning organization might be achieved.

Tools and techniques

Where a process may be seen as something that is intended to go on happening on a continuous basis, 'tools and techniques' are defined here as methods and approaches that are used in specific situations. In an organization similar situations may recur, and so the use of the technique or tool may be repeated. The differences between a 'technique' and a 'process' often form a grey area, because techniques are sometimes incorporated into a process. For example, 360° feedback may be used as a way of collecting information, but it can also be an integral part of an annual appraisal process.

The range of tools and techniques available to consultants is very wide and the few mentioned below are included to illustrate this. The list does not include those in the area of strategic management, as they have been discussed in Chapter 14.

Human resource management

360° feedback
This is a group of related techniques that measure how a manager manages by defining the behaviours needed for successful management and taking measurements in a carefully controlled way from peers, subordinates and boss.

In reality, depending on the purpose, it is not always necessary to do more than take bottom-up feedback, while for other purposes it may be desirable to break out of the internal circle and take feedback from customers and suppliers.

As mentioned, such a technique may become part of a formal appraisal process, the idea being that the totality of the approach gives a more balanced assessment of the performance of the whole person than is the case with more traditional methods. It is this use of the technique that has become very popular during the 1990s. As a technique, for gaining information for use in training programmes, to measure the organizational climate or a variety of other purposes, however, it has a much longer history and has been in use by Harbridge House (now part of Coopers & Lybrand) and Forum Group since the 1970s.

The concept is very simple, but developing validated methods, establishing the statistical databases that enable the results of the findings about an individual to be compared with those of peers and colleagues and developing approaches that are ethical and preserve confidentiality are all opportunities for something unique to be created by the consultant. This point could be repeated for any technique, but, as this would become boring, I will not do so here.

Psychometric tools

A number of these have been mentioned earlier in this chapter and so they will not be listed again here. They consist of various ways of assessing personality, very often grouping people into types. These typologies are then used to help managers understand conflict behaviour, improve the effectiveness of meetings and relate job requirements to the individual. In fact, there are hundreds of specific methods intended for different uses.

Competences

The human resources meaning of competences is not the same as core competences, discussed in Chapter 14, in the context of strategic management. Tovey (1992) defines competence as 'the application of a blend of knowledge, skills and behaviours in the context of individual job performance'. In other words, competence is one of the things that has to be done well if a person is to be effective in their job. The concept itself is not new, but it attracted new interest in the UK after the publication of an extensive report into management development (Constable and McCormack, 1987).

The competency approach is a tool rather than a technique and by itself does little. However, it can be the underpinning of management training and development, career planning, culture change and performance management as well as the management of recruitment. It is not surprising therefore that some consulting firms have developed their own methods for identifying competences.

A generic approach has been developed and published by one organization – the Management Charter Initiative (MCI) – which has done useful work in codifying the method (see, for example, MCI, 1992). However, the underlying assumption in the MCI's approach is that the key management competences are the same across all companies for people on equivalent levels. This is a weak assumption (see Hussey, 1996, page 93, for more information) and leaves plenty of scope for consultants to develop proprietary approaches that relate competences to the business needs of the organization. In addition, the whole area of professional and technical competences should be considered. Tovey (1992) illustrates both these aspects by providing a description of the methodology developed by one firm of consultants to achieve a strategic approach to competences, illustrated by case histories, and also the methods used to define the competences at various levels in the tax department of one of the world's largest oil companies.

General management

Some of these tools and techniques may be claimed by specific functions. For example many accountants and a few economists would argue that the discounted cash flow technique discussed is 'theirs', and they may well be the people who suggest its use. Its purpose is to aid management decision making, which is why it is listed as a general management tool.

Discounted cash flow

There are several techniques based on discounted cash flow principles, and the basic approach is by no means new. Its widespread use dates back to the 1960s, when it was used as a method of evaluating and comparing various capital expenditures.

It is a form of analysis that takes into account the time value of money, and is based on the fact that a unit of money today is worth more than the same unit at some time in the future, because of the earnings that could be gained if it were available today. If the money is not available until some time in the future, this opportunity has to be forgone. Thus, net streams of cash for an investment or activity are forecast into the future and discounted back to their present value, using a rate of discount that equates to the cost of capital. Several measures can be calculated, the two most common being *net present value (NPV)* and *internal rate of return (IRR)*. The former measures the net cash flows of the project over time. For example, if a discount rate of 10 per cent were used, the NPV would be zero if the project equated to the standard, negative if it went below 10 per cent and positive if it went above it. IRR is the rate of discount that would apply to achieve a zero NPV.

The basic rules of discounted cash flow are almost as well established as double-entry bookkeeping, and the more modern developments have been how to allow for risk and the extension of the approach from projects to concepts of shareholder value. It is in the use of the technique in the management of shareholder value that consultants are more likely to develop proprietary approaches as there is still a debate about certain aspects of the methodology. There are firms that specialize in this area, such as Stern Stewart and Company in the USA (see Stewart, 1991).

Benchmarking

The originator of this tool is believed to be the Xerox Corporation. G H Watson (1993) quotes the definition of benchmarking of the American Productivity and Quality Control Center (APQC, 1992): 'Benchmarking is a systematic and continuous measurement process; a process of continuously measuring an organization's business processes against business process leaders anywhere in the world to gain information which will help the organization take action to improve its performance'.

Benchmarking should not be confused with ratio analysis, although this may be a first step in indicating that improvement is possible. The aim is to study the process by which an organization achieves the better performance. It follows that this need not be a competitor's process. For example, certain companies have studied the pit stop activities of Formula 1 racing, in order to find ways in which they can speed up changeover times on a production line.

The first requirement of the method is that the organization studies and defines its own process, because only after this has been done will it be sensible for it to see what can be learned from other organizations. The final stage is to adapt what has been learned to the organization's situation. The process element is the repetition of the tool across different processes over time, in a continuous search for improvement.

Many consultancies have undertaken benchmarking assignments on behalf of clients. Some, such as Karlöf and Partners, a Swedish firm, have taken the thinking further and have a concept they call *benchlearning*, which links benchmarking to a leadership development process and training. The precise details are not important (but see Karlöf and Östblom, 1994, if you are curious), as the significance of the method lies in the way consultants use and build on standard concepts.

The balanced scorecard

Kaplan and Norton (1990 and 1996) developed the concept of the balanced scorecard as a means of controlling the total performance of an organization. The balance is achieved by the inclusion of both financial and non-financial measures. The scorecard has four quadrants:

- financial, or the perspective of the shareholders
- customer
- innovation and learning, or the ways in which the organization can continue to create value
- internal, or what is the organization good at.

Making the concept work requires that the key variables under each quadrant be identified, and goals and measures be set for each. A subsequent step is working out how to obtain the information needed to monitor progress on a regular basis.

The concept is one that is used by a number of consultancies in their work with clients. For example, Andersen Consulting promotes it as a stage in its procedure for helping organizations develop a strategic approach to training.

Other techniques and tools
Many more could be mentioned, but these are the main ones. Descriptions of the others can be found in a variety of books, including T Kempner's (1990) which covers a broad spectrum of management techniques, tools and concepts, D E Hussey's (1998) D F Channon's (1997) and R H Parker's (1992).

Developing proprietary methods

All proprietary methods should be developed with care, but the risks are not the same for all of them. A new psychometric tool, for example, requires extreme care to be taken to ensure that it is both reliable and valid, because of the serious damage that would otherwise be caused the client and the individual employees of the client.

However, a workbook that codifies an approach to help guide a client's managers through an exercise in industry analysis carries less risk as it can be used in a more flexible way and is intended to guide rather than define.

Harbridge House in Boston, USA, developed an original approach to innovation, and a brief description of the way this was done may aid those thinking about some of the issues involved. Innovation appeared to be a subject that fitted the capabilities of the firm and one for which there were clients who had need of help. It was also a subject that appeared to be current, judging by the number of books and articles on it appearing at the time. It was also observed that many clients confused innovation with creativity, which, in fact, is only one of its components. Research was the first step, and a significant sample was chosen of organizations that had innovated successfully, whether this had been in terms of products, processes or systems. Interviews were held with the managers who had taken the innovation from basic idea to action to identify what they had done to achieve this. From these interviews, two things emerged. One was a listing of management 'behaviours', or competences, that had been displayed and the other was a grouping of those behaviours into a form of change leadership model. From all this work there emerged a core result that was common to all the successful innovating managers. This was validated by discussing the findings with a different sample of successful innovators.

The firm already had a number of 360° feedback tools, and the database to back them up, as well as nearly 20 years of experience in using these approaches. It was a natural step to develop a feedback instrument to enable measurements to be taken of the degree to which managers in an organization were managing in a way that enabled innovation to take place. The models and the feedback instruments became the core of a training programme, that not only enabled participants to identify what was blocking innovation, but also to learn and apply the new behaviours needed for success. Creativity of course played a part in this, but the greatest barrier to success, which the new approach helped to overcome, was the management of the innovation from creative idea through to application. Additional attention to creativity was wasted effort unless these matters were also dealt with.

The result of this work was an approach to innovation that could be used in either a consultancy or a training mode, that addressed a real problem clients were facing and gave the firm a product that was not exactly matched by any of its competitors. The underlying concepts were not new, but the identification of what was needed, and the application of concepts to provide a specific solution, were original. Further information about the approach that was developed can be found in P Owen (1990) and B Webster (1990).

This is by no means the only appropriate way of developing proprietary material, and indeed, what constitutes the best approach will vary with the particular technique or procedure. However it does illustrate that it is something more than a bright idea, and that the firm has a duty to ensure that any method it develops, modifies or uses really does add value to the organization. This can only be achieved when those using tools, techniques and so on have a thorough understanding of the concepts that lie behind them.

Making the most of proprietary approaches

A tool, technique, method or approach can add great value for both client and the consultancy when it is in the hands of a consultant who is expert in the subject area that underpins it. It can have a negative impact when the consultant's knowledge and experience are limited to just the application of the technique and so on. This is because, in any assignment, judgements have to be made about what is appropriate for the situation and, often, even the best conceived methodology will need to be adjusted to get the best value from it in a particular situation. If all you have is a rule book and all you know is one way of doing things without any real knowledge of the underlying subject, you are unlikely to be of much use to the client.

It is also worth remembering that not only is it potentially dangerous to be overly reliant on one way of doing things, but, in many situations, the use of a number of techniques may add considerable insight. If you think of a kaleidoscope, you will see what I mean. Every time it is lifted up to the light, something new is revealed. The elements that make up the toy are unchanged, but moving them around gives a different picture. This can happen when techniques are used to help analyse a situation in, say, a marketing or strategic management assignment. Each technique looks at the issue from a different viewpoint, and it is the combination of these views that can help the client come to a betters more apt, decision than would be the case if a single technique was to be used in an inflexible way.

A technique, tool, method or approach may be inappropriate for a particular situation, in which case the consultant must be able to recognize the deficiencies and take action. We can observe this happening when we consider the many different approaches an accountant might use for costing. These include absorption costing, where an allocation or apportionment of every item of expense is added to the direct costs; direct costing, where only the variable expenses are allocated to products and fixed costs are treated as period expenses; activity-based costing, where the true costs of every activity are arrived at; and incremental costing, which is concerned with the effects of changes. None of these approaches is wrong and, equally, none of them is right for every situation. An accountant who only knew one method and tried to apply it in every situation could do irreparable harm.

As we have seen, consultants will make use of the techniques and so on that are available, develop proprietary approaches to apply these and make them more effective and may sometimes develop totally original approaches. The value of proprietary material to a consultancy may be considerable, even if there is always the dilemma of how to protect intellectual property. If the approaches are kept totally secret, it may be difficult to make clients aware that they exist. If too much is disclosed, other consultants may pick them up and use them. This is a tightrope that every consultancy that has any proprietary material has to learn to walk, but it is an area where thought should be given to what is in the best long-term interest of the firm.

References

APQC (1992) *Planning, Organizing, and Managing Benchmarking*, American Productivity and Quality Centre, Houston, Texas

Buckner (ed.) (1993) *The Portfolio of Business and Management Audits*, Strategic Direction Publishers, Zurich

Channon, D F (ed.) (1997) *Encyclopedic Dictionary of Strategic Management*, Blackwell, Oxford

Constable, J, and McCormick, R (1987) *The Making of British Managers*, British Institute of Management, London

Crosby, P B (1979) *Quality is Free*, McGraw-Hill, New York

Crosby, P B (1984) *Quality Without Tears*, McGraw-Hill, New York

Crosby, P B (1987) *Running Things*, McGraw-Hill, New York

Farrell, L C (1993) *Searching for the Spirit of Enterprise*, Dutton, New York

Hayes, R H, Wheelwright, S C, and Clark, K B (1998) *Dynamic Manufacturing: Creating the learning organization*, Free Press, New York

Hersey, P, and Blanchard, K L (1969) *Management of Organizational Behaviour*, Prentice-Hall, Englewood Cliffs, New Jersey

Henry, J (1990) 'Making the Technology-Technology Connection', in Hussey, D E (ed.) *International Review of Strategic Management*, Vol. 1, Wiley, Chichester

Hussey, D E (1996) *Business-driven Human Resource Management*, Wiley, Chichester

Hussey, D E (1998) 'Glossary of Techniques for Strategic Analysis' in Hussey, D E (ed.) *The Strategic Decision Challenge*, Wiley, Chichester

Karlöf B, and Östblom, S (1994) *Benchmarking*, Wiley, Chichester

Kempner, T (ed.) (1990) *Penguin Management Handbook*, (5th edn), Penguin Books, London. (Unfortunately this book is no longer in print and a new edition is not planned, but you should be able to find it in a library)

Kepner, C H, and Tregoe, B B (1981) *The New Rational Manager*, John Martin Publishing, London

Management Charter Initiative (1992) *Management Standards: Supervisory management standards*, MCI, London

Owen, P (1990) 'Fostering Innovation in Organizations, in Lom', C. (ed.) *Technology Strategy Resource Book*, Strategic Direction Publishers, Zurich

Parker, R H (ed.) (1992) *Macmillan Dictionary of Accounting*, Macmillan, London

Peters, T L, and Waterman,. R H (1982) *In Search of Excellence*, Harper & Row, Cambridge, MA

Porter, M E (1980) *Competitive Strategy*, The Free Press, New York

Porter, M E (1985) *Competitive Advantage*, The Free Press, New York

Stewart, G B (1991) *The Quest for Value*, Harper, New York

Tovey, L (1992) *Competency Assessment: A strategic approach*, Harbridge Consulting Group, London

Watson, G H (1993) *Strategic Benchmarking*, Wiley, New York

Webster, B (1990) 'We know we need it, but how do we do it?' in Hussey, D E, and Lowe, P (eds.) *Key Issues in Management Training*, Kogan Page, London

Wilson, A (1993) *Marketing Audit Checklists*, McGraw-Hill, Maidenhead

16

The impact of IT on consultancy practice

Kevin Long

Introduction

Traditionally, consultancy meant management consultancy, or big 'C' consultancy, and focused primarily on business and economics as target areas. Big 'C' consultancy was typically populated by industry specialists with a style and gravitas that gained them access to industry leaders and business directors. IT consultancy by comparison was mainly confined to 'guru' or 'anorak' status and dealt typically with technology in isolation from key business drivers and returns. This dichotomy between classical management consultancy with its business envisioning and the technology enablers that could possibly make such visions work in the real business world was poorly addressed, if at all. This situation was clearly present in consultancy organizations that maintained management consultancy as a separate practice from the systems parts of their businesses. It was often the situation for these consultancies that management consultants could never be understood or produced 'blue sky' solutions that could not be implemented. This very common situation frequently resulted in new business 'pull through' opportunities being lost.

Over the past ten years, this situation has changed enormously, driven in part by the accelerating pace of technological progress and the needs of industry to look to technology to provide a competitive edge. Today IT consultancy has an established and recognized role within all levels of the consultancy business and IT consultants may expect the same career opportunities and rewards as their management consultancy colleagues.

IT consultancy started as small 'c' consultancy, typified by consulting teams applying technology to an existing business solution and subsequently supporting the delivery of these systems. Only in recent years have we begun to see big 'C' IT consultants operating within the marketplace, bringing with them similar skills to those of their management consulting colleagues with business and client awareness, together with a facilitative approach to technology and enterprise architecture solutions.

Figure 16.1 shows the key influences on an IT consultancy practice. They key features of an IT consultancy practice are of two kinds:

● market facing
● inward facing.

The market-facing features include:

● the strong business drivers that underpin all IT consultancy services focus on markets, sectors and clients
● knowledge of the IT technologies that exist in the marketplace and the trends for existing and new technologies that may evolve
● they have alliances with key technology suppliers in order to gain a full understanding of particular products and potentially to combine forces to provide a full range of IT consultancy and systems services to clients and markets.

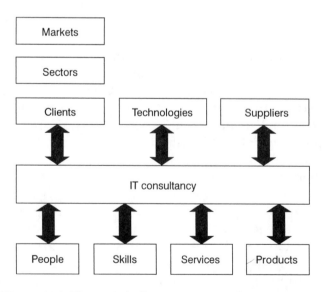

Figure 16.1 The main influences on consulting practices

The impact of IT on consultancy practice

The inward-facing features rest on the fact that IT consultancy practices are nothing without their people. Managing these consultants, their skills and knowledge is a classic knowledge management problem and one that, as a consultancy service, consultants offer to the marketplace. The final section of this chapter will go into more detail about the IT requirements for consultants and the types of applications that are put into place to fully exploit their knowledge. Some of the areas to be considered, however, include:

- people skills and competences expected of modern-day IT consultants, such as credibility, integrity, imagination, innovation, influence, facilitation and enthusiasm
- skills and knowledge of markets, sectors and technologies
- a range of IT consultancy-related services and themed products.

In the following sections, the generic IT consultancy services and supporting frameworks that are most often requested by clients are covered. The chapter will go on to review the key technologies that would be considered part of delivering those services, including information on the Internet and the outsourcing of IT functions. The chapter will finish with a discussion of IT consulting competences and how IT is being used to support consultancy work to make consultants more effective.

Framework model of an IT consultancy's services

As IT consultancy matures, consulting firms have expended a lot of effort on developing standard consultancy services and supporting frameworks. These services are both generic to meet general business requirements and specific or themed to address the needs of particular market sectors and industries, such as retail and banking. Consultancy practices further support their models and frameworks with best practice examples. All this effort is intended to provide the right level of support and information to allow IT consultants to deliver consultancy services of the expected level of detail, quality and rigour.

Figure 16.2 provides an example of a generic IT consultancy framework model that could be used to deliver consultancy via a set of general or themed services.

Each of the segments shown in the framework may be defined as follows.

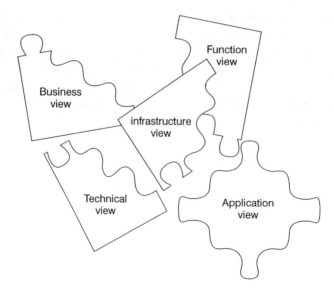

Figure 16.2 An IT consultancy framework model

Business view

The business view is a broad perspective on an organization or enterprise from which a more detailed picture can be developed, consisting of the following elements.

- **Vision** An understanding of where a business is currently within its marketplace, its core business and where it wants to be strategically in, say, two to five years' time is developed. This could be illustrated in terms of market share, scale of business or product acceptance for example.
- **Organization and role** The business is mapped in terms of an organizational hierarchy and the roles performed.
- **Location** The geographical disposition of the company – in terms of staff function and role – is covered under this heading.
- **Culture** Attempts are made to understand the business in terms of its staff, particularly in respect of empowerment and attitudes to change.

Function view

The function view looks at the core business functionality in terms of:

- **process inputs** – the location of process and actions

- **process triggers** – that is, what starts a process and the outputs from that process
- **conceptual data models** – the information that is required, processed and generated by the core business functions.

Technical view

The technical architecture area, together with its partner, application architecture view, forms the basis of an IT solution, and the consultancy that sits around it. The technical architecture area covers:

- desktop, server and mainframe hardware and operating systems
- database management systems
- networks and network protocols
- middleware and messaging architectures.

Application view

This application architecture view revisits the core business functionality in order to derive an application architecture that will support the business in terms of function and data distribution. This area includes:

- the capabilities, structure and user interfaces for application software
- the content, structure, relationships and business data rules of the organization
- the physical database design
- package selection processes and criteria.

Infrastructure view

This covers the remaining areas for a business, including:

- development and test tools and strategies
- change management strategies and tools
- non-functional requirements, including security, back-up and restore and so on
- production support strategies, tools and agreements, regarding level of service.

Using the framework

This generic framework may be developed to successive levels of detail in order to meet the needs of specific services, such as a high level for strategic work and a very detailed level for consultancy support of systems integration work.

Best practice models and examples further support the development and delivery of the frameworks and may provide IT consultants with examples, procedures, answers and warnings about pitfalls.

Another key use for such generic frameworks is that of developing the basic information required to support migration and transition models. For example, the framework approach may be used to develop both future and current state models of the business across the five areas, or views. With this information, the consultant would be in a position to plan and propose a migration and transition plan for the business. Such a model would identify and include:

- key milestones and dates
- quick wins
- costs
- resources and skills
- benefit realization points.

The overall effect, looking from the current to the future state, develops a tactical view of migration and transition, while looking back from the future state to the current highlights the strategic view.

With such generic frameworks in place, IT consultancy needs to relate and sell to its market via a set of services, themes and products. The following section develops an example of a generic IT consultancy service model.

Generic model of an IT consultancy's services

IT consultancy deals with a very wide range of business and commercial issues. In order to help understand the type of IT-related issues clients commonly seek help with, let us first discuss a generic IT consultancy model.

The model shown in Figure 16.3 illustrates the very broad range of services that an IT consultant may be called on to deliver and the variety of interrelationships that exist between those services.

Typically, IT consultancy would begin with advice on strategy and direction and then develop the remaining services of IT solutions, solution delivery and benefits realization within the strategy context. At a more detailed level, however, each of the services shown could be used in a stand-alone way in order to develop more depth and focus. The framework model developed earlier in this chapter (see Figure 16.2) would be used for guidance in these cases.

Broadly the areas above can be defined as follows.

The impact of IT on consultancy practice

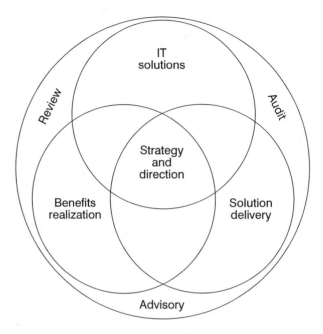

Figure 16.3 Generic model of the services an IT consultancy provides

Strategy and direction

Strategy and direction consultancy services embrace the organization as a whole and involve development of both current and future state models in business and IT terms. Typical deliverables from this area may include:

- business vision
- market analysis
- competitor analysis
- business and technical principles
- business case
- plan for action
- stakeholder identification and engagement.

IT solutions

IT solutions involves providing consultancy and other support in the development of technical and application architecture solutions for an enterprise or business. Again, the framework approach would be applied, together with IT-related knowledge in order to develop a solution or proposal.

Solution delivery

In a similar way to the IT solutions area, solution delivery provides consultancy and advice on development, implementation and roll-out strategies. Solution delivery would draw on the principles developed within the IT solutions service, say, and supplement this information by providing, for example:

● detailed architectures
● development approach and methods, such as rapid application development (RAD) and joint application development (JAD)
● testing plans and principles
● production support standards and tools
● service-level agreements and production running.

Benefits realization

All consultancy assignments presuppose benefits to a business. Inherent in all the IT consultancy services is the process of gathering information and making projections that support the benefits case over and above the actual proposed solution. The benefits realization service develops a more detailed and rigorous approach within a set of proposed consultancy solutions and plans. It would also define processes and procedures that the business could use to actively monitor and capture performance data. The benefits realization consultancy service is especially useful where business process outsourcing (BPO) is being considered as a contribution towards both the costs of running that service and as a means of measuring the performance of the supplier. (See under Outsourcing of IT functions, below, for more information on BPO.)

Review, audit and advisory

These are typically stand-alone services and include:

● reviewing current IT investment and systems in the context of technical refreshment and efficiency, for example
● auditing IT systems and infrastructures in line with regulatory requirements, such as safety critical systems for railway companies

- advisory and executive briefings on current and up-and-coming technologies and their application within a business or sector.

Clearly, these services may well lead to a request for and provision of more mainstream consultancy services.

The next section will review IT-related topics that, together with the IT consultancy services and the supporting framework mode, would provide a complete and balanced offering from an IT consultancy.

IT-related issues

Generally, clients seek the help of IT consultants principally because of business problems. These problems would traditionally result from the drive to improve productivity and profitability by improving the various processes involved in the business. Increasingly, however, the move from discrete systems to Internetworking is looking like it will realize bigger savings by building close relationships between customers, suppliers and staff.

This move is understandable, given where the IT industry has come from. We have seen three discrete generations of information technology: the mainframe, the minicomputer and the personal computer (PC). The move to Internetworking represents the fourth generation.

Internetworking advances have resulted from progress in the PC area, where we have seen computing power delivered to the desktops of business and home users. PCs feature user-friendly interfaces that make computers vastly more accessible than were mainframes and minicomputers.

Below are descriptions of a number of key technologies that IT consultants would consider using or applying in combination with the services and frameworks described earlier in order to meet the business goals of their clients. The technologies are described within the following categories:

- building blocks and components
- systems and architectures
- enabling technologies
- applications
- innovation on the Internet.

Building blocks and components

Processors and chips represent the basic building blocks of every piece of electronic equipment. This fact has resulted in an industry that is moving exceptionally quickly and developing ever more powerful processors and components. Coupled with this is the demand for ever larger amounts of reliable storage, such as redundant arrays of inexpensive disks (RAID), causing this complementary industry to grow rapidly as well.

Mobile computing drives the demand for lighter laptop computers with batteries that are safer, last longer and are rechargeable, as well as larger, higher-resolution and cheaper flat panel displays.

Telecommunications technologies that connect computers have advanced as dramatically as processors and components. Networks are more widespread, distributed and complicated in response to applications that have grown beyond simple data exchange and sharing of expensive peripherals so that they now encompass client/server systems, the Internet, multimedia and videoconferencing.

IT consultancy in these primarily covers advisory, review and audit services.

Systems and architectures

This is a key area of demand for IT consultancy and covers operating systems for hardware ranging from personal digital assistants (PDAs) to mainframes. Also included in this area are Internet applications, such as browsers, search engines and servers. Today's focus on Internetworking emphasizes the need for tools relating to security in order to access, manage and protect information as required.

Businesses are increasingly using electronic messaging, network computing and client/server systems to conduct business that was once performed manually. The Internet's success in connecting people has spurred companies to look for expansion and success on the web in terms of the delivery of information, services and products. As a result, network management and security are among the most important services requested from IT users and clients.

Enabling technologies

These are defined as the tools used to improve the creation, analysis and distribution of information.

Development tools and languages represent enabling technologies used to construct the software and applications that help automate business processes and make people more productive. These languages are increasingly based on rapid application development (RAD) techniques that encourage intensive user involvement and joint application development (JAD) techniques to facilitate shared skills and the co-responsibility that enable systems to be delivered quickly and accurately.

As businesses come to understand the realities behind knowledge working, new database query, management and analytical systems are enabling staff to compile and analyse data from a variety of sources and use it to make effective business decisions.

Groupware, work flow and document management systems also enable such workers to share information and insights anywhere and anytime as part of the enhancement of the decision-making processes. This area is one of the strongest in IT consultancy, particularly in respect of a proposed business culture and vision for change. For example, in moving a business from a classical hierarchy to a flatter, more empowered organization, groupware applications provide the added systems and access to allow this move to be supported effectively.

Applications

Key to business improvement are the applications that run across and deliver value to a business through an increasingly distributed workforce. Competition among suppliers of software products has resulted in applications that do more than simply automate existing business processes. Increasingly, they offer integrated modules with a common look and feel that are capable of being run on client/server architectures. Such are the capabilities of packaged software that extensive in-house developments are becoming rare and only considered where there may be significant commercial gain or regulatory pressures.

Internet technologies and the World Wide Web have dramatically altered business drivers and, consequently, IT consultancy. The use of the Internet and those technologies applied to intranets and even extranets for electronic commerce and business transactions of all kinds are having a dramatic effect on the business world. Where once traditional businesses would look for size and scale before embarking on a global strategy, the web and electronic commerce allowing start-up businesses to be global in attitude and reach from day 1!

Innovation on the Internet

As the Internet is now fully in the spotlight, the potential and demand for IT consultancy knowledge and services in this area are extremely high.

The Internet, including the World Wide Web and on-line services, comprises the on-line world of cyberspace – the so-called information highway. The new communications channel provides a massive electronic pipeline between businesses and consumers. From an IT consultancy point of view, it opens up exciting new possibilities that challenge the traditional ways of interacting, communicating and doing business.

The Internet and the uses to which Internet technologies can be put may be viewed as the glue holding a whole variety of technologies together that provide capability and connectivity in a way that was thought impossible only a few years ago. Some examples of this convergence are that:

- the content development and pace of new products and services are the fastest ever seen
- the web as a hypertext multimedia system is linking computer resources around the world
- the interfacing of web browsing and traditional database and transaction processing systems is realigning thoughts on ease of use, cost of ownership and integrating legacy systems
- interactive services, such as virtual reality, animation, audio/video, Java applets, and the convergence of all of these into seamless applications provide many opportunities for commerce and entertainment
- web TV and the integration of telephony, TV and the Internet into a new set of coherent services primarily aimed at content providers and electronic commerce open up all sorts of possibilities for every home.

Developers are putting these technologies to work, building innovative content and services for business, commerce, entertainment, education, information exchange and numerous other uses.

From an IT consultancy point of view, there are enormous challenges. Given the rapid pace of development, innovations can be overtaken rapidly, lasting as little as three or four months. One of the challenges for IT consultants, therefore, is to be fully conversant with these trends and know what will be sustainable and last.

Intranets, or private internets
Applying Internet technologies and innovation internally within a business as an intranet is a way of exploiting ideas and applications from the Internet, but in a more controlled way, utilizing the private networks that are available within most corporations.

The impact of IT on consultancy practice

A great many converging technologies make use of Internet technologies and the Internet architecture models, leading to business opportunities in the areas of:

- publishing and information dissemination
- browser-style graphical user interfaces that simplify and standardize on-line system dialogues, improving usage and throughput as well as reducing training costs and effort
- thin client or Net PC trends that move application processing away from the desktop, as in the PC world, to one or more application servers.
- the use of Java and ActiveX to dynamically load small application 'applets' on to those thin client terminals in order to provide the flexibility and interaction expected of PC systems, but without the complexity and high cost of ownership of modern desktop PCs.

Extranets

An extranet, or extended intranet, is the expansion of private corporate intranets to, for example, key customers and suppliers. Opening up corporate intranets in this way fosters closer partnerships as it involves sharing more information, reducing costs of doing business and increasing the visibility of a company's products and services. It also provides a vehicle for business function outsourcing (BFO), which is when certain functions that would normally be performed by, say, the external customer's own staff could be brought inside and provided by a supplier as a tightly integrated service.

Extranets allow such external entities to be drawn into the corporate network in a controlled and secure way. Examples of the use of extranets include allowing customers access to their own data and a range of applications from within the supplier's own systems. Such systems would make use of the client/browser technology as well as hypertext mark-up language (HTML) information publication capabilities.

Internet applications

Some examples of the many Internet applications in use, or starting to appear, include:

- Internet telephony
- on-line services

- business and commerce in the areas of:
  - retail
  - shipping
  - banking
  - insurance
  - investment services
  - entertainment and education
  - travel
- virtual events and virtual reality
- information services, such as magazines
- news
- telephone directory services.

Increasingly, product and application suppliers are web-enabling their products to allow modules to interconnect over the Internet or intranet and permit the use of browser-style front ends for simplicity and openness.

Information delivery

Since its beginnings, the Internet has been based on a 'pull' model of information access – that is, the user uses a web browser to 'surf' web sites for information and content. During the last year, however, an alternative 'push' model of information delivery has emerged, which means that information is delivered to a user's desktop automatically. Obvious examples of the use of the push model would be the provision of financial or stock information or latest news breaks.

Within businesses, however, this push model also has applications. In government and administration services, such as in the immigration and benefits agency areas, casework typifies the work style and the range of supporting applications. A key feature of this work is the need to perform information gathering and intelligence or deductive reasoning across large numbers of cases and related information. The use of an intranet search engine together with push technology allows cases to be stored and viewed as hypertext mark-up language (HTML) via a browser, but also for on-line analytical processing (OLAP) style searches to be launched or tagged for certain events. Push technology may then be used to inform the caseworker, sending the relevant information to the desktop once the search had been completed or when an external event has occurred on an individual case. Moreover, with the inclusion of work flow and groupware applications, these types of events could be routed to the next available caseworker as a good example of technology convergence.

Outsourcing of IT functions

IT-related outsourcing has been a prevalent activity in the USA for 15 to 20 years. In the UK and Europe, the outsourcing industry has seen very large growth over recent years. The key driver for outsourcing is the move to focus on the core business of the enterprise and buy in peripheral supporting services, such as IT functions.

The premise is that an expert external service provider should be able to provide that type of service (for example, data centre management) more efficiently and at a reduced cost than the business could do if it provided this service internally.

The European market for outsourcing would suggest that the cost premise is proving true. However the debate about what a business chooses to outsource and what it should retain goes on. There is most certainly a need for an organization to differentiate itself from, for example, the competition or to retain sufficient strategic expertise in the area that is outsourced to be able to continue to exploit its own capabilities and maximize the benefits of potential outsourcing agreements.

Apart from IT consultancy services helping businesses identify, support bids for and define their IT outsourcing arrangements, they can also aid them in deciding which capabilities businesses might retain and how they might best manage them.

Examples of options for IT-related outsourcing include:

- data centres, including mainframe and server farms
- call centres – providing the IT-related services to the data centre itself and the systems integration services to clients' existing systems
- IT departments – typically for all business analysis, development, testing, applications management and production support of new and existing systems
- FM-style outsourcing, including:
  - network supply and management
  - mainframe, server and desktop hardware and systems software supply and management.

Finally, this section would not be complete without a brief word on business process outsourcing (BPO).

Again, as a result of technology's convergence with Internet technologies and groupware and work flow applications, the potential for outsourcing discrete or related business functions becomes ever more possible. Whereas in the past the smallest unit of outsourcing would be at, say, the department level, with such new technologies the smallest unit is now a business function. A good example of this is, say, purchasing, where a supplier may actually perform the purchasing function on behalf of a client. The use of extranets here, for example, would provide the technology to support this role.

From the point of view of BPO outsourcing suppliers, this could mean that they would create businesses explicitly set up for the purpose of supplying specific functions to the marketplace and, hence, that they would be able to offer value in terms of costs, scale and ability. There remains, however, the same need for caution in this area as with departmental outsourcing, in that a business would have to analyse what its own core business functions are and be sure to retain these as its own. There are already one or two examples in America of manufacturing companies that outsourced so vigorously they found they actually did not add any value to their own products!

How consultants themselves use IT

The past five years have seen a marked improvement in the way that IT is used among IT consultants to support their own work and capabilities. Consultancy has its heritage in the individual, in that the knowledge and approach to providing IT consultancy services to the marketplace has always been very individualistic. As the market for IT consultancy services has grown so rapidly, this approach, after a time, did not allow consultancy companies to either grow apace or provide the necessary rigour and consistency.

Consultancy is not just about knowledge or the application of that knowledge to an IT consultancy opportunity. It is about improving the attitude, style and approach that an IT consultant adopts with clients and colleagues. To this end, the IT systems and applications adopted within a consultancy would include:

- knowledge and knowledge management – that is, on-line and accessible repositories for IT consultancy-related information
- skills – that is, how IT consultancy services are delivered, via frameworks and examples of best practice examples
- competences – whereas it would be extremely difficult to support the application of certain preferred competences, such as facilitation, IT could be exploited to help set and review individual objectives, as well as provide access to the company models in this respect.

The impact of IT on consultancy practice

Clearly database technology would also be used to create and maintain the sorts of information highlighted above. It is in the area of access and interpretation that IT really begins to benefit the modern IT consultancy's methods and practices.

IT consultancy has always been a highly mobile career. The impact of this is that IT consultants require significant support while on the road and out on assignments. The traditional model of providing office network access to consultancy information does not meet these needs. Add to this an IT consultant's needs for mobile technology in order to assist them in their work with clients and we have the basic ingredients for high-powered mobile computing capabilities with remote access to the consultancy practice's networks and databases.

The old model of the lone consultant working with a client is also diminishing. There is an increasing trend to provide consultancy services in the form of teams or for a consultant to at least have access to other consultants as required.

Taking all of this together, we have 'knowledge management' facilitated by means of:

- e-mail, work flow, groupware and OLAP applications
- electronic communication with the inclusion of attachments – that is, e-mail
- scheduling and disseminating work and targets using work flow applications
- groupware applications for the creation of virtual consultancy teams dedicated to a particular task
- research and analysis of disparate information using OLAP tools.

Clearly, Internet technologies provide leading-edge examples of the basic building blocks of the support systems required for IT consulting. The Internet itself, of course, represents a classical research tool and many well-known IT-related market research companies are placing their premium services on the Internet as commercial ventures.

Part 6

Different fields of consulting activity

17

Small and medium-sized firms

Rosemary Harris Loxley and Tony Page

Introduction

Small- and medium-size firms are highly important to the economy and require a distinctively different approach from consultants to that which would be used with large companies.

With large companies shedding jobs and outsourcing all but their core workforce, we are moving into a new post-industrial age in which the proportion of smaller, knowledge-based service companies is set to go on increasing. In the UK, there are 2.65 million businesses employing fewer than 200 people, out of a total of 2.70 million UK businesses. Small businesses employ nearly 70 per cent of the private-sector workforce (RSA Inquiry, 1995) and form a growing sector.

Potentially, small- and medium-size enterprises (SMEs) could be our economic dynamo. Some of them are very dynamic, generating new jobs and growing at 40–50 per cent a year, but most SMEs may be under performing, many of them without realizing it. IBM and the London Business School's survey (1994) showed that 70 per cent of companies thought they performed at world-class levels when only 2.3 per cent were actually found to do so! If as consultants we can find really effective ways of assisting these companies (both the leading firms and the laggards) to develop and maintain a world-class performance, then we are achieving something very valuable for them, for us and for the wider economy.

Does working with these companies really require a different approach? Doesn't what you already know about consulting apply just as well when you are dealing with SMEs as with large firms? Our answer is no. We will try to illustrate why.

Imagine a situation. Last week you had a briefing meeting with the MD of a small company employing 25 staff. You spent yesterday preparing a development workshop and, filled with optimism, you rose early today to arrive in time to prepare the meeting room. The management team enters and you open with some rousing words about using the workshop to create an exciting future. However, slightly disturbingly, three directors leave the room and, at coffee break, your heart sinks as the MD informs you that a big order from their major customer was cancelled this morning. The workshop is also cancelled and the MD asks you to stay on and help the directors formulate a list of actions needed today to stay in business.

This story, based on a real-life case, illustrates how consulting with SMEs is immediate and fast moving. There is not much slack in the system and priorities can shift suddenly, so you need exceptional flexibility and responsiveness. Beyond speed of reaction, there is a less obvious and more important point to make: an entirely different approach to consulting really is needed. It is no use simply importing consulting practices developed with larger organizations, you need to make a deliberate style shift. Some typical mistakes made by experienced consultants when consulting with small firms include:

- assuming that the experience and skills they have acquired in large firms can be transferred easily
- assuming that the CEO's success criteria are mainly related to growth of the company and so not finding out the personal motivations and long-term aspirations of the CEO, which are especially important if that person is the owner or a major shareholder.
- not appreciating the need for multiskilling and whole brain thinking in order to manage, at speed, all the elements that impact the business
- assuming that the directors are unprofessional amateurs who have nothing to teach and no interest in learning
- assuming that directors will want to make time for training courses laid on by educational establishments
- assuming that a set of recommendations in a report is the answer to a firm's development needs
- not recognizing that the most successful projects are the result of 'learning partner' relationships between directors and consultants
- applying short-term solutions, such as staff cuts and financial controls, without considering the loss of tacit knowledge that occurs when the experienced people are made redundant

- not questioning whether or not their own personality and values fit with those of the client – without such a fit, a productive working relationship is rarely possible.

In our experience, what makes the greatest difference to SMEs is sustained support being given to the leaders – probably extending over one year, two years or more. The familiar packages of government grant assistance tend to overlook this point, and the widely available short training courses for staff tend to leave leaders of SMEs high and dry afterwards.

When leaders of SMEs want help, they typically value a trusted generalist (a sort of GP) with whom they can have a special, but jargon-free, conversation that grows their strategic thinking capacity, leaving them better equipped to address future challenges. However, in seeking to offer this special level of attention, the question for you is how to be time-effective, how to provide a compact and practical means of delivery that does not consume too much of the client's time or profit.

In this chapter, we seek to convey an understanding of approaches to consulting with leaders of SMEs that we believe work, drawing on operating experience, case examples and research.

Why it is necessary to shed some assumptions

Many large companies, in transforming themselves for world-class performance, appear to have damaged their relationships with their employees (Cooper, 1997). We must not blindly carry assumptions from the world of large companies into SMEs. In fact, large companies may have something valuable to learn from successful smaller companies about trust and how to get the best from their people.

Take a minute to check your assumptions. Many people think that because large organizations are so complicated, smaller firms are simpler to work with. Do you? Many people think that in smaller companies it is easier or faster to bring about change? Do you?

You may remember an episode in the BBC series *Troubleshooter* in which Sir John Harvey-Jones sought to assist the Morgan car company. His thorough analysis pointed to the conclusion that Morgan needed to change radically to remain viable – reducing the handmade element, shortening its waiting list, and rationalizing and expanding production. The father and son running the company could not agree with this analysis, argued vociferously and implemented few of his recommendations.

Although the analysis step might appear easier, really effective consulting in SMEs is often neither simple, nor fast. This is particularly so when dealing with family businesses, perhaps run by second- or third-generation owners. The personal qualities and prevailing business environment that led to the founders' business success are not always apparent in the current executive team. Sometimes positions have been created to justify high salaries for family members or individuals have been given responsibilities that do not match their capabilities. This inevitably leads to decline in the performance of the functions for which they are accountable, erosion of credibility and self-esteem. In other words, damage to the business and the individual concerned result.

Let's look at an example to clarify these points.

The hotel group

Imagine you have been asked to assist a small hotel group where:

- three hotels have been inherited by four children from their parents
- two of the hotels are profitable and one is not
- a younger brother is in charge of the unprofitable hotel and he is struggling
- the siblings realize he's not right for this job, it's tearing him apart.

What do you do? A strategic analysis on their behalf? Provide a course on business analysis and managing change?

We began with one-to-one interviews in order to build a relationship with each of the directors and start to bring the issues to the surface. This was followed by a weekend workshop with the theme 'What's right for the business?'

The workshop was emotional at times. It was a family we were dealing with after all, they were facing the difficult issue of 'it's not working'. They learned that when you inherit a hotel company you cannot play at being in business, and that moving to the next phase in the company's development requires focus and commitment.

Once the workshop had identified what was right for the business, attention turned to the needs of individuals, the personalities, relationships and possible solutions. It became clear that the younger brother and the company were headed in different directions.

What would the brother do instead? He loved the hotel business. With some help, he decided his interest was in marketing. He enrolled on a degree course in marketing, funded by the company, of which he continued to be a director, obtained a degree and became a successful consultant to the hotel sector. He later obtained an MBA and is now a college lecturer.

This short case study underlines the point that SME consulting is not necessarily a cool and detached activity. You are dealing with the owners of a business who are also directors, managers and hands-on workers. They are pulled in many different directions.

Small and medium-sized firms

There may be muddled and conflicting thinking both within a single person and between people in a business team. You may, as in the hotel company example, become, for a period of time, quite deeply involved in other people's lives, their past, present and future. You can become involved in helping the relationships between people to end, or to move on to a new phase.

So, the point is, in SMEs you rely a little less on your analytical skills. You need to shed some assumptions, suspend judgement. You help the director of an SME to think through issues for themselves, you engage in their thought process and, together, produce solutions that you then support them in implementing. Later on we will describe a tool that can help you in such conversations with your client.

What issues leaders of SMEs typically want help with

The first request by a business for outside help often arises from their first major transition – when the founder realizes they can no longer control everything themselves. This marks a shift from being small to becoming medium-sized – a time to install a management structure, appoint trusted managers and delegate responsibility for the first time. So, during the last decade or thereabouts, while many large firms have been removing layers of management, successful small- and medium-sized firms have been adding layers!

As a consultant, it is important to understand the deeper implications and, therefore, the client's underlying needs when something apparently clear and rational, such as a new layer of management, is being added. There is a change in the relationship between the founder and long-standing employees, bringing more formality and distance. Usually, there is a review of the competences of senior staff, some of whom are appointed to management positions, which brings with it a perception of winners and losers. There is a formalization of accountability and performance measurement. Staff may experience feelings of rejection and betrayal while the founder experiences greater loneliness, isolation and anxiety. At the same time, the founder may be afraid of endangering loyalty and affection that has built up over the years. Spouses, being part of a tight informal network, can exert behind-the-scenes pressures to maintain the status quo. Thus, the whole transition process can be very emotionally charged – on a par with a marriage break-up.

Countless surveys have revealed the low interest of directors of SMEs in training for themselves or their staff (for example, the Price

351

Waterhouse Cranfield Project, 1996, found that 40 per cent of small firms spend 1 day or less per year on training and only 12 per cent spend 5 days or more a year on it). Local educational bodies and government grants have sought to raise awareness of the importance of training. It appears that well-intended solutions may often be marketed at SMEs without listening to them sufficiently.

So what assistance do the leaders of SMEs really want from consultants? The following is a list of the questions we have been asked most often.

• How can we become more professional, giving an image to our customers that we are bigger than we actually are, having efficient processes and systems?
• How can we manage to grow and take advantage of market opportunities without being ruined by punitive bank loans and overdrafts?
• How can we improve without taking time away from our jobs to go on training courses?
• Can you keep us up to date and aware of what is going on 'out there', recommend useful books on key topics and be our conscience about the things in our 'good intentions' box?
• How can we cope with sudden growth?
• How can we manage a particularly sensitive and difficult issue, such as a director who is no longer effective or will not be needed by the business in the future?
• How much do you charge and how can we get you for nothing using grants?

Some directors of SMEs have become keen badge collectors, recognizing that a means of winning credibility with customers is to demonstrate that their firm has a quality management system (ISO 9000), is dedicated to continuous quality improvement (TQM programme, customer service training), invests in its people (Investors in People) and is benchmarking its way, to excellence (Business Excellence Model, EFQM, Baldrige).

Other directors of SMEs remain cynical about the value of all this. Perhaps having tried ISO 9000 or Investors in People they had their fingers burned – believing the promise of business benefits, they found that they got bogged down in the onerous, bureaucratic and distracting task of writing down quality procedures or assembling an Investors in People portfolio instead.

In our experience, directors of SMEs *are* keen to learn – they know their success depends on it. It also depends on keeping focused on the business, not being distracted or sent off on interesting but irrelevant tangents. Like many of us today, they work long hours, feel swamped with information and do not feel they can devote the necessary time to reading books and going on courses.

There is potential value to each of the standardized approaches (ISO, TQM, Investors in People and so on), provided they are adopted at an appropriate stage in a firm's development. However, there are few, if any, universal rules about when is the right time – it all depends. The damage is done when a director of an SME is persuaded by a heavy sell from a specialist provider without first taking time to explore what is truly needed now.

Some form of external benchmarking is undoubtedly a good idea, given the widespread tendency to denial revealed in the IBM/LBS study (1994). Without an objective external benchmark, the SME leader is vulnerable because:

- if they do not know how bad they are, they have no incentive to improve
- there is a risk of improvements being misdirected, focused on the wrong processes
- they reinvent the wheel in ignorance of best practice
- they set targets unrealistically, either too high or too low.

Firms can draw on the benchmarking expertise that already exists in the British Quality Foundation and the firm's own local TECs/LECs and Business Links.

Benchmarking, while often necessary, is certainly not sufficient in itself. Beyond knowing how they match up with the outside world, every firm needs to know what makes it unique, how to measure its own success and how it should manage the vital relationships that will ensure its continuing success. The Centre for Tomorrow's Company provides a useful practical framework for helping companies define what makes them unique and distinctive, as shown in Figure 17.1.

Using this framework, a director of an SME finds answers to fundamental questions, such as the following.

- **Purpose** What are you in business for?
- **Vision** Where do you want this business to be in one or three or five years' time?
- **Values** What really represents success? Why is that important?
- **Measures** How will you measure success?
- **Relationships** Which are the relationships that you depend on to achieve success?
- **Licence to operate** What are the risks and dangers?

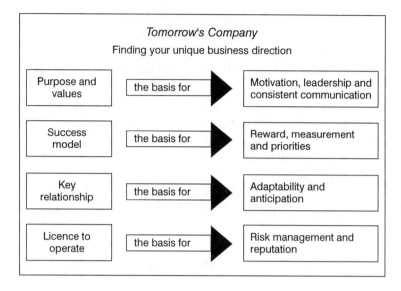

Figure 17.1: Tomorrow's Company's Framework (RSA Inquiry, 1995)

In working with a consultant, directors of SMEs seem to value a relationship with a trustworthy, well-informed and experienced outsider who can give them access to the best, most relevant learning, knowledge and new ways of thinking. In other words, the client wants you to read the books and attend the courses for them! They then need to be given a way to benefit from what you have learned.

Some government-sponsored agencies have gone some way down this route by providing personal business advisers who seek to build long-term relationships as 'business friends' to leaders of SMEs. However, the advisers are not allowed to 'do consultancy' and, in practice, they can sink to an analysis and report-writing approach, bringing with it frustration at the leaders of SMEs' attitude as they cherry-pick from the adviser's lists of recommendations.

A practical tool for entering the client's thought process

So, how do you get around the 'attitude' of the busy leader of an SME and deliver something that is highly valued and makes a profound difference to their business performance?

We believe that you start one step back, working first on whatever problem or issue is real and pressing in the business today. This means that what you are doing is classed as essential 'work' rather than 'nice to have', fanciful or tangential. Use a lot of questioning and listening to enter the client's way of thinking and follow a process that produces learning, insight and lasting impact in the client, leading on to their implementing solutions and also to their seeing their world differently in some way. This approach derives from Reg Revans' pioneering method called *action learning* (Revans, 1982), and recognizes that consultants who ask their clients questions tend to trigger more active, and therefore profound, learning in clients, than those consultants who solve the problem for their clients and serve up pre-formed solutions.

In our conversations with clients, we use a simple sequence of questions by means of which we move with the client from identifying the problem to implementing the solution. This is shown in Figure 17.2, and derives from the Kolb learning cycle (Kolb, 1979). Starting with '1. Describing current issue' – that is, the problem that is occupying the client right now, today – we move clockwise through the cycle, drawing on our shared pool of knowledge. The client reflects, gains insight, explores alternative ways forward and thinks their way towards implementing a solution. Often there is a looping back to explore new alternatives (as shown by the arrow from step 6 to step 3) after piloting or implementing something (in steps 5 and 6).

Let us look at an example of the tool in use in a control systems company.

The Control systems company

1. Describing current issue

MD: We are a control systems company with specialized industry divisions covering oil and gas, mining, water and power.
It is hard for us to be profitable because we need to fund specialists in each industry division.

2. Reflecting

MD: Some divisions are under great pressure, while others are under-utilized
Some research is duplicated in different divisions. We're wasting money reinventing wheels.

3. Exploring alternatives

Consultant: Is it possible to reduce the duplication of research without upsetting our customers?
MD: I'm not certain.
Consultant: How would you find out?
MD: We could test the idea with our customers.

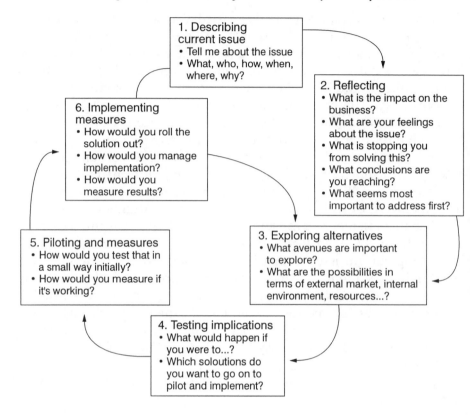

Figure 17.2 A practical tool – a sequence of questions taking clients from a problem to its solution.

4. Testing implications
A joint report from customer perception survey undertaken by consultant and market research undertaken by another agency finds the following:
- need for major changes – customers report that they love you and want to remain loyal, but need new products and are not certain you can deliver them
- losing money and goodwill by salespeople promising products that engineering/production cannot deliver

> MD: I'm seeing this differently now! We have to fund new product development. We have to get our engineers and salespeople to liaise more effectively with our customers. Let's see if our customers will help us fund new product development.

5. Piloting measures
A few salespeople and engineers began joint visits to customers, finding ways to say 'yes, but . . .' to customers – Yes we can do it, but it will take some time and some money.'

Customers are happier and some new product development is part-funded by customers.

6. Implementing measures
Joint working between salespeople and engineers and customer-funded product development become established as the norm.

In the control systems company example, the MD and consultant worked closely together, with the MD leading and the consultant supporting. Clearly this was not achieved by means of a single conversation, but the sequence of questions provides a clear route through the project.

In practice, how do you make this method work? First, agree an amount of time – say one and a half to two hours – to begin the conversation with the client, without interruptions. As it is 'work' and it is what's really important to the client right now, gaining the time is usually possible. You begin by opening your mind, shedding as many preconceptions as you can. Try to listen without making many notes at first. Treat it as a conversation in which you question the client with the aim of helping them to learn, make new connections, gain insights, rather than one of gathering data for yourself. Explain to the client the process you are using and aim to end each meeting with clarity about what the next steps are, a review of how useful the client found the meeting and a further meeting booked.

Why does it work? Well, it is a means of activating a thought process in the company leader that creates new knowledge, that can then work its way outwards into the company. The underlying process is described by I Nonaka and H Takeuchi (1995) as the 'spiral of knowledge' which has helped to make Honda, Canon, Matsushita, Sharp and NEC into highly successful world-class companies.

Essentially, what happens is that you draw your client's deep experience or tacit, unarticulated know-how to the surface, where it can be challenged, tested and changed in conversation with you, then you help the client to internalize and embed the new know-how in revised operating practices.

Why being different can add to your impact

Are some consultants better at doing this than others? It appears that the answer is 'yes'. A few years back, one of us (Rosemary) participated in action research conducted by Alistair Mant in association with HR Partnership that was seeking to explain the factors underlying the effectiveness of consultants working on government-sponsored business growth programmes with SMEs. This revealed that the greater the differences between the client and consultant, the more learning occurred. So, for example, male-female pairings were more effective than those between people of the same gender, and age differences between client and consultant were also helpful. A female consultant, for example, might say to a male MD who is reluctant to delegate, 'Still doing it, aren't you?' From a male consultant, this could provoke competitive hostility, but from a female it is perceived as a gentle but useful reminder. This suggests that the challenge experienced by the client may be as much to do with 'who you are being' as the questions you ask!

This research points to the conclusion that if you are different from the client, provided that you are reasonably confident about the difference and the client feels you are not too strange, hostile or threatening to be let into their thought process, then the more they feel positively challenged by working with you, and the more they learn and the more their business stands to gain.

Successful consulting, therefore, rests not only on your being able to enter and work within the client's thought process, but on there being a level of creative tension between you, which arises from a difference that you represent, perhaps in your age, life-stage, background or gender.

Understanding personal agendas

When an experienced colleague was recently asked what he would offer as the best advice for consulting with SMEs, he said: 'Understand the directors' motivations and all the rest falls into place!'

The most difficult, emotional and hard-to-understand moments in a business conversation with the client may also be the keys to your having the most profound impact and adding the greatest possible value to their business. Why? Because there is always a personal agenda that rarely breaks to the surface of your business conversations until something the client deeply wants is being threatened. When it does appear, you know you are on to something, but you need to handle the situation with great skill and sensitivity. In spite of this being difficult territory, you continue there knowing that when the client's personal agenda is in conflict with the business direction, they are unable to be fully effective.

Everyone has a personal agenda, but when consulting with leaders of SMEs it is particularly important to know what it is and to work with it, because, as owners as well as managers of a dynamic fast-moving business, a personal business agenda conflict can be very damaging. The following story of one of our clients serves to illustrate the influence of personal agendas.

John Roberts' personal motivation

John attended a business performance workshop with owner-managers from nine other companies. He was selling used computers. Having started the business from his kitchen table with help from his wife and a colleague from his previous job, he grew the company without any outside investment to become a team of 20 people operating from a small industrial unit.

John now needed to borrow a considerable sum of money in order to take a giant step and move into custom-built premises and then become a recognized distributor of the computers. He said this 'scares the pants off me'. At the workshop, he explored the implications of taking and not taking this step and decided to go ahead.

A recession followed this move that pushed the expanding and financially exposed company into a crisis that lasted for two to three years, but by the end of this time John had succeeded in becoming a recognized dealer. However, after problems with his original business partner, he realized he needed further investment in the business.

At this point, he began to question his own motivation and realized he was bored with running the business and dissatisfied with his life. All he had ever wanted was to establish the business, then sell it and do something different.

Now he has sold the business to a larger company and started a new, quite different business that is successfully trading in outlets in Singapore and the US. He no longer works so many hours and feels he is managing to maintain the more balanced life he was looking for.

To understand person–business conflicts as a consultant, we first have to know what motivates the leader of the SME personally. The following are some answers given by directors of SMEs to the question 'What are you in business for?'

- 'To maintain and fund the lifestyle I enjoy today.'
- 'I want to build up the business, sell it and then do something else, such as go into consultancy, become a non-executive director, start a new baby business.'
- 'I thrive on the excitement, the thrill, the buzz, doing deals, something new all the time. I get bored easily.'
- 'I just love being a hotelier/making things/selling things and so on. I couldn't see myself doing anything else.'

The range of motivations in just these few examples reminds us of the danger of making assumptions. When you assume a client wants the business to grow, do not be surprised if they point to their Rolls-Royce in the car park and their bank balance and throw your assumption back at you. The following apocryphal story underlines the dangers of a consultant ignoring the client's personal agenda:

Every day, a man goes to a lake to catch a fish for his tea. A consultant comes up to him and says, 'Why don't you catch two fish, eat one and sell one?' The man says, 'What for?' The consultant answers, 'If you do this each day, you can save up some money and start a fishing company'. The man says, 'What for?' The consultant says, 'Then you can build up the company and put in a manager.' The man says, 'What for?' 'Then you can take some time off each afternoon.' The man says, 'What for?' The consultant says, 'Then you can go fishing!'

Helping people find the business direction

We saw in the example of the hotel company earlier in this chapter how there is a need to separate the personal from the business issues and, after being clear on 'What are you in business for?', the next step is to identify, as objectively as possible, 'What's best for the business?' To understand this, it can help to stand back and take a lifetime perspective on the business.

Larry Greiner (1972) described the growth of a small company as consisting of a series of predictable crises: of leadership, autonomy, control, red tape and so on. Just as children grow into adults by going through discontinuous phases – baby, toddler, schoolchild, adolescent and so on – so do companies. Within each phase, there is relative calm and certainty followed by an unsettling crisis or revolution, marking the threshold of a new phase.

Since Greiner's work, we have become used to slimmer, flatter organizations with greater delegation and faster communication, and it may be wrong to assume that in every company crises occur in the same predictable sequence. However, the underlying idea that there are phases and each requires a different approach to managing the business seems to hold true. It is also likely that the periods of stability between crises have become shorter.

The following is an example of a company moving from one phase to the next.

Moving on

Richard Green and his brother were market traders, selling top stores' seconds and bankrupt stock. Richard was young, ambitious and intelligent. He wanted to leapfrog into a new line of business.

360

Small and medium-sized firms

He attended a business performance workshop and, after the module presented by a financial specialist, set about professionalizing both himself and the company

With help from the financial specialist he has now set up a chain of jewellery concessions in department stores throughout the UK. His brother is running the original market trading business.

At the business performance workshop he met John Roberts (see under John Roberts' personal motivation above). They have remained in contact over many years since that first meeting, as friends, helping one another through business dilemmas. From such contacts, new business possibilities constantly emerge. Richard may soon be starting a new venture in Singapore as an outlet for John Roberts' computer. Is another new phase being born? We do not know what will happen next!

As a consultant, you can help the leader of the SME find their purpose, their business path, what new phase they are entering and how best to work within this phase. You can use the Tomorrow's Company tool (see Figure 17.2) to establish what makes the company distinctive and what it needs in the current and emerging phases of development. You may use some simple analytical methods, such as:

- business position audit using SWOT analysis (which stands for strengths, weaknesses, opportunities and threats)
- outer context using PEST (which stands for political, economic, social and technological trends)
- organizational effectiveness using the McKinsey 7-S framework (strategy, structure, systems, style, staff, skills and shared values)

However, helping your client find the direction or path is not usually sufficient. You have to take people with you – the client, their colleagues on the management team, customers, suppliers, investors, even the surrounding community and, of course, all the staff.

We know from the work of Bill Bridges (1996) that it takes people time to adjust to change, to move their energy and attention away from the past into the present and future. Bridges describes a three-phase transition process of ending, neutral zone and new beginnings. This implies that you give people time to let go, let them bring something from the past with them, help them articulate what is ending both personally and in the company and encourage rites of passage, such as leaving parties and office-warming parties, to ease people into the new world that is beginning for them now.

A very valuable role for you as a consultant is to monitor where people's energy and attention is focused. Are they locked counter-productively in the past, busily engaged head-down in the present or dreaming of the future, missing the practical reality of what needs doing today?

The professional services agency

The relationships among the directors of this company had, over recent months, become fraught, tense and ineffective:

- one of the two co-founders was now chairman; his female co-founder was a director
- the Board had recently decided to bring in a new MD to help run the business
- the new MD was having difficulty establishing himself.

We began with a series of one-to-one listening conversations, not making notes, getting a feeling for what needed to take place.

This was followed by a workshop addressing the question 'What does the business need now to go forward?'

It became clear that hiring the MD had been the right thing for the business, but that the female co-founder had long since become ineffective and emotionally adrift from the development of the business. Through a misguided sense of loyalty, this had not been faced up to and had become a serious blockage. There were feelings of failure, betrayal and resentment. There had been various bizarre attempts to undermine the new organization, including an accusation of sexual harassment, (later proved to be false).

It emerged that the female co-founder no longer had a role in taking the company forward and compassionate arrangements were made to enable a parting of the ways.

In this example emotional baggage from the past was interfering with morale and performance in the present situation, preventing the company from moving forward into the future. Although the directors in this company all had advanced interpersonal skills, their relationships had become seized up and they needed a third party, not actively involved, to help move them on.

As a consultant, you are a little like a midwife, helping the client and their company through a painful transition, enabling the future, a new phase, to be born.

Growing the leaders' thinking capacity

One way of growing the leader that we have not been advocating is that of downloading knowledge and information directly, as you would if you were giving them a sort of mini-MBA course covering all the tools and methods that are known and used in business today. However, we

Small and medium-sized firms

have seen how leaders of SMEs are less interested in this type of learning than they are in the learning they can access via you while tackling work issues directly, and so described below is a special mode of conversation that achieves this.

Over a period of time, your client will have learned to work more effectively with you than without you. Your conversations give them double the brain power, access to different ways of thinking about their business problems and a sort of enthusiasm and sense of possibility. When they are getting carried away with enthusiasm, you help bring them back to the ground. When they are lost in their problems, you help inject enthusiasm and possibility. You remind them to balance the needs of the task and the people. You make them more intelligent (using the word 'intelligence' in its widest sense).

A risk arises that when you go away, the leader's thinking will revert to its old habitual patterns. It is a truism in a dynamic world that the thinking that got them through the last three years may not be the thinking they need to move ahead. Ideally, before you have left, your client will have learned new thinking habits. How, though, do you teach someone new ways of thinking?

We use a method called *brain mapping*. Leaders complete a simple self-report questionnaire to identify their preferred patterns of thinking, then these are mapped against the four quadrants of the brain to provide their personal brain map (see Figure 17.3).

Different people think in different ways. We use this information to help the leader of the SME understand how their own characteristic ways of thinking can interact most productively with others. Typically, they gain some immediate insights into why they find it hard to get on

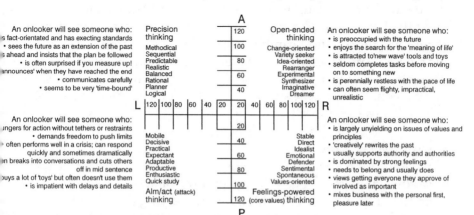

Figure 17.3 A brain map

363

with so and so. However, more importantly, they start to understand how valuable it can be to get colleagues with inherently different viewpoints to collaborate.

Conversely, they come to understand that because conflict often becomes personal and people avoid it, you get what D Leonard and S Strauss (1997) call 'comfortable clone syndrome' and fail to harness the many kinds of intelligence needed by the company to stay ahead. Using brain mapping and other personality indicators, such as Myers-Briggs (Leonard and Strauss, 1997), you start to build an understanding of how the client can lead their company as an intelligent network, drawing the greatest possible benefit from being wired up together, connected like cells in a powerful brain, accessing all of its diverse resources.

As a consultant, before being capable of using these methods effectively with a client, you will find that it is important to have gained insight into your own thought processes and what happens when you interact with others of different types. So, you need to try brain mapping and Myers-Briggs questionnaires on yourself. Recognizing that the impact and value of your work to the client depends on the rate at which you are able to learn, you might adopt an attitude towards your own professional life as a kind of 'developmental journey', in which you are constantly converting new experiences via reflection into powerful insights and uniquely appropriate new interventions. This method has been developed by one of us (Tony), using a personal learning diary, and is described in his book *Diary of a Change Agent* (Page, 1996).

Having built the leader's basic understanding of his thinking patterns, we introduce a simple practical method devised by Edward DeBono called 'six thinking hats' (DeBono, 1985), which is valuable both for new product development and strategic problem-solving. As we all know the benefits of playing devil's advocate, or 'wearing a black hat' sometimes, this method can be quick to learn and apply. We can produce better strategies and more innovative and practical solutions when, instead of using just a single black hat, we use a series of six different coloured hats in sequence to pool and focus our thinking about an issue. These are the:

- white hat – for the facts
- red hat – for feelings
- yellow hat – for optimistic thoughts, possibilities
- black hat – for pessimistic thoughts, identfiying risk, danger
- green hat – for wild, absurd, creative, lateral thinking 'outside the box'
- blue hat – for helicopter, overview, summary thinking.

When we have encouraged leaders of SMEs to use this simple way of extending their thinking habits, both in one-to-one and group situations, we find it makes a big difference. It gives permission to left-brain analysts to engage their right-brain creative and empathic talents. It makes brainstorming fun, allowing all the people in a team to achieve a better sense of involvement, and better solutions and strategies as a result.

Beyond our initial work addressing today's problems and helping the client find their path forwards into the future, we like to leave behind with our clients these ways of working and thinking that enable continuous future learning and adaptation. Clients have learned not only our working/learning conversation process, but also a great deal about ways of thinking that they have already started to teach and apply in all conversations with their people.

The business performance workshop approach

At the start of this chapter, we referred to the challenge of finding a compact and practical way to deliver your consultancy to leaders of SMEs, whose time and funds are limited. If you were to follow all the steps in the consulting process that we have described so far, you would exhaust and bankrupt many small companies or you might end up feeling resentful at the sheer amount of free consulting you were having to provide.

Our answer to this dilemma is a consortium approach, in which you bring the leaders of, typically, ten non-competing firms from a region together for a series of business performance workshops. During a single workshop, each day of your time is bringing benefits to ten companies instead of one. The benefits are further multiplied many times because of the rapid learning that occurs between participants.

An initial two-day business performance workshop would take the following form:

- the new world of business
- your personal agenda:
  - who you are?
  - what you are in business for?
  - brain mapping and personality profiles
- the working/learning conversation
- the needs of your business:
  - business past/present/future

- – working on your business issues today
- – how you measure success
- the way forward:
  - – wants and offers
  - – future workshops, group identity, network, dinners, learning events
- learning review and next steps.

Further specialist workshops are offered according to the emerging needs of participants, typically covering:

- your Tomorrow's Company strategy
- financial management
- people management
- performance measurement
- supply chain management
- Total Quality Management
- change management
- breakthrough thinking.

Each workshop is highly practical, giving leaders the chance both to focus on finding solutions for their own businesses, and also to learn from the experiences of their colleagues.

Over a 12-month period, there are five workshops, three of them one-day ones and two of them two-day ones. In addition there are two days in-company consulting (which might be taken as workshops) for each participant. A float of time is held to provide *ad hoc* assistance that is needed. Workshops are interspersed with a series of dinners, talks, company visits and other participant-organized learning events.

The programme gives you a way of delivering high value to directors of SMEs, sustained over a year, but also putting them on a path for future success with a learning and support network built round them.

There follows the story of the first group who went through this approach.

Quorn Associates

The first series of business performance workshops was held in Leicester in 1984. The directors of SMEs who participated named themselves 'Quorn Associates' and continued to meet – for learning, networking, dinners – both with spouses or partners and without, sometimes with visiting speakers.

Small and medium-sized firms

Since 1984, 144 companies in the East Midlands have taken part in business performance workshops. Many of the participants have taken their businesses forward dramatically, some have since sold their businesses, some have retired, some have become consultants, some provided business opportunities for one another or pursued opportunities together. Many of the original relationships have been maintained to the present day.

Due to the huge and growing number of SMEs and the widespread needs for these programmes, we have also become involved in expanding the delivery capacity of government agencies, by training other consultants in the business performance workshop approach.

Moving forward

Being the leader of an SME can be a lonely business. To be able to add something as a consultant, you are taking on the role of a trusted friend and mentor. The path is not easy or predictable. You are having conversations with your client that help to transform their business and their life. We have tried to simplify this process in order to communicate it clearly in this chapter, but, as the world is turbulent and frequently unclear, we're tempted to close on a cautionary note with the words of Albert Einstein who, when asked, 'How do you work?' replied 'I grope!'

By the way, do you want to know what happened to the 25-person company that cancelled their workshop at the start of this chapter? They had to make all their staff redundant. They made their offices available to staff as a sort of job shop, with the consultant's help. The MD used his contacts to place some of the staff in new jobs elsewhere. The directors continued to run the business on their own for one year. They found a part-time commercial manager who helped them through a financial restructuring. They survived! They moved on to a new phase in the company's life. They now have a much reduced cost base and are profitable again.

References

Bridges, B (1996) *Transitions*, Nicholas Brealy, London
Cooper, C (1997), *The Psychological Implications of Changing Patterns of Work*, RSA lecture, 19 November, London
DeBono, E (1985), *Six Thinking Hats*, Penguin, London
Greiner, Larry (1972) 'Evolution and Revolution as Organizations Grow', *Harvard Business Review*, July–August, p165

IBM United Kingdom Limited/London Business School (1994), *Made in Europe: A four nations best practice study*, LBS

Kolb, D A *et al.* (1979) *Organizational Psychology.* 3rd edn, Prentice-Hall, Englewood Cliffs, NJ,

Leonard, D, and Straus, S, (1997) 'Putting Your Company's Whole Brain to Work', *Harvard Business Review*, Juy–August

Lynch, D (1985) *Your High-performance Business Brain: An operator's manual*, Prentice-Hall, Englewood Cliffs, NJ

Nonaka, I, and Takeuchi, H (1995) *The Knowledge Creating Company*, Oxford University Press, Oxford

Page, T (1996) *Diary of a Change Agent*, Gower, Aldershot

Price Waterhouse, Cranfield Project, March 1996, referred to in Barrow, C (1997) *Barriers to Growth*, published by Cranfield University School of Management, Winter

Revans, R W (1982) *The Origins and Growth of Action Learning*, Chartwell-Bratt, Bromley

RSA Inquiry (1995) *Tomorrow's Company: The role of business in a changing world*, Gower, Aldershot

18

Consulting in
the public sector

Michael G Jarrett

The increasing dynamics of change in the public sector

Local authorities are increasingly faced with a multiplicity of competing objectives. They are expected to be the 'enabling authority', commissioners of services, competitive providers and regulators Isaac-Henry and Painter (1991), Gyford (1991), Flynn (1993), Audit Commission (1986), Widdicombe (1986) . These demands are made within an environment of changes in funding regimes, legislation and expectations by stakeholders, especially the public (Common, Flynn and Mellon (1992), Flynn (1993), Wilkinson and Pedler (1996), Gaster (1996)). Thus, local authorities and public sector organizations in general are faced with increasing external complexity, new and emerging managerial and organizational models, as well as the need to continue 'quality' public services at least cost.

This series of dilemmas has led to increase in the use of external consultants in the public sector. These have varied in quality and type from the increasing number of independent consultancies to the Big Six. On the operational process, there have been examples such as Andersen Consulting's work with the Department of Social Security, through to an *Economist* report on consultants that suggested, along with IT, Organization Development (OD) and consulting in the public sector were among the growth areas (*Economist* report, 1997).

It is these two areas that provide the focus for this chapter. The interest in the public sector is the principal subject, while organization development consultancy provides an additional twist for a number of reasons.

There are several excellent consultancies that provide an expert role on the strategic, task or an operational role on training skills and developing systems (see a review of current practice in O'Shea and Madigan (1997)). But it is the contention here that the most difficult domain on which to consult is strategic process, where OD is a significant consulting intervention.

The strategic aspects of OD cut to the heart of the organization: its culture, leadership, strategy and the management of change. There is considerable agreement on the importance and relatedness of these key organizational variables. Gouillart and Kelly (1995), Kanter *et al.* (1992), Beckhard and Pritchard (1992), Pettigrew and Whipp (1991), Beer *et al.* (1990), Bessant and Buckingham (1993), Thomas and Ramaswamy (1996), Peters and Waterman (1982), Kets DeVries and Miller (1986), Miller (1990), Schneider (1997), Wasdell (1997), Burke and Litwin (1992) and Miles and Snow (1978).

It is in this domain that politics and power play a significant part in organizational dynamics. In the public sector 'organizational politics' is more complex as it includes large 'P', local and national politics and this impacts on how the organization takes up its 'primary task'.

The question that this chapter explores is what is the role of the consultant in strategic OD interventions within a public sector setting? The rest of the chapter covers four areas:

- what is the impact of the changes in the organization?
- what are the implications for organization development consulting?
- what might be the roles of the consultant?
- what next?

A short case study is used to provide examples of what happens in organizations driven by political dynamics.

The impact of change can distort the 'primary task'

The changing environment of the public sector has put new strains on organizations. It has meant that they have had to take on new roles and in many ways think about what they are here to provide and what is their primary task. For example, an NHS trust that is also a teaching hospital will have its competing demands even more in profile as it attempts to reconcile these pulls, given the declining security and level of resources.

These dilemmas of policy and direction cannot be solved only by a managerial or strategic model. They are informed by values, and mandates are often in the political domain.

Widdicombe (1986), Walker (1991) and Stewart (1986) explore the different aspects and difficult role of political management and imply that such a role has an increasing relevance within public sector organizations. Bryson (1988), Pfeffer (1992), Mangham (1979), Greiner and Schein (1989) and Johnson and Scholes (1993) would all take the view that an analysis of stakeholders, coalitions, and power relations is a vital part of organizational development and change and this is more emphasized in the public sector.

Thus, rational models of organizations and of change are to be challenged by the apparent paradox of complexity, political and organizational dynamics. In most instances the enactment of these dynamics interferes with task attainment and organizational learning (see Miller and Rice (1967), Menzies (1960), Hirchhorn (1988; 1995) and Diamond (1994)).

Evidence from research based on three in-depth cases studies within the public sector suggests that strategic organizational learning is inhibited by 'defensive routines' (Jarrett, 1998). These routines are described by Chris Argyris as regular and unspoken organizational dynamics that undermine organizational learning (see Argyris (1985; 1990), Argyris and Schon (1996)). They come in several forms such as 'avoidance' of conflict or reality, inconsistencies between what people say and what they do, a resistance to thinking or reflecting and keeping the undiscussable undiscussed. In each case, the main source of these difficulties was the Board or elected members.

In addition, the organizations were poor in identifying or implementing their strategic task, they had poor political leadership and in two of the cases the political dynamics of the elected members were such that they acted as a force for instability within the organization and the strategic imperatives were undermined by the political in-fighting and insecurity of the politicians.

The case of a local authority in transition

Organizational context

Cateringham[1] was an urban, multi-cultural district council that had been through immense organizational change during the late 1980s

---

1. The organization has been heavily disguised to protect anonymity

through to the mid-1990s. It had reduced its staff headcount by 5 per cent, reduced its management structure from 20 to eight main directorates, cut services and turned around its poor public image to be now seen as a 'well managed' authority. The authority's strategic and organization development was to implement strategic, performance monitoring and review systems while also securing further sources of funding from non-traditional places such as partnership arrangements with the private sector and 'special funds' from central government and Europe.

The authority had a large political majority and the CEO had hitherto led the changes to where the group was at the time of the study, which covered a period of action research for over a year. During the time of the work the directors also used an independent consultant to increase the quality of their teamwork.

The key changes over the decade of the authority are in Table 18.1

The summary of change shows how the managerial and political dimension of change had become more important.

Managing strategic dilemmas

The elected members and the directors had made formal agreements about the strategic direction of the authority, the resource priorities and the process of decision-making that was to be followed on budgets and the strategic use of resources. The CEO and the directors had gone to great lengths to ensure the strategic decision-making process was developed. They had agreed the process with their committee chairman and had formalized how things were to be undertaken.

In the event the authority found itself having to make large scale decisions over the budget that had not come to light until a few weeks before the first cut of the budget in October 1995. The elaborate consultative process that was painstakingly agreed with elected members and officers was ditched and the final decision was made by a small group of people including the leader of the council and the CEO.

The dynamics of the strategic apex

Mintzberg (1983) refers to the organizational strategic apex as the part of the organization that makes policy, strategy and executes plans. In the case of the local authority this is invested in the elected members and the executive directors. The former set the policy agenda based on an explicit political manifesto. The latter translate these policies into action. It is this role distinction between members and directors, plus the

Consulting in the public sector

Table 18.1 A summary of the key periods of change for Cateringham District Council

	Period 1 Early 1980s	Period 2 1989/90	Period 3 1995
Driving force	Keep the workers happy	Manage for survival in crisis	Managerial realism plus political agenda
Leadership	Leader of the Council	Chris James, CEO	Chris James and Tommy Grant, Leader of the Council
Environment	Relatively stable	Turbulent	Quasi-market forces
Values	'The workers matter'	'The service matters'	'The "customers" matter'
Strategy	Single provider – monopoly supplier	Turnaround strategy – including cuts	'Mixed economy' of partnerships and provision
Skills	Political	Managerial influence	Turn policies into reality and manage the politics
Structure	Large departments	In transition – special project and ad hoc groups	Large directorates but more focused units
Staff at the top	Large management team and senior offficers	Reductions made	Slimlined to eight directorates
Style	Focus on relationship	Focus on crisis here and now	Mixture of corporate management and political management
Systems	Bureaucratic and ineffective	Budget focused – devolved to front line	Focus on management systems and politics

explicit dimension of the party political agenda, that makes consulting to such organization within the strategic apex so difficult.

There were three organizational and group dynamics operating in the strategic apex leading to this unpredictable outcome.

- The dynamic in the 'top team' of directors.
- The dynamics within the members.
- The intergroup dynamics between the two.

The dynamics of the top team

The 'top team' was not a team. Despite support from an external consultant on its processes and behaviours, it was more like a 'pseudo-team',

373

which operated at a superficial level. (Katzenbach and Smith (1993, 1994, 1997). Team members described the group as cold, lacking in trust, not focused, low on social contact and poor on task completion. During the decision-making time on strategic resources they were excluded. The time they seemed to work best and enjoyed was during a crisis or a 'rush on'.

The CEO was often in conflict with the team members, especially George Tans, the strategic director, who was often used as the scapegoat by all the members of the team and blamed for anything that went wrong with strategy.

The dynamics of the team did not help strategic task attainment nor organizational learning

The dynamic of the elected members

The ruling party had a majority. However, it did not have a unison of political opinion. This was because of different political persuasions within the majority, different political coalitions and political allegiances to the Leader of the Council, Tommy Grant. Grant had been the leader for several years and was seen as the ideal candidate for leader as he was a suitable compromise of these different competing interests. However, the disadvantage was that his leadership was easily compromised and what was agreed at the executive meeting of the political party could be easily changed when the chair of the committee finally made his or her vote.

Thus, weak leadership, in-fighting between different factions of the same political party and wider differences over philosophical and political ideology distorted the strategic task and process. Mintzberg (1983) argues that ideologically driven organizations tend to 'balkanize' or fragment and thus the organizational coherence and the nature of the consulting task become uncertain and ambiguous.

The intergroup dynamics

The dynamics between the elected members and the directors was characterised by three main features:

- The power relations between members and directors was asymmetric with members in charge.
- The in-fighting and conflict within the elected members spilt over and into the directors group and in some way mirrored the same power struggles.
- The organizational tendency to fragment at the strategic apex was counter-balanced by a coalition of Tommy Grant (the Leader of the Council) and Chris James (CEO) plus one or two others. This

constellation provided both a focus for the organization to get through the dynamics of change but at the same time undermined the strategic development of the strategic apex. This was because it perpetuated the dependency and current state of working with the CEO 'leading' along with the CEO and it also stopped learning taking place within that strategic system.

These intergroup dynamics made for a continuing unstable and uncertain organizational context

The implications for organizational consultation

The case study highlights some of the issues the consultant can face when working at the strategic apex on OD interventions. What are the implications? It suggests that the nature of the consulting task, understanding of the organization and role demands of the organizational consultant may need re-visiting.

Challenges in the consulting process

The challenge for the organizational consultant is to see the consulting task as part of a wider system so that one fully accounts for the political and organizational dynamics that impact on the work.

Secondly, in this type of context the consultant is pushed to work at the boundary of ambiguity, uncertainty and unknowing as the political and organizational dynamics are enacted. As a consultant, the challenge is to prevent pre-judging the situation, acting out of one's own anxiety and confusion, or feeling the need to have an answer or be 'expert' without a full understanding of the organizational dynamics

The third challenge and opportunity is to develop a wider repertoire of consulting style and approaches that fall within a framework of process consultation – what Schein (1991; 1995) calls a 'clinical approach', where the emphasis is still on solving the client's problem but from a deep understanding of the internal psyche of the organization and the preoccupations of its stakeholders.

Understanding organizations as complex adaptive systems

The consulting challenge opens up the possibility to work outside of the dominant organizational framework of 'strategic choice'.

The paradigm of strategic choice

Here the organization is viewed as a social system and the focus of analysis is based upon the premise that managers have 'strategic choice'. It sees answers to problems as lying outside of the organization and all the manager has to do is to scan the environment and import the most relevant solution. This is often associated with the use of consultants. Managers are seen as 'doers' and all they have to do is follow the recipe and they can make things happen. It is a 'can do' message.

The 'strategic choice' framework underpins much that might be described in the HR and training field and has a lot in common with 'leaders of transformation' literature which is available for managers and in popular management literature. It includes theories in the field of: organizational development; planned incrementalism; entreprenuerialism; learning from 'best practice' (eg Japanization); the use of external consultants and change agents and, the enterprise culture as normative practice (Wilson, 1992). These, again, broadly fall within a normative or pragmatic paradigm and in some ways deny the reality of organizational life.

Wilson (1992) notes: 'In contrast, there appears to have been relative neglect of the systemic conflict framework in which the context, history and antecedents of change are fundamental pieces of the jigsaw of evidence and understanding. Such analyses are both rare in number and inherently more difficult to research, in contrast to studies of managerial entreprenuerialism, management training and strategic choice.'

The systemic conflict framework

Here the organization is seen as a social system. However, this is characterized by conflict, politicking and inherent tensions. These tensions can operate at the individual, group or organizational level, but it is these tensions and contradictions that provide the impetus for change. Energy to support the change comes from within the single organizational unit, the ultimate goal being to achieve a new balance between the current set of conflicts (Wilson, 1992).

The organization as a complex system

Thus, the first step for organizational consultants is to revise their models of understanding organizations. A systems approach that sees organizations as having a 'primary task' and is made up of system inputs and outputs is necessary, but not a sufficient place to start.

Thus, the organization is seen as an open system with a task and it also has boundaries.

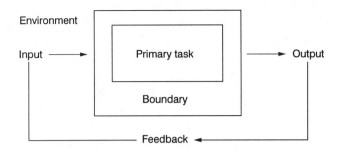

Figure 18.1 A simple 'open systems' model

'A task system is a system of activities plus the human and physical resources required to perform the activities' (Miller and Rice (1967)). It is the governing rationale for the organization.

A 'boundary' provides a delineation of one system from another or one task from another. This clear delineation or 'boundary' is essential in order to be clear about what is to be managed and to avoid confusion.

Miller and Rice (1967) also add that the system is also a series of social and psychological relationships. They described these as 'sentient relationships' where conscious and unconscious bonds are made among group members in the system, which can support or undermine the task. These relationships need to be managed, otherwise they can undermine the primary task and interfere with performance and learning.

In the case of Cateringham we see that the organization is a complex, social system and it is constantly adapting. It has elements of chaos and stability in it and systemic conflicts that arise from political and ideological conflict. To provide a valuable and lasting intervention, taking a systemic conflict view of the organization and seeing it as a complex, adaptive, non-linear system is likely to bear more fruit than seeing it in the rational strategic choice framework. The difference will be in the way the organization is diagnosed, managed, the process of consultation and the nature of the intervention itself.

The consultancy process differs in emphasis

The process of consultation in a political environment requires some change in emphasis in the consultancy process. These changes are summarized in Table 18.2. However, there are three things to which the consultant should pay additional attention.

The consultant needs to see the organization as a whole and complex system. Thus, the work of the independent consultant on the directors' teamworking seemed to draw the boundaries too closely and therefore ignored the wider systemic aspects of the organization. Thus, the intervention had not met its expectations and the directors were disappointed with the results. Information about the organizational and systemic dynamics of the team and its context provided greater insights and opportunities for the team to act and think differently about its role and task

The use of a clinical approach means that the consultant seeks to understand the internal and complex dynamics of the organization. This approach involves the use of observation, listening with free attention and being open to following the needs and interests of the client.

Finally, it requires the consultant to put their own reactions and ego to one side and provide a structure for the client to think about its progress and learning in the journey of change. In the case of Cateringham District Council, this took the form of dialogue sessions within the top team as part of the action research (Schein (1993)).

The role of the consultant

In the case material there was a role for consultancy support on the strategic process and that was unofficially provided by the research process. Schein (1991) would argue that the distinction between process consultation and a clinical approach to understanding the organization was unhelpful. Kahn (1993) also shows how difficult it is to separate these two roles in reality. Thus, it is suggested that consultants working on the strategic OD tasks in public sector organizations should also have a clinical approach to their entry processes, diagnosis, data collection, intervention and reviews.

Second, the consultant provides the role of managing the boundaries and anxieties of change at the strategic apex. This is often referred to as the 'container' role where the consultant is able to listen to the client, hear without prejudging the material, internalize the meaning of the client's predicament and reflect or feed it back in a way that the client can hear and gain insight or learning for action. (Kahn (1995), Obholzer & Roberts (1994), Stapley (1996) and Jarrett & Kellner (1996)).

Third, the consultant needs to be able to manage himself. In the role of the container, it is 'as if' the consultant provides a secure base or 'holding environment' to the organization as a parent does for a child. This allows the organization to manage and tolerate the organizational and

Table 18.2 The change in emphasis in the consulting focus

Adapted from Clarkson and Kellner, 1995, and Miller, 1997, Brunning *et al.*, 1990, Schein, 1991

Stages of consulting	Dominant model	Systemic and psychodynamic approaches
Entry	Establish relationship with client as basis for further involvement	Focus on client problem, acknowledge feelings, explore nature
Contracting	Developing a mutual contract, clarifying expectations and modus operandi	Establish needs and wants. Agree processes and milestones, not just outputs
Data Collection	Measuring organizational indices and variable	Emphasis on understanding, 'listening with the intent to understand' the social and political system and learn its history
Diagnosis	Interpret data and feedback to client, developing a joint understanding	Develop and test working hypotheses, take open systems model, interpret the psychosocial dynamics and the impact on the primary task
Implementation	Plan and carry out intervention	Participative, inclusive of organizational stakeholders and agents. Model conflict handling, value difference and validate all parties
Review	Evaluate the success of the interventions	Dialogue and feedback sessions. Collective involvement
Termination	Withdraw leaving system able to manage its own future changes	Endings are as important as the entries. Provide sustainability for insight and learning

primitive anxiety of transition, change and ambiguity. In order for the consultant to do this well, they too must have the capacity to manage ambiguity, the unknowing, and have a developed ability for self-reflection and self analysis (Berg and Smith (1998), Clarkson and Kellner (1995) and Hirschhorn (1995). These capacities are equally important for large scale, participative changes where a small group may provide that locus for reality checking and task focusing, for example in the case of Cateringham (see Wilkinson and Pedler, 1996, and Miller, 1997)

The implication is that consultants need to develop an additional perspective in their understanding of organizations and an additional skill-set in terms of taking systemic and psychodynamics organizational interventions in complex and political organizational systems. Thus, training in advanced organizational consultation processes, which have a system psychodynamic approach, along with 'clinical' supervision and personal development in this craft provides the first steps to developing new personal and professional competencies.

Conclusion

In this chapter I have tried to show the impact of public sector organizational dynamics on the consulting process. Using a case study and material from other similar studies it suggests that public sector organizations need to be understood as complex and political systems and that dominant consulting models and methodologies could be enhanced with a different and more systemic psychodynamic perspective.

The combination of an increasingly complex system and the explicit political nature of public sector organizations makes them a challenging system for organization development. There is evidence to suggest that the political dynamics may impact negatively on the primary task and that such dynamics fuel defensive routines, task avoidance and anti-learning. The systemic and psychodynamically orientated consultant can provide a strategic and 'container' role to help manage the organizational and task anxieties that come from change. This consultancy approach provides a challenge to the individual consultant (or practice) and to the profession itself, where there is often a collusive pull to be all-knowing and have all the right answers. However, in the approach presented in this chapter the value is in working on the boundary of 'unknowing', providing a 'holding environment' and insight and helping the client get to task and learn through their own work.

References

Argyris, C (1985) *Strategic Change and Defensive Routines*, Pitman, London
Argyris, C (1990) *Overcoming Organizational Defenses: Facilitating Organizational Learning*, Allyn and Bacon, Needham Height, MA

Consulting in the public sector

Argyris, C, and Schon, D A (1996) *Organizational Learning II: Theory, Method and Practice*, Addison-Wesley, Reading MA

Audit Commission for Local Authorities in England and Wales (1986) *The Competitive Council, Management Papers No.1*, Audit Commission, London

Beckhard, R, and Pritchard, W (1992) *Changing The Essence: The Art of Creating and Leading Fundamental Change in Organizations*, Jossey-Bass, San Francisco

Beer, M, Eisenstat, R A, and Spector, B (1990) 'Why Change Programs don't produce change', *Harvard Business Review*, Nov/Dec pp.158–166

Bessant, J, and Buckingham, J (1993) 'Innovation and Organizational Learning: the case of Computer-Aided Production Management', *British Journal of Management*, Vol. 4, No. 4, pp.219–234

Berg, D N and Smith, K K (1988) *The Self in Social Inquiry*, Sage, London

Brunning, H, Cole, C and Huffington C (1990) The Change Directory: Key Issues in Organizational Development

Bryson, J M (1988) *Strategic Planning for Public and Nonprofit organizations*, Jossey-Bass, San Francisco

Burke, W W (1987) *Organization Development: A Normative View*, Addison-Wesley, Reading MA

Clarkson, P, and Kellner, K, (1995) 'Danger, confusion, conflict, deficit. A framework for prioritising organizational interventions', *Organizations & People*, Vol.2, No.4

Common, R, Flynn, N, and Mellon, E (1992) *Managing Public Services: Competition and decentralisation*, Butterworth-Heinemann, Oxford

Diamond, M A (1994) *The Unconscious Life of Organizations*, Cenorium

Flynn, N (1993) *Public Sector Management*, (2nd edn.) London: Harvester Wheatsheaf

Gaster, L (1996) 'Quality Services in Local Government: a Bottom-up Approach', *Journal of Management Development*, 15, 2, 80–96

Gouillart, F J, and Kelly, J N (1995) *Transforming the Organization*, McGraw-Hill, New York

Greiner, L E, and Schein, V E (1989) *Power and Organization Development*, Addison-Wesley, Reading MA

Gyford, J (1991) 'The Enabling Council – A Third Mode', *Local Government Studies*, 17, 1, 1–5

Hirschhorn, L (1988) *The Workplace Within: Psychodynamics of Organizational Life*, London: The MIT Press

Hirschhorn, L (1995) 'A Psychodynamic Approach to Consulting', Master Class, South Bank University, London

Isaac-Henry, K, and Painter, C (1991) 'The Management Challenge in Local Government – Emerging Themes and Trends', *Local Government Studies*, 17, 3, 69–90

Jarrett, M G (1998) 'The psychodynamic of top teams and the impact on strategic organizational learning: three case studies from the public sector' Unpublished thesis, Cranfield University School of Management, Cranfield

Jarrett, M G, and Kellner, K (1996) 'Coping with uncertainty: a psychodynamic perspective on the work of top teams', *Journal of Management Development*, 15, 2, 54–68

Johnson, G and Scholes, K (1993) *Exploring Corporate Strategy*, Prentice-Hall, Englewood Cliffs, New Jersey

Kahn, W A (1993) 'Facilitating and Undermining Organizational Change: A Case Study', *Journal of Applied Behavioural Science*, 29, 1, 32–55

Kahn, W A (1995) 'Organizational Change and the Provision of a Secure Base: Lessons from the Field', *Human Relations*, 48, 5, 489 – 514

Kanter, R M, Stein, B A, and Jick, T D (1992) *The Challenge of Organizational Change: How Companies Experience it and Leaders Guide it*, Free Press, New York

Katzenbach, J R, and Smith, D K (1992) 'The delicate balance of team leadership', *McKinsey Quarterly*, 128–142

Katzenbach, J R and Smith, D K (1993) *The Wisdom of Teams: Creating the High-Performance Organization*, Harvard Business School Press, Boston MA

Katzenbach, J R, and Smith, D K (1994) 'Teams at the Top', *McKinsey Quarterly*, Spring, 71–79

Katzenbach, J R, and Smith, D K (1997) 'The Myth of Teams', *Harvard Business Review*, October

Kets de Vries, M R F, and Miller, D (1986) 'Personality, culture and organization', *Academy of Management Review*, 11, 2, 266 – 279

Mangham, I (1979) *The Politics of Organizational Change*, Associated Business Press, London

Menzies, I (1960) 'A Case in the Functioning of Social System as a Defence Against Anxiety', *Human Relations*, 13, 95–121

Micklethwait, J, and Wooldridge, A (1994) *The Witch Doctors: What the management gurus are saying, why it matters and how to make sense of it*, Heinemann, Oxford

Miles, R E, and Snow, C C (1978) *Organizational Strategy, Structure and Process*, McGraw-Hill, New York

Miller, D (1990) 'Organizational Configurations: Cohesion, Change, and Prediction', *Human Relations*, 43, 8, 771–89

Miller, E J (1997) 'Effecting Organizational Change in Large Complex Systems: A collaborative consultancy approach' in Neumann, J, Kellner, K, and Dawson-Shepherd, A (1997) (eds.) *Developing Organizational Consultancy*, Routledge, London

Miller, E J, and Rice, A K (1967) *Systems of Organization*, Tavistock Publications, London

Mintzberg, H (1983) *Power In and Around Organizations*, Prentice-Hall, New Jersey

Obholzer, A, and Roberts V Z (1994) *The Unconscious at Work: Individual and Organizational Stress in the Human Services*, Routledge, London

O'Shea, J, and Madigan, C (1997) *Dangerous Company: The Consulting Powerhouses and the Business They Save and Ruin*, Nicholas Brealey Publications Ltd, London

Peters, T J, and Waterman (Jr), R H (1982) *In Search of Excellence*, Harper and Row, New York

Pettigrew, A, and Whipp, R (1991) *Managing for Competitive Success*, Blackwell, Oxford

Pfeffer, J (1992) *Managing with Power: Politics and Influence in Organizations*, Harvard Business School Press, Cambridge, MA

Schein, E H (1991) *Legitimating Clinical Research in the Study of Organizational Culture*, Working paper (3288–91-BPS), MIT, Cambridge, MA

Schein, E H (1993) 'On Dialogue, Culture and Organizational Learning', *Organizational Dynamics*, Autumn, 40 – 51

Schein, E H (1995) 'Process consultation, action research and clinical inquiry: are they the same?', *Journal of Managerial Psychology*, 110, 6, 14–19

Schneider, W E (1997) 'Aligning strategy, culture and leadership' in Neumann, J, Kellner, K, and Dawson-Shepherd, A (1997) (eds) *Developing Organizational Consultancy*, Routledge, London

Stapley, L (1996) *The Personality of the Organization: A Psycho-Dynamic Explanation of Culture and Change*, Free Association Books, London

Stewart, J (1986) *The Management of influence – Implications for Management Development*, Local Government Training Board, Luton

Thomas, A S, and Ramaswamy, K (1996) 'Matching Managers to Strategy: Further Tests of the Miles and Snow Typology', *British Journal of Management*, 7, 3, 247–262

Walker, D (1991) *Political Management in Local Authorities: A Discussion Paper*, The Public Management Foundation, London

Wasdell, D (1997) 'The consulting organization as an advanced learning system' in Neumann, J, Kellner, K, and Dawson-Shepherd, A (1997) (eds) *Developing Organizational Consultancy*, Routledge, London

Widdicombe, D (QC) (1986) *The Conduct of Local Authority Business*. Cmnd 9797 HMSO, London

Wilkinson, D, and Pedler, M (1996) 'Whole systems development in public service', *Journal of Management Development*, 15, 2, 38–53

Wilson, D C (1992) *A Strategy of Change: Concepts and Controversies in the Management of Change*, Routledge, London

19

Large corporations

Mike Jeans and Tony Page

Introduction

When you are consulting with large corporations, you may find yourself challenged in altogether different ways to those discovered with small- and medium-sized enterprises or public-sector organizations.

Typically, a large corporation has many product lines, in many organizational units that may also be geographically dispersed across many locations and, increasingly, crossing national boundaries. Arguably this results in a similar scale of organizational complexity and inertia to that found within the public sector, but in large private-sector organizations great complexity is combined with a quite different profile of values, risks and opportunities.

Let us take an example to illustrate this point. SmithKline Beecham, a global healthcare company, has headquarters in London and Philadelphia, around 50,000 staff spread across laboratories, factories and offices in over 100 countries throughout the world developing, producing and selling a huge portfolio of products, some 'ethical', delivered by means of doctors' prescription, and others available over the counter at high street retail pharmacists. The organization was formed in 1989 when two very different organizations merged, namely the US-owned SmithKline Beckman and the UK-owned Beecham Group. In 1994, the complexity of culture, product portfolio and organization was compounded by the acquisition of a third company, Sterling Health (Bauman, Jackson and Lawrence, 1997).

It is a gross oversimplification to say that 'making profit' is the only value in a large corporation. You are dealing with a large employee population that has a wide range of national cultures, religions, climates, lifestyles, backgrounds and career aspirations. These differences mani-fest in the workplace in all sorts of ways, at times inhibiting and at other times enabling corporate performance. The large corporation usually needs to develop its own distinctive culture and values in order to engage diverse interests and transcend these differences.

If you enter a large corporation as a consultant in a naive way, you run the risk of repeating the sorts of mistakes many have made before you. Typical mistakes include those listed in Table 19.1.

Perhaps the list in Table 19.1 seems a little daunting. Consulting is not easy work to do, so there are many ways to get into difficulties and there is a constant risk to your reputation as a consultant, carrying with it the loss of possible future business with both current and prospective clients. The scale of the opportunity is great and therefore so is the downside risk.

Table 19.1 Some typical mistakes and solutions to them

Typical mistake	Consequence	Advice
Taking things at face value	Solutions fail because based on partial data	Differentiate opinion from fact
Misreading the power structure	Recommendations not adopted because not accepted by key influencers	Find out how decisions made in reality rather than the theory of the organigram. Map the roles/relationships in the client's system
Ignoring personal agendas	Objective solutions are blocked	Discover and take account of the personal/career drivers of key players
Overplaying the politics	Getting sucked into covert games, setting people up, running your own agenda not the client's	Understand but don't play the politics, aim for total transparency of what you're up to
Scope creep	Clients ask 'Could you also look at this?', loss of focus, unrealistic client expectations	Be clear with yourself and others about the boundaries of your assignment
Overstaying your welcome	Client starts to get used to you being around, but you've gone past the point of adding the greatest value. Reputation of your firm is damaged when client realizes!	Make a clear agreement with the client about the end point of the assignment.

385

For example, a consultant facilitating a successful visioning workshop with a divisional management team in any medium-sized organization, might gain a chance to run that workshop with another divisional team. In a large corporation there are potentially more divisional teams, but the increased opportunity does not end there. In fact, in this example, there are at least three sources of leverage:

- selling across the organization, replicating the visioning workshop in other divisions
- selling through the value stream, for example, from visioning workshop on managing information systems, to a workshop on IT strategy, leading on to a business process re-engineering project with change programme management.
- optimizing consultant ratios, bringing less expensive junior people in to facilitate future workshops and projects.

A company such as Shell, with annual turnover of $108 billion, is one of a handful of very large multinationals that, between them, control more money and so, arguably, are more powerful than many national governments. The large consulting firms are in business relationships with the world's largest 500 companies that are both lucrative and long-term. So, there is plenty at stake. Make a small mistake, lose one of these clients and the lost lifetime revenue to you and your firm can run into many hundreds of millions of pounds!

On the other hand, by learning from the experience of others (some of which is offered in this chapter), you could avoid many of the worst mistakes and distinguish yourself as a highly respected consultant. You could find yourself in strategic engagements with one or more large corporations producing high client value combined with high consulting profits arising from the combination of good billings with low selling costs.

Between us, we have around 40 years' experience of consulting with large corporations covering both the business/financial and the organizational/people perspectives. We believe that:

- consulting with large corporations is challenging and different because no one member of staff has the total picture. Each person is selective about the data they hold and has only a partial view
- you are increasingly involved in creating change directly, helping the client to implement, rather than simply producing, recommendations;
- you have to achieve a broad and integrated view, to build an objective business case based on concrete data;

- you are constantly balancing task and process, business and people issues;
- the high risk/high reward nature of consultancy work with large corporations adds to the importance of adopting a totally professional and ethical approach (see Chapter 2, Part I).

Although one of us has roots in accountancy and the other in psychology, we have both learned that our success in consulting depends on working from an integrated view of people and business. Stirring people to change without a clear business case is a pointless, confusing wind-up. Providing an objective business case for change without an effective process for engaging people in it is also totally ineffective.

Having set out this challenge, in the rest of this chapter we offer some ideas, practical methods and guidance, supported with examples of consulting with large corporations.

Understanding your context and role

In today's competitive world, traditional boundaries between sectors – such as those between petrol retailers and supermarkets – are dissolving as every organization strives to increase its effectiveness and efficiency in order to remain viable. Sustainable success depends on delivering shareholder value by means of effective management of the vital business relationships with customer, employee, supplier and community. This challenge has been referred to as protecting and growing the 'licence to operate' (RSA Inquiry, 1995). Rarely can this be achieved without implementing radical change by, for example, outsourcing non-core functions, fundamental process redesign, or participating in mergers and acquisitions. You can see this everywhere. Global mergers are in the news among the already large Big Six accountancy firms. Also British Airways is waiting to hear the decision of European commissioners regarding its proposed merger with American Airlines. Guinness has gained the go ahead for its merger with Grandmet. The privatized electricity and water utilities seem to be in a constant state of alertness for mergers and takeovers. Not so long ago, Glaxo merged with Wellcome. Meanwhile, BT's plans to go global via a merger with MCI have been thwarted.

During its life, each large corporation develops its own unique character. There is no reason to expect that Unilever, Ciba Specialty Chemicals or IBM share anything more than quite superficial similarities. Also, each displays its own pattern of inertia when exposed to the need for change. Some organizations with power concentrated at the centre behave more like supertankers, requiring lots of lead time and huge amounts of energy in order to change direction, but then again it can be no less challenging to realign many semi-autonomous units like smaller, well-captained vessels in a flotilla.

Finding a metaphor that captures your understanding of the unique character and means of engaging with each organization (as in the supertanker and flotilla example just mentioned) in answer to the question 'What is this organization like?' is an important early step in any consulting engagement (Morgan, 1986).

Once you feel you have some understanding of the broad character of the organization, expect it to be constantly challenged, to be regularly reframing your understanding and continuously learning. This is inevitable, given both the fast-changing external environment and the wide range of underlying differences that are constantly present in workstyle, values and beliefs arising from the rich mix of people and expertise present.

It is also important for you to build an understanding of the informal side of the organization – that is, how things are really done as opposed to how things are done in theory, as depicted by the organizational chart. When you are meeting people in the client's organization, you can quickly extend your practical knowledge of it by using the following three simple questions.

- Who do you report to?
- Who do you see most often?
- Who do you rely on to get your job done?

Having started to understand the context for your consultancy work in this way, one of the early questions you must answer is why the organization needs a consultant anyway. Clearly the reasons will be particular to each situation, but there are some broad trends to be aware of.

After more than a decade of downsizing and outsourcing, large corporations are leaner. As a result, they have fewer of their own resources and so find it more acceptable to look outside for help than they used to.

As we have seen, large corporations are more aware of the importance of competitiveness, benchmarking and the need to change fast than ever before. They want help from outside consultants who have seen the mistakes other organizations have made, who know what is emerging as best practice and who can help them make change happen.

Large corporations

During the 1980s, the large consulting firms achieved a massive expansion by developing 'T-shaped' specialist consultants – those with vertical depth of specialism combined with a horizontal breadth of understanding of the business as a whole. Now, in the late 1990s, large corporations have a new mix of requirements from their consultants:

- specialist knowledge (such as of SAP and Baan systems software) that is needed for a couple of years only – organizations with a lean philosophy prefer to resource this via short-term contracts or by calling on consultants
- transformation programme management skills, requiring generalists who can draw in and co-ordinate a whole range of more specialist consultants
- Board-level generalist skills, requiring non-executive director-type mentors for the managing and other directors.

A large consultancy engagement nowadays might include a partner as a full-time programme manager, other partners and consultants engaged as specialists – some of them also full-time, others on a more short-term, as needed basis. The project may run for two or three years and the fees may run into millions.

In addition to understanding the organizational context, and your own consultancy role, it is valuable to step back from time to time and consider how the many client and consultant roles of your assignment might interact to produce value. In Figure 19.1 you will find an example of a method called 'mapping the client system'.

To do this exercise yourself, take a sheet of paper, draw a vertical line down the middle. In the centre, draw a circle and write your name and role title (if you have one) inside it. On the left-hand side, list the names and titles of all the client's people you interact with on the project. Classify these if you can into:

- **power figures** people who say 'Yes' or 'No' to allocation of resources
- **gatekeepers** people who control access to power figures
- **problem owners** people in whose patch a problem is located
- **agents** people trying to initiate some constructive action
- **client** the person who commissions the work and pays the fees.

Now list all the names and titles of the people involved in the assignment from your own organization (and other consultants). Draw lines between all the roles to indicate who is interacting with whom.

Try to express the unique contribution you are making to the project. Identify any system blockages or breakdowns and consider how these can best be addressed.

Identifying your sponsor

There is a key sponsor – a person who is ultimately in charge of all decisions and resources – for each of the three phases in a consultancy engagement, which are selling, undertaking and delivering. For fuller coverage of the stages and roles involved in the selling process, see Rackham, 1987. See Figure 19.2 for a matrix you can use to set out who is the key sponsor for each phase.

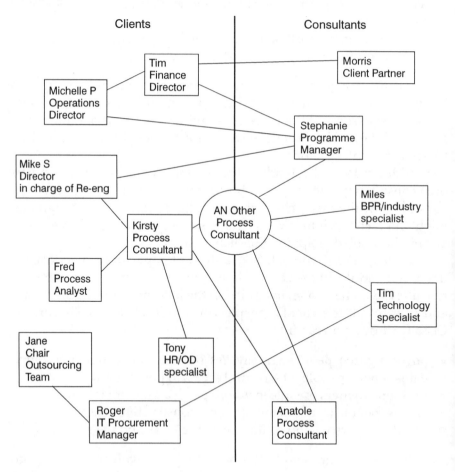

Figure 19.1: Mapping the client system

Large corporations

Sponsor/Stage	Selling	Undertaking	Delivering
Originator of work	K	I	I
Arranger of work	I	K	I
Implementer of work	I	I	K
Payer of work	I	I	I

Key:
K = Key sponsor
I = Influencer

Figure 19.2 Matrix showing the roles of the client's key sponsor and influencers during the phases of a consulting engagement.

During the selling phase – which is that leading up to a decision being made to commence an engagement – it is likely that a number of the client's personnel will be contacted. The key sponsor in this phase is the person who makes the decision to engage consultants. This may not necessarily be the person most affected by your work or, indeed, the person you have the most contact with during the engagement or even the person to whose budget the fees will be charged – though all these individuals may influence the decision. The following story of the food manufacturer is an example of what happens during the selling phase.

The food manufacturer

A major UK-based food manufacturer had a number of subsidiaries. One of these subsidiaries had experienced problems with its costing system and stock valuations. Given that it had operated on very tight margins (less than 5 per cent) supplying national supermarket chains, cost control and early identification of adverse trends were crucial to the company's profitability.

The holding company was well aware of the problem and had decided to seek consultancy assistance. It had additionally decided which firm to appoint. The subsidiary was unhappy, both about the engagement itself and the firm to be appointed. It felt that the holding company was imposing its will.

While unable to forestall the engagement, the subsidiary did manage to gain permission for a competitive quote to be obtained. The holding company, while agreeing to this, still anticipated that the work would be given to its preferred consultancy firm. A tendering process was agreed and issued to the two firms. It was to culminate in a presentation to a selection panel comprising representatives of both the holding company and the subsidiary.

The consultancy firm that had been asked for a competitive quote gained knowledge of the background during its process of gathering data and views prior to making the presentation. The firm knew that it had to satisfy a number of individuals that their requirements would be taken into account:

- the Finance Director of the holding company (commissioning the work)
- the Finance Director of the subsidiary (paying for the work)
- the Chief Management Accountant of the subsidiary (agreeing to any recommendations resulting from the work)
- the Factory Manager of the subsidiary (having to implement any new system and being judged by the resulting output).

Great care was taken to listen to all these individuals during the tendering process. The result was a unanimous decision by the selection panel to choose the quote from the competitor firm. Not only did it correctly identify the relevant sponsors, but, also, the original firm chosen by the holding company thought that the tendering process was a ritual and it had been predetermined to award the work to them.

Of course this was not the end of the story. During the undertaking of work and drawing up the recommendations, the needs of the various sponsors had to continue to be addressed. Expectations had been aroused and had to be managed and met.

Having been commissioned to do the work, the second phase begins – 'undertaking'. The process of data collection and analysis commences. This usually occurs both by requesting actual data to be provided and by interviewing the client's staff.

The key sponsor in this phase is the person who gives permission for data to be released and agrees to the interview programme. This might not be the same person who was the key sponsor during the selling phase.

This sponsor needs to be kept informed of progress, advised of any obstacles encountered, informed of any attempts to increase or decrease the scope of the work and so on. In the event of the consultants being unable to resolve any issues with this sponsor, it may well be necessary to revert to the key 'selling' sponsor.

The key sponsor in the next – 'delivering' – phase is the person responsible for accepting your recommendations and implementing them. Again, this will not necessarily be the same person who was the key 'selling' or 'undertaking' sponsor. You need to maintain close contact with this sponsor during the course of the engagement so that recommendations contain no surprises. 'Rolling the wicket before going in to bat' with your recommendations is usually vital to success in terms of gaining acceptance.

As a useful quick exercise, review a recent consultancy engagement known to you. Identify the key sponsor(s) and influencers in each of the three phases.

Understanding politics

Having understood who the sponsor is in any one phase, you also need to become aware of how the political system works. 'Politics' can be defined as any activity concerned with the acquisition of power. 'Company/organizational politics' are therefore concerned with the activities of an individual or group of individuals seeking to gain or retain power within an organization.

The character of some organizations is open – encouraging candid discussion, allowing people to express personal interests and concerns, bringing covert issues into public view, people helping one another to succeed both individually and collectively. Other organizations – often those that claim to be more task-focused – however, discourage the expression of personal agendas and thereby push politics underground into a covert role.

In large corporations the sheer size and complexity of the organization means that the opportunities for its personnel to play politics are enormous. When the organization is in a stable state, people may constantly be seeking to advance or preserve their own positions or status. When an organization is in a state of change, careers may be threatened and new opportunities exist to acquire power, so personal interests are in play. Consultants who are brought in to assist an organization to implement change should be very sensitive to issues such as these.

Any behaviour may or may not be an example of political activity – it all depends on the context. It is a reasonable rule of thumb to assume that the person is innocent until you start to observe a repeating pattern. Here are some signs to look out for:

- statements being made about other individuals' views and the validity of these views
- selective data being used to prove a point
- minutes of meetings being tailored to suite an individual's viewpoint
- rejection, on apparently logical grounds, of reasoned arguments
- personal agendas predominating over the corporation's agendas
- opinions being stated as factual evidence
- timing meetings so that people cannot be present
- lobbying activity
- pre-emptive actions prohibiting wider debate.

The following example illustrates the political dimension to a consulting engagement.

The multinational group

The group operated along lines adopted by many multinationals, namely, operating a matrix organization structure, with staff reporting along geographical, product and functional lines. Having said this, the operating companies in individual countries enjoyed high levels of delegated powers, even empowerment.

Matrix structures are both complicated and provide fertile ground for political activity, with the reporting lines crossing over each other. Additionally, staff at head office could be divided, rather simplistically, into three groups:

- those returning from many years in operating companies to spend their remaining service coasting until retirement, with their career behind them
- those spending two or three years at head office, gaining experience of its activities, prior to returning to an operating company, with their careers ahead of them
- those whose careers, both behind and ahead of them, were entirely spent in head office.

The motives of individuals, and their resulting politics, differed within each of these groups.

The head office commissioned a consultancy to recommend a management information system that could operate throughout the corporation. The concept was that each operating company could submit information on-line to head office. It would be capable of consolidation by geographic area and product line. Functional reporting, where required, would also be satisfied.

A system was designed, but its implementation failed – primarily for political reasons:

- individual operating companies resented having to supply information to head office, fearing this would result in increased interference in their affairs;
- geographical areas feared that product information could result in the product line organization achieving dominance over the geographical organization
- the system required compatibility of IT software throughout the group, and there was fear that this would result in IT policy being increasingly centralized;
- at least two of the three groups of head office personnel were disinclined to do anything that would 'rock the boat' and, at best, make life uncomfortable, at worst, damage their future plans.

There are two questions that arise from this example:

- Could the political problems have been avoided?
- Should the consultancy have been engaged in the first place?

The key for the consultant is to recognize that these activities are occurring and not to become unwittingly involved. Seek to model a non-political style, being up front about your concerns, needs and interests and providing a climate in which other people can also feel safe about expressing their true concerns. Transparency in your dealings with the client should result in political damage limitation.

Finally, it is important to identify whether or not you are engaging in a highly politically sensitive or politically active organization. This is one area of risk to be aware of from the outset.

Managing risk

If clients never had any problems, the consultancy industry would probably not exist. These problems, or issues, can manifest themselves in a variety of ways for which there is a variety of solutions. However, if the client is unable to find a solution, it follows that, by undertaking to find one, the consultant is taking a risk – that of also failing to do so.

It follows, too, that the more difficult the problem, the greater the risk in undertaking to resolve it. It can also be argued that the greater the problem, the more a client may be willing to pay for its solution. If a consultancy practice wishes to undertake higher value-added engagements, it is therefore likely to expose itself to greater risk.

The complexity of larger organizations and the sheer size of their operations lead to the likelihood of issues being of a greater magnitude and the associated risk being greater, too. Risk management is therefore a real necessity. It should not be seen as a reason for not undertaking a piece of work, but, rather, as a means of enabling the work to be performed. The only way to avoid risk completely is not to undertake the work at all, but then cash flow will suffer!

The key to good risk management is an early assessment of where the risks may occur. Once identified, these risks may then be managed. It may be helpful to classify risk into five main categories:

- clients
- engagement
- methodologies
- people
- fees/contract

and to look at those risks that are arguably peculiar to working with large corporations.

Large clients are likely to be complicated organizations and there will be consequent risks if the politics and power structures are not understood. Most large corporations will have used, and possibly misused, consultants in the past. They may have preconceived ideas about how to use consultants – and these may not tie in with your own!

All engagements carry a degree of risk or else consultancy help would not have been sought. Large corporations tend to have skilled resources so the fact that they have a need for external help must be carefully examined. It could be that a solution is being sought for an immensely difficult issue. The likelihood of finding such a solution must be assessed.

Methodologies that are well proven should reduce risk and are often used for the engagements commissioned by large corporations. They should never, however, be forcefully applied as this can increase the risk of ignoring the fundamental issue. Conversely, lack of a methodology may increase risk.

Matching your people to the needs of the client and the engagement is usually key to its success. Large corporations may have great variety among their staff and the matching of consultants – in terms of skills, knowledge, character – to clients' staff is likely to be an investment of time that pays dividends.

Finally, there are risks associated with fees and contracts. Large corporations are usually creditworthy, but they can also have systems and procedures that can cause delays in payment – and endless queries about bills! They may also wish to impose their own procedures and contracts, including liability clauses, that may not be to your liking.

In conclusion, all consultancy engagements are intrinsically risky. A clear identification and analysis of these risks (before an engagement is agreed to) should lead to risk management actions and processes being put in place.

Programme management

In recent years, many large corporations have embarked on fundamental and sustained programmes of transformation. Typically, such organizations require help from consultants in developing, initiating, leading and managing such programmes. This help can draw heavily on the resources of any consultancy firm and requires an in-depth understanding of how to manage complicated programmes.

Gaining commitment to a major transformation from a large corporation is never easy – be it a 'flotilla' or a 'supertanker'. Indeed, many chief executives, when faced with a decision as to whether or not to set such a transformation in motion, ask themselves two fundamental questions.

- 'In order for the process to start, I shall have to let go. How can I prevent corporate anarchy from breaking out and the organization self-destructing?'

Large corporations

- 'How can I take people with me?'

The key to success is achieving alignment of purpose throughout the process. To do this, there must be a clearly defined process. One of the simplest, but most powerful, models has been supplied by N Tichy and S Sherman (1995) who describe three steps:

- awakening
- envisioning
- re-architecting.

K Blanchard and T Waghorn (1997), similarly, identify three steps:

- envision
- propose
- deliver.

This set of steps probably assumes that the 'awakening' step has already occurred.

Without this alignment of purpose, a multitude of problems can arise, such as:

- personal agendas predominating over corporate agendas
- lack of clear sponsorship
- unconnected and possibly conflicting projects being commissioned
- confusion and low morale among staff
- confused messages to the marketplace and loss of customers.

Take, for example, a hypothetical manufacturing company that, by common consent, is 'bleeding to death'. Margins are down, staff turnover is high, market share is being lost, management is pressurized, resulting in a disastrous bottom line. The Board is unanimous – 'We have to change!' Consultants are engaged and charged with drawing up recommendations and reporting back to the Board. The report is duly presented and, at its heart, recommends that a massive cost-cutting exercise be embarked upon, primarily based on a reduction in headcount. One can imagine the consequent dialogue among Board members:

Finance Director:	'Marvellous, just what we need. This should increase margins and profitability.'
Marketing and Sales Director:	'Fantastic, but only if it enables us to retain current margins, reduce selling prices and increase market share.'

Personnel Director:	'What's that going to do to staff turnover – increase it still further. Who is going to manage the redundancy – me, I suppose! Then there's the costly effect on work-force morale . . .'
Production Director:	'Not only that, but most of the people are in my area, so I'll be having to cut back. Fat chance of meeting any increased product demand.'
Chief Executive:	!!!!!!!?????

Perhaps it was the right recommendation, but now not only is the company bleeding to death, but there is also blood in the boardroom.

Imagine what it might feel like operating as a consultant in such an environment – indeed, you might question if you should have taken on an engagement for a client in such a situation. Ask yourself how you might have diagnosed that this was the situation, how you might rectify it or how you disentangle yourself if you do not realize the situation at the outset.

Assuming that there is a defined process in place, the consultant can contribute to each stage in a number of ways. Some of these are as follows:

Awakening
- Collecting and presenting data to demonstrate that the status quo is not an option and that a transformation is required.
- Facilitating workshops where the data is presented and consensus on the causes and need for change are agreed.

Visioning
- Undertaking studies of potential strategies for the future organization.
- Gaining commitment to the agreed vision.
- Designing programmes to communicate the vision.

Re-architecting
- Determining the projects required to build the new organization that matches the vision.
- Designing the overall implementation programme (resources, training, project interfaces and so on).

Large corporations

- Assisting with the implementation (process and projects).

In order to manage the transformation programme successfully, it is necessary to understand:

- the organization itself and what it is trying to achieve
- the component parts (projects) of the programme and how they interact
- the different roles of the individuals concerned with the projects.

An organization is not a structure, but, rather, a system. One part of this system cannot be changed without an impact being made on the other parts of the system. Systems are difficult to explain in words alone as they are multidimensional, whereas language is essentially linear. Figure 19.3 shows one way of describing an organization that was developed by Mike Jeans and others at KPMG.

In any transformation programme, an organization seeks to align its vision with the changed marketplace. The organizational system needs to be designed to achieve that vision. Each of the component parts may need to be altered, but should remain coherent with each other.

A way of describing such a programme in visual terms is shown in Figure 19.4.

A programme manager is appointed to oversee the whole programme. This role requires skills and experience beyond that of a project manager. The success of the programme will demand an understanding of each of the elements depicted in Figures 19.3 and 19.4.

The projects shown in Figure 19.4 are sometimes described as the 'task' elements. A successful programme manager appreciates the importance of each task, but also of the wider 'process', being aware of the connections and interdependencies of the tasks making up the whole programme. Thus, Figure 19.4 also shows the 'process' element underpinning the various projects that in total, contribute to the overall transformation programme. Figure 19.5 gives an alternative depiction of this, but, in addition, shows that the whole programme is one of dynamic interaction.

While individual projects may relate to each other and be interdependent, it can be seen that all change processes cut across all the projects. Such processes can include culture change, behavioural/attitude change, sponsorship programmes, communications and so on. To manage such a programme in a large corporation represents an enormous challenge to a consultant and requires business knowledge, consulting skills and depth of experience of the highest order.

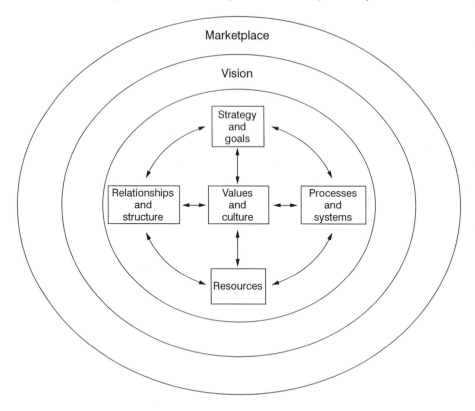

Figure 19.3 A visual way of describing an organization

Working with counterparts

Increasingly, consultants are engaged on a basis of working *with* the client rather than *for* the client – which sometimes manifests itself in doing something *to* the client. Phrases such as 'collaborative working', 'partnering', 'client ownership', 'knowledge transfer' and so on are becoming widespread.

The use of counterparts is another example of this trend, though there can be other reasons and many of them particularly associated with large corporations. Counterparts are individuals from the client's staff who work with the consultants as members of the project team, usually on a full-time basis.

It is important to understand why the use of counterparts has come about. The reasons include:

Large corporations

Transformation programme management					
Project 1 BPR	Project 2 Performance measures	Project 3 IT systems	Project 4 Supply chain	Project 5 Recruitment	Project 6 etc. ...
Process (change) management					

Figure 19.4 A visual way of describing a transformation programme

- **reduced fees** by using client's personnel to undertake some of the work, the external fees for an engagement may be reduced
- **industry/client knowledge** a client's personnel can often bring key industry/client knowledge to the project being undertaken
- **knowledge transfer** by working alongside consultants, a client's staff gain understanding of the approach/methodology being used and may be able to apply this to subsequent work, thus reducing dependence on the consultants
- **ownership** by being involved in the project, a client's staff will share in the result, creating a sense of ownership and thereby reduce the need for the consultants to sell their conclusions
- **personal development** exposure to consultants and their way of working can form a valuable part of the development of individuals. Depending on the project, those individuals can also gain a broader understanding of the organization for which they work.

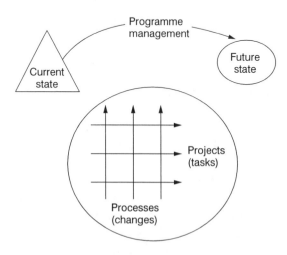

Figure 19.5 Transformation programmes are a dynamic interactive process.

Perhaps the most special and distinctive form of working with counterparts is a method that draws deeply on the separate knowledge and experience possessed by a client and a consultant, combining their thinking in a fast, real-time process that produces valuable, mould-breaking and unique solutions to the problem or issue under discussion. This is called a *generative conversation* (Page, 1996).

Depending on the reason for using counterparts, the criteria for selection to fulfil the role will vary, but individuals could be chosen because they:

- have been identified for career progression and would gain from the experience
- are highly regarded within the organization and their involvement in the project will be viewed positively
- have the interpersonal skills to work in a consultancy role and are committed team members
- have a sound knowledge of the organization and the industry in which it operates.

Above all else, individuals should not be chosen simply because they are 'available'. Indeed, the reasons for such availability would need to be questioned closely.

Creating conditions for engaging people

Given all that we now know about managing complicated programmes in large corporations, would it be true to say that bringing people on board has become a predictable and reliable process? No – far from it. The process (change) management component shown in Figure 19.5 is not easily reducible to a set of well-ordered steps. In fact, it is more of an art than a science.

We might all prefer our success to be applauded when we have ticked off everything on our list of predefined tasks. Unfortunately, as consultants, we are usually judged on outcomes. One of the most important measures of our success is whether or not we create the right conditions for people affected by the programme to come on board and put their energy behind making it succeed. There is lots to learn from consultants who have not attended sufficiently to this aspect.

Staff in most large corporations – now delayered and downsized – are still having severe difficulties adjusting to new demands. Cary Cooper

(1997) identified that two thirds of all managers in the UK have experienced a major organizational change in the last 12 months, and there is a growing gap in the perceptions of this between two groups: directors and above, senior managers and below. The first group judges the company's position to be better following the changes, whereas the second group judges the position to be worse.

Cooper's research also indicates that the increase in reported profits following organizational change is accompanied by a reduction in loyalty, morale, motivation and security, plus an increase in working beyond the contracted hours and a growing concern about the impact of work on home life. This represents a form of damage to the goodwill in the employee relationship that carries with it a future cost. Even among CEOs, an astonishing 25 per cent reported a desire to leave their current job because of its impact on family life and a wish to engage in some other less disruptive form of work, such as consultancy!

Eric Miller (1997) highlights the psychological withdrawal in the workplace since the arrival of the performance culture of the 1980s and 1990s. To counter this, companies have launched countless mission and values programmes, attempting to win hearts and minds, but, beneath superficial shows of commitment, they have produced deeper feelings of anxiety, cynicism, resistance, detachment, depression and alienation.

Is it OK to produce psychological withdrawal or do we need people to be present and engaging themselves fully in their work? Plainly in unpredictable, challenging times, when, increasingly, we are engaged in service-based knowledge work, we do want people to be present, alive, engaged in their tasks.

What do you need to know about the conditions that produce presence and human engagement?

Learning the art of engagement involves educating your senses, becoming perceptive, making fine discriminations. Everyone has different needs in a change programme, so do not judge others by your own needs. Understand your own needs by talking with other consultants and reflecting privately using a diary method (Page, 1996). Many consultants enjoy the thrill of the new and are bored easily by stability. Your clients may be oriented differently. If they are, you stand little chance of persuading them to enjoy uncertainty; you have to begin from where *they* are.

Effective consultants – skilful in the art of engaging people – observe how people are behaving as the wider programme advances, find out and acknowledge their feelings, encourage them to face realities, support them in discovering options and making choices.

Do not make the mistake of ignoring or diminishing the achievements of the past. Bill Bridges' (1996) work on transitions reminds us that you have to give people time after an outside change (such as a new organizational structure or an office move) to make an inner change, a mental readjustment. It helps if you honour successes from the past, perhaps having a celebratory party to mark an ending. It also helps if you let people bring something of the past with them – a photograph, procedure, memento. Primitive rites of passage performed this function, allowing lives to move on. If you don't let people manage their endings, they do not move on – their minds remain stuck in the past.

Recognize that you have an important role in coaching the leaders, helping them to find the right balance between providing certainty and a clear direction, and leaving problems for others to solve. Thereby, you are treating people as adults, demonstrating trust and giving them a reason to be involved.

Remain in close contact with as many of the people and groups affected by a programme as possible. Then, you will be in touch with their concerns and be able to reflect these in programme priorities. For example, you will know whether or not you need to put more resources into communicating, training, rewards, or thanks and recognition.

While most programmes are deficient in many ways, there are four fundamental conditions that any person needs if they are to come on board with a change programme:

- a sense of dissatisfaction with the status quo
- a sense of the future state being attractive, desirable
- knowing what the first steps are and judging these to be feasible
- perception that the benefits exceed all the costs.

The more experience you gain as a consultant, the more you will become practised in helping people express their own feelings and values in relation to a change that is affecting them. Although this might appear to be distracting them from the task or wallowing in the past, you may come to realize that these conversations, properly conducted, help them to let go of an old order, bring about ownership of the task and speed up its accomplishment.

Such conversations can happen in one-to-one situations and in small groups, but, increasingly, large numbers of people are assembled in special workshop-style meetings to create together the changes that their organization needs to make to achieve fast, simultaneous alignment. There are several proven large-scale intervention processes that you can

Large corporations

learn to use. Such meetings need not be confined to groups comprised of a single stakeholder, such as employees, and can be more powerful if they involve representatives from several of the vital relationships, such as customers, suppliers, investors, employees and community (Bunker and Alban, 1997).

Shaping the future

Large corporations are an increasingly important force in the world. An effective strategic engagement with a large corporation, while probably complicated and lasting a long time, plays an important part in shaping the future of that organization and its dealings with its employees, customers, investors, suppliers and the wider community. This important work can be deeply satisfying and rewarding.

We have underlined the importance of dealing with the large corporation as a whole system in which the parts interact, in which changes in one part cause effects in other parts. Some consultants address their task quite narrowly, from a single professional viewpoint – be it finance, sales, IT or human resources. We hope that, regardless of your own professional background, what we have described here will help you take an integrated view of the consulting role, and better manage the risks involved. More than this, we hope that by reading this you have found some extra ways to rise to the larger opportunity, to create more effective conditions for engaging people, to generate greater value, and make a positive difference.

Our closing words come from a satisfied client and underline the challenge you face:

> You need to understand that we are a graveyard for consultants! But your consultants were able to operate at 30,000 feet and at ground level – and to know when they were required to operate at each level.

Good luck!

References

Bauman, B, Jackson, P, and Lawrence, J, (1997) *From Promises to Performance: A Journey of Transformation at SmithKline Beecham*, Harvard Business School Press, Boston
Blanchard, K, and Waghorn, T, (1997) *Mission Possible*, McGraw-Hill, New York
Bridges, B (1996) *Transitions*, Nicholas Brealey, London

Bunker, B B, and Alban, B T (1997) *Large Group Interventions: Engaging the whole system for rapid change*, Jossey-Bass, San Francisco

Cooper, C (1997) *The Psychological Implications of Changing Patterns of Work*, RSA lecture, 19 November, London

Miller, E (1997) *From Dependency to Autonomy*, Maresfield Curnow Brainstrust, London

Morgan, G (1986) *Images of Organizations*, Sage, London

Page, T (1996) *Diary of a Change Agent*, Gower, Aldershot

Rackham, N (1987) *Making Major Sales*, Gower, Aldershot

RSA Inquiry (1995) *Tomorrow's Company: The role of business in a changing world*, Gower, Aldershot

Tichy, N, and Sherman, S (1995) *Control Your Destiny or Someone Else Will: How Jack Welch is making General Electric the world's most competitive corporation*, HarperCollins, London

20

Management consultancy for voluntary organizations

Pesh Framjee

This chapter examines the voluntary sector and particularly charities, which make up the bulk of this sector. Discussion will focus primarily on the particular nuances of the voluntary sector, for it is these peculiarities that a consultant working in the sector should know about.

In broad terms, the voluntary sector encompasses all organizations where there is voluntary governance, that is where the senior governing body works on a voluntary basis. This is particularly the case with charities.

What is a charity?

There is no precise legal definition of 'charity', however Lord MacNaghten observed in the Pemsel Case in 1891 that 'of all words in the English language bearing a popular as well as a legal signification, I am not sure there is one which is unmistakably as technical a meaning in the strictest sense of the term, that is a meaning clear and distinct peculiar to the Law as understood and administered in this country . . .'

A number of cases have established what is charitable and what is not. The Charities Act 1993 defines a charity as 'any institution, corporate or not, which is established for charitable purposes and is subject to the control of the High Court in exercise of the Court's jurisdiction with respect to charity'. The Pemsel case referred to above laid down the four heads of charity.

1. The relief of poverty.
2. Advancement of education.

3. Advancement of religion.
4. Any purposes beneficial to the community generally.

Apart from a peculiar exception for poor relation charities, most charities must pass 'the public benefit' test.

Constitutional forms

A charity can be set up broadly in three different ways:

- by trust deed
- as an unincorporated association
- as an incorporated body.

Incorporation is usually under the Companies Act with the charity being incorporated as a company limited by guarantee. Incorporation can also be under the acts relating to friendly and industrial providence societies by royal charter or by special act of parliament.

An unincorporated association has no legal persona; it is usually just a group of people who have come together with a common objective. The trustees themselves enter into any contracts with third parties and ownership of assets is vested in the names of holding trustees.

An unincorporated association has a simplicity that is appealing to smaller organizations that want to come together in a flexible way, but it is not suitable for organizations that own assets and enter into a lot of contracts with third parties.

Therefore, incorporation is recommended for charities that enter into contracts with third parties, employ staff and own property. The main difference between an unincorporated and an incorporated charity is that the latter has a legal persona, this means that any contracts such as employment contracts, property contracts, contracts to purchase or provide services, etc., are entered into by the charity rather than the trustees themselves. It also simplifies the question of ownership of assets since in an unincorporated association any assets have to be held in the name of holding trustees or duly appointed nominees. This can often be complicated, requiring change when trustees change.

Similarly, an incorporated charity can enter into legal actions and sue and be sued in the name of the charity rather than the name of the individual trustees. Trustees can be held personally liable to third parties for debts to the charity. These liabilities can arise in two ways, through breaches of contracts or through tort. In certain circumstances such liability can even extend to the members if it could be established that they were primarily responsible for the action that gave rise to the liability. A number of unincorporated charities include, in their constitution, a clause entitling trustees to be indemnified against losses out of the charity's assets as long as these losses do not arise from negligence or fraud. This means that where trustees have acted reasonably and properly they can use the charity's funds to meet these liabilities. However, where such funds are insufficient, the trustees may be personally liable.

A recent case, Marston Thompson and Eversted PLC v Bend and others, highlights the problem. A rugby club borrowed money to finance a new clubhouse. The loan was secured by a mortgage of the club's property held in the name of the four trustees who acknowledged receipt of the money in their capacity as trustees. The club was unable to repay the debt and the lender claimed the trustees were personally liable. The trustees forwarded the argument that the lender's claim could only be satisfied out of the club's assets. The court disagreed, holding that the trustees were liable for the full extent of the debt.

There is a further measure of protection provided to trustees regarding breaches of trust and this is found in Section 61 of the Trustee Act 1925. This section states, *inter alia*, 'if it appears to the court that a trustee, whether appointed by the court or otherwise, is or may be personally liable for any breach of trust but has acted honestly or reasonably, and ought fairly to be excused for the breach of trust and for omitting to obtain the directions of the court in the matter in which he committed such a breach, the court may relieve him either wholly or partly from personal liability for the same.'

How limited is limited?

A limited liability company gives an added measure of protection to trustees, but should not be seen as a method of removing all liability. Most charity companies are limited by guarantee. This means there are no shares and instead the members each guarantee to contribute to the company's debts up to a specified limit. Unfortunately, this sometimes gives a sense of false security. The liability of the guarantors is the extent they would have to pay in the event of the charity being wound up; it has little to do with the liability of the directors as trustees of the charity. Furthermore, the memorandum of many charitable companies includes a clause that draws aside the corporate veil and limits further the perceived protection of incorporation.

The directors of a limited company can avail themselves of Section 727 of the Companies Act 1985 which offers similar statutory protection to that offered by the Trustees Act, but in addition they also have to consider the concept of 'wrongful trading' introduced by Section 214 of the Insolvency Act 1986. This means the directors may be held personally liable for debts incurred by a company which has gone into insolvent liquidation. This liability will arise if they continued trading when they knew or ought to have known that there was no reasonable prospect of the company avoiding insolvent liquidation. Directors should be aware of wrongful trading but I know of no case where it has been used with a charitable company limited by guarantee.

Governance structures

A peculiarity of the voluntary sector is the two tier of governance/management structure. Governance is by a board of trustees. If the charity is incorporated as a company they may be directors for Companies Act purposes, but they will also be trustees for charity law purposes. A survey of trustees a few years ago found that approximately 75 per cent of trustees did not realize they were trustees. Many of the respondents thought that they were governors, council members, etc, and failed to see that they were also trustees with the associated responsibilities.

Section 97 of the Charities Act 1993 defines trustees as 'persons having the general control and management of the administration of a charity'. This can sometimes be misleading as in reality larger charities have paid management who deal with the day-to-day administration and management. The definition is intended to cover all categories of charity from small to large and, in the larger charities, whilst trustees may delegate day-to-day management, they cannot abdicate their ultimate responsibility for the control of it.

There is no stereotype structure for effective governance in a voluntary organization. Much will depend on the nature of the organization: its size, the stage in its life cycle, the level of management support available, and the time available for trustees' involvement, etc.

Generally, where there is paid management, trustees should not get over-involved in the day-to-day business of the charity and should focus on the big issues and lay down the strategy and policy for the organization.

The level of trustee involvement in setting the detailed agenda will differ from charity to charity. For example, charities that deal with a medical ailment might often have members on the trustee board who know much about the ailment and the needs of those afflicted by it. They, or family members, may belong to the beneficiary class of the charity. In these circumstances it is not unusual for trustees to get actively involved with assessing the needs of those that are being served by the charity. On the other hand, consider an overseas charity – trustees may not have a detailed understanding of the needs of those they are serving and it is more likely that management and field staff decide what is really needed.

It is important for any consultant working in the voluntary sector to understand the different perspectives and to realize that a charity has many stakeholders. These would include:

1. the governing body
2. management
3. staff
4. funders and donors
5. beneficiaries and service-users.

In some cases, perspectives of these individuals will be different and in carrying out any piece of consultancy it is always useful to find out whether there is a particular agenda in mind and whether there are some sacred cows which cannot be altered because of the fundamental nature of the organization.

Regulatory regime

Voluntary organizations have to comply with many laws and regulations. Normally these will include employment law, health and safety, contract law, etc. In addition are a number of other laws which impact particularly on this sector. Most importantly they are caught by fundamental tenets of trust law which pre-date much of the codified law to which I have just referred. Charities also have to comply with the Charities Act 1992 and 1993. It is important for any consultant working within the sector to be aware of the general principles of charity law, so that when advice is given in one area it does not impinge on these fundamental principles that govern the charity. The Charities Act 1993 is the main consolidating Act and covers the duties and powers of the Charity Commissioners, the peculiar rules relating to charity land (see below), the charity accounting, auditing and reporting regime and other miscellaneous provisions. In addition the rules governing charitable fund-raising and public collections are to be found in the Charities Act 1992.

Accounting and reporting

In February 1995 the Home Office published draft regulations on the new accounting, auditing and reporting regime under the Charities Act 1993 (the Regulations). The consultation period ended on 17 May 1995 and new Regulations were published in October 1995 to come into force for accounting periods beginning on or after 1 March 1996.

To facilitate a better understanding of the Regulations, they should be read with the revised Statement of Recommended Practice (SORP) on accounting by charities.

Although the objectives of charity accounting have remained unchanged, experience has shown that the original guidelines needed to be strengthened and clarified in certain areas. The thrust of the changes stems from the desire for greater accountability of all the resources entrusted to a charity.

Many of these concepts mirror important aspects of trust law and, to comply with that law, charities are expected to maintain records that should allow much of the information required by the SORP to be easily obtained. In many areas the requirements are virtually identical to the original SORP 2 but additional clarification and refinements have been made so that the accounting treatment and public presentation reflects the legal requirement and the needs of users of charity accounts.

Complying with the SORP

The Regulations stipulate the minimum accounting requirement for charities that are not also companies, in effect the statutory framework. The revised SORP will, as best practice for all charities, provide the flesh on the bones. The accounting regulations and the SORP have been drafted to ensure that compliance with the SORP will ensure full compliance with the accounting regulations. Although the SORP, being recommended practice, is not mandatory, the Charity Commissioners have explained that they would expect charities to comply with the requirements unless another SORP which is more specific to them is published. Charity accounts should specifically note compliance with the SORP as part of the accounting policies.

Charities with income under £100,000, if preparing accounts on a receipts and payment basis, can adopt a simplified basis. It is important to recognize that the SORP only applies to material items.

Furthermore, in certain cases a departure from the principles of the SORP may be necessary to give a true and fair view, and in such cases the departure should be explained stating the reasons for such departure.

When considering the principles expressed in the SORP, readers should understand the underlying reasons for the recommendations and adopt a common sense approach to their application. Narrow and rigid interpretations are often made on certain aspects when clearly this is not the rationale behind those aspects. Above all, a charity's accounts should be transparent and the accounting policies and the notes should explain what has been done.

In addition to the Charity SORP there are other SORPs that are applicable to specific classes of charities. There are SORPs for Universities, Housing Associations and Unit Trusts (the last should be followed by Common Investment Funds). This material does not cover these specific SORPs and concentrates on the accounting for charities that do not have to follow alternative regimes.

Relationship with accounting standards

Statements of Standard Accounting Practice (SSAPs) and more recently issued Financial Reporting Standards (FRSs) are together seen as being authoritative statements on accounting practice. They aim to narrow the areas of difference and variety in the accounting treatments of the matters with which they deal to ensure that accounts are prepared on a broadly similar basis. They are applicable to all financial statements, which are intended to give a true and fair view of the organization's state of affairs at the balance sheet date and of income and expenditure for the financial period ending on that date. Compliance with accounting standards will normally be required if financial statements are to give a true and fair view.

It is important to recognize that many charities are already following the principles of the revised SORP as indication of best practice since nothing in the new SORP conflicts with existing accounting principles. In fact the SORP has received the 'negative franking' from the Accounting Standards Board.

The SORP specifically does not reiterate all the principles of generally accepted accounting practice. Therefore charities preparing accounts to give a true and fair view must also consider Accounting Standards.

Relationship with other legislation

The SORP has been written to ensure that it is in line with the accounting requirements of the Charities Act 1993. In fact charities preparing accounts under the SORP will automatically meet the Charities Act accounting requirements.

In addition, there is nothing in the SORP that would be unacceptable for charitable companies. In certain cases a summary income and expenditure account may be required (see Section on Charity Law).

The purpose of a set of accounts

Many charity accountants have long complained that the traditional income and expenditure account did not reflect or explain fully all the financial activities of the charity. They consider that the very nature of raising and using of charity resources requires a different approach from that of commercial profit oriented companies.

Charities do not usually have shareholders with an equity interest, so matters such as distributable profit and dividends do not feature. A charity's resource providers do not usually expect a direct return on their donations. The users of charity financial statements need to assess the services that the charity is providing and its ability to continue providing them. The accounts should also show how the trustees have discharged their stewardship responsibilities during the year, and whilst it may be that the bottom line surplus or deficit provides some of this information, any presentation that focuses on such a bottom line tends to ignore some fundamental differences between accounting for charities and commercial organizations.

With most commercial organizations, the bottom line profit for the year is vitally significant. To some extent it measures performance, and users of accounts justifiably turn to it to ascertain the results for the period. Revenue and costs are matched because there is a strong relationship between them; for example, sales in a period are matched with the cost of those sales as they are interdependent.

Charities, unless they are receiving fees or funding for specific work, are not usually in the business of directly matching income and expenditure. They do not generally work towards a particular result for the year end date. For example, a charity that receives income in the last few months of the accounting period would rightly include the income in that period's accounts notwithstanding that the expenditure funded by this money may not be incurred until later accounting periods. Therefore, to emphasise a bottom line at a particular point in time could be misleading as income and expenditure in a given period are often not directly linked and may bear little or no resemblance to each other.

There are certain charities where matching of their activities may be appropriate, for example, fee income from residential care matched with costs of residential care. However, even with these the inclusion of voluntary income or expenditure which is not related to the fee income can often skew the bottom line.

Furthermore, the traditional income and expenditure account with the historical distinction between revenue and capital does not always adequately explain a charity's activities. The motive of capital expenditure may be different from commercial companies, which usually invest in fixed assets to generate income whereas a charity may invest in fixed assets as part of its primary purpose, eg building hospices, purchasing wetlands, etc. This difference may be quite important to certain charities whose *raison d'être* requires them to incur significant capital expenditure on a recurring basis.

In certain years a charity may use income to purchase fixed assets and since this expenditure, being of a capital nature, will not be shown in the income and expenditure account, it might appear that it has a surplus. In fact the charity might have spent large amounts on fixed assets, which may be as important to its mission as is the other revenue expenditure shown in the income and expenditure account. Therefore judging the charity on the bottom line criteria can often be misleading.

The statement of financial activities – the rationale

In recognition that charities do not generally have any one single indicator of performance comparable to a business enterprise bottom line, it is perhaps more important to consider changes in the *nature* as well as the *amounts* of the net resources of a charity. This, coupled with other information about the charity's efforts and accomplishments, will assist in assessing performance. Accordingly, the SORP and the Regulations recommend a primary statement that records all the resources entrusted to the charity and reflects all the financial activities in the period under review. The proposals are that this statement will be called the Statement of Financial Activities (SOFA) (SORP para 69 et seq).

In producing the SORP, this departure from an 'operating' statement format had to be carefully considered and certain options were considered. For example, that the reporting statement should be divided into two parts, a statement of 'operations' and a statement of other changes in net assets. The suggestion was that the first statement would report operating income and expenses and would be followed by another statement that would report all other income, expenses, gains and losses. There is however no consensus on how to define an operating measure and on which income and expenses should be included or excluded from 'operations'.

For example, some would include in 'operations' only donations and resources available for current period use, whether restricted or not. Others suggested the exclusion of restricted income if the restrictions were not met in the current period. Some would exclude from 'operations', revenues, gains or losses from non-recurring, unexpected or unusual events such as a very large legacy.

Many example accounts produced by charities show that distinctions based on operations tend to be arbitrary and are dependent on the impossible task of trying to match a charity's total income and total expenditure when in most cases no such matching is possible or even desirable. Hence the SOFA tries to move away from giving undue emphasis to the bottom line based on matching, and focuses instead on the periodic measurement of the changes in both the nature and amounts of all the net resources of a charity.

Some charities, usually those providing services, do try and match income and expenditure such as costs of and revenues from housing services or costs and fees from education. However, the format of a traditional income and expenditure account that lists separately the income and the expenditure does not really assist these charities since it merely lists all revenue such as donations and also fee income and then deducts all revenue expenditure. Consequently, no direct matching is possible and, inevitably, these charities link by way of notes the revenue and costs where they are directly attributable. This practice, which shows whether there has been a surplus or deficit on a particular activity where matching is appropriate and useful, should continue where it is applicable.

Fund accounting

The distinction between income and capital permeates through trust law. Income includes all resources that become available to the charity and that the trustees are legally required to apply in furtherance of the charitable purposes within a reasonable time. Capital, on the other hand, must be invested or retained.

In addition, due to the constraints of trust law and the important matter of donor imposed restrictions, it is vital that users of the accounts can see what the increase or decrease in net resources represents. A charity may, for example, have maintained the level of its net assets only because it received restricted income earmarked for a particular purpose, which compensated for a significant decrease in general income. This would not be obvious in the traditional single column format, which usually does not distinguish between the types of funds. It is important, to ensure compliance with the terms of the special trusts and funds, that the accounts assist this understanding.

Many charities receive significant amounts of restricted resources and these restrictions often affect types and levels of service. Consequently, information about the change in the nature of net assets is vitally useful in assessing a charity's ability to respond to short term needs or higher levels of service. Therefore, the recommendations are that the resources of a charity should be grouped according to the restrictions on their use as follows:

- unrestricted funds
  These are funds available for general use and include those that have been designated for particular purposes by the trustees of a charity.
- restricted income funds
  These are funds which are restricted for particular purposes, either by the wishes of the donor or by the nature of the appeal. Therefore those preparing and auditing charity accounts will have to consider carefully appeal literature, direct mail and other forms of solicitation to ascertain whether income received as a result of the solicitation should be restricted.
- capital funds
  These funds are funds which are not for direct application. Where the trustees have no power to apply capital as income it will be permanent endowment. Where the trustees have a power to expend it if necessary, this will be expendable endowment. Expendable endowment should be treated as capital until the right to expend it is exercised, in which case it should be transferred to income prior to application.

Appendix 3 to the SORP provides a useful explanation on the principles of Fund Accounting and the definition of income and capital are covered in the glossary.

Operating structures

Charities function under many different structures; again this will depend on the type of charity and perhaps age and development. Some charities operate through a tight, centralized structure with all fundraising and service provision being managed and controlled centrally. On the other hand a number of charities operate through a very decentralized structure of fundraising and/or service provision. The question of control, monitoring and accountability of branches and decentralized operating units is one that has often been ignored by the voluntary sector.

Charity Branches

The question of accounting for branches is one that has often been glossed over by charities and their auditors. The SORP, while not changing the rules, will make important clarification on what is expected.

There will of course be differing practice based on the different type of charity/branch relationship and the activities carried out by the branch. Some charities use branches primarily to raise funds and public awareness while some charities also use their branches to carry out their charitable objectives. Some are truly independent whilst others clearly are not.

The original SORP stated that, *'The annual report of a charity should contain information on all the activities and funds of the charity and its non-autonomous branches. If a charity has some branches which are autonomous and which are therefore not dealt with in the report, this fact should be explained.'*

To a purist the term 'autonomous branch' is a misnomer and confuses the issue. Either the 'group' is autonomous or it is a branch of the main charity. In practice, the distinction may appear to be blurred.

It is of fundamental importance to ascertain whether the branches are part of the main charity or are autonomous entities, such as groups of 'friends'. In many cases this may not be as straightforward as it may seem. The charity may believe that the 'branch' is part of the charity whereas the individuals running the 'branch' may consider themselves autonomous and resent 'interference' from headquarters.

Autonomous or not?

The glossary to the SORP and the notes published with the regulations explain the importance of establishing the status of branches. The question of whether a branch is autonomous or not is usually a matter of legal fact. The attitude of branch members or of head office is not the deciding factor. The constitution of the parent charity and/or the branches may assist, but where it remains silent it may be difficult to establish the legal status. Here are some points to consider:

- Does the branch carry out its activities using the name and/or charity registration number of the main charity?
- Does the branch avail itself of the fiscal benefits of being part of the main charity?
- Who 'owns' funds held at a local branch, particularly what would happen if the branch were to close?
- If a legal action were to be taken out, would it be against the branch or the parent charity?
- Can the branch disburse funds as it pleases and could it support another charity?
- Does the parent charity appoint members to the branch committee?
- Does the parent charity have the right to exercise significant influence over the operating and financial policy of the branch?

The answers to these questions will usually indicate whether a branch is truly autonomous and should guide the accounting treatment. Suffice it to say that many charities have treated their branches as autonomous but on considering the questions above it can be seen that they should be treated as part of the charity.

The argument is that any money raised using the charity's name must belong to the charity and that the branch is acting as custodian in a trustee capacity. The proponents of this view believe that while fundraising groups or indeed individuals may be autonomous as to the processes which they may adopt to raise funds, it nonetheless would appear that funds raised under the charity's banner are properly regarded as held in trust for the charity from the moment of their receipt. Thus even a separate legal entity administered by or on behalf of the parent charity whose funds are held for specific purposes which correspond to the parent charity could require 'consolidation'.

On the other hand, some charity branches are quite clearly separate legal entities and may even be registered as separate charities, in which case they could be connected charities with common purposes. There may also be instances in which funds raised locally are not raised for one specific charity but may be applied separately and distributed amongst a number of charities. Similarly, fund raising is often carried out by independent individuals or 'friends of' a charity or hospital who, while they may be collecting for a cause, are collecting in their own name. In these situations legal title and beneficial interest in the funds does not pass until a decision is made at local level.

Unfortunately, in some cases the answers are not so clear cut. For example, one individual may do a sponsored run for a charity and collect funds in a particular village. Clearly, this person is holding those funds on trust for the charity, which does not necessarily know about these funds. The individual then sends the funds in to the charity. Perhaps this continues with more individuals in the same village raising funds on an ad hoc basis. Gradually they may change from being a loose collection of people to a more formalized branch, receiving support from, and raising funds in the name of, the main charity. Consequently, there may be no clear cut-off as to when this change takes place. In all cases the individual circumstances, the materiality of the transactions and the substance will have to be considered.

Overseas operations

A number of charities operate overseas through branches, linking organizations, field projects and so on. There appears to be a degree of confusion over how they should report and account for these operations. Many of the issues are similar to matters of UK branch accounting but there are some special issues which need to be considered.

Essentially, at the extremes, there are two models that charities adopt. The first is where the overseas operation is clearly within the control and operating activities of the UK charity. In this case remittances and finances sent overseas are merely a transfer between different bank accounts belonging to the charity until they are actually expended overseas by the charity as part of its own operations.

The second case is where the charity transfers funds, be they by way of grant or project funding, to other organizations overseas. In this case the funds leave the control of the charity as soon as they are received by the other organization. The charity may of course have some form of reporting requirement from the recipient organization to ensure that the funds are being used as intended. However, this in itself will not mean that the funds are within the control of the organization

There is a third variation that causes even more confusion. This is where an overseas operation is run jointly by two charities.

It is important to determine the legal status of the overseas operations. It may be thought that if the overseas operation has a separate legal entity then it is separate and distinct from the UK operation. This is not always the case, local laws might require the setting up of a separate legal organization although to all intents and purposes that organization is part and parcel of the UK charity, albeit located overseas.

The issue of control is extremely important. If the UK charity controls the overseas charity then this would indicate that for financial reporting purposes the overseas operation should be reported as part of the charity.

In essence, if the UK charity can exert dominant influence over the local operation there should be presumption of control. Dominant influence is the right to give directions with respect to the operating and financial policies of the other undertaking.

It is all-important to consider who is controlling the operation and who is carrying it out. If it is part and parcel of the main charity then the overseas operation's activities must be reported in the accounts of the main charity. Similarly, this will affect the exercise of financial and operational control. In essence, if the UK charity falls under this model where it controls the overseas operations, then there are a range of issues which it must consider. If on the other hand the charity is merely making a grant or donation to a local entity that is not within its control, and is carrying out its own activities, then it is not part of the UK charity.

Other issues

The legal status of branches has been discussed at length in the charity sector. There is increasing support for the view that a branch that derives the benefits of carrying out its activities under the banner of the charity should report all its activities as part of the charity.

There is more than the issue of presentation to consider. The important issue is that of stewardship and accountability of charity funds.

In all cases a charity should receive regular returns from its branches and carefully review these to ensure that the branches are operating at optimum efficiency. For example, interest and bank charges might be more favourable if negotiated by the charity after pooling all its accounts.

A branch's actions reflect on the parent charity and without imposing onerous restrictions on their branches, charities should try and make the branch officers appreciate the need for prompt remittances, comprehensive returns and good financial control over income and expenditure and bank accounts.

Charities will probably find that attempts to increase the accountability of branches may meet with some resistance since branch officials may perceive this as interference. It is therefore important that the issues are handled sensitively so as not to alienate supporters. Most branch members should agree with the changes if they can see that they are necessary and go hand-in-hand with enhanced support. Invariably, the structure should be one that complies with the rules and is expedient in the best interest of both the charity and the branch.

Finally, the accounting policy adopted by the charity should be properly disclosed. Users of the report and accounts should be able to gain an understanding of the accounting treatment adopted to report on the activities carried out by the charity and its operating entities be they autonomous or not.

Cost ratios

Any discussion on charities would be incomplete without reference to the ubiquitous cost ratios. The charity world and the giving public have an obsession with questions such as, how much is spent on administration? How much is going directly to the beneficiaries? And people turn to the accounts or to published statistics to try and measure a charity's efficiency.

Some believe that there should be regulations as to how much a charity can spend on its overheads. To dispel the fears of inefficiency and wastefulness there must be accountability. Accountability demands honesty and old prejudices and misconceptions have to be dispelled. The public is often led to believe that a charity's effectiveness can be measured by how much of the income is spent on charitable objectives. Minimal overheads are meant to mean that the charity is effective. Due to a lack of performance information, inputs are used to evaluate performance.

The relative lack of performance accountability highlights a pressing need in the sector. Annual accounts and management information reports are very successful at measuring inputs such as wages and salaries, heat and lighting, printing and stationery and so on. They say very little about outputs and more importantly outcomes and the effect of an organization's performance on its stakeholders.

Very often the information is not comparable, some charities allocate the costs of their finance departments and others do not. Even if all charities were using a similar method it would be wrong to compare different charities on this basis.

It is time more charities provided different measures of effectiveness and also educated the public that charities cannot be run on a shoestring and that there is nothing wrong in incurring expenditure to ensure that there is a proper infrastructure.

At the same time there is a need to ensure that we are seen to be fair in allocating costs. Recently there has been concern in the USA that charities are masking their true fund-raising costs by allocating large elements of their costs such as direct mail costs to headings such as 'public awareness' and 'information dissemination'. It is important that charities do not abuse the flexibility offered by the new recommendations and do not misallocate costs to purely 'window dress' the accounts.

Above all, whatever method is used, the accounting policies should provide a clear explanation.

Taxation

Contrary to popular misconception, charities are not automatically exempt from taxation. Charities are in fact affected by income/corporation tax, VAT, employee taxes, and capital gains tax. There are of course fiscal benefits associated with charitable status and charities should ensure that they are aware of the opportunities and pitfalls.

Primarily, it is important for a charity to consider carefully where its income has come from, whether it is doing anything in exchange for the income and how it is spending its money. When considering the tax and legal position of charities, the concept of being established 'for charitable purposes only' is used time and time again in tax legislation but this phrase is not defined in any legislation. Consequently one has to turn to case law.

Both the Inland Revenue and HM Customs & Excise have provided useful leaflets on charity matters.

Conclusion

A chapter of this length can merely scratch the surface when considering the voluntary factor. It must be recognized that this is a very complex sector carrying out many activities. It is highly unlikely that a consultant will have expertise in all areas, but all consultants must be aware that if they advise on one aspect they may be falling foul of rules in another.

21

Consulting internationally

James Hall

Introduction

Management consultancy has traditionally been an industry with an international flavour, and the life of the consultant has long been characterized by extensive foreign travel. However, a closer look at the past international nature of consultancy shows it to have been limited in many ways. Often, the consultant's forays abroad were limited to projects on behalf of a domestic client, rather than interacting with the local business community. Some international brand names in consultancy often proved to be little more than an international franchise linking together a largely autonomous federation of local partnerships. Other consultancies' 'international' presence was highly patchy, and conforming rather too closely to the limits of a former colonial empire.

Nowadays, it is increasingly difficult for any major consultancy to operate in such a piecemeal or disjointed fashion. If your consultancy focus is towards the top of the market – the larger international organizations that make up the Forbes Global 500 – then it must take account of the way in which those organizations are going through profound changes, changes that are making them increasingly global in perspective.

Going global

The old paradigm of the 'multinational' is falling away as these companies 'go global'. Organizations that were multinational operated largely as federations of national businesses: these national businesses would report to a common parent, but with varying degrees of connection and autonomy. Links between the national units themselves would be minimal, or completely mediated through 'head office'. Now these divisions are breaking down as the multinationals move to become single, integrated global businesses.

In Europe we can see some of these forces at work as national businesses come to terms with the single market, but this is a trend that spreads well beyond Europe. Functions such as sales, marketing, distribution, manufacturing are all increasingly run on a global basis. This is a long term trend, in reaction to a wide variety of global stimuli: some of these may be more emotional than real, such as the end of the Cold War. However, moves towards Economic and Monetary Union, and the creation of the single market, are very real in their effects on business and the ability of national companies to compete.

To design in one country, manufacture in another and sell in a third is no longer regarded as anything other than the norm. With this sort of client activity taking place there is obvious pressure on consulting organizations to respond. This does not mean simply picking up the change projects as clients reorganize and globalize – it is imperative that we think and organize in the same way in our own businesses.

Over the last few years, the major consulting organizations have faced up to this recognition and started to organize globally to varying degrees. One should not underestimate the size of this task, which involves bringing together a number of different organizations from different backgrounds and organizational structures. Not only that, but organizations can vary in their degrees of difference, depending on the looseness of the consulting federation.

Andersen Consulting

In meeting this challenge, Andersen Consulting has had a significant advantage. It was already highly global and highly integrated: this is partly an effect of our focus on common training and methodologies. However, there has also been a firm-wide evolution, first from a close federation of national business to an integrated regional businesses, and now onwards to a global business.

The history of Andersen Consulting

Although the history of the partnership can be traced back to 1913, Andersen Consulting is relatively young, being incorporated as a separate business unit within the Arthur Andersen Worldwide organization in 1989. At that time it was organized in three geographic units: Europe (including the Middle East, Africa and India), Asia Pacific and the Americas.

Within the geographic units, there were three levels of organization: by service line, industry sector and country practice. Despite Andersen Consulting's common recruitment and training practices, each country business had developed along subtly different lines. However, it is worth noting that the practice has always maintained a global cost sharing model, to which other consulting practices are only now moving.

However, forces both within and outside Europe put pressure on this structure. National companies were rapidly spreading their operations across Europe while foreign multinationals increasingly viewed Europe as a single operating area. The demand of such clients for, for example, single-point, single currency billing for delivery in multiple countries was something with which many multinational companies, in many industries, found difficult to cope.

A few years ago Andersen Consulting partners recognized that a pan-European operation was fast becoming the norm for some industries. Others, on the other hand, such as national health care providers, would clearly take some time to cross even national boundaries. It was also recognized that, while there was a good deal of convergence between individual countries, others were moving at different rates, and indeed in some cases the gap was widening. While the need for Europe-wide communication, co-operation and knowledge sharing was also recognized, the structure of a European organization sitting 'above' largely autonomous country units and co-ordinating this was also felt to be unworkable. There was also a recognizable degree of duplication in resource and overheads between countries.

The EMEAI (Europe, Middle East, Africa, India) geographical unit therefore regrouped itself into three major regional units: Maritime, West Europe and South Europe. Wherever possible, operating countries were grouped in tiers that reflected their differing maturity as consulting markets and cultural links.

At the same time Andersen Consulting's historical focus, on the interface between strategy implementation and IT, was naturally evolving into a Business Integration model: this coincided with a business plan that rested on longer-term partnerships with a smaller customer base drawn from the very largest companies. There were also developments in pricing, moving from time-based fee rates to value-pricing contracts, which could equally operate on a shared-risk, fixed fee or even an equity stake basis.

While making the move to a regional structure, the organization moved to more of a balanced scorecard approach for assessing performance of both units and partners. This was to encourage such non-financially measurable behaviours as teaming and contributions to knowledge capital, while investment in electronic infrastructure helped to underpin the new structures and minimize the need for excessive travel.

This regional structure was a step towards the global structure which we have now implemented. Creating a global organizational structure is very much the final stage in a process: the organization must create common discourses and common processes before making the leap to a common organization.

It is not an area of organizational development in which there are clear precedents to follow. Andersen Consulting is probably at the vanguard of executing what it is to be a global organization. However, we feel confident that common principles apply and other organizations will ultimately follow a similar path.

The satellite system

The first stage is the 'hub and spoke' or satellite system, in which the international faces of the firm are run very much as offshoots from the national parent. This system will inevitably fall victim to its own success. It collapses when the satellites become too complex and large scale. This throws up a dual challenge: you have to manage locally, but at the same time you have to create a global network.

The global network

This network consists of centres each with their own specific operations, but tied together into a specific whole: the aim is to create a consulting operation capable of giving a single global response to a large global organization.

However, it is important to remember that the global consulting organization is not an anonymous 'supranational' or 'transnational' entity.

For all the application of global methodologies and IT infrastructures, consultancy is at heart a people business, made up of people, who each live locally and participate in their local culture. It is important that the global entity is in return supportive of its local geographical units as much as they support the global whole.

The integration of local people with the global firm is extremely important for clients. For example, Andersen Consulting was recently successful in a bid for a project with a large government institution in Hungary. There were many factors involved, but the key to the success of the bid was our combination of global expertise with local presence: other bidders could offer global strengths but no local presence, or alternatively had strong local roots but lacked the global experience the client wished to draw upon.

Consultancy can no longer work on the model of 'parachuting in' teams of consultants who live out of hotels for a few weeks before disappearing forever. It is culturally and economically impractical to do all consultancy work on a fly-in basis.

Everyone is local somewhere – consultants don't exist in some kind of cyberspace – and as consultants we want to be active and engaged in our local community.

This is true in even the most globalized of industries. We consider ourselves to be worldwide experts in the pharmaceuticals sector: this type of work is to some extent independent of geography but we have also created a real presence in the local markets we serve. Our teams are not country-independent, but rather are teams that exist across a large number of countries, not just serving global clients but also bringing global skills to bear on local clients. In many areas, such as PTT, railways, banks or insurance, clients need, and demand, exposure to global best practices.

The differences between clients within this global market can be enormous. Take two car manufacturers Andersen Consulting encountered in Asia. One was working towards a goal of being 'best in class' in the Asian market. This goal was achievable with local people and local skills. The other, however, was ready to move onto the global stage and wanted to be world class: this brought with it a totally different set of challenges.

However, one of the effects of globalization is that the time-lag between the most sophisticated markets and countries and the rest is rapidly shrinking. Some players are able to take the opportunity of skipping several stages of technology and are moving straight to state of the art solutions. There is obviously a limit to the speed at which this can be done, but it is not impossible.

Similar considerations apply to the 'wave of ideas' in consulting and advanced managerial and strategic theory. Some commentators take this to be a simple movement of ideas from an American genesis, to Europe and then on to progressively less sophisticated markets. This type of thinking is typical of those who are still working with the 'hub and spoke' paradigm. The hub and spoke model tends to assume that good ideas start at the centre, and work their way out to the (by implication) 'far flung' rim. The network organization, by contrast, recognizes that good ideas can come from any part of the network, and that the challenge is to disseminate them as quickly as possible and simultaneously to all other parts of the network. It is possible for a global consultancy organization such as Andersen Consulting to have 'centres of excellence', which are spread all over the network. These may well stem from strong local roots or experiences, for example the groundbreaking work in the UK in privatization and deregulation, or the piloting of IT concepts in the United States, or the strength of the Japanese in process management.

Consultancy is not a straightforward product that can be packaged and exported in uniform cartons. A consultancy buyer in France is not looking for a repackaged American concept, but strong ideas which may come from the US or from France or equally from anywhere in the global network where leading-edge work is being done.

Managing such a global network is one of the greatest challenges in building the global consulting organization; desirable as it might seem from some angles, one can't do everything from one giant central base and constantly fly one's people around the world.

A key component of global consulting is therefore the use of technology and knowledge management techniques to disseminate knowledge around the globe. But note that this is still a two-way process, which very much depends on a strong local presence drawing information from local environments and feeding it into the network.

This is not just a technical fix involving wires and satellites; it also requires strong underpinnings in order for a culture of sharing to develop, not merely on a tit-for-tat basis, but in the sense of creating a global pool of knowledge capital.

The forces of globalization are changing the structure of the consultancy market. It is clear that organizations like ourselves, that can bring to bear global abilities, will develop and prosper. On the other hand, there is always room for the small niche consultancy organization, whether the niche is organized along local or industry or functional lines.

However, the middle market, which has always been under pressure, will find it increasingly difficult to survive, lacking the focus of a small niche capability or the global presence of the larger firms. Medium to national or even purely regional consultancies will find themselves squeezed between those two extremes, and will either disappear or be forced to consolidate in an attempt to reach global scale.

Much has also been written of the challenge from so called 'virtual' players. Developments in technologies such as email raise the possibility that smaller consultancies or even individual consultants will configure themselves in ways that will allow them to challenge the largest firms. The idea of smaller firms giving way to virtual networks sounds very attractive, and undoubtedly some will pull it off. However, it is hard to overstate the challenge of such a venture. The issues range far beyond technology and our ability to physically connect people: it's about creating cultures and disciplines that are consistent: common practices, common processes: do the members of the network think about problems in the same way?

It is true there are lots of opportunities to tackle problems on a global scale, but this also requires very strong common processes on a global scale.

In my view, a single integrated management structure, rather than a decentralized network, is the only way to achieve this.

For example, in my own management role within Andersen Consulting I have, effectively, two jobs. As managing partner in the UK, I represent Andersen Consulting in the UK and the UK firm in Andersen Consulting; but I am also a member of a global team responsible for technology capabilities across product lines.

This is not to underrate the benefits of technology: a number of things have had to come together to allow us to be global in our operations, and without those technical developments neither we nor our clients could have achieved global scale.

Some of these developments are not without their downsides. In a global organization projects can 'follow the sun', passing from timezone to timezone as different teams start their day: the downside of this is that it's a 24-hour day – it's always midday somewhere, and there's always someone somewhere who is wide awake and needs to talk to you!

Conclusion

In conclusion, it is important to see globalization in consulting, not as an alternative to local operations, but as an extension and strengthening of the local firm.

Consulting internationally

Take currency issues: if local revenues are offset by local costs, fluctuations in currency values are manageable, far more so than when costs in one country are offset by revenue in another. Diversity of currencies is one issue to manage: Economic and Monetary Union will only take 20 countries out of the 70 in our equation.

Even more challenging is the issue of managing diversity within such an organization. Andersen Consulting employs 53,000 people, who between them represent every shade of opinion. These range from consultants who do not want to travel extensively, to those who see this as a fantastic opportunity to embed themselves in another culture for a while. Our organization has to be able to respond to that variety.

Career management and promotion management needs to be done in an integrated fashion. At one time, a consultant who spent time 'abroad' – a word increasingly difficult to define in this context – risked being left out of the promotion loop at home. It's important that our processes do not allow that to happen: increasingly the reverse is the case; people who do spend time abroad who will be on the promotion fast track – they'll have gained the insights that won't be available to those who stay put.

However, consulting internationally brings its own challenges for individuals: maintaining 'equality of reward' is a complex balancing act across economies, which vary considerably in terms of cost and standard of living, tax regimes and so forth. Some regions of the world, which are vital in consulting terms, also carry a degree of personal risk for the consultant.

Global consultancy is not about homogenising the world economy to a single set of business practices. One of the paradoxes of globalization is that it is creating pressure for more, not less, regional identity.

Within Andersen Consulting we can watch this collision and cross fertilization of world cultures in action. Our worldwide partners are learning a tremendous amount from us – as indeed we are learning about them.

22

The role of the internal consultant

Margaret Neal and Christine Lloyd

Introduction

This chapter explores the role of the internal management consultant –
focusing on some of the essential capabilities, skill sets and values that
the successful internal consultant will need to possess and demonstrate.
In addition, some of the organizational considerations that may need to
be explored before using internal consultants are highlighted.

Some of the challenges and dilemmas that confront the internal consultant (as opposed to an external consultant) are further explored through
the medium of four case studies that illustrate some of the key skills and
competences required to manage relationships and potential conflicts of
interest in a professional and ethical way. Because of our particular experience and expertise, we have drawn from our own careers in the field of
organization development, but much of our learning is relevant to internal consultants in other fields – such as management consultancy.

The chapter will endeavour to capture relevant learning from these
different interventions and then move to career options – for example,
what are the routes into and out of internal consultancy?

Finally, some relevant survival techniques for 'taking care of yourself'
and remaining 'fighting fit' to cope with the demands of the internal
consultant's role are explored, together with some practical tips to those
embarking on this at times frustrating, yet always rewarding journey.

Overview of challenges and contribution

There is a need for the individual to be clear on their capabilities, preferences and values and the way in which they feel it is possible or
appropriate to contribute to the organization.

The role of the internal consultant

For example, internal consultants need to gain satisfaction from a 'behind the scenes' role – achieving results through others and encouraging leaders within the organization to gain recognition for work which may have demanded enormous time and effort from the internal consultant.

A successful intervention by the internal consultant should be 'seamless' in its delivery and impact – the extent and nature of the influence bring imperceptible. Those who need frequent visible recognition for their efforts or need to feel openly rewarded would be ill advised to become an internal consultant.

Internals will often need to demonstrate resilience in the face of adversity if things are deemed to have 'gone wrong'. They may be 'blamed' or 'held responsible', with the client often taking the credit for success. The role can often appear to be an unrewarding and thankless task.

Independence is another essential quality of a successful internal consultant. Over the long term, internals will not be valued for their contribution if they are perceived as 'following the party line' or 'promoting' a particular approach in their consultancy work. It is essential that the client always retains ownership of his or her issues and that the internal does not attempt to control, 'take over' or encourage 'dependency' in their relationship.

Related to this client-focused approach in every aspect of the internal's work, is the need to be able to speak the client's language, understand the nature of the business and have the skill and experience to be able to help with business solutions (*not* what the internal may think is right).

There is, however, a balance to be achieved between support and challenge to the client. The internal will soon suffer loss of reputation if he or she is perceived as colluding with the client, rather than providing a suitable challenge – ultimately for the client's benefit.

An internal will also need to be prepared to take risks and be the 'lone voice' rather than enjoying a 'cosy' relationship with clients. Anyone who has a need to be liked, or who has strong needs for harmony in working or business relationships should reflect on their resilience to cope with the potential loneliness of the internal role.

Essential requirements of the internal role are personal integrity and the ability to preserve client confidentiality – even if political pressures are exerted to divulge confidential information. Anyone who finds it difficult to handle highly confidential data with sensitivity will be unable to build a reputation as a person of integrity in dealing with consultancy situations.

433

Finally, drive and energy are essential requirements for the success-ful internal to cope with often unpredictable and demanding patterns of work.

Why might an organization opt for an internal consultancy unit?

Before exploring the specific nature of the internal role, one issue to address is why certain companies choose to create an internal consul-tancy unit, or at least individual consultant roles. Arguments for the internal unit or role include cost effectiveness, closeness to the business, trustworthy advice and the retention of competences internally. However, internal consultancy units can also suffer from lack of inde-pendence, be regarded as too insular or become, inappropriately, a 'parking lot' for surplus managers and executives.

In recent years however, an increasing number of organizations have decided to create an 'in-house' consultancy capability. So what are the differentiating features of the internal consultant's role?

The specific nature of the 'internal' role

The internal consultant's role is primarily differentiated by being part of the system to which it is giving advice, guidance and support. This poses a number of challenges such as how to retain independence and how to avoid colluding with the status quo in the organization. In work-ing across the whole organization, the internal consultant must be aware of the interdependencies between all the sub-systems and the risks of both influencing and being influenced by them.

The role of the internal consultant can take many forms, varying from strategic influencer to internal service provider to auditor. The nature of the role may be influenced by whether it is seen as a commercial entity (being required to recover costs with or without profit) or as a free resource available to the organization. This will affect the demand and supply of services and the use/perception of the role by the rest of the organization.

In many situations, the nature of the role can be determined by the individual, although clear contracting is required with the major client/sponsor.

The nature of reporting can also vary. Some internal consultants or consultancy groups report to the chief executive, where they fulfil a broad business improvements role. Other, more specialized groups, report to functional heads such as HR, finance or strategy and planning. This positioning is often perceived as important in terms of internal influencing and power.

What then are the specific advantages of the internal? Often they are seen as a more acceptable and effective alternative to a mass of external consultants descending on the organization. Their value lies in knowing the organization, its processes and its people. They understand context and culture and are likely to be sensitive to what will and will not work.

Being able to see the whole picture of the organization, internal consultants are often able to influence longer-term strategic direction and also follow-through on the consequences of implementation, resulting in more of a feeling of belonging and a sense of achievement. Over a period of time internal consultants often earn trust and credibility, being valued for their commitment to the longer term success of the organization and trusted with internally confidential information.

The internal is also capable of retaining learning within the organization and transferring capability and best practice across the organization. There are, however, a number of downsides to be considered. The risk of collusion with, or infection by, the internal culture is significant. There are numerous examples of internal consultants going 'native' by adopting the behaviours of their clients' systems and failing to provide that independent challenge. Internals, over a period of time, may also create dependency with their clients or feel pressure to conform to the existing power-base.

There are also risks in starting to own the 'content' of the agenda rather than focusing on the quality of the processes within the organization. The risk of getting too hands-on is also a very real one. Therefore, the challenge of remaining at the 'strategic level' and not being sucked into day-to-day operational activities is ever present. Certainly in a non-commercial environment, the perception of the internal as a 'free resource' can lead to over-loading and under-valuing.

Skills and competences

Both externals and internals require a number of common competences such as customer focus, energy, enthusiam and mastery of the appropriate tools and techniques. What then are some of the differentiating competencies?

Extremely well developed systems-thinking and awareness of organizational dynamics are critical for the internal. Equally important, as hinted at in the introduction, is a deep awareness of their own biases and values in the consulting process in order to retain as independent a view as possible. The ability to think conceptually, extracting simple patterns from the internal complexities of organizations is also critical.

The courage to challenge internal direction and decisions while still sustaining effective working relationships is also essential. The ability to confront within a long-term relationship is a skill that needs to be nurtured and developed.

There is a greater need for the internal (as opposed to the external) consultant to demonstrate the ability to coach, share best practice and transfer skills across the organization. One of the key roles of the internal is to enhance internal capabilities over a prolonged period of time. Resilience, energy and optimism are key characteristics. There is no hiding place for the truly professional internal consultant.

Case studies

The following four case studies illustrate some of the key requirements that the *internal* consultant will need to demonstrate (managing relationships, handling typical dilemmas) and the skills and competences that may be needed.

The case studies address the following representative situations.

- Retaining independence and integrity, even when confronted with political issues or senior managers trying to exercise their power.
- Working in partnership with external consultants for the benefit of the organization.
- Taking risks based on a belief in one's professional judgement and experience (often presenting a lone voice against apparently overwhelming odds).
- Leveraging learning and development across the organization (rather than retaining one's individual know-how and expertise).

Each case study looks at:

- the details of the situation
- the approach followed by the internal consultant
- the outcomes and the learning.

Retaining independence and integrity in working with clients

This case study explores the need for the internal consultant to retain integrity and confidentiality at all times and not be pressured into collusion by responding in a particular way by clients (managers) in the system who are far more senior and in a position to provide feedback which may impact on rewards and future career prospects for the internal.

The situation

The internal, through previous contacts with the Head of Information Services, was called in to help with an interpersonal relationship problem that had developed between two of his senior managers and was beginning to affect their business performance.

Previously, the two managers had been level in the organizational hierarchy but because of a reorganization one was now reporting to the other. The reorganization also called for new ways of working, and more demanding 'deliverables' rather than the 'old style' of networking and a relaxed approach to achievement of targets. 'The bottom line' had become more visible and challenging. It became clear that effective communication between all three managers had broken down and that there was an impasse. The internal consultant, through personal knowledge of two of the managers, was immediately sensitive to the potential problems inherent in the request for assistance. For example, there could have been a hidden agenda for the most senior manager, a skilful political operator, who might have wanted to use the internal consultant to instigate the removal of a manager perceived as 'difficult' from the organization.

There is always a need for the internal to be aware and sensitive to 'hidden agendas' and 'power plays' which may be at work and avoid being manipulated into a position that compromises his or her independence and integrity.

The internal needs to understand and respect the needs of the client, organization and the individuals involved, yet adopt a 'whole-picture' approach, which is objective and attempts to address the best interests of all concerned.

Sensing the tension in the situation, in which emotions were 'running high', the internal opted for one-to-one sessions with each indidividual instead of an initial meeting with all three managers together. This allowed each person to speak freely about his hoped for outcomes, preferences and aspirations for the future.

Resisting pressures to 'go into print' about the content of these meetings, the internal recommended that a positive next step could be for each manager to complete a Myers Briggs Type Indicator questionnaire, which would provide some individual insights into the situation of 'impasse'.

After this, there could be a meeting of all three managers, facilitated by the internal consultant – the purpose of which would be to agree a way forward that was acceptable to the three managers. (It had emerged in discussions that the most senior manager was concerned that each person should be contributing in a full and effective way, that the manager who perceived himself as being demoted in the reorganization had a need for his professionalism and expertise to be recognized and valued and his status as a world class expert in his field be acknowledged. The third manager, having recently taken over responsibility for a new area, had needs to be kept informed so that he was not surprised at important meetings to hear what his former colleague and his team were engaged in and could avoid public embarrassment.)

The key issues to be resolved were:

• support and recognition needs
• communication and openness about relevant activities
• clarification about roles and targets and deliverables (what was expected from each person to achieve business results)
• ways of giving and receiving constructive feedback about performance
• learning to understand individual motivations and avoid making assumptions that intentions were negative.

A month after the preliminary one-to-one discussions the meeting took place. What would represent a successful outcome and the agenda were discussed and agreed in real time.

The internal adopted a style of openness, yet independence in facilitating the discussion – being scrupulous not to appear to be siding with any individual. Encouragement was also given to each individual to make eye contact and be open about expressing needs and wants from the situation. 'Contracting' was also encouraged (ie 'What I need from you is . . .' 'What I'm prepared to do to support you . . .' 'How will we measure progress/success together?')

At stages, as agreements were reached, and at the end of the meeting, the internal summarized what had been agreed and checked again for understanding and 'buy in'. In addition, the internal also agreed to draft a brief statement of intent for the three managers to which they could commit. (This was done after the meeting and after a few minor additions and amendments it was agreed as 'the way forward' for all.)

Key learning points
The need for the internal to:

• stay objective
• independent
• scrupulously honest in not playing people off against each other or trying to gain favour by siding with the most senior manger
• not be intimidated by the seniority of the clients
• preserve confidentiality of any one-to-one discussions with individuals *unless* there is expressed permission to do so
• listen carefully and summarize accurately in the diagnosis of the situation
• create opportunities for clients to reach their own solutions rather than telling them what's best for them.

Working in partnership with external consultants

This case study explores how an internal and external consultant work together effectively, each making different, but complementary, contributions to a successful outcome.

The role of the internal consultant

The situation

The director of a service organization employing 1000 people decided to accelerate his organizational change process by running a three-day workshop for his leadership team focusing on their own personal development.

The internal organization development consultant was asked to lead the design and implementation of this activity and decided early in the process to use the design phase as well as the workshop itself as an opportunity for leadership development.

In order to do this, a design team of key internal players was formed to work on the initial design. Led by the internal consultant, the team identified the key leadership capabilities required for the future and the gaps in the current leadership profiles. Based on this understanding, a high level design for the workshop was created. The involvement of a number of senior managers in the design secured their ownership and commitment.

At this stage, an external consultant familiar with the organization was contracted to provide an external challenge to the design and to bring in external experience for the detailed session design. The external was able to provide insights and teachings from how other organizations have tackled such issues and share thinking on current tools and techniques.

The request for external support at this stage could have proved difficult. Some externals want to be involved right at the beginning and may want to take the major lead in such an activity. Agreeing the relative roles of internal and external consultants is an area which requires attention.

However, in this case the internal and external consultants had already developed a good working relationship. The internal had access to all the key players in the organization and a deep understanding of the current organizational issues, while the external provided independent challenge and external best practices.

During the preparation for the workshops the external consultant focused on detailed design work and session content, using the high level design prepared by the internal team as a framework. The internal consultant focused on identifying individuals to lead specific sessions and spending time coaching them on their role.

At the workshop itself, the external focused on the overall design and flow of the workshop, re-designing where necessary, whilst the internal consultant coached and gave feedback to the individual session leaders. The division of these responsibilities enabled each of them to focus on certain aspects of the workshop, whilst retaining the integrity of the whole design. They frequently met during breaks to exchange thoughts, ideas and feedback, modifying sessions where appropriate.

Following the workshop, the internal consultant focused primarily on managing the follow-through and integrating actions into the organizational systems. The external provided objective feedback on the process and outcomes of the workshops and suggested possible future actions from a more distant perspective.

Key learning points

An internal–external partnership can be a highly effective way of operating. Once a personal relationship of trust has been established and there is a strong fit of personal values and beliefs, they can work as a seamless partnership within the organization. Working styles need not necessarily be similar, in fact a contrast is often helpful, but their deeply held convictions and assumptions must be congruent.

Beyond the working relationship of designing and implementing activities, this partnership can also develop into one of mutual support and challenge, resulting in personal development for both individuals.

Tensions can emerge, particularly if either individual starts using his or her position to 'work' the power systems in the organization without involving the other. Difficulties also occur when either party starts to view the other as inferior or less competent. Mutual respect for their respective roles and the individual is essential from both sides.

Creating learning and development opportunities across the organization

This case study describes how the internal role can be used to create development opportunities across the whole organization and illustrates how valuable learning can be retained with the organization.

The situation

An organization decided to create an internal consultancy unit and initially recruited a professional consultant from the external market with wide ranging consultancy skills and experience. In setting up the unit, this individual decided not to recruit further professional consultants but rather use the unit as a development opportunity for existing staff.

The professional's role would be primarily acting as a coach to the newly created team. The unit was resourced by identifying some individuals of high potential from within the organization and also by advertising a number of roles for open application. The final team of six, from a variety of functional backgrounds, were selected for their enthusiasm, systemic thinking and relationship-building skills.

The newly appointed professional (now the internal consultant) began by identifying the key skills required by the team. It was decided to develop these by forming an Action Learning group consisting of six members of the new team and six other individuals from the wider organization. The key topics which were covered were diagnostic skills, workshop design and facilitation, team effectiveness and individual coaching.

Initially, the internal consultant identified the work activities for the team through key people in the organization. Where possible, the internal consultancy team worked in pairs in order to provide support and challenge for each other. The internal consultant was always in the background for help, advice and support.

One of the key challenges was to convey to the newly formed team that, although there were some specific consultancy tools and techniques that could be helpful, their existing knowledge, skills and gut feelings were of critical importance. They needed to use what they already had as well as developing new skills.

The role of the internal consultant

Some of the areas in which the team struggled included: 'letting go' of their own agendas, not using the role to 'promote' themselves and learning how to facilitate rather than 'prescribe'. These struggles were not surprising considering a number of the team had been recruited because they were regarded as ambitious high fliers.

Many of the individuals in the team initially found the experience frustrating. They had volunteered to join the team to 'make things happen' and be released from the bureaucracy of line management. Learning to achieve results from a facilitation model rather than a control model was a real challenge. They really began to understand the difference between positional influence and personal influence.

The initial appointments were for 18 to 24 months and then individuals moved on to positions in the mainstream organization. For a few, the consultancy world was a magnet and they moved out into external consultancies. In most cases, however, the individuals moved back into the organization, retaining their learning and sharing their skills with others.

Having to live with the consequences of their results was also an important driver for the team. They could not just 'walk away' from implementation as they often found themselves managing it on their return to a line position.

Key learning points

From the perspective of the professional internal consultant, this was a tough role. Developing and coaching a group of 'raw' recruits is a challenging prospect requiring time, energy and determination, but reaping rewarding results. A group of individuals, some verging on arrogance, underwent experiences that deeply affected their future managerial and leadership styles, as well as contributing to the effectiveness of the organization.

Most people can develop consultancy skills. There is no specific magic or mystique. A lot of the skill is in learning to 'let go' and trusting one's own judgement and intuition. However, after developing two groups of internal consultants over a period of three years, the internal consultant, although richer from the experience, moved on – exhausted and drained.

Preserving professionalism

The situation

A request for assistance with a workshop was received from another internal (based at a different location) with high 'control' needs and a 'commanding' facilitation style.

When the two internals met it became clear the 'the workshop' was a significant and large-scale event, which would potentially contribute to the transformation of the research and technology organization into a global organization supporting the chemicals business.

During the planning stage, the internal who had initiated the request admitted to feeling out of his depth with the prospect of designing an event for 70 to 80 people, many of whom were destined to be leaders in the new organization.

441

The more experienced internal recognized the opportunity to use open space technology rather than a more structured 'conference' approach, but needed to persuade the other internal that the benefits that could accrue would outweigh the risks (ie a untried approach, inviting 'ownership' by the participants rather than the facilitators and appearing to be 'soft' to a group of highly analytical research scientists).

Convinced of the value of the approach for a workshop of this kind, the internal consultant set about coaching the less experienced colleague to feel more comfortable with the ambiguity that the approach presented.

Once he felt more relaxed about a co-facilitating role where the outcomes could not be guaranteed, the next challenge was to gain the support of the sponsor of the event (including financial backing). This was a highly intelligent senior manager, who although young, clearly felt more comfortable with an autocratic leadership style.

This became far more challenging to the internal – especially in the face of constant questioning from the sponsoring manager as to whether the approach would work. The internal used considerable design skill experience, as well as expertise in large scale interventions, not to 'promote' the approach as the solution, but to explain the practicalities, processes and the roles of the facilitators and those who might offer to run sessions. Those involved in planning for the event were carefully briefed on what to expect and told that there would be no guarantees of success, but that the chances of gaining greater commitment from the participants and 'follow through' of agreed actions would be far higher.

There were times during the planning phase when it would have been far easier to revert to a highly structured programme and run the event as a formal conference with a series of input sessions – following an 'old style' information giving, controlled 'passive participants' model.

There was a strong need for the internal to retain independence and a belief in the open space technology approach which would give 'ownership' to all participants and provide an opportunity for them to do some real work during the time frame of the event – with far more likelihood of continued commitment to any action plans devised than if 'top-down' approaches were imposed.

Additionally, what felt like a huge burden of responsibility was placed on the shoulders of the internal consultant since the sponsor and other facilitators were 'hands-off' and keeping their options open until they could reasonably allow themselves to feel optimistic that this was an appropriate approach to take. Coaching and support to them had to be maintained throughout and 'a sense of calm' transmitted by the internal. Once the event was underway, the professional decisions made by the internal were vindicated.

The approach was embraced with enthusiasm by the group (who were prepared to contribute, offfer sessions, work on real actions and build support networks for the future amongst the leadership team) although at times coaching had to be offered to all participants.

The less experienced internal also needed coaching and support throughout the event (which lasted three days). For example, questions such as: 'Shall I go and tell them what to do?' had to be fielded with the response: 'Why not let them decide for themselves?' by the experienced internal, as well as taking care of all the logistics of a group of 80 people meeting at an off-site hotel location.

The role of the internal consultant

The need was for the experienced internal consultant to be very much 'back seat' and 'hands off', in managing the process *not* the content, and acting as support and coach to some of the key players and stakeholders. One of the greatest rewards for this was, perhaps, the genuinely surprised reaction of the sponsor: 'It works! It works!' Following the event, the most senior manager present declared that it was 'the best workshop he had ever attended'. He was impressed by the energy and leadership shown by everyone and appreciated that the approach could be more fun and more rewarding than a formal event – so long as it was appropriate to the needs. The fellow internal facilitator acknowledged that he had 'learned a lot' and had probably been given much of the credit for the success of the workshop by the organization.

Key learning points

- 'Stick to your guns', although it is necessary to feel confident about the process being proposed.
- Stay calm. Do not be panicked by pressure from others to revert to more tried and tested approaches.
- Be prepared for a multi-faceted role: coach; support; counsellor; 'sheep dog' (at times!); cheerleader; challenger; adviser to senior managers, and be ready to tolerate the ambiguity and manage the potential stress in that.
- Remember that: 'nothing breeds success like success'. Having established credibility, the internal consultant was able to work with leaders in that part of the business to ensure 'carry over' of the learning back into the organization.
- Calculated risk taking can yield enormously positive results in pushing forward acceptable boundaries within an organization and resulting in real development.

Career paths and opportunities

There are many routes into, through and out of the internal consultant's role.

Those who make an early career decision to follow a consultancy path may enter through the MBA route. People emerging from this route will possess a sound grounding in business concepts and techniques, but may initially lack organizational experience, especially if they have entered this route relatively young. The more formal grounding of an MBA needs to be complemented with real experience of organizational dynamics and human behaviour.

Alternatively, deeper experience within a specific function, or preferably a range of functions, will give an individual insights into the more complex nature of organizations. The combination of multi-functional experience and the ability to diagnose systems and build effective relationships provides an excellent basis for internal organizational consulting.

A third entry route may be from external to internal consultant. Externals who feel a need to identify more closely with an organization or build a base of power and influence from within an organization may take this route.

Once within an organization, the career path for an internal can be limited. A move into a line-role is always a possibility, although the 'professional' internal is likely to want to remain in a consulting role. One option is to move roles across organizations in the same way that an internal manager may move roles within an organization. Contracting for 3 to 5 years with an organization and then moving on is one way of retaining some independence and exposure to a variety of organizational styles. In this way, the internal consultant builds up a portfolio of experience across a number of organizations or sectors.

Moving back into a line role has already been mentioned as an option for leaving the internal consulting role. Equally, a move into an external consultancy is another route; either into a consultancy company or as an independent external. The move from internal to external is a difficult decision and, hopefully, this chapter has given some insights into the major differences between the two consultancy roles.

These career choices can be difficult and pose a number of dilemmas. Too long in internal consultancy roles may result in alienation from the 'line' roles. Once in the external consulting world, it may be difficult to re-enter organizational life, although there are numerous examples of people doing both successfully.

The internal role in many respects is on the 'edge' of the organization; it requires specific skills and personal traits. It is often energizing, frustrating, rewarding and demoralizing – all at the same time. Whether the ultimate choice is to 'remain on the edge', move back into a line role or make the move into the external world, experience as an internal will provide exciting challenges and opportunities for personal growth and development.

Survival techniques for the internal consultant

In conclusion, some techniques are offered for taking care of yourself – bearing in mind some of the challenges of the role already discussed.

1. Suitable support networks

In view of the potential loneliness of the role, it is essential for the internal to have suitable support networks (or supportive individuals) either within or outside of the organization. Following the principle of 'taking care of the carers' you will need to be able to discuss difficult situations with someone you trust, let off steam or receive support and encouragement during those down times or, even stronger, moments of dark despair.

2. Balance

Related to appropriate support is the need to achieve a balance between work and home life – ensure that you are physically fit and have the stamina to work long hours, perhaps travel extensively and yet still enjoy your home life and leisure activities. You will bring more to the role if you have a separate social life and contacts from your work with clients, as well as sport or leisure interests, which give you different perspectives and horizons.

3. Physical and mental fitness

Positive thinking is a 'must' for internal consultants, as well as having deep resources of energy and stamina.

4. Continuously learn

You will need to be very aware of your own capabilities and where you need to develop skills.

Competence builds confidence!

Try to ensure that you preserve time to develop your own professionalism. You will need to keep abreast of current trends and developments in your area of expertise in order to avoid becoming insular in your thinking and therefore less able to make effective contributions.

For example, being able to adopt a 'whole systems' approach, or focus on 'process' rather than 'content' in your consultancy work or being able to work with clients to devise business-related solutions.

Always think of yourself as 'You PLC' – having options will allow you to retain your independence and constantly explore alternative paths and opportunities.

5. Tolerate ambiguity

If you have 'high control needs', or have even been described as a control freak, you will need to work hard on this to become an effective internal consultant. You will need to develop your own creativity and tolerance of ambiguity to survive the 'slings and arrows of outrageous fortune' (or, perhaps more accurately, cope with some of the attacks and criticisms which will be levelled at you occasionally).

Some of the situations that you may encounter, which may place great demands on your ability to cope with ambiguity are:

- living with blank sheets of paper when embarking on a design
- not knowing for certain what the outcomes of a large scale intervention will be
- not receiving timely feedback following an intervention so that you are left wondering whether the client regarded it as a success or not.

As already indicated, if you have high controlling needs and regularly feel that you want to take charge of a situation, if you have a need for glory and/or recognition, or if you prefer routine (and may be dissatisfied with modest financial rewards for your efforts) then it is unlikely that the internal consultant's role would hold appropriate attraction for you.

If, however, you enjoy creativity and open-ended situations; coaching others and achieving results through them; making a real difference every time and working in a client focused way, then internal consultancy could be something for you. It will give you:

- valuable experience
- the opportunity to work in different situations within and outside of your organization
- the scope to establish long term relationships and continuity within the organization
- the chance to contribute to the business results of the organization

as well as plenty of hard work, variety and challenge – if you choose to accept it.

Part 7

Looking forward to the next century

23

Challenges and prospects: a SWOT analysis of the consultancy industry as it approaches the millennium

Mick James

Introduction

One of the paradoxes of the consultancy industry is that the agents of change have themselves been the slowest to adapt. The metaphor of the cobbler's children having no shoes has become something of a cliché, in the industry, with the internal management of consultancy firms appearing positively archaic in contrast to the practices they urge their clients to adopt.

This is now changing. Consultants have accepted the need to take their own medicine and are reinventing themselves to cope with the internal and external pressures they face. Consultants recognize that the rapid pace of change in the global economy and the ever-varying demands of clients mean that, in order to survive, it may be necessary to completely reinvent the consultancy industry every few years.

Strengths

The consultancy industry is currently stronger than it has ever been, with most of the large firms reporting record fee incomes. The industry as a whole has achieved around 15 per cent growth over the last few years, but this has regularly been exceeded by the larger players. Niche consultancies have also flourished, and the sole practitioner sector seems to have an almost limitless capacity to absorb redundant executives or independent-minded defectors from the big players.

Not only that, but the larger companies have begun a round of consolidation, which is beginning to spread to the rest of the industry. Although the mergers (between Coopers & Lybrand and Price Waterhouse, and between Ernst & Young and KPMG) have been reported in terms of the union of the Big Six audit firms, in fact the motivation behind them was completely consultancy driven. There is little or no benefit in building global audit and tax practices, given that tax and accounting regimes vary so much around the world. In fact, the main obstacle to these mergers has been the problems associated with combining the audit businesses, what with hostility from the regulators and the need to choose between competing clients.

The globalization of business has left what used to be known as the Big Six consultancies in an enviable position – the existence of multinational partnerships is an excellent foundation on which to build global services. Consultants are thus able to market their own experiences in globalization to clients that wish to follow the same path. Multinational consultants can also take advantage of the fact that the different economies they operate in are at different stages of development and moving at different rates, so the lifecycle of consultancy techniques and expertise can be greatly extended. An example of this is how British firms were able to sell their skills in privatization to Eastern Europe. Emerging markets, such as India and China, offer fertile ground to grow new practices, at first by helping Western firms establish themselves there and later by consulting with local industries exposed to new forces of competition and deregulation.

Demand for consultancy is at an all-time high as firms, having stripped out layers of middle management and other staff, lack the resources to undertake change projects internally. Many have no wish to embark on lengthy learning curves for projects they will never repeat and so prefer instead to draw on consultants' pools of expertise and the programme, risk and change management skills that come with them.

The big consultancies have also been adept at moving into new businesses – the growth of outsourcing being an example of this. From the simple management of IT systems, this has now become a full service business, offering clients the chance to outsource virtually any business process.

One of the main drivers of the growth in consultancy has been the increasing dependence of business on IT. The selection and installation of IT systems by large corporations is now dominated by consultancy firms, which can field both armies of implementers and provide the change management and so-called 'soft skills' on which successful implementation depends. The era of large, bespoke software implementations may be coming to an end, but consultants have compensated by investing in packaged software skills and developing strong relationships with software suppliers.

This blurring of the lines between IT and business strategy has opened the field of consultancy to new entrants from the world of IT. This has not been successful in all cases, but a major factor in the resurgence of IBM has been its development – in the space of five years – of a global consulting group that can stand toe to toe with the Big Six and Andersen Consulting. Other companies with roots in the IT services and outsourcing industries have successfully staked out ground in the world of consultancy. Names such as Sema and Cap Gemini Sogeti are now well established in consultancy. Most notable among these is EDS, which, with its purchase and successful integration of the venerable AT Kearney consultancy, at a stroke transformed itself into a global force in consulting.

Other, more esoteric forms of consultancy are also flourishing. The strategy houses – led by McKinsey – show no sign of relinquishing their hold on the top of the consultancy value chain, and have resisted most attempts by their cousins in the process world to buy their way into this market. Indeed, they have begun to encroach on other areas of boardroom advice. At the time of writing, a bitter and prolonged 'turf war' is underway between the strategy consulting and advertising and marketing industries, which the strategy consultants show every sign of winning. Strategy houses (notably McKinsey) also have a record of providing managerial (and occasionally political) leadership to their clients in the form of 'alumni', who provide valuable networking contacts for the next generation of consultants.

Niche consultancies and sole practitioners have done very well in the 1990s. Niche consultancies – often formed by experienced consultants who found themselves underused or under-rewarded in bigger firms – have proved adept at developing a depth of resource in their chosen field that can match, or even surpass, that of a top firm. The increasing prevalence of alliances, partnerships and 'co-opetition' allows them to operate successfully in a world of mega-consultancies. It is not unusual to find a six- or ten-man firm operating as head contractor or programme manager in a project involving one or more of the big firms.

Sole practitioners benefit from these arrangements, too. It is by no means true to suggest that small consultant equals small client. However, equally, many former executives have found more rewarding lives as external consultants, perhaps working with local firms or contacts from their former industry.

So, at the moment, the consultancy industry is on top of the world, sitting on vast reserves of expertise at the moment when clients are crying out for help to change, adapt and grow. Even without such contingent issues as the year 2000 crisis or European economic and monetary union, the prospects for profitable growth in consulting would seem to be assured for years to come.

Weaknesses

Unfortunately, the consultancy industry is in some danger of becoming a victim of its own success. Demand for consulting services is at an all-time high, but who is to staff all these assignments? Recruitment is the major headache of heads of consulting practices, and has been for at least the last two years. The crisis presents firms with a number of dilemmas.

There is no shortage of candidates for consultancy vacancies. Indeed, it is the profession of choice among European graduates, and many experienced executives would willingly exchange middle management or redundancy for the life of a consultant. However, the supply of quality candidates is limited. Consultancies could easily employ people, but at the risk of compromising the quality of assignments and provoking a backlash. Nor is flourishing a chequebook the answer. So far, the consultancies have tried to avoid getting into bidding wars (although there are signs of salary inflation among MBA graduates going into strategy houses). The results of such a salary war would be disastrous, encouraging 'job-hopping' and disaffectedness among existing staff. It would also create a higher salary bill with no ultimate increase in resources and little prospect of passing on the overhead to clients by increasing day rates.

The consultancy industry also has a number of structural weaknesses, which, if not rectified soon, may grow into major problems. As a people business, the consultancy industry has never, until now, been capital-intensive. Consultancies' ability to raise capital has been limited by their partnership status or by ownership via obscure trust arrangements, such as is the case for PA Consulting. Nor have those consultancies that have gone for stock market listing found it to be an easy experience. It is hard to put a firm value on an enterprise that has assets that can literally walk out the door, leading to extreme volatility in share price. It is not unknown for listed consultancy firms to find that their market capitalization has dropped below the value of the buildings they occupy.

In the past, this was not such an issue, but now the costs of maintaining global infrastructures and moving into emerging markets require large, up front investments. It is rumoured that at least one of the Big Six mergers was prompted by one firm's lack of cash to match its global ambitions.

Globalization has exposed major consultancy firms in unexpected ways. Behind multinational audit and consulting brands there were often little more than collections of largely autonomous national franchises. Building genuine global infrastructures and cultures has occupied a considerable amount of management resource in recent years, and it will continue to do so. The Big Six have found their illustrious history as audit firms to be something of a ball and chain. Anyone setting up an international consultancy today would be unlikely to pick a partnership structure and would hardly wish to bolt on an audit and tax practice. Partnership has advantages – particularly in terms of motivation, empowerment and commitment to the firm – but the consensus nature of decision making in a partnership makes the management of global enterprises highly unwieldy, and major internal disagreements can be, at best, paralysing or, at worst, destructive. The quantum leap involved in becoming a partner – from employee to owner-manager – can also be highly divisive within a firm, and many larger consultancies are working to develop alternative career paths that do not involve partnership or encourage an 'up or out' culture.

Non-partnership firms – which may often be 'national champions', such as Roland Berger in Germany or PA Consulting in the UK – can also be exposed by globalization, their international reach limited by linguistic or regional focus. Niche consultancies and sole practitioners suffer from the 'one pair of hands' syndrome, and may be frozen out in a world in which size itself becomes a competitive weapon.

We have not discussed medium-sized consultancy firms so far. In fact, the lack of a flourishing middle ground is a perennial structural feature of consultancy and a problem that sooner or later any growing consultancy firm must face. Between the big firms, with their global reach and international brands, and the niche players, with their focus and flexibility, lies an uncrossable no man's land. The current wave of consolidation is increasing this polarization.

A further internal weakness of the profession is the lack of a significant female presence, particularly at managerial level. Recent figures are not available, but it is unlikely that the 11 per cent proportion of women in the profession reported 5 years ago in the UK has increased by very much.

A breakdown of the figures (from a joint IMC/*Management Consultancy* magazine survey) at first gave signs of hope: the age profile showed near equality in the younger reaches of the profession. However, it soon became clear that this age profile was not the result of past recruitment attitudes. The consultant's lifestyle itself was driving women out of the profession in large numbers or forcing them to make an unenviable choice between career and family. The pressures of the consultant's lifestyle also take their toll on men and, taken together, 'lifestyle-related losses' exacerbate the resourcing crisis.

Opportunities

The major opportunity for the consultancy industry now is to capitalize on the massive demand for consultancy projects while it lasts. In essence, the problem is the same for the sole practitioner as it is for the biggest partnership: to get the maximum leverage out of limited human resources.

The larger consultancies have recognized that they are, in essence, knowledge industries, and most are enthusiastic early adopters of knowledge management techniques (the combination of IT, software, techniques and culture to liberate and disseminate the knowledge capital of a business). Consultants used to spend a great deal of time reinventing the wheel – knowledge captured in assignments was hidden in inaccessible reports and separate practice areas were not aware of each others' knowledge resources. Using e-mail, groupware and intranet technology, together with cultural change designed to encourage sharing, consultancies can gain greater mileage from their existing knowledge assets. (As a bonus, the expertise gained in knowledge management projects can also be sold on to clients.)

Consultants are increasingly recognizing the need to use their intellectual assets in a more proactive way, rather than merely passively responding to customer needs. 'Thought leadership' programmes range from the publication of articles in academic journals to the design of complicated consultancy offerings based on economic projections of the mid-term futures of entire industries.

The 1990s will be seen as the era in which consultants finally began 'taking their own medicine', analysing and changing their own work practices. This has partly been forced upon them by outside events, but also reflects the way in which the processes of modern consultancy are well-suited to taking advantage of the possibilities of technology.

As consultancies globalized, they were faced with the task of linking disparate businesses in different time zones and attempting to create a coherent cultural and operational unit. Consultants have always been 'road warriors', racking up the frequent flyer points, but the increasing strains of globalization threatened to break working and personal relationships and, ultimately, the individuals themselves.

Building a private international communications infrastructure is an expensive task, but some of the larger consultancies had embarked on this task when the Internet came to the rescue. Consultants were enthusiastic early adopters of Internet technology, which enabled the quick and effective creation of worldwide communications and knowledge-sharing applications.

Working via the Internet has numerous advantages for both large and small consultancies. For the biggest firms, it can help eliminate the need to transfer resources around the world by creating teams that, although geographically scattered and in different time zones, use e-mail and shared databases to work together. Working in multiple time zones can be turned to advantage. An urgent project can 'follow the sun', with a distant team picking up the reins in the morning as their colleagues on the other side of the world go to bed.

Small consultancies are benefiting from the Internet too, and we are seeing the growth of 'virtual consultancies' as sole practitioners band together – possibly on an *ad hoc* basis – to create the skills and location mix demanded by assignments they would not be able to handle alone. It is too early to say whether or not these networks will grow to significantly threaten the mega-consultancies.

Consultants are also experimenting with 'new ways of working' to increase their effectiveness. This can range from simple expedients such as 'hot-desking' – an obvious solution in an industry where most people work on-site with clients – to more complicated solutions designed to accommodate different lifestyles. Flexible human resource policies are one way to alleviate the skills crisis by making it possible for previously alienated workers to come back into the consultancy fold.

Sideways expansion into other areas of professional services is also proving tempting for many of the larger firms. Although closely watched by regulators, some of the larger players have already made inroads into areas such as law and corporate finance.

As mentioned earlier, the emerging markets offer growth opportunities for consultancies. There are also untapped areas nearer home. The high costs of sale and desire for economies of scale are, as we have seen, pushing the bigger firms into consolidation. This leaves some interesting gaps in the market. It has traditionally been difficult for the bigger firms to service the SME sector. Experiments such as Ernst & Young's 'consultancy lite' service, Ernie, distributed via the Internet, have only been partially successful. The consolidation of larger firms and their concentration on a small client list consisting of the largest firms in the world leaves many quite large enterprises out in the cold as they are too small for the big guys, but also too big for the niche players. This raises three possibilities:

- the big firms will discover an effective way to service this sector
- smaller consultancies will learn to network to capitalize on this opportunity
- we will see the development for the first time of a genuine middle tier of consultancies.

Other consultancies are exploring new ways of working with clients. The shift of emphasis from advice to implementation in consultancy work brings with it a desire by the client for more commitment and risk-sharing from the consultant. This can be particularly attractive for the smaller client that may not have the cash to pay until some savings or benefits have been achieved. Daily rate, fee-based consulting is now only one alternative to fixed-fee or performance-related assignments. Some assignments are even rewarded by an equity share in the client's business. Of particular note is an outsourcing/consultancy contract recently signed between EDS/AT Kearney and Rolls-Royce Aerospace. This began with an initial payment of several millions of pounds by the consultant to the client for the transfer of staff and equipment. This is followed up by a ten-year period of consultancy work to achieve profitability goals, and only then will money flow back to the consultancy. Clearly these types of arrangement make significant demands on cash flow and so increase the opportunity for the big players to increase their grip.

Threats

The consultancy industry is so ill defined that threats are both hard to identify and resist. Last year's threats are this year's stalwarts of the industry. For example, the accountancy firms did it and now the IT industry has its tanks parked on the lawn. In the past, consulting firms could laugh at outsiders with fat chequebooks as attempting to hire

Challenges and prospects

your way into the industry has rarely been anything other than disastrous. Now that consultancy is more capital-intensive, however, they cannot afford to be so complacent.

The major threats to the industry, though, are internal. The current round of consolidation must be seen as highly risky as the attempt to merge service industries can all too often end up as 2 + 2 = 2 (or even less). Thus, the firms that are merging to catch Andersen Consulting may find themselves falling even further behind as they become embroiled in internal issues.

The audit-based firms are increasingly finding their background in accountancy a handicap, as witnessed by Andersen's long-running attempt to sever for ever the ties that bind them to Arthur Andersen. But where Andersen leads, others will follow. It seems likely that, in future, the remainder of the Big Six will wish to separate from their audit business, and the ease or difficulty with which this is achieved will determine their competitiveness.

The second question is, where will this consolidation lead? There is, by definition, only a limited number of global 500 clients. The more consultancies' financial structures compel them to consult only to this sector, the more overheated the competitive brew will become. Similarly, at the other end of the scale, the continual influx of redundant executives and new-minted MBAs into sole practitioner consultancy may undermine profitability in this sector.

The position of national players is even more ambiguous. Will they be swamped by the multinationals or will their local knowledge enable them to survive? The global firms face a curious dilemma: the adoption of global methodologies and cultures that enable them to succeed may also alienate them from their clients. The big consultancies may have to learn to reverse the ecological slogan and learn how to act globally while still thinking like the locals.

Like any industry, consultancy is not immune to recession, though often the nature of the business offers some cushioning. Clients still need help in recessions, even though it is of a different nature. For example, a human resources consultancy that offered both executive search and outplacement services might smooth out some of the fluctuations of the cycle. Consultants have also been lucky as the effects of the recession in the UK were alleviated by local government and central government work, and the opening up of new markets in Eastern Europe. In the future, political change cannot be expected to come so readily to the rescue, and an increasingly global economy leaves global firms exposed to the possibility of near-simultaneous recession in all their markets.

Already the allure of emerging markets has been tarnished by financial instability in the Far East.

Consultants are also vulnerable to changes in business trends. Niche consultancies in particular can suffer from the 'up like a rocket, down like a stick' syndrome, as their brand of consultancy becomes the latest trend and then disappears from clients' agendas. It is possible that the current trend for outsourcing all but core business processes may reverse, but, in that case, there would still be work for consultants in managing the 'insourcing' process.

A more serious threat is that change itself will be seen as a core business process. Many firms, after all, have committed themselves to a process of continual change. As a result, they are now in competition with the consultancy profession for the same pool of intelligent, change-oriented individuals. The old distinction between the change-averse line manager and the project-oriented consultant no longer holds. In the extreme case, the need for change work may become so continuous that it makes sense to establish an internal consultancy rather than continually look outside for assistance.

Conclusion

Short of a massive worldwide recession – and even this would have its compensations – it is difficult to foresee any major obstacles to the onward march of consultants. All the indicators are in their favour, and it seems as if, in the long run, we will all be consultants of one kind or another. The only thing that could seriously threaten the profession of change is if the world as a whole entered a period of protracted stasis. 'What if things stopped changing?' is an interesting intellectual proposition, but not one that many consultants are making contingency plans for.

Index

Index

Index

Index

Index

Index

Index

Peters, Tom   58, 234, 264, 314
PIMS   119
political changes   53–5
political environment   369–83
political system   393–5
politics of organizational change   255–7
politics of revelation   262
politics of salvation   262
population groups   61
Porter, Michael   10–11, 106, 114, 291, 313
Porter's five forces   285, 287–8
Porter's three generic strategies   288–9
Porter's value chain model   290–91
Practical Business Re-engineering   294,
   303
Prahalad, C K   299
presentations   103–4, 134–6
   checklist   103–4
   format   134
   length and content   134–5
   preparation   135–6
   venue   135
   visual aids   135
Price Waterhouse   25
principle of transparency   38–9
principle of vulnerability   38
problem solving   313
process approach   311, 312
process skills   161–2
process specialist role   83–4
processes   317–18
product development   15
product improvement   63
Production Engineering Consultants (P-E
   Consultants)   8
production-oriented company   170
productivity   8, 203
profession, essential characteristics   5–6
professional staffing of consultancy   98
professionalism   31–7
profitability   204–8
programme management   396–9
project control   217
project implementation   216–17
project management   212–17
project organizing   214–16
project planning   93–4, 213–14
project team   153–4
promotion of consultancy   183
promotion procedures (staff)   236
proposal
   amending   129
   analysis   104

anticipated benefits of assignment
   95–7
preparing   94–102
presenting   102–4
problem specification   95
results expected   97
proprietary approach   312–14
   developing   322–3
   implementing   324–5
psychological aspects   142–3
psychometric tools   319
public relations (PR)   186–7
public sector
   dynamics of change   369–70
   primary task   370–71
   role of consultant   378–80

quality management   352
Quorn Associates   366–7

rapid application development (RAD)
   techniques   337
Rappaport, A   294
recommendations
   implementation failure   139–46
   involving the client   128–9
recruitment   232–3
redundant arrays of inexpensive disks
   (RAID)   336
Re-engineering the Corporation   11
regional economies   57
remuneration   237
report writing   130–33, 265
   culture and language   132–3
   graphic material   133
   simplicity   133
   structure   131–2
research   183
   methodology   122–3
researcher role   83
resistance to change   255–8
revenue   18–21, 198–200
reward strategy   237
Rise and Fall of Strategic Planning, The   301
risk management   395–6
role modelling   254
Rolls-Royce PLC   59–60
round tables technique   149
routine analysis   107
Rowntree, Seebohm   8

salaries   200–202
sales-oriented company   170

466

Index

Index of Advertisers

So what, we're an
IT services consultancy

Putting a value on consultancy

The success of the transaction between customer and consultant, and the continued growth of the management consultancy industry rests on the simple premise that '**customers pay for what they value.**'

No amount of self-regulation, acquisition of professional qualifications or attempts to define with any exactitude the range of services will serve by themselves to change customer perceptions.

So what do customers value; and how can consultants continue to provide that value?

Answering the first question is easy - customers value what they don't have in-house, or what they have decided is not central to their business. So they buy the services of lawyers or corporate financiers or accountants or any number of other experts. These experts, armed with their knowledge and professional experience interpret and apply the complex rules of their profession by advising the customer on a specific course of action to achieve a desired outcome. In this respect all advisers offer a similar service and for many organisations, consultancy has become an anchor in an unpredictable world.

To understand the second question we should consider the origins of consultancy and the changes that the industry has undergone over the years.

The emerging consultancy tradition

In the early days the most successful large companies were those which had developed a "fleetness-of-foot" - having a financial infrastructure which enabled commercial opportunism, leverage of financial assets and damage limitation of external bureaucracies and financial legislation. Thus the large accountancy practices, whose growth was already spurred on by the audit requirements set out under company law, spawned consultants who helped plan the strategic development and operational capability of organisations to flex the financial infrastructure. These consultancy services became so important that a whole new service industry developed.

In more recent times, the most successful organisations are those which have effective and efficient IT infrastructures and which demonstrate "fleetness-of-foot" in leveraging commercial advantage from information. Hence the success of consultancy practices such as ours whose parent companies are in information systems and computing, is helping to improve that "fleetness-of-foot" through technical solutions.

What about the next generation of consulting?

Almost certainly those practices with a global capability, employing consultants who have the capacity to understand complex multi-cultural organisations and the ability to manage not just information systems but the knowledge within organisations.

472

The New age of business consulting

And customers don't just value advice and expertise, they also value **applied expertise**. The recent trend of divesting non-core businesses to the outsourcers and the growing dependence on buying-in 'business-theme' operational fixes such as preparation for the Euro and the management of environmental issues, has opened up opportunities for consultants in broader business areas.

The outsourcing of services - IT and now increasingly non-IT - requires long-term contractual relationships and has precipitated the move towards risk sharing and partnership arrangements between customer and supplier. Gone are the days of mere provision of without prejudice advice, here are the days of "money where your mouth is" and consultancy organisations staking their reputations on the intellect and ability of their consultants.

For this is the nub of consulting - customers buy the intellect of their consultants. An intellect which is not necessarily better than the customers' but one which increases the organisation's intellectual capital in by bringing a diversity of experience and expertise and a capacity to make objective decisions. The consultant, or consultancy practice, who fails to do this, has failed its customer and, ultimately, failed its peers.

New behaviours, new consulting skills, new

What are the constituents of the increased intellectual capital provided by management consultants from the IT services world? Are they any different from that provided by their predecessors from the accounting world?

Absolutely. As we know, organisations in yesterday's world were concerned about how to get the best out of the interaction of people and processes (mainly financial).

Today's world is of course about the interaction of people with processes but it is also about the interaction with technology which is hugely more complex. Two sets of behaviours must now be managed, those of the people and those of the technology.

Whilst technology is far, far away from replacing all aspects of human endeavour, it can be argued that for people and technology to work together to best effect, technology is increasingly required to exhibit some characteristics of the people it has replaced. It is only the consultant from the IT services environment who can orchestrate, understand, predict, manipulate, exploit and engage the inherent behaviours of systems and software, so that technology interacts with people to perform exactly as the organisation demands.

It is not just the technical knowledge which is paramount. Of vital importance is the appreciation of the wider business environment and how the two are glued together.

This appreciation of the wider business environment is what the customer values. This is this knowledge that we have and which we manage for the benefit of our customers. This is the new consulting skill of the new business age and, increasingly, the intellectual capital which customers pay for.